MISSISSIPPI WRITERS
An Anthology

Mississippi Writers: An Anthology

CONSULTING EDITORS

JANE HOGUE BRUCKMEIER	*Phil Hardin Foundation,* Meridian
DR. NORMA GOLDSTEIN	*Mississippi State University,* at Meridian
GWEN HITT	*Collins Middle School*
MABLE HOSKINS	*Meridian High School*
LAURA HYCHE	*Meridian High School*
LINDA LOFTON	*Newton Elementary School*
GAY MORGAN	*Jones Junior High School,* Laurel
CYNTHIA RAWSON	*Southeast Lauderdale High School,* Meridian
DIANE REYNOLDS	*Northwest Junior High School,* Meridian
EMMA RICHARDSON	*Mississippi School for Math and Science,* Columbus
CAROL ROBBINS	*Meridian Community College*

MISSISSIPPI WRITERS

An Anthology

Edited by
DOROTHY ABBOTT

UNIVERSITY PRESS OF MISSISSIPPI
Jackson and London

Center for the Study of Southern Culture Series

94 93 92 91   4 3 2 1
The paper in this book meets the guidelines for permanence and durability
of the Committee on Production Guidelines for Book Longevity of the Council
on Library Resources.
Copyright © 1991 by the
University Press of Mississippi
All rights reserved
Manufactured in the United States of America

Most of the selections in this anthology previously appeared in *Mississippi
Writers: Reflections of Childhood and Youth*, a collection edited by Dorothy
Abbott and published by the University Press of Mississippi. Four volumes
comprise the collection: volume I, fiction; volume II, nonfiction; volume III,
poetry; and volume IV, drama.
Publication of this volume has been made possible through the generosity of the
Phil Hardin Foundation, the National Endowment for the Humanities, and the
contributors to the NEH Challenge Grant to the University Press of Mississippi.

Library of Congress Cataloging-in-Publication Data

Mississippi writers : an anthology / edited by Dorothy Abbott.
      p.   cm. — (Center for the Study of Southern Culture series)
      ISBN 0-87805-479-0 (cloth). — ISBN 0-87805-503-7 (pbk.)
      1. Mississippi—Literary collections.   2. American
literature—20th century.   3. American literature—Mississippi.
4. Children—Literary collections.   5. Youth—Literary collections.
I. Abbott, Dorothy, 1944–   II. Series.
PS558.M7M54   1991
810.8'09762—dc20   90-28947
                                                                          CIP
British Library Cataloging-in-Publication data available
ISBN: 0-87805-479-0

CONTENTS

Contents

THE MISSISSIPPI WRITERS SERIES

SINCE 1983 the Phil Hardin Foundation directors have made grants to support the publication of Dorothy Abbott's *Mississippi Writers: Reflections of Childhood and Youth*. This four-volume series recognizes the accomplishments of our state's authors. The series also introduces young Mississippians to our state's literary heritage, and the values revealed in that heritage.

The major values, themes, and situations found in these writings, however, have substantial significance beyond the borders of our state—as Mr. Faulkner demonstrated with his "postage stamp of native soil." This series, then, to the extent that its pieces touch the human heart and give expression and meaning to human experience, may encourage a love of good literature and develop interest in the craft of writing.

The Phil Hardin Foundation is honored to join with other Mississippians to make possible the publication of this volume and the *Mississippi Writers* Series, from which most of the selections are drawn. Mississippians can accomplish more working together than working alone.

C. Thompson Wacaster
The Phil Hardin Foundation

TWENTIETH-CENTURY MISSISSIPPI WRITERS

THE WRITERS FEATURED on these pages have all spent an important part of their lives in Mississippi and have published creative or interpretive literature—fiction, poetry, drama, literary essays— that has received critical attention.

Alligator
Jack Butler b. 1944

Benton County
James Autry b. 1933

Batesville
John Nixon, Jr. b. 1924
James Seay b. 1939

Brookhaven
Cid Ricketts Sumner 1890–1970

Carrollton
Elizabeth Spencer b. 1921

Carthage
Katherine Bellamann
1877–1956

Centreville
Anne Moody b. 1940

Charleston
Robert Herring b. 1938

Clarksdale
Lerone Bennett, Jr. b. 1928

Cleveland
Wirt Alfred Williams b. 1921

Clinton
Robert Canzoneri b. 1925
Barry Hannah b. 1942
Evans Harrington b. 1925

Sterling D. Plumpp b. 1940
Jes Simmons b. 1954

Columbus
Samuel Prestridge b. 1952
Paul Ruffin b. 1950
Luke Wallin b. 1943
Tennessee Williams 1911–1983

Como
Stark Young 1881–1963

Corinth
Frances Gaither 1889–1955
Etheridge Knight b. 1931
Thomas Hal Phillips b. 1922

D'Lo
Patrick D. Smith b. 1927

DeSoto County
Walter Malone 1866–1915

Greenville
William Attaway 1911–1986
Charles G. Bell b. 1916
William Burt b. 1950
William Hodding Carter II
1907–1972
David Lewis Cohn 1897–1960
Ellen Douglas
(Josephine Ayres Haxton)
b. 1921
Shelby Foote b. 1916

Brooks Haxton b. 1950
Angela Jackson b. 1951
Bern Keating b. 1915
Beverly Lowry b. 1938
Walker Percy 1916–1990
William Alexander Percy
1885–1942
Jessie Schell b. 1941

Greenwood
Mildred Spurrier Topp
1897–1962

Grenada
Rebecca Hood–Adams b. 1949

Hattiesburg
Frederick Barthelme b. 1943
Elliott Chaze b. 1915
Sybil Estes b. 1942
William Mills b. 1935
Chester Sullivan b. 1939

Hazlehurst
Charles Henri Ford b. 1913

Hermanville
Maxwell Bodenheim 1892–1954

Hinds County
John A. Williams b. 1925

Holcomb
Gloria Norris

Holly Springs
Karen Mitchell b. 1955

Itta Bena
Lewis Nordan b. 1939

Jackson
Anne Carsley b. 1935
Turner Cassity b. 1929

Richard Ford b. 1944
Beth Henley b. 1952
Frank Smith b. 1918
John Stone b. 1936
Mildred D. Taylor
Margaret Walker b. 1915
Jerry Ward b. 1943
Eudora Welty b. 1909
James Whitehead b. 1936

Liberty
Will Davis Campbell b. 1924

Lumberton
James Howell Street 1903–1954

Macon
T. R. Hummer b. 1950
Ben Ames Williams 1889–1953

Magnolia
Martha Lacy Hall b. 1923

McComb
Charlie Braxton b. 1961

Meridian
Winifred Farrar b. 1923
Edwin Granberry b. 1897
William Edward Kimbrough
1918–1965

Natchez
Alice Walworth Graham b. 1905
J. Edgar Simmons b. 1921
Julius Thompson b. 1946
Richard Wright 1908–1960

Ocean Springs
Al Young b. 1939

Oxford
John Faulkner 1901–1963

William Faulkner 1897–1962
Dean Faulkner Wells b. 1936

Pace
besmilr brigham
(Bess Miller Moore) b. 1923

Philadelphia
Turner Catledge 1901–1983

Piney Woods
Virgia Brocks-Shedd b. 1943

Pontotoc
Borden Deal b. 1922

Port Gibson
Berry Morgan b. 1919

Shelby
Charles East b. 1924

Soso
Rebecca Hill b. 1944

Starkville
Stephen Owen b. 1946

Sunflower
Craig Claiborne b. 1920

Tula
Larry Brown b. 1951

Tunica
Charlaine Harris b. 1951

Verona
Perrin Holmes Lowery b. 1923

Vicksburg
D. C. Berry b. 1942
Mart Crowley b. 1935
Harris Dickson 1868–1946
Ellen Gilchrist b. 1935

Water Valley
Hubert Creekmore 1907–1966

Yazoo City
Reuben G. Davis 1888–1966
Willie Morris b. 1934

INTRODUCTION

ELIZABETH WHITLOCK

I MOVED to Mississippi in January of 1969 and found violets blooming near my front door. What a change from the snow and ice we had left behind in Nashville! Month after month, my husband, three children, and I enjoyed the ever-blooming bouquets that the former owners had provided. Watching the forsythia and the wisteria, the day lilies and the banana plant by our carport, we learned to love our new home and state. The pleasure we took in the area's physical beauty was only one aspect of our appreciation, however. We looked on as Mississippians managed a crippling ice storm, turning it into a time for frolicking down ice-covered streets on garbage can lids; we observed the resilient spirits of the victims of Hurricane Camille.

As we traveled through the state, we searched the creeks for fossils, climbed the hills near Yazoo, and camped on the sandy beaches of the coast. Whatever landscape we desired, Mississippi provided. With our children, we hiked through wooded portions of the Natchez Trace and found lush ferns and rich carpets of moss; on the coast we felt the tug of the gulf's undertow, listened to the seagulls scream, and followed the intricate tracks of the terns along the white sands.

Wanting to know more about the literary legends that enriched the heritage of this state, I began to read books by Mississippi writers, beginning with Welty and Faulkner. Before long, I had read the works of Morris, Wright, Walker, Whitehead, Douglas, Spencer, Williams, and others. As my appreciation for the vast body of Mississippi literature increased, I began to wonder just why Mississippi had so many successful authors. I found that many other people had tried to answer the same question.

One of the primary influences, of course, is the storytelling legacy of the South, with its legend-filled history of affluence and poverty, stability and change, and oneness and conflict with the land. Mississippi writers are, in some ways, the scribes for that vast oral tradition. Just as the churchmen recorded the ballads and riddles of the Anglo-Saxon era, these men and women rework the story for the published form, pulling from gossip, from family tales, and from small-town news the incidents of interest around which they build their fiction, poems, and essays. These literary philosophers record not only the Mississippi they experience; they also describe the impact that such events as the importing of the slaves or the intrusion of the carpetbaggers or the developments of the twentieth century have had on individuals. Using the wealth of available material, these writers inform us about the nature of Mississippians and show us how native sons and daughters have confronted difficult situations over the years. Some of their characters sing the blues, while others establish a code of behavior that prevents any overt reference to family weakness; but all adjust to meet the conflicts that they face.

Faulkner, in his Nobel Prize acceptance speech, pays tribute to the quality so obviously present in Mississippi material: man's ability to prevail. Wishing to use the moment at the "pinnacle" of his success to encourage other writers to turn from the fear of being "blown up" to the study of "the human heart in conflict with itself," he focuses on the ability of the successful Mississippi writers to look closely at the individuals they create in an effort to determine just how the universal truths of love, honor, pity, pride, compassion, and sacrifice apply.

Many writers choose to reflect the influence of indigenous settings and themes in the rich, compressed form of poetry; others approach this subject matter through prose. Whatever the genre, Mississippians speak in a rich dialect, filled with sound devices, allusions, and images. As a teacher, I have been fascinated with how the microcosm of Mississippi literature allows for a broad study of the literary genres. Dorothy Abbott, in the *Mississippi Writers: Reflections of Childhood and Youth* series, devoted a volume each to fiction, nonfiction, poetry, and drama. As an individual in search of a better understanding of her adopted state, I am fascinated by the themes that run through the works.

One of the most compelling themes I have found in the selections in this volume is the music of the people. In William Attaway's *Blood on the Forge*, Melody sings the blues to fight away the gut-grabbing poverty that the family must endure as a result of having to satisfy the whims of the white man, Mr. Johnston. Melody's music provides him with a dignity that allows him to rise above the poverty, hunger, and anger that are so devastating to those around him.

Sterling D. Plumpp sings the blues in much the same voice that defines the character of Melody. In "Blues," he writes of coming from the womb "All red/and underfed," and concludes with a determination to "just sing, feel pain, and keep/going ahead"; in "I Hear the Shuffle of the People's Feet" he claims "i live tyranny down /by swinging with jazz." Etheridge Knight has another octave to add to his musical statement. He sings, in "A Poem for Myself," of having left the Mississippi mud and of his decision to return, "This time to stay for good."

In "Jazzy St. Walk: An improvisational poem," Charlie Braxton captures the feelings of depression and desolation that find expression in the blues. Using capital letters only to affirm his condition and isolation, he spaces his words to suggest the ache of loneliness he feels. In a similar poetic form, Angela Jackson sets forth a different view of being black. In "Make/n My Music," she celebrates her race, affirming the value of the spirituals, of "hav/n fun," finding Billie Holiday, and learning how to cry. Al Young's poem "A Little More Traveling Music" claims that the radio music—"Colored music, rhythmic & electrifying"—and "all that motherly music" has enabled him to make "out the sound of my own background music."

In these works, music is presented as a means of coping with life's frustrations. The prevalence of poverty, combined with ignorance and cruelty, forms a second theme. Sybil Pittman Estess has mixed emotions about her cousin Leon who suffered from epilepsy and whose entrapment in poverty was represented by the well he descended to his death in order to satisfy the taunts of the "loud crowd." Unable to watch "Leon in black water," she fled to her grandmother; she still has trouble when she relives the experience. Confessing that as a child she hated him, Estess presents his story empathetically, revealing a sense of oneness with him.

Larry Brown's Mr. Parker, in "Old Frank and Jesus," feels that his many worries, including money problems, are becoming insurmountable. Contemplating a picture of Jesus, he wonders what it would have been like to be present at the crucifixion and to offer some small help to Him. He moves toward helping himself by firing the gun he has borrowed from Hulet and escaping from his own frustrations.

Poverty is also one of the by-products of bigotry; and even though Richard Wright, in the selection from *Black Boy*, focuses more upon his pangs of hunger than upon the racial injustices he experienced as a child, his youthful craving for vanilla wafers and meat while he lived on a diet of mush and gravy, peanut roast, and greens and lard was directly linked to his being black.

Poverty, however, need not always be crippling; it can also be a source of determination and strength. Wright diligently pursued an education by reading good books and made himself into a writer who had a wealth of words at his fingertips. He not only understood the emotions he wanted to share; he also possessed the vocabulary needed for expression. Sarty Snopes, in William Faulkner's "Barn Burning," has a similar ability to rise above the poverty and pettiness of his early years. Reared by Abner Snopes, who resorted to the burning of barns to express his anger and frustration, Colonel Sartoris Snopes becomes the antithesis of his father and develops high moral standards. The intense hunger Sarty feels as the story opens with his father's trial in the midst of the heavy scents of cheese and meat in the old country store does not weaken his sense of family loyalty. His willingness to fight the taunters who sneeringly whisper "barn burner" intensifies the conflict he faces when he decides to warn Major de Spain about Abner's decision to burn the barn even though he knows his action might bring about the death of his own father.

Less dramatic examples of the successful war against poor beginnings are almost nostalgic in tone. Karen Mitchell's poem "The Eating Hill" tells of a child and her grandmother going for some "eating dirt, special dirt" that was "quick and easy to fill"; and Charlie Braxton's memories of childhood reestablish a sense of pride in who he is. His ironic conclusion in "Childhood Remembrances" is that the cowboys never were his heroes, so the mocking of the "rich boys from across the tracks" cannot keep from him a sense of pride about his life, even though being poor has meant substituting a hydrant for a pool and paper caps for guns. Virgia Brocks-Shedd's description of childhood in "Southern

Roads/City Pavements" conveys the good feelings that a family gets from picking and selling blackberries, listening to stories, raising their own food, and visiting with each other. The "dusty or muddy, good southern roads" are the foundation of her life and of her children's lives as they learn from her memories.

The eras of conflict and change in Mississippi have found expression in its writers' work. In an almost chant-like fashion, Margaret Walker, in "For My People," tells of the games she and her friends played and of the songs they sang to ward off tension; and in *Jubilee* Walker tells how Vyry had to adapt to the cruel world of slavery, with its jealousy and illness. In Shelby Foote's *Shiloh*, the narrator, Luther, faces his first battle of the Civil War. Thinking how proud General Johnson's mother would be if she could see her son in his uniform, Luther reveals the contrasts between the life he had before the war and the one he must experience on the battlefield.

Faulkner's "A Rose for Emily" also deals with the problems that accompany change. His Miss Emily Grierson is so much a part of the past that she cannot adjust to the present. Frustrated over the new generation's demands that she pay taxes she believes have been excused, she refuses to accept the civic responsibility just as she has refused to believe that her father is dead. In an attempt to preserve the attention she has received from Homer Barron, she feeds him arsenic and places him on a bed where she visits his decaying body, leaving one of her iron-gray hairs on the pillow next to him. Since gentlemen callers are no longer a frequent occurrence, she assures herself of a permanent guest.

Hodding Carter, in the selection from *Southern Legacy*, bridges the years by offering insight into the intense frustration his grandmother's generation felt about the changes that followed the Civil War, while at the same time pointing out how wrong an extension of those attitudes would be in modern times. He recalls a visit with his maternal grandmother, who, defending the Ku Klux Klan, told him how she made her husband's Klan robes almost single-handedly. Carter believes that every family has someone just like his grandmother who remembers the Civil War and blends fact and fancy to create legend. He describes the impact on southern "aristocrats" and their heirs of the loss of property that would have been handed down through the generations. In talking to his own northern-born sons about the injustices they witness on their arrival in the South, he identifies the "stubborn legacy" as a "tragically employed excuse for wrongs since committed and right things left undone."

William Mills, in an elegy addressed to his great-grandfather, remembers the men who fought for the South and who "leaked away" a "salt blood [that]/Moved now down the Pascagoula" to embrace the earth; he describes the fear, the disease, and the hunger that they faced. Al Young also addresses the character of the individual in the selection from *Bodies & Soul*. Through the voice of his second-grade teacher Miz Chapman, the "scolder and molder" of his youth, he presents a challenge to the children to learn so that they may overcome the heritage of slavery that she has so vividly presented. Ending with echoes of the Twenty-third Psalm, he recognizes that he must yet identify his enemies, but vows to "learn to be strong, clever, and swift or forever play dead."

In "Growing Out of Shadow," Margaret Walker remembers being five and wondering why the history books glorified the white race and why churches, hospitals, schools, and cemeteries were segregated. As a young adult, she recognized her limited understanding when she discovered that "there are poor white working people exploited by rich white people." While working in Chicago, she realized that "whites suffer psychologically from the problem of race prejudice as much as Negroes"; and she began to understand the role that prejudice plays in keeping people divided and disadvantaged.

Lerone Bennett, Jr., desires the same equality for the races that Walker would like to see. The question in his piece "Have We Overcome?" receives a negative reply. He notes that some changes have taken place or he would not be expressing his criticism to a white audience at the University of Mississippi; but he argues that we have overcome only the river and must now cross the sea. In his address, he pays tribute to "the James Merediths, the Fannie Lou Hamers, the Aaron Henrys, the Margaret Walker Alexanders, and the brave children of the SNCC" who have helped bring about that change by staying in Mississippi. He encourages his fellow participants in the 1978 Chancellor's Symposium on Southern History to recognize the "political, economic, and social realities of the twentieth century" and to admit that having only a few gifted blacks enrolled in a predominantly white university run by a white board and faculty is not "overcoming."

The theme of conflict and change runs through many other works as well. In Paul Ruffin's "The Rolling Store," regret is expressed for the sort of change that contributes to an old woman's isolation. In *The Freedom Kick*, Shelby Foote notes that the mother's conception of the importance of freedom and voting to her family and race differs from the narrator's judgment decades later that "it seems like they dont mean so much as they did back then when the Kluxers [were] riding the roads to take them from you." Anne Moody, in *Coming of Age in Mississippi*, writes of the great value freedom has. She tells of the price she had to pay when she made the choice to speak up for her belief that she, who could tutor the white children in math, had a right to eat at the Woolworth's lunch counter.

Richard Wright also demands the opportunity to become an independent individual in "Almos' a Man." Turning from family and responsibility, Dave buys a gun and sets out on his own to try to break with the oppressive sharecropper existence of his youth. The children Mildred Taylor describes in *Roll of Thunder, Hear My Cry* have enough pride to be offended by the used books and the derogatory labeling of their race that they find on the issue cards in the fronts of the books. Both Karen Mitchell, who grieves for the loss of a young woman killed in a church in "Birmingham, Alabama: 1963" and Jerry Ward, Jr., who warns, "Don't be fourteen/ black and male in Mississippi," recognize the need for change.

Ellen Douglas's story "On the Lake" considers the effects of the historical and cultural differences between black people and white people. Estella is superstitious in a way that Anna cannot comprehend, and her defense of that view of life threatens to open a gap between the two women. Their friendship survives a nearly disastrous episode, though Anna feels guilt about her own actions in relation to the black woman.

The difficulties of being young are explored in several pieces. In "Testimony of Pilot," Barry Hannah's narrator reflects upon the challenges he and his friends faced while growing up during World War II. Tennessee Williams's one-act play *This Property Is Condemned* presents Tom listening helplessly as Willie describes her existence in the condemned building where she entertains the railroad men who had once visited her now-deceased older sister. Ten-year-old Rhoda, in Ellen Gilchrist's "Revenge," suffers the frustration of being a girl who is denied access to her brother's Broad Jump Pit. The young narrator in Eudora Welty's "A Memory" watches a "common" family cavorting on the sand nearby while she remembers a boy with whom she has been in love, and she suddenly realizes the disparity between real life and an idealized image. The youth in James Whitehead's "He Remembers Something from the War" understands why his grandfather, who has been his father figure while his father was fighting the Germans and his mother was going to the movies to see the war his father was fighting, gets drunk to escape the memory of the bloody body in the alley and the possible parallel of his son's death on the battlefields of Europe.

Some conflicts find expression in a lighter tone. In "Piano Lessons," John Stone recounts his childhood difficulties with a demanding teacher and his desire to "disguise myself as a clarinet, /march past her in the crowd/lining the street for parades/and blow her eardrums out/with a high held G." Stephen Owen describes the de-masking of a group of students who make discoveries about themselves while sitting in a circle and discussing *Lord of the Flies*. Ovid Vickers creates a character sketch of two interesting women: Lola Forest, an entertainer of men, and Miss Pearl Parkerson, a teacher who taught her students "to sing and to spell/to read and to write/to cypher and to parse" until "one day the state/required a degree."

Another broad theme that runs through Mississippi literature is the role of the family and its influence upon the individual. Eudora Welty links family and books in her reminiscence "A Sweet Devouring." She praises her mother for allowing her to read anything "except *Elsie Dinsmore*" in the public library and her great-aunt in Virginia, "who understood better about needing more to read than you could read," for sending her a bound volume of magazines. She comments upon her grandfather's gift of a dollar so that she could buy the book of her choice and about the lesson she learned when she chose to buy ten cheap books instead of one with greater literary value. Comparing herself to the little girl in Maria Edgeworth's *The Purple Jar*, she decides that the Kress books are as empty as the jar without its purple water. She then reaches for her mother's twenty-four-volume set of Mark Twain.

Dean Faulkner Wells also remembers gifts that were a part of her family Christmas with William Faulkner. She mentions several that she prepared for him after he requested that he be given homemade items. She then describes the Christmas that Faulkner gave her a plaid skirt that was a part of her heritage. She remembers, "I put it on whenever I was sad or scared, or whenever I needed to be strong or brave. . . . I cried when I couldn't wear it anymore." The skirt, the food, and the games are all a part of the wonderful memories of the family time she spent with Faulkner.

Anne Carsley's family consisted of her father and her aunt. She remembers the times that she and her father laughed together about her getting tickled in church, their visits with family, and the occasions when she discovered how much she despised hypocrisy as she sensed her cousin's attempts to keep the truth from her. John Nixon, Jr., had a family that protected him from the hardships of the depression. He admits to having no sense of the financial difficulties that followed the crash of 1929. The only crash he remembers was that of the bottled brew that his mother took behind the barn and smashed when he was five years old. Stark Young and Richard Ford both think about family by remembering the mothers they have lost. Young, in "Written at My Mother's Grave," wishes he could have had her longer; and Ford, in "My Mother, A Memory," recognizes that he will always have his mother because she has become a part of him.

Related to the theme of family is the role that gossip, legend, and storytelling play in the works of Mississippi writers. Gossip entertains, informs, and forms. Mississippi's warm climate and relatively unindustrialized society make possible more social contact among its citizens. Shared personal experiences often become almost legendary before the final telling, and fabulous tales may feature characters of heroic stature; but gossip plays another role in the southern lifestyle, too. James A. Autry, in "Genealogy," begins with an attention-getting incremental repetition of "who you were and who you will become/and not just who you are" to suggest that the listeners in their "shaking of heads/the tightening of lips/the widening of eyes" predetermine the character of "the unborn children," almost sending them to the penitentiary as soon as they are born because they are "gonna end up there anyway." Autry understands another aspect of gossip as well; these people who talk can also forgive and can even "talk" the character of a person into acceptability. He concludes with "Through it all/communities new and old watch and judge and make sure/ the names are in order and everyone understands."

Eudora Welty also uses gossip to form acceptable impressions. The narrator of "Why I Live at the P.O." fights a fruitless verbal battle with Stella-Rondo who returns home with her daughter Shirley-T and talks herself into the role of the much-loved prodigal daughter by adjusting the facts so that they support her instead of her sister. She views gossip from quite a different angle in "The Little Store," as she realizes that her visits to the source of delightful sights and smells were also providing her with a memory that involved the unfinished story of the Sessions family who disappeared without explanation from her life.

Because of "talk," the young girl in Elizabeth Spencer's "The Day Before" goes off to school aware of the fact that she comes from a smart family and is expected to continue the tradition of learning. Her loving relatives provide her with a new pencil box, as well as expectations of success; and they pave the way for her building of knowledge and memories that she can always recall by flicking the hidden catch and revealing "a great hidden world."

Samuel Prestridge, in "How to Tell a Story," uses a tongue-in-cheek tone to maintain that the writer must gossip about his own life, claiming truth for his tales to make them the most vivid experiences. This technique is not unfamiliar to writers. Willie Morris, for example, blends fact and fiction in almost everything he writes. In *Good Old Boy*, he combines real people such as his elementary teacher Miss Abbott with fictional characters such as Spit McGee; and he exaggerates humorous moments from his past, including the episode when his teacher was hit in the head with a softball. Truth merges with legend in *North Toward Home* when he relates his moments of glory as the town's seer, the Phantom.

The storytelling tradition in Mississippi tends to create legends. Margaret Walker's title character in "Molly Means" possesses the supernatural powers of the black arts, and the "gal" in "Kissie Lee" is the best shot in Mississippi. Tales of the absurd also appear. Beginning with a simple memory, Ellen Gilchrist, in "The Best Meal I Ever Had Anywhere," embroiders the tale so elaborately that she creates a hilarious scene. Remembering in her childhood being seated on dictionaries and encyclopedias so that she could reach the table, she recalls Pierce Noblin's wiring of "the salt shaker to a dry cell battery" and Dolly's almost dying from "a fishbone caught in her throat," and claims to remember stabbing "Bunky in the knee/with Onnie Maud's pearl handled wedding fork." William Burt uses a different kind of humor in "Hank and Peg." His narrator's memory is filled with the t-shirts, crew cuts, and games of his youth. He relates how, out of boredom, he and the kid next door would tease the Boston terrier Peg until she snapped back, perhaps reminding herself of earlier days when she was "Peg the fighter/Triumphant/Cat killer."

Of all the themes that run through Mississippi literature, the most important may be the people's relationships to the land. Jack Butler in "Preserves" pays tribute to his mother, whose dedication to her family kept her picking beans and berries, canning and storing them during the summer, and feeding them to her family during the cold barren months of winter. He testifies to the quality of her love as she "plucks the difficult word of a berry" and brings "home /voluminous tribute" that she breaks "into speech." Deeply attached to the land in a different way, Jesse and Skeeter, in James Street's "Weep No More, My Lady," listen to "the moonlight symphony of swamp creatures" and submerge themselves in the privacy of its rich growth. There the young man is able to develop the values that will allow him to meet a moral challenge and emerge the winner.

William Alexander Percy's love for the land is an obvious element in his work. He describes taking "to the levee in sheer lonesomeness and confusion of soul." Paul Ruffin's poem "Frozen Over" describes the rare opportunity for a Mississippi child to "walk on water"; and the discovery and reburial of Indian treasures, along with the narrator's wish to "connect all of this," are recounted in Jes Simmons's "Indian Mound."

I have many reasons to be pleased that my family moved to Mississippi, and one of the most important is the opportunity I have had to study the works of her writers. Sharing the experiences of those who lived through more troubled times, I can better understand the forces that operated upon them, and I am better able to view the problems through their eyes. I believe that the selections in this volume provide an important cross section of those ideas and that a journey through its pages will enrich even the casual reader.

Mississippi Writers
An Anthology

One

FICTION

Blood on the Forge

WILLIAM ATTAWAY

HE NEVER HAD a craving in him that he couldn't slick away on his guitar. You have to be native to the red-clay hills of Kentucky to understand that. There the guitar players don't bother with any fingering; they do it by running a knife blade up and down the stops. Most of the good slickers down where he was born would say that a thin blade made the most music. But he liked the heft of a good, heavy hog sticker. It took a born player to handle one of those. And maybe that's why his mother changed his name to Melody when he got old enough for a name to mean something beside "Come get tit."

Nineteen-nineteen—early spring: the last time, there among the red-clay hills, he was to reach down his guitar. It was a hunger craving yanking at his vitals. That wasn't unusual; share-cropping and being hungry went together. He had never thought about white pork, molasses and salt water cornbread as food anyhow. They were just something to take the wrinkles out of his stomach. Maybe thinking like that had something to do with his not growing up tall and hefty like his half brothers, Big Mat and Chinatown—that and making music when he should have been fighting over the little balls of fat left in the kettle.

Chinatown was in the dust by the shack, playing mumblety-peg with the hog sticker. His back was flattened against a tin patent-medicine sign that covered the chinks in the cabin. Because the tin held the heat of the last sun he rubbed his back up and down and grinned. His gold tooth flashed. There had never been anything wrong with his teeth; he had just had a front one pulled to make space for the gold.

Melody plopped down on the lopsided stoop and arranged his guitar. Chinatown looked out of the corners of his little slant eyes.

"What blues you chordin'?"

"Hungry blues." And Melody plucked the thrown hog sticker out of the air.

"Won't be no more hungry blues come night."

Hattie came and stood in the doorway. She was Big Mat's wife. The marks on her told that much. But although she was hardly bigger than Melody's music box nobody could take the spunk out of her. She leaned against the doorjamb and rubbed one bare foot against the other.

"I hear what you say, China."

"What you hear I say?"

"That you goin' out stealin' come night."

"You hear wrong, woman. I say ain't gonna be no more hungry blues, come night. An' you know why?"

"'Cause we be doin' ninety days on the road gang for your thievin'?"

"Naw," squealed Chinatown, "'cause, come night, we all be sleepin'." He laughed, and his gold tooth shone as he laughed, only you couldn't call it laughter by his face. His slant eyes and the tight skin drawing the lips back off his teeth made laughing his natural look.

"Maybe Mat bring somethin' back." Hattie sighed. "He gone over Moaningreen way to kill them ailin' hogs for Mr Johnston."

"Maybe he git a whole hog," said Chinatown. "They gonna die anyways."

"Mr Johnston ain't givin' niggers no well hog an' he ain't givin' 'em no sick hog. He ain't givin' 'em no hog a-tall." And with that Melody struck up a chord, running his knife the full length of the guitar. It was mellow, like the sound of hound dogs baying across a river.

> *Done scratched at the hills,*
> *But the 'taters refuse to grow....*
> *Done scratched at the hills,*
> *But the 'taters refuse to grow....*
> *Mister Bossman, Mister Bossman,*
> *Lemme mark in the book once mo'....*

There were more verses like that than any one man knew. And after each verse the refrain:

Hungry blues done got me listenin' to my
love one cry. . . .
Put some vittles in my belly, or yo' honey
gonna lay down and die. . . .

He quit singing to just slick a little while. There was no need to think; his hand wouldn't stop until it had found every minor chord in the box.

"It ain't no two ways about it," breathed Hattie. "Blues sure is a help."

"Hungry blues ain't nothin'," he told her, never stopping. "It ain't like you tryin' to blues away a love cravin' that git so mixed up with the music you can't know which is which."

"Lawd, now!" she breathed.

"Ain't never hear tell of a creeper singin' no love blues," said Chinatown through his golden grin.

"Ain't never seen no creeper without razor marks on him somewhere, you mean," said Hattie.

"There ain't no mark on me."

"Well, what you lay that to?"

"Reckon I jest too slick to git caught."

"You jest got more space to cook up devilment than anybody else. A body ought to be 'shamed to lay round in the dust all day, lettin' his two brothers go out in the fields and earn his somethin'-to-eat for him."

"I lazy, and they smart." He grinned. "I lazy and hungry—they smart and hungry." He helped his point with a bigger grin.

Hattie did not know what to say. She fussed around with her feet. Then, snorting, she went into the shack. Chinatown winked at Melody.

From the southwest came a flock of coots, flying high, straining forward like all water fowl. All day they had been passing overhead, curving north. It would not be long before the wild ducks and geese would make the same passage. Chinatown looked up.

"When coots come afore the duck tomorrow goin' to bring bad luck." Extending his hands, he sighted along an imaginary rifle. "Bop! Bop! Bop!" He settled back, satisfied with the number of coots he had killed in his mind.

Hattie popped into the doorway. She had thought of the right answer for Chinatown. "It ain't needin' for none of us to be hungry, an' you with a hunk of gold in your mouth."

Chinatown looked scared, and Hattie watched him with satisfaction. She knew he would rather die than part with that shiny tooth but she was out to plague him.

"Maybe it ain't worth nothin'," he mumbled.

"It worth a full belly."

He could not look at her eyes. His toes searched the dust.

"I know what," she said.

"What?" mumbled Chinatown.

"Tonight I talk to Big Mat, so he yank it outen your head and take it in to Madison."

Chinatown half rose. "No!" His voice went into falsetto and cracked. "I work in the bossman's fields all season for that tooth."

Hattie backed. "Onliest time you stir since is to look at that gold in the glass." She disappeared in the shack.

He sat back against the tin. After a time he mumbled, "Ain't no use in a man stirrin' round and gettin' all lathered up. He ain't gittin' no place."

He was talking to himself, but Hattie heard and called out, "Now what you tryin' to say?"

"Only seem like good sense to stay where you was in the first place and save yourself the trouble of comin' back."

She came to the door again. "How the crop goin' to git made?"

"We jest niggers, makin' the white man crop for him. Leave him make his own crop, then we don't end up owin' him money every season."

"Lawd, you never will be no good!" Hattie sighed. "Maybe you git straightened out if you gits a woman of your own to feed."

Melody entered the conversation in an old song:

> Now the berry always sweeter
> on the other man's bush....
> What you reckon make that?

Chinatown guffawed. "Now that there the truth."

"Your poor dead maw musta had a conjure, to set a bad egg like you without spoilin' the brook," she said.

"Better be careful not to say nothin' 'bout Maw when Big Mat around," Chinatown warned.

"Sure said he'd belt you," put in Melody.

"An' I ain't never knowed Mat to grin when he say somethin'," said Chinatown.

"Mat know he in the wrong," she scolded.

"Forgit about it," advised Melody.

"I got cause to talk as much as I please."

"Jest forgit about it."

"Mat jest afeared I goin' to talk about how come we ain't got no mule and what the reason we ain't got nothin' to cook up in the house."

To cut Hattie off Melody started up another spell of the blues. Maw hadn't been in the ground but about four weeks. Neither of them wanted to hear any talk about her or that mule. Talk brought back the homemade burial box, the light rain falling and the thud of falling clods still ringing in their ears as they went homeward across the pastures, before sunup Maw out pushing that one-mule plow, Chinatown sitting around in the dust, Melody dodging the fields for his guitar. They thought of it now. She had dropped dead between the gaping handles of the plow. The lines had been double looped under her arms, so she was dragged through the damp, rocky clay by a mule trained never to balk in the middle of a row. The mule dragged her in. The rocks in the red hills are sharp. She didn't look like their maw any more. Hattie went to work on the body with yellow hog-fat soap. Chinatown and Melody sat against the house and cried. Big Mat went away for a long time. He came back hog wild and he took a piece of flint rock and tore the life out of that mule, so that even the hide wasn't fit to sell.

Melody had fallen out on the ground and vomited and for three days afterward he couldn't hold food on his stomach. The sight of blood always acted on him like that.

Four weeks had stopped them from wailing. It was better for her to be in heaven, was Hattie's word on their maw, than making a crop for Mr Johnston. . . . Still, you couldn't stop her from working. If that mule went to the same place she did she probably started in right away to plow for God.

Mr Johnston said that they could not have any more food credit. He claimed their share of the crop for the next two years in payment for his mule. He didn't say where the crop was coming from when there was no animal to plow with. He didn't say how they were going to eat without food credit. All they could do was to wait for him to change his mind.

Hattie had kept at Big Mat, driving him crazy with her talk, blaming him for everything. One day it had taken both Chinatown and Melody to keep him from lighting into her with the butt end of a hoe. But he swore he'd belt her if she even mentioned Maw again.

Melody sang softer and softer. Soon he was just singing for himself. Going onto verse fifty, or thereabout, he got weary and barely hit the stings. He looked away over the rolling country to the place where the sun had about given up fighting the dark hills. Most of the country beyond Vagermound Common was bunched with crab-apple trees, posing crookedly, like tired old Negroes against the sky. Big Mat was going to come walking out of those hills, over the Vagermound Common, down the red, packed road that wound past their door. He was going to have a greasy sack over his shoulders, Melody hoped. To keep from hoping too hard about that sack he made out to play the wish game with Chinatown.

"China," he half sang, "you know where I wish I was at now?"

Chinatown hunched forward in the dust. He liked the wishing game. They had played at it all their lives, most times wishing they were at the grand places pictured in the old newspapers that livened the walls of the shack.

"Where at?" He grinned eagerly.

"Me—me," pondered Melody, "me—I wish I was in town. That's it—smack in town—and it's a Saturday noontime."

"What you be doin'?"

"Jest standin'—all made out in a white-checkered vest and a ice-cream suit, and you can't hardly see the vest for a gold watch chain. I got on shoes, too—yeller shoes with dimes in the toes. Man, man!"

"The gals is passing by. . . ." Chinatown tried to help.

"Naw, that ain't till evenin'. Now I aimin' to shoot some pool."

"You can't shoot no pool."

"But I wish I can," said Melody.

"Ain't you aimin' to make no music?"

"Jest aimin' to shoot some pool," he told him. "Course, I got my guitar with me, jest in case. But I'm feelin' too good to make my guitar cry."

"Now ain't that awful you can't make no music, and you feelin' good?" sympathized Chinatown.

"It don't make no never mind, 'cause my box is shinin' with silver, and the stops all covered with mother-of-pearl. An' everybody see me say that must be Mr Melody. They say howdy to Mr Dressin'-man Melody."

Hattie was in the doorway again.

"Stuff!" she snorted, but she was listening hard.

"What you do, come night?" asked Chinatown.

Melody thought hard and struck a long chord to make his thoughts swell with the music.

"Come night—come night... Well, I guess I spark around the gals and drink a little corn. Maybe I'm on a church picnic. The gal and me has got our bellies full and slipped away in the bushes at the edge of the river. Had the corn in my pocket all the time."

Chinatown had a pucker around his slant eyes.

"Goin' to drink anythin' but corn?" he asked hopefully.

Chinatown wanted him to put a bottle of red pop into the story. Chinatown lived on red pop whenever they were in Masonville. He had loved it from the first bottle given him by a white man who thought it would be funny to see a little slant-eyed pickaninny drink red pop. When asked how he liked it Chinatown had told the man:

"Taste kinda like your foots is 'sleep."

He was right.

"I say you goin' to drink anythin' but corn?" repeated Chinatown.

"Jest corn." Then, seeing how Chinatown was caught in the story, he added: "Maybe I mix it with a little red pop though."

"That make it good." Chinatown grinned.

It was deep dusk.

"Wish night gone and real night come on." Hattie sighed. "Guess I light the rag for Big Mat." Melody looked up, caught by the rhythm of her words. She went in to light the scrap in a dish of black tallow. The kerosene had been gone a long time.

Chinatown took an old quid out of his pocket. He wrapped it in a dried corn husk and tied the cigar-shaped mass with Johnson grass.

"Smoke always spoil my feelin' for eatin'," he said. He called to Hattie: "Hand me out a lighted stick."

"What you want a fire stick for?" she called back.

"Gonna set the house on fire." He laughed.

Grumbling, she brought a glowing twig.

"Ain't but one place you coulda got any tobacco," she said. "You done found one of Mat's hunks o' chewin' tobacco and crumbled it up."

"That's right," he said.

"Mat take the hide off you."

"What for? He chewed this piece already about ten times."

"Well, can't say I hold no blame. . . . What I wouldn't give for a pinch of snuff under the lip!"

"Wish night gone and real night come on," Melody repeated. "That sound like the blues, Hattie."

"Too bad you didn't bring some wish snuff back with you from Wish Town," was her answer.

"Night creep up like a old woman," Melody said softly to himself. "Can't see her—can't hear her. She jest creep up when your back turned."

"Smoke makin' me light in the head. My stomach growlin'. Guess that mean I got fast business in some white man's smoke-house." Chinatown snuffed his smoke. He got to his feet, cleaning his hands by spitting on them and wiping them on his overalls.

"She got on a black skirt," Melody dreamed. "She black, too, so's you can't see her legs when she shackle her skirt to the floors o' the earth."

"Keep the kettle bilin', Hattie," said Chinatown. "Bilin' water for meat or for buckshots."

Melody began to sway.

"At night the hills ain't red no more. There ain't no crab-apple trees squat in the hills, no more land to hoe in the red-hot sun—white the same as black. . . . Where the mule gone at? He only a voice in the pasture land. . . ."

Of a sudden he became conscious of what he was doing. He grabbed for the guitar. "Listen, China; listen, Hattie—listen what I'm doin'." He went on lightly: "Now the chigger ain't nothin' but bite. All the crickets is is a big chirp in the grass. Night bird call out the deathwatch. . . . Night-flyers is glow buckles on the garters of old creepin' night. The mosquitoes is her swamp-fever sting. . . . But it don't last long, 'cause she say, 'Git along,' an' be nothin', 'cause black ain't nothin', an' I is black. . . ."

"Hallo, hallo . . ." It came like an echo lost in the hills beyond Vagermound.

Hattie was peering into the night, listening.

"Hallo, hallo . . ." the echo answered itself.

"It's Big Mat," she cried.

"Well, git the kettle bilin', woman," cried Chinatown. "He ain't holler lessen he got somethin' in a sack."

> *Nigger, nigger never die.*
> *Black face and shiny eye,*
> *Kinky hair and pigeon toe—*
> *That the way the nigger go. . . .*

Because he was blacker than his half brothers the white share croppers' kids had sung that little chant at him. They had said that Big Mat's father must have been a lump of charcoal. And Big Mat had learned to draw to a safe distance within himself everything that could be hurt. The years had given him a shell. But within that tight *casure* his emotions were under great pressure. Sometimes they broke through, and he filled with red madness—like a boar at mating—hog wild. Few folks had seen him like that. To almost everybody but his close kin he was a stupid, unfeeling giant, a good man to butcher hogs and veal cattle. Melody alone knew him completely. Melody, from his dream world, could read the wounds in Big Mat's eyes.

Now seven carcasses glistened on the sacks at Big Mat's feet. Flies struggled in the sticky blood that oozed from the box of entrails. He threw the chain around the hind leg of the last hog. Passing the free end of the chain over the low branch of a tree, he began to hoist the struggling, squealing animal off the ground. Out of the corners of his eyes he saw Mr Johnston and the riding boss. Mr Johnston had always been a landowner, but the riding boss had been a poor white share cropper. Big Mat remembered him as a little ragged boy singing the hated chant. The two men stood in the shade of the barn, mixing their talk and spit. That talk was about him. He could see it in their little gestures. So he bent closer to the chain, lifting the hog in easy jerks. When the hog was well off the ground Mat fastened the chain to a stake and reached down into the box of guts for his knife.

"Oh, Mat," called Mr Johnston.

"Yessuh?" Mat waited.

Mr Johnston came toward him.

"This here's the last hog, ain't it?"

"This the brood sow, suh."

"Well, I want to catch her blood."

Mat went and got a bucket and set it under the hanging animal.

"Figger to make some blood sausages," said Mr Johnston. "Damn good eatin' when they made right."

Mr Johnston stood watching while Big Mat wiped the knife across the hog's teats. The animal had grown quiet. Its little eyes sucked back out of sight. The snout dripped a rope of saliva halfway to the ground. Big Mat touched the hog's neck tentatively with the point of the knife. The animal quivered. The shining rope broke and made a bubble on the ground.

"Mr Johnston."

"What is it, Mat?"

"This here the last hog, and the sun almost down. I was jest wonderin'——"

"Say what's on your mind, boy," said Mr Johnston.

"My folks is waitin'——"

"For what?"

"For me, Mr Johnston. They hungry. . . ."

"Go on."

"If I could jest scald this one and leave the butcherin' until tomorrow—take somethin' home to my folks. . . ."

Mr Johnston spat his quid into the box of entrails.

"Well, that there's a good idee, Mat. What you figger on takin' home?"

"Why, anythin' you gives me, suh." Mat played the knife over the sow's throat. The animal held its breath and then gagged. Saliva ran like unraveling silk.

"What makes you think I'm goin' to give you anythin', Mat?"

Bit Mat did not answer.

Mr Johnston said, "It ain't my fault your folks ain't got nothin' to eat."

The knife point found a spot on the hog's neck.

"I figger this here labor can jest go on what you owe me for my mule."

The blade slid out of sight. The haft socked against the bristled neck. A quick wiggle of the knife found the great blood vessel. Big Mat drew the blade. Dark blood gushed in its wake. Mr Johnston looked admiringly.

"You know the needs of a knife, Mat," he said.

Big Mat stood watching the hog bleed. He shifted the bucket a trifle with his toe.

"Mr Johnston."

"Yes, Mat?"

"How we goin' to make a crop this year? We already late on plowin'."

Mr Johnston grinned. "Well, Mat, I figger on you all makin' a good crop with corn and molasses cane."

"We got to have a mule, suh."

Mr Johnston's eyes grew small and sharp. "Looka here, I contract with you for a crop. It ain't my business how you make it. Them hills has always growed a crop and they'll grow one this season if you folks have to scratch it outen the bare rocks."

So Big Mat told him what he already knew about the land: "It ain't jest the mule, suh. It's everythin'. Wind and rain comin' outen the heavens ever' season, takin' the good dirt down to the bottoms. Last season over the big hill the plow don't go six inches in the dirt afore it strike hard rock. Stuff jest don't come up like it use to. Us'll have a hard time makin' it on our share, mule or no—a hard time. . . ."

Mr Johnston caught Big Mat with his eyes. He came forward. Big Mat looked doggedly into the hard eyes. For a long second they hung on the edge of violence.

Mr Johnston said, "You ain't kickin', are you, Mat?"

Big Mat's eyes dropped to the bloody entrails. He presented a dull, stupid exterior.

"Nosuh, I ain't kickin'."

Mr Johnston smiled and drew out a plug. He bit a chaw and settled it in his cheek to soften.

"Mat," he said, "you know I don't have nothin' but niggers work my land. You know why?"

"Nosuh."

"Well, they's three reasons: niggers ain't bothered with the itch; they knows how to make it the best way they kin and they don't kick none."

The hog suddenly started its final death struggles. It threshed about on the chain, throwing blood in a wide circle. Mr Johnston jumped back. Big Mat grabbed hold of the animal's ears and held the big body steady.

"They don't jump till they 'most dead," said Big Mat.

Mr Johnston laughed. "What I say jest past your understandin', Mat—slips off your head like water offen a duck's back."

"Yessuh."

"You a good boy though. What I really come over here for is to tell you I'm goin' to let you have a mule tomorrow."

"Yessuh." Big Mat's outward self did not change, but his heart jumped. A mule was life.

"An' about what's on the book against you—you send them brothers of yourn over here. They can work some of it off. Give them fifty cents a week to boot. That'll keep you goin'."

"Yessuh."

"You kin take along a bag of them guts when you go. Throw the rest of them back to the other hogs."

Mr Johnston started toward the house. He turned. "Oh, Mat, my ridin' boss tells me there some jacklegs around, lyin' to the niggers about how much work they is up North. Jest you remember how I treat you and don't be took in by no lies."

It was dark when Big Mat picked up his greasy sack and started for home. The moon would not be up yet, but he knew the rolling hills by night. His feet would find the road. Deep inside him was his familiar hatred of the white boss, but the thought of a mule was hot, like elderberry wine. Against the dark sky the darker crab-apple trees kept pace with him as he walked. When he reached the edge of Vagermound Common he threw back his head and gave a long "Hallo . . . hallo . . ."

Old Frank and Jesus

LARRY BROWN

MR. PARKER'S on the couch, reclining. He's been there all morning, almost, trying to decide what to do.

Things haven't gone like he's planned. They never do.

The picture of his great-grandpa's on the mantel looking down at him, a framed old dead gentleman with a hat and a long beard who just missed the Civil War. The picture's fuzzy and faded, with this thing like a cloud coming up around his neck.

They didn't have good photography back then, Mr. P. thinks. That's why the picture looks like it does.

Out in the yard, his kids are screaming. They're just playing, but to Mr. P. it sounds like somebody's killing them. His wife's gone to the beauty parlor to get her hair fixed. There's a sick cow in his barn, but he hasn't been down to see about her this morning. He was up all night with her, just about. She's got something white and sticky running out from under her tail, and the vet's already been out three times without doing her any good. He charges for his visits anyway, though, twenty-five smacks a whack.

That's . . . seventy-five bucks, he thinks, and the old white stuff's just pouring out.

Mr. P. clamps his eyes shut and rolls over on the couch, feels it up. He had cold toast four hours ago. He needs to be up and out in the cotton patch, trying to pull the last bolls off the stalks, but the bottom's dropped out because foreign rayon's ruined the market. He guesses that somewhere across the big pond, little Japanese girls are sewing pants together and getting off from their jobs and meeting boyfriends for drinks and movies after work, talking about their supervisors. Maybe they're eating raw fish. They did that on Okinawa after they captured the place and

17

everything settled down. He was on Okinawa. Mr. P. got shot on Okinawa.

He reaches down and touches the place, just above his knee. They were full of shit as a Christmas turkey. Eight hundred yards from the beach under heavy machine-gun fire. No cover. Wide open. They could have gotten some sun if they'd just been taking a vacation. They had palm trees. Sandy beaches. No lotion. No towels, no jamboxes, no frosty cool brewskies. They waded through water up to their necks and bullets zipped in the surf around them killing men and fish. Nobody had any dry cigarettes. Some of their men got run over by their own carriers and some of the boys behind shot the boys in front. Mr. P. couldn't tell who was shooting whom. He just shot. He stayed behind a concrete barrier for a while and saw some Japanese symbols molded into the cement, but he couldn't read them. Every once in a while he'd stick his head out from behind the thing and just shoot.

He hasn't fired a shot in anger in years now, though. But he's thinking seriously about shooting a hole in the screen door with a pistol. Just a little hole.

He knows he needs to get up and go down to the barn and see about that cow, but he just can't face it today. He knows she won't be any better. She'll be just like she was last night, not touching the water he's drawn up in a barrel for her, not eating the hay he's put next to her. That's how it is with a cow when they get down, though. They just stay down. Even the vet knows that. The vet knows no shot he can give her will make her get up, go back on her feed. The vet's been to school. He's studied anatomy, biology. Other things, too. He knows all about animal husbandry and all.

But Mr. P. thinks him not much of a vet. The reason is, last year, Mr. P. had a stud colt he wanted cut, and he had him tied and thrown with a blanket over his head when the vet came out, and Mr. P. did most of the cutting, but the only thing the vet did was dance in and out with advice because he was scared of getting kicked.

The phone rings and Mr. P. stays on the couch and listens to it ring. It's probably somebody calling with bad news. That's about the only thing a phone's good for anyway, Mr. P. thinks, to let somebody get ahold of you with some bad news. He knows people just can't wait to tell bad news. Like if somebody dies, or if a man's cows are out in the road, somebody'll be sure to pick up the nearest phone and call somebody else and tell him or her all about it. And they'll tell other things, too. Personal things. Mr. P. thinks it'd probably be better to just not have a phone. If you didn't have a phone, they'd have to come over to your house personally to give you bad news, either drive over or walk. But with a phone, it's easy to give it to you. All they have to do's just pick it up and call, and there you are.

But on second thought, he thinks, if your house caught on fire and you needed to call up the fire department and report it, and you didn't have a phone, there you'd be again.

Or the vet.

The phone's still ringing. It rings eight or nine times. Just ringing ringing ringing. There's no telling who it is. It could be the FHA. They hold the mortgage on his place. Or, it could be the bank. They could be calling again to get real shitty about the note. He's borrowed money from them for seed and fertilizer and things and they've got a lien. And, it could be the county forester calling to tell him, Yes, Mr. Parker, it's just as we feared: your whole 160-acre tract of pine timber is heavily infested with the Southern pine beetle and you'll have to sell all your wood for stumpage and lose your shirt on the whole deal. It rings again. Mr. P. finally gets up from the couch and goes over to it. He picks it up. "Hello," he says.

"Hello?"

"Yes," Mr. P. says.

"Mr. Marvin Parker," the phone says.

"Speaking," says Mr. P.

"Jim Lyle calling, Mr. Parker. Amalgamated Pulpwood and Benevolent Society? Just checking our records here and see you're a month behind on your premium. Just calling to check on the problem, Marv."

They always want their money, Mr. P. thinks. They don't care about you. They wouldn't give a damn if you got run over by a bush hog. They just want your money. Want you to pay that old premium.

"I paid," Mr. P. says. He can't understand it. "I pay by bank draft every month."

A little cough comes from the phone.

"Well yes," the voice says. "But our draft went through on a day when you were overdrawn, Mr. Parker."

Well kiss my ass, Mr. P. thinks.

Mr. P. can't say anything to this man. He knows what it is. His wife's been writing checks at the Fabric Center again. For material. What happened was, the girls needed dresses for the program at church, capes and wings and things. Plus, they had to spend $146.73 on a new clutch and pressure plate for the tractor. Mr. P. had to do all the mechanical stuff, pull the motor and all. Sometimes he couldn't find the right wrenches and had to hunt around in the dirt for this and that. There was also an unfortunate incident with a throw-out bearing.

Mr. P. closes his eyes and leans against the wall and wants to get back on the couch. Today, he just can't get enough of that couch.

"Can I borrow from the fund?" says Mr. P. He's never borrowed from the fund before.

"Borrow? Why. . . ."

"Would it be all right?" Mr. P. says.

"All right?"

"I mean would everything be fixed up?"

"Fixed up? You mean paid?" says the voice over the phone.

"Yes," says Mr. P. "Paid."

"Paid. Why, I suppose. . . ."

"Don't suppose," says Mr. P. He's not usually this ill with people like Jim Lyle of APABS. But he's sick of staying up with that cow every night. He's sick of his wife writing checks at the Fabric Center. He's sick of a vet who's scared of animals he's sworn to heal. He doesn't want Jim Lyle of APABS to suppose. He wants him to know.

"Well, yes sir, if that's the way. . . ."

"All right, then," Mr. P. says, and he hangs up the phone.

"Goodbye," he says, after he hangs it up. He goes back to the couch and stretches out quick, lets out this little groan. He puts one forearm over his eyes.

The kids are still screaming at the top of their lungs in the yard. He's worried about them being outside. There's been a rabies epidemic: foaming foxes and rabid raccoons running amuck. Even flying squirrels have attacked innocent people. And just last week, Mr. P. had to take his squirrel dog off, a little feist he had named Frank that was white with black spots over both eyes. He got him from a family of black folks down the road and they all swore up and down that his mama was a good one, had treed as many as sixteen in one morning. Mr. P. raised that dog from a puppy, played with him, fed him, let him sleep on his stomach and in front of the fire, and took him out in the summer with a dried squirrel skin and let him trail it all over the yard before he hung it up in a tree and let him tree it. He waited for old Frank to get a little older and then took him out the first frosty morning and shot a squirrel in front of him, didn't kill it on purpose, just wounded it, and let old Frank get ahold of it and get bitten in the nose because he'd heard all his life that doing that would make a squirrel dog every time if the dog had it in him. And old Frank did. He caught that squirrel and fought it all over the ground, squalling, with the squirrel balled up on his nose, bleeding, and finally killed it. After that he hated squirrels so bad he'd tree every squirrel he smelled. They killed nine opening day, one over the limit. Mr. P. was proud of old Frank.

But last week he took old Frank out in the pasture and shot him in the head with a .22 rifle because his wife said the rabies were getting too close to home.

Now why did I do that? Mr. P. wonders. Why did I let her talk me into shooting old Frank? I remember he used to come in here and lay down on my legs while I was watching "Dragnet." I'd pat him on the head and he'd close his eyes and curl up and just seem happy as anything. He'd even go to sleep sometimes, just sleep and sleep. And he wouldn't mess in the house either. Never did. He'd scratch on the door till somebody let him out. Then he'd come back in and hop up here and go to sleep.

Mr. P. feels around under the couch to see if it's still there. It is. He just borrowed it a few days ago, from his neighbor, Hulet Steele. He doesn't even know if it'll work. But he figures it will. He told Hulet he wanted it for rats. He told Hulet he had some rats in his corncrib.

Next thing he knows, somebody's knocking on the front door. Knocking hard, like he can't even see the kids out in the yard and send them in to call him out. He knows who it probably is, though. He knows it's probably Hereford Mullins, another neighbor, about that break in the fence, where his cows are out in the road. Mr. P. knows the fence is down. He knows his cows are out in the road, too. But he just can't seem to face it today. It seems like people just won't leave him alone.

He doesn't much like Hereford Mullins anyway. Never has. Not since that night at the high school basketball game when their team won and Hereford Mullins tried to vault over the railing in front of the seats and landed on both knees on the court, five feet straight down, trying to grin like it didn't hurt.

Mr. P. thinks he might just get up and go out on the front porch and slap the shit out of Hereford Mullins. He gets up and goes out there.

It's Hereford, all right. Mr. P. stops inside the screen door. The kids are still screaming in the yard, getting their school clothes dirty. Any other time they'd be playing with old Frank. But old Frank can't play with them now. Old Frank's busy getting his eyeballs picked out right now probably by some buzzards down in the pasture.

"Ye cows out in the road again," says Hereford Mullins. "Thought I'd come up here and tell ye."

"All right," says Mr. P. "You told me."

"Like to hit em while ago," says Hereford Mullins. "I'd git em outa the road if they's mine."

"I heard you the first time," says Mr. P.

"Feller come along and hit a cow in the road," goes on Hereford Mullins, "he ain't responsible. Cow's ain't sposed to be in the road. Sposed to be behind a fence."

"Get off my porch," says Mr. P.

"What?"

"I said get your stupid ass off my porch," Mr. P. says.

Hereford kind of draws up, starts to say something, but leaves the porch huffy. Mr. P. knows he'll be the owner of a dead cow within two minutes. That'll make two dead cows, counting the one in the barn not quite dead yet that he's already out seventy-five simoleans on.

He goes back to the couch.

Now there'll be a lawsuit, probably. Herf'll say his neck's hurt, or his pickup's hurt, or something else. Mr. P. reaches under the couch again and feels it again. It's cold and hard, feels scary.

Mr. P.'s never been much of a drinking man, but he knows there's some whiskey in the kitchen cabinet. Sometimes when the kids get colds or the sore throat, he mixes up a little whiskey and lemon juice and honey and gives it to them in a teaspoon. That and a peppermint stick always helps their throats.

He gets the whiskey, gets a little drink, and then gets another pretty good drink. It's only ten o'clock. He should have had a lot of work done by now. Any other time he'd be out on the tractor or down in the field or up in the woods cutting firewood.

Unless it was summer. If it was summer he'd be out in the garden picking butter beans or sticking tomatoes or cutting hay or fixing fences or working on the barn roof or digging up the septic tank or swinging a joe-blade along the driveway or cultivating the cotton or spraying or trying to borrow some more money to buy some more poison or painting the house or cutting the grass or doing a whole bunch of other things he doesn't want to do anymore at all. All he wants to do now's stay on the couch.

Mr. P. turns over on the couch and sees the picture of Jesus on the wall. It's been hanging up there for years. Old Jesus, he thinks. Mr. P. used to know Jesus. He used to talk to Jesus all the time. There was a time when he could have a little talk with Jesus and everything'd be all right. Four or five years ago he could. Things were better then, though. You could raise cotton and hire people to pick it. They even used to let the kids out of school to pick it. Not no more, though. Only thing kids wanted to do now was grow long hair and listen to the damn Beatles.

Mr. P. knows about hair because he cuts it in his house. People come in at night and sit around the fire in his living room and spit tobacco juice on the hearth and Mr. P. cuts their hair. He talks to them about cotton and cows and shuffles, clockwise and counter-clockwise around the chair they're sitting in, in his house shoes and undershirt and overalls and snips here and there.

Most of the time they watch TV, "Gunsmoke" or "Perry Mason." Sometimes they watch Perry Como. And sometimes, they'll get all involved and interested in a show and stay till the show's over.

One of Mr. P.'s customers—this man who lives down the road and doesn't have a TV—comes every Wednesday night to get his haircut. But Mr. P. can't cut much of his hair, having to cut it every week like that. He has to just snip the scissors around on his head some and make out like he's cutting it, comb it a little, walk around his head a few times, to make him think he's getting a real haircut. This man always comes in at 6:45 P.M., just as Mr. P. and his family are getting up from the supper table.

This man always walks up, and old Frank used to bark at him when he'd come up in the yard. It was kind of like a signal that old Frank and Mr. P. had, just between them. But it wasn't a secret code or anything. Mr. P. would be at the supper table, and he'd hear old Frank start barking, and if it was Wednesday night, he'd know to get up from the table and get his scissors. The Hillbillies always come on that night at seven, and it takes Mr. P. about fifteen minutes to cut somebody's hair.

This man starts laughing at the opening credits of the Hillbillies, and shaking his head when it shows old Jed finding his black gold, his Texas tea, just as Mr. P.'s getting through with his head. So by the time he's finished, the Hillbillies have already been on for one or two minutes. And then, when Mr. P. unpins the bedsheet around this man's neck, if there's nobody else sitting in his living room watching TV or waiting for a haircut, this man just stays in the chair, doesn't get up, and says, "I bleve I'll jest set here and watch the Hillbillies with ya'll since they already started if ya'll don't care."

It's every Wednesday night's business.

Mr. P. doesn't have a license or anything, but he actually does more than a regular barber would do. For one thing, he's got some little teenincy scissors he uses to clip hairs out of folks' noses and ears. Plus, Mr. P.'s cheaper than the barbers in town. Mr. P.'ll lower your ears for fifty cents. He doesn't do shaves, though. He's got shaky hands. He couldn't shave a balloon or anything. He could flat shave the damn Beatles though.

Mr. P.'s wondering when the school bus will come along. It's late today. What happened was, Johnny Crawford got it stuck in a ditch about a mile down the road trying to dodge one of Mr. P.'s cows. They've called for the wrecker, though, on Mr. P.'s phone. They gave out that little piece of bad news over his phone, and he thinks he heard the wrecker go down the road a while ago. He knows he needs to get up and go down there and fix that fence, get those cows up, but he doesn't think he will. He thinks he'll just stay here on the couch and drink a little more of this whiskey.

Mr. P. would rather somebody get him down on the ground and beat his ass like a drum than to have to fix that fence. The main thing is, he doesn't have anybody to help him. His wife has ruined those kids of his, spoiled them, until the oldest boy, fourteen, can't even tie his own shoelaces. Mr. P. can say something to him, tell him to come on and help him go do something for a minute, and he'll act like he's deaf and dumb. And if he does go, he whines and moans and groans and carries on about it until Mr. P. just sends him on back to the house so he won't have to listen to it. Mr. P. can see now that he messed up with his kids a long time ago. He's been too soft on them. They don't even know what work is. It just amazes Mr. P. He wasn't raised like that. He had to work when he was little. And it was rough as an old cob back then. Back then you couldn't sit around on your ass all day long and listen to a bunch of long-haired hippies singing a bunch of rock and roll on the radio.

Mr. P.'s even tried paying his kids to get out and help him work, but they won't do it. They say he doesn't pay enough. Mr. P.'s raised such a rebellious bunch of youngsters with smart mouths that they'll even tell him what the minimum wage is.

Even if his oldest boy would help him with the fence, it'd still be an awful job. First off they'd have to move all the cows to another pasture so they could tear the whole fence down and do it right. And the only other pasture Mr. P.'s got available is forty acres right next to his corn patch. They'd probably push the fence down and eat his corn up while he's across the road putting up the new fence, because his wife won't run cows. Mr. P.'s run cows and run cows and tried to get his wife out there to help him run cows and she won't hardly run cows at all. She's not fast enough to head one off or anything. Plus, she's scared of cows. She's always afraid she's going to stampede them and get run over by a crazed cow. About the only thing Mr. P.'s wife is good for when it comes to running cows is just sort of jumping around, two or three feet in any direction, waving her arms, and hollering, "Shoo!"

Mr. P. can't really think of a whole lot his wife *is* good for except setting his kids against him. It seems like they've fought him at every turn, wanting to buy new cars and drive up to Memphis to shop and getting charge accounts at one place and another and wanting him to loan money to her old drunk brother. Mr. P. doesn't know what the world's coming to. They've got another damn war started now and they'll probably be wanting his boys to go over there in a few more years and get killed or at the very least get their legs blown off. Mr. P. worries about that a good bit. But Mr. P. just worries about everything, really. Just worries all the time. There's probably not a minute that goes by when he's awake that he's not worrying about something. It's kind of like a weight he's carrying around with him that won't get off and can't get off because there's no way for it *to* get off.

The whiskey hasn't done him any good. He hoped it would, but he really knew that it wouldn't. Mr. P. thinks he knows the only thing that'll do him any good, and it won't be good.

He wonders what his wife'll say when she comes in and sees him still on the couch. Just him and Jesus, and grandpa. She's always got something to say about everything. About the only thing she doesn't say too much about is that guy who sells the siding. Mr. P.'s come up out of the pasture on the tractor four or five times and seen that guy coming out of the house after trying to sell some siding to his wife. She won't say much about him, though. She just says he's asking for directions.

Well, there the bus is to get his kids. Mr. P. can hear it pull up and he can hear the doors open. He guesses they got it out of the ditch all right. He could have taken his tractor down there and maybe pulled it out, but he might not have. A man has to be careful on a tractor. Light in the front end like they are, a man has to be careful how he hooks onto something.

Especially something heavy like a school bus. But the school bus is leaving now. Mr. P. can hear it going down the road.

It's quiet in the house now.

Yard's quiet, too.

If old Frank was in here now he'd be wanting out. Old Frank. Good little old dog. Just the happiest little thing you'd ever seen. He'd jump clean off the ground to get a biscuit out of your hand. He'd jump about three feet high. And just wag that stubby tail hard as he could.

Old Frank.

Mr. P. thinks now maybe he should have just shot his wife

instead of old Frank when she first started talking about shooting old Frank. Too late now.

Mr. P. gets another drink of the whiskey and sees Jesus looking down at him. He feels sorry for Jesus. Jesus went through a lot to save sinners like him. Mr. P. thinks, Jesus died to save me and sinners like me.

Mr. P. can see how it was that day. He figures it was hot. In a country over there like that, it was probably always hot. And that cross He had to carry was heavy. He wonders if Jesus cried from all the pain they put Him through. Just thinking about anybody being so mean to Jesus that He'd cry is enough to make Mr. P. want to cry. He wishes he could have been there to help Jesus that day. He'd have helped Him, too. If he could have known what he knows now, and could have been there that day, he'd have tried to rescue Jesus. He could have fought some of the soldiers off. But there were probably so many of them, he wouldn't have had a chance. He'd have fought for Him, though. He'd have fought for Jesus harder than he'd ever fought for anything in his life, harder than he fought on the beach at Okinawa. Given his own blood. Maybe he could have gotten his hands on a sword, and kept them away from Jesus long enough for Him to get away. But those guys were probably good sword-fighters back then. Back then they probably practiced a lot. It wouldn't have mattered to him, though. He'd have given his blood, all of it, and gladly to help Jesus.

The kids are all gone now. Old Frank's gone. His wife's still at the beauty parlor. She won't be in for a while. He gets another drink of the whiskey. It's awful good. He hates to stop drinking it, but he hates to keep on. With Jesus watching him and all.

The clock's ticking on the mantel. The hair needs sweeping off the hearth. He knows that cow's still got the white stuff running out from under her tail. But somebody else'll just have to see about it. Maybe the guy who sells the siding can see about it.

Mr. P. figures he ought to make sure it'll work first, so he pulls it out from under the couch and points it at the screen door in back. Right through the kitchen.

He figures maybe they won't be able to understand that. It'll be a big mystery that they'll never figure out. Some'll say Well he was making sure it'd work. Others'll say Aw it might have been there for years. They'll say What was he doing on the couch? And, I guess we'll have to go to town for a haircut now.

They'll even talk about how he borrowed it from Hulet for rats.

Old Frank has already gone through this. He didn't understand it. He trusted Mr. P. and knew he'd never hurt him. Maybe Mr. P. was a father to him. Maybe Mr. P. was God to him. What could he have been thinking of when he shot his best friend?

What in God's name can he be thinking of now?

Mr. Parker, fifty-eight, is reclining on his couch.

On the Lake

ELLEN DOUGLAS

LATE SUMMER IN Philippi is a deadly time of year. Other parts of the United States are hot, it is true, but not like the lower Mississippi Valley. Here the shimmering heat—the thermometer standing day after day in the high nineties and the nights breathless and oppressive—is compounded, even in a drought, by the saturated air. Thunderheads, piling up miles high in the afternoon sky, dwarf the great jet planes that fly through them. The air is heavy with moisture, but for weeks in July and August there is no rain.

In July, Lake Okatukla begins to fall. The lake, named from a meandering bayou that flows into it on the Arkansas side, bounds the town of Philippi on the west. It was once a horseshoe-shaped bend of the Mississippi, but its northern arm is blocked off from the river now by the Nine-Mile Dike, built years ago when a cut-through was made to straighten the river's course. The southern arm of the lake is still a channel into the Mississippi, through which pass towboats pushing strings of barges loaded with gravel, sand, cotton, scrap iron, soybeans, fertilizer, or oil.

In August, the lake drops steadily lower, and at the foot of the levee mud flats begin to appear around the rusty barges that serve as Philippi's municipal terminal and around the old stern-wheeler moored just above them that has been converted into the Philippi Yacht Club. The surface of the mud, covered with discarded beer cans, broken bottles, and tangles of baling wire, cracks and scales like the skin of some scrofulous river beast, and a deathlike stench pervades the hot, still air. But the lake is deep and broad—more than a mile wide at the bend, close to the town—and fifty feet out from the lowest mud flat the steely surface water hides unplumbed black depths.

Late in August, if rain falls all along the course of the Mississip-

29

pi, there will be a rise of the lake as the river backs into it. The mud flats are covered again. The trees put on pale spikes of new growth. The sandbars are washed clean. Mud runnels steam from the rain-heavy willow fronds, and the willows lift their heads. The fish begin to bite. For a week or two, from the crest of the rise, when the still water begins to clear, dropping the mud that the river has poured into the lake, until another drop has begun to expose the mud flats, Lake Okatukla is beautiful—a serene, broad wilderness of green trees and bright water, bounded at the horizon by the green range of levee sweeping in a slow curve against the sky. Looking down into the water, one can see through drifting forests of moss the quick flash of frightened bream, the shadowy threat of great saw-toothed gar. In the town, there has been little to do for weeks but wait out the heat. Only a few Negroes have braved the stench of the mud flats for the sake of a slimy catfish or a half-dead bream. After the rise, however, fishermen are out again in their skiffs, casting for bass around the trunks of the big willow trees or fishing with cane poles and minnows for white perch along the fringe willows. Family parties picnic here and there along the shore. The lake is big—twelve miles long, with dozens of curving inlets and white sandy islands. Hundreds of fishermen can spend their day trolling its shores and scarcely disturb one another.

One morning just after the August rise a few years ago, Anna Glover set out with two of her three sons, Ralph and Steve, and one of Ralph's friends, Murray McCrae, for a day on the lake. Her oldest son, who at fifteen considered himself too old for such family expeditions, and her husband, Richard, an architect, for whom summer was the busiest season of the year, had stayed behind. It was early, and the waterfront was deserted when Anna drove over the crest of the levee. She parked the car close to the Yacht Club mooring float, where the Glovers kept their fishing skiff tied up, and began to unload the gear—life jackets for the children, tackle box, bait, poles, gas can, and Skotch cooler full of beer, soft drinks, and sandwiches. She had hardly begun when she thought she heard someone shouting her name. "Miss Anna! Hey, Miss Anna!" She looked around, but, seeing the whole slope of the levee empty and no one on the deck of the Yacht Club except Gaines Williamson, the Negro bartender, she called the children back from the water's edge, toward which they had run as soon as the car stopped, and began to distribute the gear among them to carry down to the float.

Anna heaved the heavy cooler out of the car without much effort and untied the poles from the rack on the side of the car, talking as she worked. At thirty-six, she looked scarcely old enough to have three half-grown sons. Her high, round brow was unlined, her brown eyes were clear, and her strong, boyish figure in shorts and a tailored shirt looked almost like a child's. She wore her long sandy-brown hair drawn into a twist on the back of her head. Ralph and his friend Murray were ten; Steve was seven. Ralph's straight nose, solemn expression, and erect, sway-backed carriage made him look like a small preacher. Steve was gentler, with brown eyes like his mother's, fringed by a breathtaking sweep of dark lashes. They were beautiful children, or so Anna thought, for she regarded them with the most intense, subjective passion. Murray was a slender, dark boy with a closed face and a reserve that to Anna seemed impregnable. They were picking up the gear to move it down to the Yacht Club float when they all heard someone calling, and turned around.

"Ralph! Hey there, boys! Here I am, up here!" the voice cried.

"It's Estella, Mama," Ralph said. "There she is, over by the barges."

"Hi, Estella!" Steve shouted. He and Ralph put down the poles and cooler and ran along the rough, uneven slope of the levee, jumping over the iron rings set in the concrete to hold the mooring lines and over the rusty cables that held the terminal barges against the levee.

"Come on, Murray," Anna said. "Let's go speak to Estella. She's over there fishing off the ramp."

Sitting on the galvanized-iron walkway from the levee to the terminal, her legs dangling over the side of the walkway ten feet above the oily surface of the water, was Estella Moseby, a huge and beautiful Negro woman who had worked for the Glover family since the children were small. She had left them a few months before to have a child and had stayed home afterward, at James', her husband's, insistence, to raise her own family. It was the first time that Anna or the children had seen her since shortly after the child was born. Estella held a long cane pole in one hand and with the other waved toward Anna and the children. Her serene, round face was golden brown, the skin flawless even in the cruel light of the August sun, her black hair pulled severely back to a knot on her neck, her enormous dark eyes and wide mouth smiling with pleasure at the unexpected meeting. As the children approached, she drew her line out of the water and pulled herself up by the cable that served as a side rail for the walkway. The walk creaked under her shifting weight. She was fully five feet ten inches tall—at least seven inches taller than Anna—and loomed above the heads of the little group on the levee like an amiable golden giantess, her feet set wide apart to support the weight that fleshed her big frame. Her gaily flowered house dress, printed with daisies and morning-glories in shades of blue, green, and yellow, took on the very quality of her appearance, as if she were some tropical fertility goddess robed to receive her worshippers.

"Lord, Estella," Anna said. "Come on down. We haven't seen you in ages. How have you been?"

"You see me," Estella said. "Fat as ever." She carefully wrapped her line around her pole, secured the hook in the cork, and came down from her high perch to join the others on the levee. "Baby or no baby, I got to go fishing after such a fine rain," she said.

"We're going on a picnic," Steve said.

"Well, isn't that fine," Estella said. "Where is your brother?"

"Oh, he thinks he's too old to associate with us any more," Anna said. "He *scorns* us. How is the baby?"

The two women looked at each other with the shy pleasure of old friends long separated who have not yet fallen back into the easy ways of their friendship.

"Baby's fine," Estella said. "My cousin Bernice is nursing him. I said to myself this morning, 'I haven't been fishing since I got pregnant with Lee Roy. I *got* to go fishing.' So look at me. Here I am sitting on this ramp since seven this morning and no luck."

Steve threw his arms around her legs. "Estella, why don't you come *work* for us again?" he said. "We don't like *anybody* but you."

"I'm coming, honey," she said. "Let me get these kids up a little bit and I'll be back."

"Estella, why don't you go fishing with us today?" Ralph said. "We're going up to the north end of the lake and fish all day."

"Yes, come on," Anna said. "Come on and keep me company. You can't catch any fish around this old barge, and if you do they taste like fuel oil. I heard the bream are really biting in the upper lake—over on the other side, you know, in the willows."

Estella hesitated, looking out over the calm and shining dark water. "I ain't much on boats," she said. "Boats make me nervous."

"Oh, come on, Estella," Anna said. "You know you want to go."

"Well, it's the truth, I'm not catching any fish sitting here. I got two little no-'count bream on my stringer." Estella paused, and then she said, "*All* y'all going to fish from the boat? I'll crowd you."

"We're going to find a good spot and fish off the bank," Anna said. "We're already too many to fish from the boat."

"Well, it'll be a pleasure," Estella said. "I'll just come along. Let me get my stuff." She went up on the walkway again and gathered up her tackle where it lay—a brown paper sack holding sinkers, floats, hooks, and line, and her pole and a coffee can full of worms and dirt.

"I brought my gig along," Ralph said as they all trudged across the levee toward the Yacht Club. "I'm going to gig one of those great big buffalo or a gar or something."

"Well, if you do, give it to me, honey," Estella said. "James is really crazy about buffalo the way I cook it." Pulling a coin purse out of her pocket, she turned to Anna. "You reckon you might get us some beer in the Yacht Club? A nice can of beer 'long about eleven o'clock would be good."

"I've got two cans in the cooler," Anna said, "but maybe we'd better get a couple more." She took the money and, while Murray and Ralph brought the skiff around from the far side of the Yacht Club, where it was tied up, went into the bar and bought two more cans of beer. Estella and Steve, meanwhile, carried the fishing gear down to the float.

Gaines Williamson, a short, powerfully built man in his forties, followed Anna out of the bar and helped stow their gear in the little boat. The children got in first and then helped Estella in. "Lord, Miss Estella," he said, "you too big for this boat, and that's a fact." He stood back and looked down at her doubtfully, sweat shining on his face and standing in droplets on his shaven scalp.

"I must say it's none of your business," Estella said.

"We'll be all right, Gaines," Anna said. "The lake's smooth as glass."

The boys held the skiff against the float while Anna got in, and they set out, cruising slowly up the lake until they found a spot that Estella and Anna agreed looked promising. Here, on a long, clean sandbar fringed with willows, they beached the boat. The children stripped off their life jackets, pulled off the jeans they wore over their swimming trunks, and began to wade.

"You children wade here in the open water," Estella ordered. "Don't go over yonder on the other side of the bar, where the willows are growing. You'll bother the fish."

She and Anna stood looking around. Wilderness was all about them. As far as they could see on either side of the lake, not even a road ran down to the water's edge. While they watched, two white herons dragged themselves awkwardly into the air and flapped away, long legs trailing. The southern side of the sandbar, where they had beached the boat, had no trees growing on it, but the edge of the northern side, which curved in on itself and out again, was covered with willows. Here the land was higher. Beyond a low hummock crowned with cottonwood trees, Anna and Estella discovered a pool, twenty-five yards long and nearly as wide, that had been left behind by the last rise, a few days before. Fringe willows grew all around it, and the fallen trunk of a huge cottonwood lay with its roots exposed on the ground, its whole length stretched out into the still water of the pool.

"Here's the place," Estella said decidedly. "Shade for us, and fringe willows for the fish. And looka there." She pointed to the fallen tree. "If there aren't any fish under *there* . . ." They stood looking down at the pool, pleased with their find.

"I'll go get our things," Estella said. "You sit down and rest yourself, Miss Anna."

"I'll come help you."

The two women unloaded the boat, and Anna carried the cooler up the low hill and left it in the shade of one of the cottonwood trees. Then they gathered the fishing tackle and took it over to a shady spot by the pool. In a few minutes, the children joined them, and Anna passed out poles and bait. The bream were rising to crickets, and she had brought a wire cylinder basket full of them.

"You boys scatter out, now," Anna said. "There's plenty of room for everybody, and if you stay too close together you'll hook each other."

Estella helped Steve bait his hook, then baited her own and dropped it into the water as close as she could get it to the trunk of the fallen tree. Almost as soon as it reached the water, her float began to bob and quiver.

"Here we go," she said in a low voice. "Take it under, now. Take it under." She addressed herself to the business of fishing with such delight and concentration that Anna stopped in the middle of rigging a pole to watch her. Even the children, intent on finding places for themselves, turned back to see Estella catch a fish. She stood over the pool like a priestess at her altar, all expectation and willingness, holding the pole lightly, as if her fingers could read the intentions of the fish vibrating through line and pole. Her bare arms were tense, and she gazed down into the still water. A puff of wind made the leafy shadows waver and tremble on the pool, and the float rocked deceptively. Estella's arms quivered with a jerk begun and suppressed. Her flowery dress flapped around her legs, and her skin shone with sweat and oil where the sunlight struck through the leaves across her forehead and down one cheek.

"Not yet," she muttered. "*Take* it." The float bobbed and went under. "Aaah!" She gave her line a quick, short jerk to set the hook; the line tightened, the long pole bent, and she swung a big bream out onto the sand. The fish flopped off the hook and down the slope toward the water; she dropped the pole and dived at it, half falling. Ralph, who had been watching, was ahead of her, shouting with excitement, grabbing up the fish before it could flop back into the pool, and putting it into Estella's hands, careful to avoid the sharp dorsal fin.

"Look, boys, look!" she cried happily. "Just look at him!" She held out the big bream, as wide and thick as her hand, marked with blue around the gills and orange on its swollen belly. The fish twisted and gasped in her hand while she got the stringer.

She slid the metal end of the stringer through one gill and out the mouth, secured the other end to an exposed root of the fallen tree, and dropped the fish into the water, far enough away so that the bream's thrashing would not disturb their fishing spot.

"Quick now, Miss Anna," she said. "Get your line in there. I bet this pool is full of bream. Come on, boys, we're going to catch some fish today."

Anna baited her hook and dropped it in. The children scattered around the pool to their own places. In an hour, the two women had caught a dozen bream and four small catfish, and the boys had caught six or seven more bream. Then for ten minutes no one got a bite, and the boys began to lose interest. A school of minnows flashed into the shallow water at Anna's feet, and she pointed them out to Estella. "Bream are gone," she said. "They've quit feeding, or we wouldn't see any minnows."

Anna laid down her pole and told the children they could swim. "Come on, Estella," she said. "We can sit in the shade and watch them and have a beer, and then in a little while we can move to another spot."

"You aren't going to let them swim in this old lake, are you, Miss Anna?" Estella said.

"Sure. The bottom's nice and sandy here," Anna said. "Murray, your mama said you've got to keep your life preserver on if you swim." She said to Estella in a low voice, "He's not much of a swimmer. He's the only one I would worry about."

The children splashed and tumbled fearlessly in the water, Ralph and Steve popping up and disappearing, sometimes for so long that Anna, in spite of what she had said, would begin to watch anxiously for their blond heads.

"I must say, I don't see how you stand it," Estella said. "That water scares me."

"Nothing to be scared of," Anna said. "They're both good swimmers, and so am I. I could swim across the lake and back, I bet you, old as I am."

She fished two beers out of the Skotch cooler, opened them, and gave one to Estella. Then she sat down with her back against a cottonwood tree, gave Estella a cigarette, took one herself, and leaned back with a sigh. Estella sat down on a fallen log, and the two women smoked and drank their beer in silence for a few minutes. The breeze ran through the cottonwoods, shaking the leaves against each other. "I love the sound of the wind in a cottonwood tree," Anna said. "Especially at night when you wake up and hear it outside your window. I remember there was one outside the window of my room when I was a little girl, so close to the house I could climb out the window and get into it." The breeze freshened and the leaves pattered against each other. "It sounds cool," Anna said, "even in August."

"It's nice," Estella said. "Like a nice, light rain."

"Well, tell me what you've been doing with yourself," Anna said. "When are you going to move into your new house?"

"James wants to keep renting it out another year," Estella said. "He wants us to get ahead a little bit. And you know, Miss Anna, if I can hang on where I am we'll be in a good shape. We can rent that house until we finish paying for it, and then when we move we can rent the one we're in, and, you know, we own that little one next door, too. With four children now, we got to think of the future. And I must say, with all his old man's ways, James is a good provider. He looks after his own. So I go along with him. But, Lord, I can't stand it much longer. We're falling all over each other in that little tiny place. Kids under my feet all day. No place to keep the baby quiet. And in rainy weather! It's worse than a circus. I've gotten so all I do is yell at the kids. It would be a rest to go back to work."

"I wish you *would* come back to work," Anna said.

"No use talking about it," Estella said. "James says I've got to stay home at least until Lee Roy gets up to school age. And you can see for yourself I'd be paying out half what I made to get somebody to keep mine. But I'll tell you, my nerves are tore up."

"It takes a while to get your strength back after a baby," Anna said.

"Oh, I'm strong enough," Estella said. "It's not that." She pulled a stalk of Johnson grass and began to chew it thoughtfully. "I've had something on my mind," she said, "something I've been meaning to tell you ever since the baby came, and I haven't seen you by yourself—"

Anna interrupted her. "Look at the fish, Estella," she said. "They're really kicking up a fuss."

There was a wild, thrashing commotion in the water by the roots of the cottonwood tree where Estella had tied the stringer.

Estella watched a minute. "Lord, Miss Anna," she said, "something's after those fish. A turtle or something." She got up and started toward the pool as a long, dark, whiplike shape flung itself out of the water, slapped the surface, and disappeared.

"Hey," Anna said, "it's a snake! A snake!"

Estella looked around for a weapon and hastily picked up a short, heavy stick and a rock from the ground. Moving lightly and easily in spite of her weight, she ran down to the edge of the water, calling over her shoulder, "I'll scare him off. I'll chunk him. Don't you worry." She threw the rock into the churning water, but it had no effect. "Go, snake. Leave our fish alone." She stood waving her stick threateningly over the water.

Anna came down to the pool now, and they both saw the whiplike form again. Fearlessly, Estella whacked at it with her stick.

"Keep back, Estella," Anna said. "He might bite you. Wait a minute and I'll get a longer stick."

"Go, snake!" Estella shouted furiously, confidently. "What's the matter with him? He won't go off. Go, you crazy snake!"

Now the children heard the excitement and came running across the beach and over the low hill where Estella and Anna had been sitting, to see what was happening.

"A snake, a snake!" Steve screamed. "He's after the fish. Come on, y'all! It's a big old snake after the fish."

The two older boys ran up. "Get 'em out of the water, Mama," Ralph said. "He's going to eat 'em."

"I'm scared he might bite me," Anna said. "Keep back. He'll go away in a minute." She struck at the water with the stick she had picked up.

Murray looked the situation over calmly. "Why don't we gig him?" he said to Ralph.

Ralph ran down to the boat and brought back the long, barb-pointed gig. "Move, Estella," he said. "I'm gonna gig him." He struck twice at the snake and missed.

"Estella," Anna said, "I saw his head. He can't go away. He's swallowed one of the fish. He's caught on the stringer." She shuddered with disgust. "What are we going to do?" she said. "Let's throw away the stringer. We'll never get him off."

"All them beautiful fish! No, *Ma'am*," Estella said. "Here, Ralph, he can't bite us if he's swallowed a fish. I'll untie the stringer and get him up on land, and then you gig him."

"I'm going away," Steve said. "I don't want to watch." He crossed the hill and went back to the beach, where he sat down alone and began to dig a hole in the sand.

Ralph, wild with excitement, danced impatiently around Estella while she untied the stringer.

"Be calm, child," she said. She pulled the stringer out of the water and dropped it on the ground. "Now!"

The snake had indeed tried to swallow one of the bream on the stringer. Its jaws were stretched so wide as to look dislocated; its body was distended behind the head with the half-swallowed meal, and the fish's head could still be seen protruding from its mouth. The snake, faintly banded with slaty black on a brown background, was a water moccasin.

"Lord, it's a cottonmouth!" Estella cried as soon as she had the stringer out on land, where she could see the snake.

A thrill of horror and disgust raised the hair on Anna's arms. The thought of the helpless fish on the stringer sensing its enemy's approach, and then of the snake, equally and more grotesquely helpless, filled her with revulsion. "Throw it away," she commanded. And then the thought of the stringer with its living burden of fish and snake struggling and swimming away into the lake struck her as even worse. "No!" she said. "Go on. Kill the snake, Ralph."

Ralph paid no attention to his mother but stood with the long gig poised, looking up at Estella for instructions.

"Kill him," Estella said. "Now."

He drove the gig into the snake's body behind the head and pinned it to the ground, where it coiled and uncoiled convulsively, wrapping its tail around the gig and then unwrapping it and whipping it across the sand.

Anna mastered her horror as well as she could with a shake of her head. "Now what?" she said calmly.

Estella got a knife from the tackle box, held the dead but still writhing snake down with one big foot behind the gig on its body and the other on its tail, squatted, and deftly cut off the fish's head where it protruded from the gaping, fanged mouth. Then she worked the barbed point of the gig out of the body, picked the snake up on the point, and stood holding it away from her.

Ralph whirled around with excitement and circled Estella twice. "We've killed a snake," he chanted. "We've killed a snake. We've killed a snake."

"Look at it wiggle," Murray said. "It keeps on wiggling even after it's dead."

"Yeah, a snake'll wiggle like that for an hour sometimes, even with its head cut off," Estella said. "Look out, Ralph." She swept the gig forward through the air and threw the snake out into the pool, where it continued its aimless writhing on the surface of the water. She handed Ralph the gig and stood watching the snake for a few minutes, holding her hands away from her sides to keep the blood off her clothes. Then she bent down by the water's edge and washed the blood from her hands. She picked up the stringer, dropped the fish into the water, and tied the stringer to the root of the cottonwood. "There!" she said. "I didn't have no idea of throwing away all them—*those* beautiful fish. James would've skinned me if he ever heard about it."

Steve got up from the sand now and came over to his mother. He looked at the wiggling snake, and then he leaned against his mother without saying anything, put his arms around her, and laid his head against her side.

Anna stroked his hair with one hand and held him against her with the other. "It was a moccasin, honey," she said. "They're poison, you know. You have to kill them."

"I'm hungry," Ralph said. "Is it time to eat?"

Anna shook her head, gave Steve a pat, and released him. "Let me smoke a cigarette first and forget about that old snake. Then we'll eat."

Anna and Estella went back to the shade on the hill and settled themselves once more, each with a fresh can of beer and a cigarette. The children returned to the beach.

"I can do without snakes," Anna said. "Indefinitely."

Estella was still breathing hard. "I don't mind killing no snake," she said happily.

"I never saw anything like that before," Anna said. "A snake getting caught on a stringer, I mean. Did you?"

"Once or twice," Estella said. "And I've had 'em get after my stringer plenty of times."

"I don't see how you could stand to cut the fish's head off," Anna said, and shivered.

"Well, somebody had to."

"Yes, I suppose I would have done it if you hadn't been here." She laughed. "*Maybe.* I was mighty tempted to throw the whole thing away."

"I'm just as glad I wasn't pregnant," Estella said. "I'm glad it didn't happen while I was carrying Lee Roy. I would have been *helpless.*"

"You might have had a miscarriage," Anna said. She laughed again, still nervous, wanting to stop talking about the snake but not yet able to, feeling somehow that there was more to be said. "Please don't have any miscarriages on fishing trips with me," she went on. "I can do without that, too."

"Miscarriage!" Estella said. "That's not what I'm talking about. And that reminds me, what I was getting ready to tell you when we saw the snake. You know, I said I had something on my mind?"

"Uh-huh."

"You remember last summer when you weren't home that day, and that kid fell out of the tree in the yard, and all?"

"How could I forget it?" Anna said.

"You remember you spoke to me so heavy about it? Why didn't I stay out in the yard with him until his mama got there, instead of leaving him laying on the ground like that, nobody with him but Ralph, and I told you I couldn't go out there to him—couldn't look at that kid with his leg broke, and all—and you didn't understand why?"

"Yes, I remember," Anna said.

"Well, I wanted to tell you I was *blameless,*" Estella said. "I didn't want you to know it at the time, but I was pregnant. I *couldn't* go out there. It might have *marked* my child, don't you see? I might have bore a cripple."

"Oh, Estella! You don't believe that kind of foolishness, do you?" Anna said.

"*Believe* it? I've seen it happen," Estella said. "I know it's true." She was sitting on the fallen log, so that she towered above Anna, who had gone back to her place on the ground, leaning against the tree. Now Estella leaned forward with an expression of intense seriousness on her face. "My aunt looked on a two-headed calf when she was carrying a child," she said, "and her child had six fingers on one hand and seven on the other."

Anna hitched herself up higher, then got up and sat down on the log beside Estella. "But that was an accident," she said. "A coincidence. Looking at the calf didn't have anything to do with it."

Estella shook her head stubbornly. "This world is a mysterious place," she said. "Do you think you can understand everything in it?"

"No," Anna said. "Not everything. But I don't believe in magic."

"All this world is full of mystery," Estella repeated. "You got to have respect for what you don't understand. There are times to be brave and times when you go down helpless in spite of all. Like that snake. You were afraid of that snake."

"I thought he might bite me," Anna said. "And besides, it was so horrible the way he was caught."

But Estella went on as if she hadn't heard. "You see," she said, "there are things you overlook. Things, like I was telling you about my aunt, that are *true*. My mother in her day saw more wonders than that. She knew more than one that sickened and died of a spell. And this child with the fingers, I know about him for a fact. I lived with them when I was teaching school. I lived in the house with that kid. So I'm not taking any chances."

"But I thought you had lost your head and got scared because he was hurt," Anna said. "When the little boy broke his leg, I mean. I kept thinking it wasn't like you. That's what really happened, isn't it?"

"No," Estella said. "It was like I told you."

Anna said no more, but sat quiet a long time, lighting another cigarette and smoking calmly, her face expressionless. But her thoughts were in a tumult of exasperation, bafflement, and outrage. She tried unsuccessfully to deny, to block out, the overriding sense of the difference between herself and Estella, borne in on her by this strange conversation so foreign to their quiet, sensible friendship. She had often thought, with pride both in herself and in Estella, what an accomplishment their friendship was, knowing how much delicacy of feeling, how much considera- tion and understanding they had both brought to it. And now it seemed to her that it was this very friendship, so carefully nurtured for years, that Estella had unwittingly attacked. With a few words, she had put between them all that separated them, all the dark and terrible past. In the tumult of Anna's feelings there rose a queer, long-forgotten memory of a nurse she had once had as a child—the memory of a brown hand thrust out at her, holding a greasy black ball of hair combings. "You see, child, I saves my hair. I ain't never th'owed away a hair of my head."

"Why?" she had asked.

"Bad luck to th'ow away combings. Bad luck to lose any part of yourself in this old world. Fingernail parings, too. I gathers them up and carries them home and burns them. And I sits by the fire and watches until every last little bitty hair is turned plumb to smoke."

"But why?" she had asked again.

"Let your enemy possess one hair of your head and you will be in his power," the nurse had said. She had thrust the hair ball into her apron pocket, and now, in the memory, she seemed to be brushing Anna's hair, and Anna remembered standing restive under her hand, hating, as always, to have her hair brushed.

"Hurry up," she had said. "Hurry up. I got to go."

"All right, honey. I'm through." The nurse had given her head one last lick and then, bending toward her, still holding her arm while she struggled to be off and outdoors again, had thrust a dark, brooding face close to hers, had looked at her for a long, scary moment, and had laughed. "I saves your combings, too, honey. You in my power."

With an effort, Anna drew herself up short. She put out her cigarette, threw her beer can into the lake, and stood up. "I reckon we better fix some lunch," she said. "The children are starving."

By the time they had finished lunch, burned the discarded papers, thrown the bread crusts and crumbs of potato chips to the birds, and put the empty soft-drink bottles back in the cooler, it had begun to look like rain. Anna stood gazing thoughtfully into the sky. "Maybe we ought to start back," she said. "We don't want to get caught in the rain up here."

"We're not going to catch any more fish as long as the wind is blowing," Estella said.

"We want to swim some more," Ralph said.

"You can't go swimming right after lunch," Anna said. "You might get a cramp. And it won't be any fun to get caught in the rain. We'd better call it a day." She picked up one of the poles and began to wind the line around it. "Come on, kids," she said. "Let's load up."

They loaded their gear into the skiff and dropped the stringer full of fish in the bottom. Anna directed Murray and Steve to sit in the bow, facing the stern. Estella got in cautiously and took the middle seat. Anna and Ralph waded in together, pushing the skiff off the sandbar, and then got into the stern.

"You all got your life jackets on?" Anna said, glancing at the boys. "That's right."

Ralph pulled on the recoil-starter rope until he had got the little motor started, and they headed down the lake. The heavily loaded skiff showed no more than eight inches of freeboard, and as they cut through the choppy water, waves sprayed over the bow and sprinkled Murray and Steve. Anna moved the tiller and headed the skiff in closer to the shore. "We'll stay close in going down," she said. "Water's not so rough in here. And then we can cut across the lake right opposite the Yacht Club."

Estella sat still in the middle of the skiff, her back to Anna, a hand on each gunwale, as they moved steadily down the lake, rocking with the wind-rocked waves. "I don't like this old lake when it's windy," Estella said. "I don't like no windy water."

When they reached a point opposite the Yacht Club, where the lake was a little more than a mile wide, Anna headed the skiff into the rougher open water. The wind, however, was still no more than a stiff breeze, and the skiff was a quarter of the way across the lake before Anna began to be worried. Spray from the choppy waves was coming in more and more often over the bow; Murray and Steve were drenched, and an inch of water sloshed in the bottom of the skiff. Estella had not spoken since she had said "I don't like no windy water." She sat perfectly still, gripping the gunwales with both hands, her paper sack of tackle in her lap, her worm can on the seat beside her. Suddenly a gush of wind picked up the paper sack and blew it out of the boat. It struck the water and floated back to Anna, who reached out, picked it up, and dropped it by her own feet. Estella did not move, although the sack brushed against her face as it blew out. She made no attempt to catch it. She's scared, Anna thought. She's so scared she didn't even see it blow away. And Anna was frightened herself. She leaned forward, picked up the worm can from the seat beside Estella, dumped out the worms and dirt, and tapped Estella on the shoulder. "Here," she said. "Why don't you bail some of the water out of the bottom of the boat, so your feet won't get wet?"

Estella did not look around, but reached over her shoulder, took the can, and began to bail, still holding to the gunwale tightly with her left hand.

The wind freshened, the waves began to show white at their tips, the clouds in the south raced across the sky, darker and darker. But still, although they could see sheets of rain far away to the south, the sun shone on them brightly. They were now almost halfway across the lake. Anna looked over her shoulder toward the quieter water they had left behind. Along the shore of the lake, the willow trees tossed in the wind like a forest of green plumes. It's just as far one way as the other, she thought, and anyhow there's nothing to be afraid of. But while she looked back, the boat slipped off course, no longer quartering the waves, and immediately they took a big one over their bow.

"Bail, Estella," Anna said quietly, putting the boat back on course. "Get that water out of the boat." Her mind was filled with one paralyzing thought: She can't swim. My God, Estella can't swim.

Far off down the channel she saw the Gay Rosey Jane moving steadily toward the terminal, pushing a string of barges. She looked at Murray and Steve in the bow of the boat, drenched, hair plastered to their heads. "Just sit still, boys," she said. "There's nothing to worry about. We're almost there."

The wind was a gale now, and the black southern sky rushed toward them as if to engulf them. The boat took another wave over the bow, and then another. Estella bailed mechanically with the coffee can. They were still almost half a mile out from the Yacht Club. The boat's overloaded, and we're going to sink, Anna thought. My God, we're going to sink, and Estella can't swim.

"Estella," she said, "the boat will not sink. It may fill up with water, but it won't sink. Do you understand? It is all filled with cork, like a life preserver. It won't sink, do you hear me?" She repeated herself louder and louder above the wind. Estella sat with her back turned and bailed. She did not move or answer, or even nod her head. She went on bailing frantically, mechanically, dumping pint after pint of water over the side while they continued to ship waves over the bow. Murray and Steve sat in their places and stared at Anna. Ralph sat motionless by her side. No one said a word. I've got to take care of them all, Anna thought. Estella kept on bailing. The boat settled in the water and shipped another wave, wallowing now, hardly moving before the labored push of the motor. Estella gave a yell and started to rise, holding to the gunwales with both hands.

"Sit down, you fool!" Anna shouted. "*Sit down!*"

"We're gonna sink!" Estella yelled. "And I can't swim, Miss Anna! I can't swim!" For the first time, she turned, and stared at Anna with wild, blind eyes. She stood all the way up and clutched the air. "I'm gonna drown!" she yelled.

The boat rocked and settled, the motor drowned out, another wave washed in over the bow, and the boat tipped slowly up on its side. An instant later, they were all in the water and the boat was floating upside down beside them.

The children bobbed up immediately, buoyant in their life jackets. Anna glanced around once to see if they were all there. "Stay close to the boat, boys," she said.

And then Estella heaved out of the water, fighting frantically, eyes vacant, mouth open, the broad expanse of her golden face set in mindless desperation.

Anna got hold of one of the handgrips at the stern of the boat and, with her free hand, grabbed Estella's arm. "You're all right," she said. "Come on, I've got hold of the boat."

She tried to pull the huge bulk of the Negro woman toward her and guide her hand to the grip. Estella did not speak, but lunged forward in the water with a strangled yell and threw herself on Anna, flinging her arms across her shoulders. Anna felt herself sinking and scissors-kicked strongly to keep herself up, but she went down. Chin-deep in the water, she threw back her head and took a breath before Estella pushed her under. She hung on to the grip with all her strength, feeling herself battered against the boat and jerked away from it by Estella's struggle. This can't be happening, she thought. We can't be out here drowning. She felt a frantic hand brush across her face and snatch at her nose and hair. My glasses, she thought as she felt them torn away. I've lost my glasses.

Estella's weight slid away, and she, too, went under. Then both women came up and Anna got hold of Estella's arm again. "Come on," she gasped. "The *boat*."

Again Estella threw herself forward, the water streaming from her head and shoulders. This time Anna pulled her close enough to get hold of the grip, but Estella did not try to grasp it. Her hand slid, clawing, along Anna's wrist and arm; again she somehow rose up in the water and came down on Anna, and again the two women went under. This time, Estella's whole thrashing bulk was above Anna; she held with all her strength to the handgrip, but felt herself torn away from it. She came up behind Estella, who was now clawing frantically at the side of the skiff, which sank down on their side and tipped gently toward them as she pulled at it.

Anna ducked down and somehow got her shoulder against Estella's rump. Kicking and heaving with a strength she did not possess, she boosted Estella up and forward so that she fell sprawling across the boat. "*There!*" She came up as the rocking skiff began to submerge under Estella's weight. "*Stay* there!" she gasped. "*Stay* on it. For God's . . ."

But the boat was under a foot of water now, rocking and slipping away under Estella's shifting weight. Clutching and kicking crazily, mouth open in a soundless prolonged scream, eyes staring, she slipped off the other side, turned her face toward Anna, gave a strange, strangled grunt, and sank again. The water churned and foamed where she had been.

Anna swam around the boat toward her. As she swam, she realized that Ralph and Steve were screaming for help. Murray floated in the water with a queer, embarrassed smile on his face, as if he had been caught at something shameful. "I'm not here," he seemed to be saying. "This is all just an embarrassing mistake."

By the time Anna got to Estella, the boat was a couple of yards away—too far, she knew, for her to try to get Estella back to it. Estella broke the surface of the water directly in front of her and immediately flung both arms around her neck. Nothing Anna had ever learned in a lifesaving class seemed to have any bearing on this reasonless two hundred pounds of flesh with which she had to deal. They went down. This time they stayed under so long, deep in the softly yielding black water, that Anna thought she would not make it back up. Her very brain seemed ready to burst out of her ears and nostrils. She scissors-kicked again and again with all her strength—not trying to pull loose from Estella's clinging but now more passive weight—and they came up. Anna's head was thrust up and back, ready for a breath, and the instant she felt the air on her face, she took it, deep and gulping, swallowing some water at the same time, and they went down again. Estella's arms rested heavily—trustingly, it seemed—on her shoulders. She did not hug Anna or try to strangle her but simply kept holding on and pushing her down. This time, again deep in the dark water, when Anna raised her arms for a strong downstroke, she touched a foot. One of the boys was floating above their heads. She grabbed the foot without a thought and pulled with all her strength, scissors-kicking at the same time. She and Estella popped out of the water. Gasping in the life-giving air, Anna found herself staring into Steve's face as he floated beside her, weeping.

My God, I'll drown him if he doesn't get out of the way, she thought. I'll drown my own child. But she had no time to say even a word to warn him off before they went down again.

The next time up, she heard Ralph's voice, high and shrill and almost in her ear, and realized that he, too, was swimming close by, and was pounding on Estella's shoulder. "Estella, let go, let go!" he was crying. "Estella, you're drowning Mama!" Estella did not hear. She seemed not even to try to raise her head or breathe when their heads broke out of the water.

Once more they went under and came up before Anna thought, I've given out. There's no way to keep her up, and nobody is coming. And then, deep in the lake, the brassy taste of fear on her tongue, the yielding water pounding in her ears: *She's going to drown me. I've got to let her drown, or she will drown me*. She drew her knee up under her chin, planted her foot in the soft belly, still swollen from pregnancy, and shoved as hard as she could, pushing herself up and back and Estella down and away. Estella was not holding her tightly, and it was easy to push her away. The big arms slid off Anna's shoulders, the limp hands making no attempt to clutch or hold.

They had been together, close as lovers in the darkness or as twins in the womb of the lake, and now they were apart. Anna shot up into the air with the force of her shove and took a deep, gasping breath. Treading water, she waited for Estella to come up beside her, but nothing happened. The three children floated in a circle and looked at her. A vision passed through her mind of Estella's body drifting downward, downward through layers of increasing darkness, all her golden strength and flowery beauty mud-and-water-dimmed, still, aimless as a drifting log. I ought to surface-dive and look for her, she thought, and the thought of going down again turned her bowels to water.

Before she had to decide to dive, something nudged lightly against her hand, like an inquiring, curious fish. She grabbed at it and felt the inert mass of Estella's body, drained of struggle, floating below the surface of the water. She got hold of the belt of her dress and pulled. Estella's back broke the surface of the water, mounded and rocking in a dead man's float, and then sank gently down again. Anna held on to the belt. She moved her feet tiredly to keep herself afloat and looked around her. I can't even get her face out of the water, she thought. I haven't the strength to lift her head.

The boat was floating ten yards away. The Skotch cooler, bright red-and-black plaid, bobbed gaily in the water nearby. Far, far off she could see the levee. In the boat it had looked so near and the distance across the lake so little that she had said she could easily swim it, but now everything in the world except the boat, the children, and this lifeless body was unthinkably far away. Tiny black figures moved back and forth along the levee, people going about their business without a thought of tragedy. The whole sweep of the lake was empty, with not another boat in sight

except the Gay Rosey Jane, still moving up the channel. All that
had happened had happened so quickly that the towboat seemed
no nearer than it had before the skiff overturned. Murray floated
in the water a few yards off, still smiling his embarrassed smile.
Steve and Ralph stared at their mother with stricken faces. The
sun broke through the shifting blackness of the sky, and at the
same time a light rain began to fall, pattering on the choppy
surface of the lake and splashing into their faces.

All her senses dulled and muffled by shock and exhaustion,
Anna moved her feet and worked her way toward the boat,
dragging her burden.

"She's gone," Steve said. "Estella's drowned." Tears and rain
streamed down his face.

"What shall we do, Mama?" Ralph said.

Dimly, Anna realized that he had sensed her exhaustion and
was trying to rouse her.

"Yell," she said. "All three of you yell. Maybe somebody . . ."

The children screamed for help again and again, their thin,
piping voices floating away in the wind. With her last strength,
Anna continued to work her way toward the boat, pulling Estella
after her. She swam on her back, frog-kicking, and feeling the
inert bulk bump against her legs at every stroke. When she
reached the boat, she took hold of the handgrip and concentrated
on holding on to it.

"What shall we do?" Ralph said again. "They can't hear us."

Overcome with despair, Anna let her head droop toward the
water. "No one is coming," she said "It's too far. They can't hear
you." And then, from somewhere, dim thoughts of artificial
respiration, of snatching back the dead, came into her mind and
she raised her head. Still time. I've got to get her out *now,* she
thought. "Yell again," she said.

"I'm going to swim to shore and get help," Ralph said. He
looked toward his mother for a decision, but his face clearly
showed that he knew he could not expect one. He started
swimming away, his blond head bobbing in the rough water. He
did not look back.

"I don't know," Anna said. Then she remembered vaguely that
in an accident you were supposed to stay with the boat. "She's
dead," she said to herself. "My God, she's dead. My fault."

Ralph swam on, the beloved head smaller and smaller on the vast expanse of the lake. The Gay Rosey Jane moved steadily up the channel. They might run him down, Anna thought. They'd never see him. She opened her mouth to call him back.

"Somebody's coming!" Murray shouted. "They see us. Somebody's coming. Ralph!"

Ralph heard him and turned back, and now they saw two boats racing toward them, one from the Yacht Club and one from the far side of the lake, across from the terminal. In the nearer one they saw Gaines Williamson.

Thirty yards away, something happened to Gaines' engine; it raced, ground, and died. Standing in the stern of the rocking boat, he worked frantically over it while they floated and watched. It could not have been more than a minute or two before the other boat pulled up beside them, but every moment that passed, Anna knew, might be the moment of Estella's death. In the stern of the second boat they saw a wiry white man wearing a T shirt and jeans. He cut his engine when he was beside them, and, moving quickly to the side of the boat near Anna, bent over her in great excitement. "Are you all right?" he asked. He grabbed her arm with a hard, calloused hand and shook her as if he had seen that she was about to pass out. "Are you all right?" he asked again, his face close to hers.

Anna stared at him, scarcely understanding what the question meant. The children swam over to the boat, and he helped them in and then turned back to Anna. "Come on," he said, and took hold of her arm again. "You've got to help yourself. Can you make it?"

"Get this one first," she said.

"What?" He stared at her with a queer concentrated gaze, and she realized that he had not even seen Estella.

She hauled on the belt, and Estella's back broke the surface of the water, rolling, rocking, and bumping against the side of the boat. "I've got somebody else here," she said.

He grunted as if someone had hit him in the stomach. Reaching down he grabbed the back of Estella's dress, pulled her toward him, got one hand into her hair, raised her face out of the water, and, bracing himself against the gunwale, held her there. Estella's peaceful face turned slowly toward him. Her mouth and eyes were closed, her expression was one of deep repose. The man stared at her and then at Anna. "My God," he said.

"We've got to get her into the boat," Anna said. "If we can get her where we can give her artificial respiration . . ."

"It's Estella," Steve said. "Mama had her all the time." He began to cry again. "Let go of her hair," he said. "You're hurting her."

The three children shifted all at once to the side of the boat where the man was still holding Estella, and he turned on them sternly. "Get back," he said "Sit *down*. And sit still."

The children scuttled back to their places. "You're hurting her," Steve said again.

"It's all right, son," the man said. "She can't feel a thing." To Anne, in a lower voice, he said, "She's dead."

"I'll push and you pull," Anna said "Maybe we can get her into the boat."

He shifted his position, bracing himself as well as he could in the rocking boat, rested Estella's head on his own shoulder, and put both arms around her. They heaved and pushed at the limp body, but they could not get her into the boat. The man let her down into the water again, this time holding her under the arms. A hundred yards away, Gaines still struggled with his engine.

"Hurry up!" the man shouted. "Get on over here. We can't lift this woman by ourselves."

"Fishing lines tangled in the screw!" Gaines shouted back. His engine caught and died again.

"We're going to have to tow her in," the man said. "That fellow can't start his boat." He reached behind him and got a life jacket. "We'd better put this on her," he said. They worked Estella's arms into the life jacket and fastened the straps. "I've got a rope here somewhere," he said. "Hold her a minute. Wait." He handed Anna a life jacket. "You put one on, too." While he still held Estella by the hair, Anna struggled into the life jacket, and then took hold of the straps of Estella's. Just then, Gaines got his engine started, raced across the open water, and drew up beside them.

The two boats rocked in the rough water with Anna and Estella between them. Anna, with a hand on the gunwale of each, held them apart while the two men, straining and grunting, hauled

Estella's body up out of the water and over the gunwale of Gaines' boat. Gaines heaved her legs in. She flopped, face down, across the seat and lay with one arm hanging over the side, the hand trailing in the water. Anna lifted the arm and put it in the boat. Then the white man pulled Anna into his boat. As he helped her over the side, she heard a smacking blow, and, looking back, saw that Gaines had raised and turned Estella's body and was pounding her in the belly. Water poured out of her mouth and, in reflex, air rushed in.

The boats roared off across the lake toward the Yacht Club. The white man's was much the faster of the two, and he quickly pulled away. As soon as they were within calling distance, he stood up in the boat and began to yell at the little group gathered on the Yacht Club mooring float. "Drowned! She's drowned!" he yelled. "Call an ambulance. Get a resuscitator down here. Hurry!"

They drew up to the float. He threw a rope to one of the Negroes standing there and jumped out. Anna dragged herself to a sitting position and stared stupidly at the crowd of Negroes. Gaines Williamson pulled up behind them in the other boat.

"Give us a hand," the white man said. "Let's get her out of there. My God, she's huge. Somebody lend a hand."

To Anna it seemed that all the rest of the scene on the float took place above and far away from her. She saw legs moving back and forth, heard voices and snatches of conversation, felt herself moved from one place to another, but nothing that happened interrupted her absorption in grief and guilt. For the time, nothing existed for her except the belief that Estella was dead.

Someone took her arm and helped her onto the float while the children climbed up by themselves. She sat down on the splintery boards, surrounded by legs, and no one paid any attention to her.

"I saw 'em." The voice of a Negro woman in the crowd. "I was setting on the levee and I saw 'em. You heard me. 'My Lord save us, some folks out there drowning,' I said. I was up on the levee and I run down to the Yacht Club..."

"Did somebody call an ambulance?" the white man asked.

"I run down here to the Yacht Club, like to killed myself running, and..."

"How..."

"Gay Rosey Jane swamped them. Never even seen them. Them towboats don't stop for nobody. See, there she goes. Never seen them at all."

"Still got a stitch in my side. My Lord, I like to killed myself running."

"Anybody around here know how to give artificial respiration?"

"I was sitting right yonder on the terminal fishing with her this morning. Would you believe that?"

"God have mercy on us."

"Oh, Lord. Oh, Lord God. Lord God."

"Have mercy on us."

A young Negro in Army khakis walked over to where the white man and Gaines Williamson were trying to get Estella out of the bulky jacket. "We'll cut it off," he said calmly. He pulled a straight razor from his pocket, slit one shoulder of the life jacket, pushed it out of the way, and straddled Estella's body. "I know how," he said. "I learned in the Army." He arranged her body in position—lying flat on her stomach, face turned to the side and arms above her head—and set to work, raising her arms and then her body rhythmically. When he lifted her body in the middle, her face dragged on the splintery planks of the float.

Anna crawled through the crowd to where Estella lay. Squatting down without a word, she put her hands under Estella's face to protect it from the splinters. It passed through her mind that she should do something about the children. Looking around, she saw them standing in a row at one side of the float, staring down at her and Estella—no longer crying, just standing and staring. Somebody ought to get them away from here, she thought vaguely, but the thought left her mind and she forgot them. She swayed, rocked back on her heels, sat down suddenly, and then lay on her stomach, her head against Estella's head, her hands cradling the sleeping face.

Who's going to tell James, she thought. Who's going to tell him she's dead? And then, I. I have to tell him. She began to talk to Estella. "Please, darling," she said. "Please, Estella, breathe." Tears of weakness rolled down her face, and she looked up above the forest of legs at the black faces in a circle around them. "She's got four babies," she said. "*Babies*. Who's going to tell her husband she's dead? Who's going to tell him?" And then, again, "Please, Estella, breathe. Please breathe."

No one answered. The young Negro soldier continued to raise the limp arms and body alternately, his motions deliberate and rhythmical, the sweat pouring off his face and dripping down on his sweat-soaked shirt. His thin face was intent and stern. The storm was over, the clouds to the west had blown away, and the sun had come out and beat down bright and hot, raising steamy air from the rain-soaked float.

A long time passed. The soldier giving Estella artificial respiration looked around at the crowd. "Anybody know how to do this? I'm about to give out." He did not pause or break the rhythm of his motions.

A man stepped out of the crowd. "I can do it," he said. "I know how."

"Come on, then," the soldier said. "Get down here by me and do it with me three times, and then, when I stop, you take over. Don't break it."

"Please, Estella," Anna said. "Please."

"One . . . Two . . ."

She felt someone pulling at her arm and looked up. A policeman was standing over her. "Here, lady," he said. "Get up off that dock. You ain't doing no good."

"But the splinters will get in her face," Anna said. "I'm holding her face off the boards."

"It ain't going to matter if her face is tore up if she's dead," the policeman said. "Get up."

Someone handed her a towel, and she folded it and put it under Estella's face. The policeman dragged her to her feet and took her over to a chair near the edge of the float and sat her down in it. He squatted beside her. "Now, who was in the boat?" he said. "I got to make a report."

Anna made a vague gesture. "We were," she said.

"Who is 'we,' lady?"

"Estella and I and the children."

"Lady, give me the names, please," the policeman said.

"Estella Moseby, the Negro woman. She used to work for me and we *asked* her, we asked her—" She broke off.

"Come on, who else?"

Anna stared at him, a short, bald man with shining pink scalp, and drum belly buttoned tightly into his uniform. A wave of nausea overcame her, and she saw his head surrounded by the shimmering black spokes of a rimless wheel, a black halo. "I'm going to be sick," she said. Collapsing out of the chair onto the dock, she leaned her head over the edge and vomited into the lake.

He waited until she was through and then helped her back into her chair. "Who else was with you?" he said.

"My two children, Ralph and Steve," she said. "Murray McCrae. I am Mrs. Richard Glover."

"Where is this McCrae fellow? He all right?"

"He's a little *boy*," Anna said. "A child. He's over there somewhere."

"You sure there wasn't nobody else with you?"

"No. That's all," Anna said.

"Now, give me the addresses, please. Where did the nigger live?"

"For God's sake," Anna said. "What difference does it make? Go away and let me alone."

"I got to make my report, lady."

Ralph tugged at Anna's arm. "Mama, hadn't I better call Daddy?" he said.

"Yes," she said. "Yes, I guess you had." Oh, God, she thought, he has to find out. I can't put it off. Everybody has to find out that Estella is dead.

Anna heard a commotion on the levee. The steadily increasing crowd separated, and two white-jacketed men appeared and began to work over Estella. Behind them, a woman with a camera snapped pictures.

"What are they taking *pictures* of her for?" Anna asked.

Then she heard her husband's voice shouting, "Get off the damn raft, God damn it! Get off. You want to sink it? Get back there. You want to drown us all?"

The policeman stood up and went toward the crowd. "What the hell?" Anna heard him say.

"And put that camera up, if you don't want me to throw it in the lake." Anna's husband was in a fury of outrage, and concentrated it for the moment on the woman reporter from the local newspaper, who was snapping pictures of Estella.

"You all right, Anna?" Richard asked her.

The people on the float were scuttling back to the levee, and the reporter had disappeared. Anna, who was still sitting where the policeman had left her, nodded, and opened her mouth to speak, but her husband was gone before she could say anything. She felt a wave of self-pity. He didn't even stay to help me, she thought.

Then, a moment or an hour later—she did not know how long—she heard a strange high-pitched shriek from the other end of the float. What's that, she thought. It sounded again—a long, rasping rattle and then a shriek. Does the machine they brought make that queer noise?

"She's breathing," somebody said.

"No," Anna said aloud to nobody, for nobody was listening. "No. She's dead. I couldn't help it. I let her drown. Who's going to tell James?"

The float was cleared now. Besides Estella and Anna, only the two policemen, the two men from the ambulance, and Gaines Williamson were on it. The man who had rescued them was gone. The crowd stood quietly on the levee.

"Where is Richard?" Anna said. "Did he leave?"

No one answered.

The long, rasping rattle and shriek sounded again. Gaines Williamson came over to where Anna was sitting, and bent down to her, smiling kindly. "She's alive, Mrs. Glover," he said. "She's going to be all right."

Anna shook her head.

"Yes, Ma'am. She's moving and breathing, and yelling like crazy. She's going to be all right."

Anna got up shakily. She walked over to where the men were working Estella onto a stretcher.

"What's she doing?" she said. "What's the matter with her?"

Estella was thrashing her arms and legs furiously, mouth open, eyes staring, her face again the mask of mindless terror that Anna had seen in the lake. The rattle and shriek were her breathing and screaming.

"She must think she's still in the water," one of the men said. "Shock. But she's O.K. Look at her kick."

Anna sat down on the float, her knees buckling under her, and someone pulled her out of the way while four men carried the stretcher off the float and up the levee toward the ambulance.

Richard reappeared at the foot of the levee and crossed the walkway to the Yacht Club float. He bent down to help her up. "I'm sorry I had to leave you," he said. "I had to get the children away from here and find someone to take them home."

"My God," Anna said. "She's alive. They said she would be all right."

Later, in the car, she said to her husband, "She kept pushing me down, Richard. I tried to hold her up, I tried to make her take hold of the boat. But she kept pushing me down."

"It's all right now," he said. "Try not to think about it any more."

The next day, when Anna visited Estella in the hospital, she learned that Estella remembered almost nothing of what had happened. She recalled getting into the skiff for the trip home, but everything after that was gone.

"James says you saved my life," she said, in a hoarse whisper, "and I thank you."

Her husband stood at the head of her bed, gray-haired and dignified in his Sunday suit. He nodded. "The day won't come when we'll forget it, Miss Anna," he said. "God be my witness."

Anna shook her head. "I never should have taken you out without a life preserver," she said.

"Ain't she suppose to be a grown woman?" James said. "She suppose to know better herself."

"How do you feel?" Anna asked.

"Lord, not a square inch on my body don't ache," Estella said. She laid her hands on the mound of her body under the sheet. "My stomach!" she said, with a wry laugh. "Somebody must've jumped up and down on it."

"I reckon that's from the artificial respiration," Anna said. "I had never seen anyone do it that way before. They pick you up under the stomach and then put you down and lift your arms. And then, too, I kicked you. And we must have banged you up some getting you into the boat. Lord! The more I think about it, the worse it gets. Because Gaines hit you in the stomach, too, as soon as he got you into the boat. That's what really saved your life. As soon as he got you into the boat, he hit you in the stomach and got rid of a lot of the water in your lungs and let in some air. I believe that breath you took in Gaines' boat kept you alive until we got you to the dock."

"You kicked me?" Estella said.

"We were going down," Anna said, feeling that she must confess to Estella the enormity of what she had done, "and I finally knew I couldn't keep you up. I kicked you in the stomach hard, and got loose from you, and then when you came up I grabbed you and held on, and about that time they saw us and the boats came. You passed out just when I kicked you, or else the kick knocked you out, because you didn't struggle any more. I reckon that was lucky, too."

Estella shook her head. "I can't remember anything about it," she whispered. "Not anything." She pointed out the window toward the smokestack rising from the opposite wing of the hospital. "Seems like last night I got the idea there's a little man up there," she said. "He peeps out from behind the smokestack at me, and I'm afraid of him. He leans on the smokestack, and then he jumps away real quick, like it's hot, and one time he came right over here and stood on the window ledge and looked in at me. Lucky the window was shut. I said 'Boo!' and, you know, he fell off! It didn't hurt him; he came right back. He wants to tell me something, yes, but he can't get in." She closed her eyes.

Anna looked anxiously at James.

"They still giving her something to keep her quiet," he said. "Every so often she gets a notion somebody trying to get in here."

Estella opened her eyes. "I thank you, Miss Anna," she said. "James told me you saved my life." She smiled. "Seems like every once in a while I heard your voice," she said. "Way off. Way, way off. You're saying, 'I'll save you, Estella. Don't be afraid. I'll save you.' That's all I can remember."

Barn Burning

WILLIAM FAULKNER

THE STORE IN which the Justice of the Peace's court was sitting smelled of cheese. The boy, crouched on his nail keg at the back of the crowded room, knew he smelled cheese, and more: from where he sat he could see the ranked shelves close-packed with the solid, squat, dynamic shapes of tin cans whose labels his stomach read, not from the lettering which meant nothing to his mind but from the scarlet devils and the silver curve of fish—this, the cheese which he knew he smelled and the hermetic meat which his intestines believed he smelled coming in intermittent gusts momentary and brief between the other constant one, the smell and sense just a little of fear because mostly of despair and grief, the old fierce pull of blood. He could not see the table where the Justice sat and before which his father and his father's enemy (*our enemy* he thought in that despair; *ourn! mine and hisn both! He's my father!*) stood, but he could hear them, the two of them that is, because his father had said no word yet:

"But what proof have you, Mr. Harris?"

"I told you. The hog got into my corn. I caught it up and sent it back to him. He had no fence that would hold it. I told him so, warned him. The next time I put the hog in my pen. When he came to get it I gave him enough wire to patch up his pen. The next time I put the hog up and kept it. I rode down to his house and saw the wire I gave him still rolled on to the spool in his yard. I told him he could have the hog when he paid me a dollar pound fee. That evening a nigger came with the dollar and got the hog. He was a strange nigger. He said, 'He say to tell you wood and hay kin burn.' I said, 'What?' 'That whut he say to tell you,' the nigger said. 'Wood and hay kin burn.' That night my barn burned. I got the stock out but I lost the barn."

"Where is the nigger? Have you got him?"

"He was a strange nigger, I tell you. I don't know what became of him."

"But that's not proof. Don't you see that's not proof?"

"Get that boy up here. He knows." For a moment the boy thought too that the man meant his older brother until Harris said, "Not him. The little one. The boy," and, crouching, small for his age, small and wiry like his father, in patched and faded jeans even too small for him, with straight, uncombed, brown hair and eyes gray and wild as storm scud, he saw the men between himself and the table part and become a lane of grim faces, at the end of which he saw the Justice, a shabby, collarless, graying man in spectacles, beckoning him. He felt no floor under his bare feet; he seemed to walk beneath the palpable weight of the grim turning faces. His father, stiff in his black Sunday coat donned not for the trial but for the moving, did not even look at him. *He aims for me to lie,* he thought, again with that frantic grief and despair. *And I will have to do hit.*

"What's your name, boy?" the Justice said.

"Colonel Sartoris Snopes," the boy whispered.

"Hey?" the Justice said. "Talk louder. Colonel Sartoris? I reckon anybody named for Colonel Sartoris in this country can't help but tell the truth, can they?" The boy said nothing. *Enemy! Enemy!* he thought; for a moment he could not even see, could not see that the Justice's face was kindly nor discern that his voice was troubled when he spoke to the man named Harris: "Do you want me to question this boy?" But he could hear, and during those subsequent long seconds while there was absolutely no sound in the crowded little room save that of quiet and intent breathing it was as if he had swung outward at the end of a grape vine, over a ravine, and at the top of the swing had been caught in a prolonged instant of mesmerized gravity, weightless in time.

"No!" Harris said violently, explosively. "Damnation! Send him out of here!" Now time, the fluid world, rushed beneath him again, the voices coming to him again through the smell of cheese and sealed meat, the fear and despair and the old grief of blood:

"This case is closed. I can't find against you, Snopes, but I can give you advice. Leave this country and don't come back to it."

His father spoke for the first time, his voice cold and harsh, level, without emphasis: "I aim to. I don't figure to stay in a country among people who..." he said something unprintable and vile, addressed to no one.

"That'll do," the Justice said. "Take your wagon and get out of this country before dark. Case dismissed."

His father turned, and he followed the stiff black coat, the wiry figure walking stiffly from where a Confederate provost's man's musket ball had taken him in the heel on a stolen horse thirty years ago, followed the two backs now, since his older brother had appeared from somewhere in the crowd, no taller than the father but thicker, chewing tobacco steadily, between the two lines of grim-faced men and out of the store and across the worn gallery and down the sagging steps and among the dogs and half-grown boys in the mild May dust, where as he passed a voice hissed:

"Barn burner!"

Again he could not see, whirling; there was a face in a red haze, moonlike, bigger than the full moon, the owner of it half again his size, he leaping in the red haze toward the face, feeling no blow, feeling no shock when his head struck the earth, scrabbling up and leaping again, feeling no blow this time either and tasting no blood, scrabbling up to see the other boy in full flight and himself already leaping into pursuit as his father's hand jerked him back, the harsh, cold voice speaking above him: "Go get in the wagon."

It stood in a grove of locusts and mulberries across the road. His two hulking sisters in their Sunday dresses and his mother and her sister in calico and sunbonnets were already in it, sitting on and among the sorry residue of the dozen and more movings which even the boy could remember—the battered stove, the broken beds and chairs, the clock inlaid with mother-of-pearl, which would not run, stopped at some fourteen minutes past two o'clock of a dead and forgotten day and time, which had been his mother's dowry. She was crying, though when she saw him she drew her sleeve across her face and began to descend from the wagon. "Get back," the father said.

"He's hurt. I got to get some water and wash his..."

"Get back in the wagon," his father said. He got in too, over the tail-gate. His father mounted to the seat where the older brother already sat and struck the gaunt mules two savage blows with the peeled willow, but without heat. It was not even sadistic; it was exactly that same quality which in later years would cause his descendants to over-run the engine before putting a motor car into motion, striking and reining back in the same movement. The wagon went on, the store with its quiet crowd of grimly watching men dropped behind; a curve in the road hid it. *Forever* he thought. *Maybe he's done satisfied now, now that he has* . . . stopping himself, not to say it aloud even to himself. His mother's hand touched his shoulder.

"Does hit hurt?" she said.

"Naw," he said. "Hit don't hurt. Lemme be."

"Can't you wipe some of the blood off before hit dries?"

"I'll wash to-night," he said. "Lemme be, I tell you."

The wagon went on. He did not know where they were going. None of them ever did or ever asked, because it was always somewhere, always a house of sorts waiting for them a day or two days or even three days away. Likely his father had already arranged to make a crop on another farm before he . . . Again he had to stop himself. He (the father) always did. There was something about his wolflike independence and even courage when the advantage was at least neutral which impressed strangers, as if they got from his latent ravening ferocity not so much a sense of dependability as a feeling that his ferocious conviction in the rightness of his own actions would be of advantage to all whose interest lay with his.

That night they camped, in a grove of oaks and beeches where a spring ran. The nights were still cool and they had a fire against it, of a rail lifted from a nearby fence and cut into lengths—a small fire, neat, niggard almost, a shrewd fire; such fires were his father's habit and custom always, even in freezing weather. Older, the boy might have remarked this and wondered why not a big one; why should not a man who had not only seen the waste and extravagance of war, but who had in his blood an inherent voracious prodigality with material not his own, have burned everything in sight? Then he might have gone a step farther and thought that that was the reason: that niggard blaze was the living fruit of nights passed during those four years in the woods hiding from all men, blue or gray, with his strings of horses (captured horses, he called them). And older still, he might have divined the true reason: that the element of fire spoke to some deep mainspring of his father's being, as the element of steel or of

powder spoke to other men, as the one weapon for the preserva-
tion of integrity, else breath were not worth the breathing, and
hence to be regarded with respect and used with discretion.

But he did not think this now and he had seen those same
niggard blazes all his life. He merely ate his supper beside it and
was already half asleep over his iron plate when his father called
him, and once more he followed the stiff back, the stiff and
ruthless limp, up the slope and on to the starlit road where,
turning, he could see his father against the stars but without face
or depth—a shape black, flat, and bloodless as though cut from tin
in the iron folds of the frockcoat which had not been made for
him, the voice harsh like tin and without heat like tin:

"You were fixing to tell them. You would have told him." He
didn't answer. His father struck him with the flat of his hand on
the side of the head, hard but without heat, exactly as he had
struck the two mules at the store, exactly as he would strike
either of them with any stick in order to kill a horse fly, his voice
still without heat or anger: "You're getting to be a man. You got to
learn. You got to learn to stick to your own blood or you ain't
going to have any blood to stick to you. Do you think either of
them, any man there this morning, would? Don't you know all
they wanted was a chance to get at me because they knew I had
them beat? Eh?" Later, twenty years later, he was to tell himself,
"If I had said they wanted only truth, justice, he would have hit
me again." But now he said nothing. He was not crying. He just
stood there. "Answer me," his father said.

"Yes," he whispered. His father turned.

"Get on to bed. We'll be there tomorrow."

To-morrow they were there. In the early afternoon the wagon
stopped before a paintless two-room house identical almost with
the dozen others it had stopped before even in the boy's ten
years, and again, as on the other dozen occasions, his mother and
aunt got down and began to unload the wagon, although his two
sisters and his father and brother had not moved.

"Likely hit ain't fitten for hawgs," one of the sisters said.

"Nevertheless, fit it will and you'll hog it and like it," his father
said. "Get out of them chairs and help your Ma unload."

The two sisters got down, big, bovine, in a flutter of cheap
ribbons; one of them drew from the jumbled wagon bed a

battered lantern, the other a worn broom. His father handed the reins to the older son and began to climb stiffly over the wheel. "When they get unloaded, take the team to the barn and feed them." Then he said, and at first the boy thought he was still speaking to his brother: "Come with me."

"Me?" he said.

"Yes," his father said. "You."

"Abner," his mother said. His father paused and looked back— the harsh level stare beneath the shaggy, graying, irascible brows.

"I reckon I'll have a word with the man that aims to begin to-morrow owning me body and soul for the next eight months."

They went back up the road. A week ago—or before last night, that is—he would have asked where they were going, but not now. His father had struck him before last night but never before had he paused afterward to explain why; it was as if the blow and the following calm, outrageous voice still rang, repercussed, divulging nothing to him save the terrible handicap of being young, the light weight of his few years, just heavy enough to prevent his soaring free of the world as it seemed to be ordered but not heavy enough to keep him footed solid in it, to resist it and try to change the course of its events.

Presently he could see the grove of oaks and cedars and the other flowering trees and shrubs where the house would be, though not the house yet. They walked beside a fence massed with honeysuckle and Cherokee roses and came to a gate swinging open between two brick pillars, and now, beyond a sweep of drive, he saw the house for the first time and at that instant he forgot his father and the terror and despair both, and even when he remembered his father again (who had not stopped) the terror and despair did not return. Because, for all the twelve movings, they had sojourned until now in a poor country, a land of small farms and fields and houses, and he had never seen a house like this before. *Hit's big as a courthouse* he thought quietly, with a surge of peace and joy whose reason he could not have thought into words, being too young for that: *They are safe from him. People whose lives are a part of this peace and dignity are beyond his touch, he no more to them than a buzzing wasp: capable of stinging for a little moment but that's all; the spell of this peace and dignity rendering even the barns and stable and cribs which belong to it impervious to the puny flames he might contrive*...this, the peace and joy, ebbing for an instant as he looked again at the stiff black back, the stiff and implacable limp of the figure which was not dwarfed by the house, for the reason that it had never looked big anywhere and which now, against the serene columned backdrop, had more than ever that impervious quality of some-thing cut ruthlessly from tin, depthless as though, sidewise to the sun, it would cast no shadow. Watching him, the boy remarked the absolutely undeviating course which his father held and saw the stiff foot come squarely down in a pile of fresh droppings where a horse had stood in the drive and which his father could have avoided by a simple change of stride. But it ebbed only for a moment, though he could not have thought this into words either, walking on in the spell of the house, which he could even want but without envy, without sorrow, certainly never with that raven-ing and jealous rage which unknown to him walked in the ironlike black coat before him: *Maybe he will feel it too. Maybe it will even change him now from what maybe he couldn't help but be.*

They crossed the portico. Now he could hear his father's stiff foot as it came down on the boards with clocklike finality, a sound out of all proportion to the displacement of the body it bore and which was not dwarfed either by the white door before it, as though it had attained to a sort of vicious and ravening minimum not to be dwarfed by anything—the flat, wide, black hat, the formal coat of broadcloth which had once been black but which had now the friction-glazed greenish cast of the bodies of old house flies, the lifted sleeve which was too large, the lifted hand like a curled claw. The door opened so promptly that the boy knew the Negro must have been watching them all the time, an old man with neat grizzled hair, a linen jacket, who stood barring the door with his body, saying, "Wipe yo foots, white man, fo you come in here. Major ain't home nohow."

"Get out of my way, nigger," his father said, without heat too, flinging the door back and the Negro also and entering, his hat still on his head. And now the boy saw the prints of the stiff foot on the doorjamb and saw them appear on the pale rug behind the machinelike deliberation of the foot which seemed to bear (or transmit) twice the weight which the body compassed. The Negro was shouting "Miss Lula! Miss Lula!" somewhere behind them, then the boy, deluged as though by a warm wave by a suave turn of carpeted stair and a pendant glitter of chandeliers and a mute gleam of gold frames, heard the swift feet and saw her too, a lady—perhaps he had never seen her like before either—in a gray, smooth gown with lace at the throat and an apron tied at the waist and the sleeves turned back, wiping cake or biscuit dough from her hands with a towel as she came up the hall, looking not at his father at all but at the tracks on the blond rug with an expression of incredulous amazement.

"I tried," the Negro cried. "I tole him to..."

"Will you please go away?" she said in a shaking voice. "Major de Spain is not at home. Will you please go away?"

His father had not spoken again. He did not speak again. He did not even look at her. He just stood stiff in the center of the rug, in his hat, the shaggy iron-gray brows twitching slightly above the pebble-colored eyes as he appeared to examine the house with brief deliberation. Then with the same deliberation he turned; the boy watched him pivot on the good leg and saw the stiff foot drag round the arc of the turning, leaving a final long and fading smear. His father never looked at it, he never once looked down at the rug. The Negro held the door. It closed behind them, upon the hysteric and indistinguishable woman-wail. His father stopped at the top of the steps and scraped his boot clean on the edge of it. At the gate he stopped again. He stood for a moment, planted stiffly on the stiff foot, looking back at the house. "Pretty and white, ain't it?" he said. "That's sweat. Nigger sweat. Maybe it ain't white enough yet to suit him. Maybe he wants to mix some white sweat with it."

Two hours later the boy was chopping wood behind the house within which his mother and aunt and the two sisters (the mother and aunt, not the two girls, he knew that; even at this distance and muffled by walls the flat loud voices of the two girls emanated an incorrigible idle inertia) were setting up the stove to prepare a meal, when he heard the hooves and saw the linen-clad man on a fine sorrel mare, whom he recognized even before he saw the rolled rug in front of the Negro youth following on a fat bay carriage horse—a suffused, angry face vanishing, still at full gallop, beyond the corner of the house where his father and brother were sitting in the two tilted chairs; and a moment later, almost before he could have put the axe down, he heard the hooves again and watched the sorrel mare go back out of the yard, already galloping again. Then his father began to shout one of the sisters' names, who presently emerged backward from the kitchen door dragging the rolled rug along the ground by one end while the other sister walked behind it.

"If you ain't going to tote, go on and set up the wash pot," the first said.

"You, Sarty!" the second shouted. "Set up the wash pot!" His father appeared at the door, framed against that shabbiness, as he had been against that other bland perfection, impervious to either, the mother's anxious face at his shoulder.

"Go on," the father said. "Pick it up." The two sisters stooped, broad, lethargic; stooping, they presented an incredible expanse of pale cloth and a flutter of tawdry ribbons.

"If I thought enough of a rug to have to git hit all the way from France I wouldn't keep hit where folks coming in would have to tromp on hit," the first said. They raised the rug.

"Abner," the mother said. "Let me do it."

"You go back and git dinner," his father said. "I'll tend to this."

From the woodpile through the rest of the afternoon the boy watched them, the rug spread flat in the dust beside the bubbling wash-pot, the two sisters stooping over it with that profound and lethargic reluctance, while the father stood over them in turn, implacable and grim, driving them though never raising his voice again. He could smell the harsh homemade lye they were using; he saw his mother come to the door once and look toward them with an expression not anxious now but very like despair; he saw his father turn, and he fell to with the axe and saw from the corner of his eye his father raise from the ground a flattish fragment of field stone and examine it and return to the pot, and this time his mother actually spoke: "Abner. Abner. Please don't. Please, Abner."

Then he was done too. It was dusk; the whippoorwills had already begun. He could smell coffee from the room where they would presently eat the cold food remaining from the mid-afternoon meal, though when he entered the house he realized they were having coffee again probably because there was a fire on the hearth, before which the rug now lay spread over the backs of the two chairs. The tracks of his father's foot were gone. Where they had been were now long, water-cloudy scoriations resembling the sporadic course of a lilliputian mowing machine.

It still hung there while they ate the cold food and then went to bed, scattered without order or claim up and down the two rooms, his mother in one bed, where his father would later lie, the older brother in the other, himself, the aunt, and the two sisters on pallets on the floor. But his father was not in bed yet. The last thing the boy remembered was the depthless, harsh silhouette of the hat and coat bending over the rug and it seemed to him that he had not even closed his eyes when the silhouette was standing over him, the fire almost dead behind it, the stiff foot prodding him awake. "Catch up the mule," his father said.

When he returned with the mule his father was standing in the black door, the rolled rug over his shoulder. "Ain't you going to ride?" he said.

"No. Give me your foot."

He bent his knee into his father's hand, the wiry, surprising power flowed smoothly, rising, he rising with it, on to the mule's bare back (they had owned a saddle once; the boy could remember it though not when or where) and with the same effortlessness his father swung the rug up in front of him. Now in the starlight they retraced the afternoon's path, up the dusty road rife with honeysuckle, through the gate and up the black tunnel of the drive to the lightless house, where he sat on the mule and felt the rough warp of the rug drag across his thighs and vanish.

"Don't you want me to help?" he whispered. His father did not answer and now he heard again that stiff foot striking the hollow portico with that wooden and clocklike deliberation, that outrageous overstatement of the weight it carried. The rug, hunched, not flung (the boy could tell that even in the darkness) from his father's shoulder struck the angle of wall and floor with a sound unbelievably loud, thunderous, then the foot again, unhurried and enormous; a light came on in the house and the boy sat, tense, breathing steadily and quietly and just a little fast, though the foot itself did not increase its beat at all, descending the steps now; now the boy could see him.

"Don't you want to ride now?" he whispered. "We kin both ride now," the light within the house altering now, flaring up and sinking. *He's coming down the stairs now,* he thought. He had already ridden the mule up beside the horse block; presently his father was up behind him and he doubled the reins over and slashed the mule across the neck, but before the animal could begin to trot the hard, thin arm came around him, the hard, knotted hand jerking the mule back to a walk.

In the first red rays of the sun they were in the lot, putting plow gear on the mules. This time the sorrel mare was in the lot before he heard it at all, the rider collarless and even bareheaded, trembling, speaking in a shaking voice as the woman in the house had done, his father merely looking up once before stooping again to the hame he was buckling, so that the man on the mare spoke to his stooping back:

"You must realize you have ruined that rug. Wasn't there anybody here, any of your women..." he ceased, shaking, the boy watching him, the older brother leaning now in the stable door, chewing, blinking slowly and steadily at nothing apparently. "It cost a hundred dollars. But you never had a hundred dollars. You never will. So I'm going to charge you twenty bushels of corn against your crop. I'll add it in your contract and when you come to the commissary you can sign it. That won't keep Mrs. de Spain quiet but maybe it will teach you to wipe your feet off before you enter her house again."

Then he was gone. The boy looked at his father, who still had not spoken or even looked up again, who was now adjusting the loggerhead in the hame.

"Pap," he said. His father looked at him—the inscrutable face, the shaggy brows beneath which the gray eyes glinted coldly. Suddenly the boy went toward him, fast, stopping as suddenly. "You done the best you could!" he cried. "If he wanted hit done different why didn't he wait and tell you how? He won't git no twenty bushels! He won't git none! We'll gather hit and hide hit! I kin watch..."

"Did you put the cutter back in that straight stock like I told you?"

"No, sir," he said.

"Then go do it."

That was Wednesday. During the rest of that week he worked steadily, at what was within his scope and some which was beyond it, with an industry that did not need to be driven nor even commanded twice; he had this from his mother, with the difference that some at least of what he did he liked to do, such as splitting wood with the half-size axe which his mother and aunt had earned, or saved money somehow, to present him with at Christmas. In company with the two older women (and on one afternoon, even one of the sisters), he built pens for the shoat and the cow which were a part of his father's contract with the landlord, and one afternoon, his father being absent, gone somewhere on one of the mules, he went to the field.

They were running a middle buster now, his brother holding the plow straight while he handled the reins, and walking beside the straining mule, the rich black soil shearing cool and damp against his bare ankles, he thought *Maybe this is the end of it. Maybe even that twenty bushels that seems hard to have to pay for just a rug will be a cheap price for him to stop forever and always from being what he used to be;* thinking, dreaming now, so that his brother had to speak sharply to him to mind the mule: *Maybe he even won't collect the twenty bushels. Maybe it will all add up and balance and vanish—corn, rug, fire; the terror and grief, the being pulled two ways like between two teams of horses—gone, done with for ever and ever.*

Then it was Saturday; he looked up from beneath the mule he was harnessing and saw his father in the black coat and hat. "Not that," his father said. "The wagon gear." And then, two hours later, sitting in the wagon bed behind his father and brother on the seat, the wagon accomplished a final curve, and he saw the weathered paintless store with its tattered tobacco- and patent-medicine posters and the tethered wagons and saddle animals below the gallery. He mounted the gnawed steps behind his father and brother, and there again was the lane of quiet, watching faces for the three of them to walk through. He saw the man in spectacles sitting at the plank table and he did not need to be told this was a Justice of the Peace; he sent one glare of fierce, exultant, partisan defiance at the man in collar and cravat now, whom he had seen but twice before in his life, and that on a galloping horse, who now wore on his face an expression not of rage but of amazed unbelief which the boy could not have known was at the incredible circumstance of being sued by one of his own tenants, and came and stood against his father and cried at the Justice: "He ain't done it! He ain't burnt..."

"Go back to the wagon," his father said.

"Burnt?" the Justice said. "Do I understand this rug was burned too?"

"Does anybody here claim it was?" his father said. "Go back to the wagon." But he did not, he merely retreated to the rear of the room, crowded as that other had been, but not to sit down this time, instead, to stand pressing among the motionless bodies, listening to the voices:

"And you claim twenty bushels of corn is too high for the damage you did to the rug?"

"He brought the rug to me and said he wanted the tracks washed out of it. I washed the tracks out and took the rug back to him."

"But you didn't carry the rug back to him in the same condition it was in before you made the tracks on it."

His father did not answer, and now for perhaps half a minute there was no sound at all save that of breathing, the faint, steady suspiration of complete and intent listening.

"You decline to answer that, Mr. Snopes?" Again his father did not answer. "I'm going to find against you, Mr. Snopes. I'm going to find that you were responsible for the injury to Major de Spain's rug and hold you liable for it. But twenty bushels of corn seems a little high for a man in your circumstances to have to pay. Major de Spain claims it cost a hundred dollars. October corn will be worth about fifty cents. I figure that if Major de Spain can stand a ninety-five dollar loss on something he paid cash for, you can stand a five-dollar loss you haven't earned yet. I hold you in damages to Major de Spain to the amount of ten bushels of corn over and above your contract with him, to be paid to him out of your crop at gathering time. Court adjourned."

It had taken no time hardly, the morning was but half begun. He thought they would return home and perhaps back to the field, since they were late, far behind all other farmers. But instead his father passed on behind the wagon, merely indicating with his hand for the older brother to follow with it, and crossed the road toward the blacksmith shop opposite, pressing on after his father, overtaking him, speaking, whispering up at the harsh, calm face beneath the weathered hat: "He won't git no ten bushels neither. He won't git one. We'll..." until his father glanced for an instant down at him, the face absolutely calm, the grizzled eyebrows tangled above the cold eyes, the voice almost pleasant, almost gentle:

"You think so? Well, we'll wait till October anyway."

The matter of the wagon—the setting of a spoke or two and the tightening of the tires—did not take long either, the business of the tires accomplished by driving the wagon into the spring branch behind the shop and letting it stand there, the mules nuzzling into the water from time to time, and the boy on the seat with the idle reins, looking up the slope and through the sooty tunnel of the shed where the slow hammer rang and where his father sat on an upended cypress bolt, easily, either talking or listening, still sitting there when the boy brought the dripping wagon up out of the branch and halted it before the door.

"Take them on to the shade and hitch," his father said. He did so and returned. His father and the smith and a third man squatting on his heels inside the door were talking, about crops and animals; the boy, squatting too in the ammoniac dust and hoof-parings and scales of rust, heard his father tell a long and unhurried story out of the time before the birth of the older brother even when he had been a professional horsetrader. And then his father came up beside him where he stood before a tattered last year's circus poster on the other side of the store, gazing rapt and quiet at the scarlet horses, the incredible poisings and convolutions of tulle and tights and the painted leers of comedians, and said, "It's time to eat."

But not at home. Squatting beside his brother against the front wall, he watched his father emerge from the store and produce from a paper sack a segment of cheese and divide it carefully and deliberately into three with his pocket knife and produce crackers from the same sack. They all three squatted on the gallery and ate, slowly, without talking; then in the store again, they drank from a tin dipper tepid water smelling of the cedar bucket and of living beech trees. And still they did not go home. It was a horse lot this time, a tall rail fence upon and along which men stood and sat and out of which one by one horses were led, to be walked and trotted and then cantered back and forth along the road while the slow swapping and buying went on and the sun began to slant westward, they—the three of them—watching and listening, the older brother with his muddy eyes and his steady, inevitable tobacco, the father commenting now and then on certain of the animals, to no one in particular.

It was after sundown when they reached home. They ate supper by lamplight, then, sitting on the doorstep, the boy watched the night fully accomplish, listening to the whippoorwills and the frogs, when he heard his mother's voice: "Abner! No! No! Oh, God. Oh, God. Abner!" and he rose, whirled, and saw the altered light through the door where a candle stub now burned in a bottle neck on the table and his father, still in the hat and coat, at once formal and burlesque as though dressed carefully for some shabby and ceremonial violence, emptying the reservoir of the lamp back into the five-gallon kerosene can from which it had been filled, while the mother tugged at his arm until he shifted the lamp to the other hand and flung her back, not savagely or viciously, just hard, into the wall, her hands flung out against the wall for balance, her mouth open and in her face the same quality of hopeless despair as had been in her voice. Then his father saw him standing in the door.

"Go to the barn and get that can of oil we were oiling the wagon with," he said. The boy did not move. Then he could speak.

"What . . ." he cried. "What are you . . ."

"Go get that oil," his father said. "Go."

Then he was moving, running, outside the house, toward the stable: this the old habit, the old blood which he had not been permitted to choose for himself, which had been bequeathed him willy nilly and which had run for so long (and who knew where, battening on what of outrage and savagery and lust) before it came to him. *I could keep on,* he thought. *I could run on and on and never look back, never need to see his face again. Only I can't. I can't,* the rusted can in his hand now, the liquid sploshing in it as he ran back to the house and into it, into the sound of his mother's weeping in the next room, and handed the can to his father.

"Ain't you going to even send a nigger?" he cried. "At least you sent a nigger before!"

This time his father didn't strike him. The hand came even faster than the blow had, the same hand which had set the can on the table with almost excruciating care flashing from the can toward him too quick for him to follow it, gripping him by the back of his shirt and on to tiptoe before he had seen it quit the can, the face stooping at him in breathless and frozen ferocity, the cold, dead voice speaking over him to the older brother who leaned against the table, chewing with that steady, curious, sidewise motion of cows:

"Empty the can into the big one and go on. I'll catch up with you."

"Better tie him up to the bedpost," the brother said.

"Do like I told you," the father said. Then the boy was moving, his bunched shirt and the hard, bony hand between his shoulderblades, his toes just touching the floor, across the room and into the other one, past the sisters sitting with spread heavy thighs in the two chairs over the cold hearth, and to where his mother and aunt sat side by side on the bed, the aunt's arms about his mother's shoulders.

"Hold him," the father said. The aunt made a startled movement. "Not you," the father said. "Lennie. Take hold of him. I want to see you do it." His mother took him by the wrist. "You'll hold him better than that. If he gets loose don't you know what he is going to do? He will go up yonder." He jerked his head toward the road. "Maybe I'd better tie him."

"I'll hold him," his mother whispered.

"See you do then." Then his father was gone, the stiff foot heavy and measured upon the boards, ceasing at last.

Then he began to struggle. His mother caught him in both arms, he jerking and wrenching at them. He would be stronger in the end, he knew that. But he had no time to wait for it. "Lemme go!" he cried. "I don't want to have to hit you!"

"Let him go!" the aunt said. "If he don't go, before God, I am going up there myself!"

"Don't you see I can't?" his mother said. "Sarty! Sarty! No! No! Help me, Lizzie!"

Then he was free. His aunt grasped at him but it was too late. He whirled, running, his mother stumbled forward on to her knees behind him, crying to the nearer sister: "Catch him, Net!

Catch him!" But that was too late too, the sister (the sisters were twins, born at the same time, yet either of them now gave the impression of being, encompassing as much living meat and volume and weight as any other two of the family) not yet having begun to rise from the chair, her head, face, alone merely turned, presenting to him in the flying instant an astonishing expanse of young female features untroubled by any surprise even, wearing only an expression of bovine interest. Then he was out of the room, out of the house, in the mild dust of the starlit road and the heavy rifeness of honeysuckle, the pale ribbon unspooling with terrific slowness under his running feet, reaching the gate at last and turning in, running, his heart and lungs drumming, on up the drive toward the lighted house, the lighted door. He did not knock, he burst in, sobbing for breath, incapable for the moment of speech; he saw the astonished face of the Negro in the linen jacket without knowing when the Negro had appeared.

"De Spain!" he cried, panted. "Where's..." then he saw the white man too emerging from a white door down the hall. "Barn!" he cried. "Barn!"

"What?" the white man said. "Barn?"

"Yes!" the boy cried. "Barn!"

"Catch him!" the white man shouted.

But it was too late this time too. The Negro grasped his shirt, but the entire sleeve, rotten with washing, carried away, and he was out that door too and in the drive again, and had actually never ceased to run even while he was screaming into the white man's face.

Behind him the white man was shouting, "My horse! Fetch my horse!" and he thought for an instant of cutting across the park and climbing the fence into the road, but he did not know the park nor how high the vine-massed fence might be and he dared not risk it. So he ran on down the drive, blood and breath roaring; presently he was in the road again though he could not see it. He could not hear either: the galloping mare was almost upon him before he heard her, and even then he held his course, as if the very urgency of his wild grief and need must in a moment more find him wings, waiting until the ultimate instant to hurl himself aside into the weed-choked roadside ditch as the horse thundered past and on, for an instant in furious silhouette against the stars, the tranquil early summer night sky which, even before the shape of the horse and rider vanished, stained abruptly and violently upward: a long, swirling roar incredible and soundless, blotting the stars, and he springing up and into the road again, running again, knowing it was too late yet still running even after he heard the shot and, an instant later, two shots, pausing now without knowing he had ceased to run, crying "Pap! Pap!", running again before he knew he had begun to run, stumbling, tripping over something and scrabbling up again without ceasing to run, looking backward over his shoulder at the glare as he got up, running on among the invisible trees, panting, sobbing, "Father! Father!"

At midnight he was sitting on the crest of a hill. He did not know it was midnight and he did not know how far he had come. But there was no glare behind him now and he sat now, his back toward what he had called home for four days anyhow, his face toward the dark woods which he would enter when breath was strong again, small, shaking steadily in the chill darkness, hugging himself into the remainder of his thin, rotten shirt, the grief and despair now no longer terror and fear but just grief and despair. *Father. My father,* he thought. "He was brave!" he cried suddenly, aloud but not loud, no more than a whisper: "He was! He was in the war! He was in Colonel Sartoris' cav'ry!" not knowing that his father had gone to that war a private in the fine old European sense, wearing no uniform, admitting the authority of and giving fidelity to no man or army or flag, going to war as Malbrouck himself did: for booty—it meant nothing and less than nothing to him if it were enemy booty or his own.

The slow constellations wheeled on. It would be dawn and then sun-up after a while and he would be hungry. But that would be tomorrow and now he was only cold, and walking would cure that. His breathing was easier now and he decided to get up and go on, and then he found that he had been asleep because he knew it was almost dawn, the night almost over. He could tell that from the whippoorwills. They were everywhere now among the dark trees below him, constant and inflectioned and ceaseless, so that, as the instant for giving over to the day birds drew nearer and nearer, there was no interval at all between them. He got up. He was a little stiff, but walking would cure that too as it would the cold, and soon there would be the sun. He went on down the hill, toward the dark woods within which the liquid silver voices of the birds called unceasing—the rapid and urgent beating of the urgent and quiring heart of the late spring night. He did not look back.

A Rose for Emily

WILLIAM FAULKNER

I

WHEN MISS EMILY GRIERSON died, our whole town went to her funeral: the men through a sort of respectful affection for a fallen monument, the women mostly out of curiosity to see the inside of her house, which no one save an old manservant—a combined gardener and cook—had seen in at least ten years.

It was a big, squarish frame house that had once been white, decorated with cupolas and spires and scrolled balconies in the heavily lightsome style of the seventies, set on what had once been our most select street. But garages and cotton gins had encroached and obliterated even the august names of that neighborhood; only Miss Emily's house was left, lifting its stubborn and coquettish decay above the cotton wagons and the gasoline pumps— an eyesore among eyesores. And now Miss Emily had gone to join the representatives of those august names where they lay in the cedar-bemused cemetery among the ranked and anonymous graves of Union and Confederate soldiers who fell at the battle of Jefferson.

Alive, Miss Emily had been a tradition, a duty, and a care; a sort of hereditary obligation upon the town, dating from that day in 1894 when Colonel Sartoris, the mayor—he who fathered the edict that no Negro woman should appear on the streets without an apron—remitted her taxes, the dispensation dating from the death of her father on into perpetuity. Not that Miss Emily would have accepted charity. Colonel Sartoris invented an involved tale to the effect that Miss Emily's father had loaned money to the town, which the town, as a matter of business, preferred this way of repaying. Only a man of Colonel Sartoris' generation and thought could have invented it, and only a woman could have believed it.

When the next generation, with its more modern ideas, became mayors and aldermen, this arrangement created some little dissatisfaction. On the first of the year they mailed her a tax notice. February came, and there was no reply. They wrote her a formal letter, asking her to call at the sheriff's office at her convenience. A week later the mayor wrote her himself, offering to call or to send his car for her, and received in reply a note on paper of an archaic shape, in a thin, flowing calligraphy in faded ink, to the effect that she no longer went out at all. The tax notice was also enclosed, without comment.

They called a special meeting of the Board of Aldermen. A deputation waited upon her, knocked at the door through which no visitor had passed since she ceased giving china-painting lessons eight or ten years earlier. They were admitted by the old Negro into a dim hall from which a stairway mounted into still more shadow. It smelled of dust and disuse—a close, dank smell. The Negro led them into the parlor. It was furnished in heavy, leather-covered furniture. When the Negro opened the blinds of one window, they could see that the leather was cracked; and when they sat down, a faint dust rose sluggishly about their thighs, spinning with slow motes in the single sun-ray. On a tarnished gilt easel before the fireplace stood a crayon portrait of Miss Emily's father.

They rose when she entered—a small, fat woman in black, with a thin gold chain descending to her waist and vanishing into her belt, leaning on an ebony cane with a tarnished gold head. Her skeleton was small and spare; perhaps that was why what would have been merely plumpness in another was obesity in her. She looked bloated, like a body long submerged in motionless water, and of that pallid hue. Her eyes, lost in the fatty ridges of her face, looked like two small pieces of coal pressed into a lump of dough as they moved from one face to another while the visitors stated their errand.

She did not ask them to sit. She just stood in the door and listened quietly until the spokesman came to a stumbling halt. Then they could hear the invisible watch ticking at the end of the gold chain.

Her voice was dry and cold. "I have no taxes in Jefferson. Colonel Sartoris explained it to me. Perhaps one of you can gain access to the city records and satisfy yourselves."

"But we have. We are the city authorities, Miss Emily. Didn't you get a notice from the sheriff, signed by him?"

"I received a paper, yes," Miss Emily said. "Perhaps he considers himself the sheriff. . . I have no taxes in Jefferson."

"But there is nothing on the books to show that, you see. We must go by the—"

"See Colonel Sartoris. I have no taxes in Jefferson."

"But, Miss Emily—"

"See Colonel Sartoris." (Colonel Sartoris had been dead almost ten years.) "I have no taxes in Jefferson. Tobe!" The Negro appeared. "Show these gentlemen out."

II

So she vanquished them, horse and foot, just as she had vanquished their fathers thirty years before about the smell. That was two years after her father's death and a short time after her sweetheart—the one we believed would marry her—had deserted her. After her father's death she went out very little; after her sweetheart went away, people hardly saw her at all. A few of the ladies had the temerity to call, but were not received, and the only sign of life about the place was the Negro man—a young man then—going in and out with a market basket.

"Just as if a man—any man—could keep a kitchen properly," the ladies said; so they were not surprised when the smell developed. It was another link between the gross, teeming world and the high and mighty Griersons.

A neighbor, a woman, complained to the mayor, Judge Stevens, eighty years old.

"But what will you have me do about it, madam?" he said.

"Why, send her word to stop it," the woman said. "Isn't there a law?"

"I'm sure that won't be necessary," Judge Stevens said. "It's probably just a snake or a rat that nigger of hers killed in the yard. I'll speak to him about it."

The next day he received two more complaints, one from a man who came in diffident deprecation. "We really must do something about it, Judge. I'd be the last one in the world to bother Miss Emily, but we've got to do something." That night the Board of Aldermen met—three graybeards and one younger man, a member of the rising generation.

"It's simple enough," he said. "Send her word to have her place cleaned up. Give her a certain time to do it in, and if she don't . . ."

"Dammit, sir," Judge Stevens said, "will you accuse a lady to her face of smelling bad?"

So the next night, after midnight, four men crossed Miss Emily's lawn and slunk about the house like burglars, sniffing along the base of the brickwork and at the cellar openings while one of them performed a regular sowing motion with his hand out of a sack slung from his shoulder. They broke open the cellar door and sprinkled lime there, and in all the outbuildings. As they recrossed the lawn, a window that had been dark was lighted and Miss Emily sat in it, the light behind her, and her upright torso motionless as that of an idol. They crept quietly across the lawn and into the shadow of the locusts that lined the street. After a week or two the smell went away.

That was when people had begun to feel really sorry for her. People in our town, remembering how old lady Wyatt, her great-aunt, had gone completely crazy at last, believed that the Griersons held themselves a little too high for what they really were. None of the young men were quite good enough for Miss Emily and such. We had long thought of them as a tableau, Miss Emily a slender figure in white in the background, her father a spraddled silhouette in the foreground, his back to her and clutching a horsewhip, the two of them framed by the backflung front door. So when she got to be thirty and was still single, we were not pleased exactly, but vindicated; even with insanity in the family she wouldn't have turned down all of her chances if they had really materialized.

When her father died, it got about that the house was all that was left to her; and in a way, people were glad. At last they could pity Miss Emily. Being left alone, and a pauper, she had become humanized. Now she too would know the old thrill and the old despair of a penny more or less.

The day after his death all the ladies prepared to call at the house and offer condolence and aid, as is our custom. Miss Emily met them at the door, dressed as usual and with no trace of grief on her face. She told them that her father was not dead. She did that for three days, with the ministers calling on her, and the doctors, trying to persuade her to let them dispose of the body. Just as they were about to resort to law and force, she broke down, and they buried her father quickly.

We did not say she was crazy then. We believed she had to do that. We remembered all the young men her father had driven away, and we knew that with nothing left, she would have to cling to that which had robbed her, as people will.

III

She was sick for a long time. When we saw her again, her hair was cut short, making her look like a girl, with a vague resemblance to those angels in colored church windows—sort of tragic and serene.

The town had just let the contracts for paving the sidewalks, and in the summer after her father's death they began the work. The construction company came with niggers and mules and machinery, and a foreman named Homer Barron, a Yankee—a big, dark, ready man, with a big voice and eyes lighter than his face. The little boys would follow in groups to hear him cuss the niggers, and the niggers singing in time to the rise and fall of picks. Pretty soon he knew everybody in town. Whenever you heard a lot of laughing anywhere about the square, Homer Barron would be in the center of the group. Presently we began to see him and Miss Emily on Sunday afternoons driving in the yellow-wheeled buggy and the matched team of bays from the livery stable.

At first we were glad that Miss Emily would have an interest, because the ladies all said, "Of course a Grierson would not think seriously of a Northerner, a day laborer." But there were still others, older people, who said that even grief could not cause a real lady to forget *noblesse oblige*—without calling it *noblesse oblige*. They just said, "Poor Emily. Her kinsfolk should come to her." She had some kin in Alabama; but years ago her father had fallen out with them over the estate of old lady Wyatt, the crazy woman, and there was no communication between the two families. They had not even been represented at the funeral.

And as soon as the old people said, "Poor Emily," the whispering began. "Do you suppose it's really so?" they said to one another. "Of course it is. What else could..." This behind their hands; rustling of craned silk and satin behind jalousies closed upon the sun of Sunday afternoon as the thin, swift clop-clop-clop of the matched team passed: "Poor Emily."

She carried her head high enough—even when we believed that she was fallen. It was as if she demanded more than ever the recognition of her dignity as the last Grierson; as if it had wanted that touch of earthiness to reaffirm her imperviousness. Like when she bought the rat poison, the arsenic. That was over a year after they had begun to say "Poor Emily," and while the two female cousins were visiting her.

"I want some poison," she said to the druggist. She was over thirty then, still a slight woman, though thinner than usual, with cold, haughty black eyes in a face the flesh of which was strained across the temples and about the eyesockets as you imagine a lighthouse-keeper's face ought to look. "I want some poison," she said.

"Yes, Miss Emily. What kind? For rats and such? I'd recom—"

"I want the best you have. I don't care what kind."

The druggist named several. "They'll kill anything up to an elephant. But what you want is—"

"Arsenic," Miss Emily said. "Is that a good one?"

"Is... arsenic? Yes, ma'am. But what you want—"

"I want arsenic."

The druggist looked down at her. She looked back at him, erect, her face like a strained flag. "Why, of course," the druggist said. "If that's what you want. But the law requires you to tell what you are going to use it for."

Miss Emily just stared at him, her head tilted back in order to look him eye for eye, until he looked away and went and got the arsenic and wrapped it up. The Negro delivery boy brought her the package; the druggist didn't come back. When she opened the package at home there was written on the box, under the skull and bones: "For rats."

IV

So the next day we all said, "She will kill herself"; and we said it would be the best thing. When she had first begun to be seen with Homer Barron, we had said, "She will marry him." Then we said, "She will persuade him yet," because Homer himself had remarked—he liked men, and it was known that he drank with the younger men in the Elks' Club—that he was not a marrying man. Later we said, "Poor Emily" behind the jalousies as they passed on Sunday afternoon in the glittering buggy, Miss Emily with her head high and Homer Barron with his hat cocked and a cigar in his teeth, reins and whip in a yellow glove.

Then some of the ladies began to say that it was a disgrace to the town and a bad example to the young people. The men did not want to interfere, but at last the ladies forced the Baptist minister—Miss Emily's people were Episcopal—to call upon her. He would never divulge what happened during that interview, but he refused to go back again. The next Sunday they again drove about the streets, and the following day the minister's wife wrote to Miss Emily's relations in Alabama.

So she had blood-kin under her roof again and we sat back to watch developments. At first nothing happened. Then we were sure that they were to be married. We learned that Miss Emily had been to the jeweler's and ordered a man's toilet set in silver, with the letters H.B. on each piece. Two days later we learned that she had bought a complete outfit of men's clothing, including a nightshirt, and we said, "They are married." We were really glad. We were glad because the two female cousins were even more Grierson than Miss Emily had ever been.

So we were not surprised when Homer Barron—the streets had been finished some time since—was gone. We were a little disappointed that there was not a public blowing-off, but we believed that he had gone on to prepare for Miss Emily's coming, or to give her a chance to get rid of the cousins. (By that time it was a cabal, and we were all Miss Emily's allies to help circumvent the cousins.) Sure enough, after another week they departed. And, as we had expected all along, within three days Homer

Barron was back in town. A neighbor saw the Negro man admit him at the kitchen door at dusk one evening.

And that was the last we saw of Homer Barron. And of Miss Emily for some time. The Negro man went in and out with the market basket, but the front door remained closed. Now and then we would see her at a window for a moment, as the men did that night when they sprinkled the lime, but for almost six months she did not appear on the streets. Then we knew that this was to be expected too; as if that quality of her father which had thwarted her woman's life so many times had been too virulent and too furious to die.

When we next saw Miss Emily, she had grown fat and her hair was turning gray. During the next few years it grew grayer and grayer until it attained an even pepper-and-salt iron-gray, when it ceased turning. Up to the day of her death at seventy-four it was still that vigorous iron-gray, like the hair of an active man.

From that time on her front door remained closed, save during a period of six or seven years, when she was about forty, during which she gave lessons in china-painting. She fitted up a studio in one of the downstairs rooms, where the daughters and grand-daughters of Colonel Sartoris' contemporaries were sent to her with the same regularity and in the same spirit that they were sent to church on Sundays with a twenty-five-cent piece for the collection plate. Meanwhile her taxes had been remitted.

Then the newer generation became the backbone and the spirit of the town, and the painting pupils grew up and fell away and did not send their children to her with boxes of color and tedious brushes and pictures cut from the ladies' magazines. The front door closed upon the last one and remained closed for good. When the town got free postal delivery, Miss Emily alone refused to let them fasten the metal numbers above her door and attach a mailbox to it. She would not listen to them.

Daily, monthly, yearly we watched the Negro grow grayer and more stooped, going in and out with the market basket. Each December we sent her a tax notice, which would be returned by the post office a week later, unclaimed. Now and then we would see her in one of the downstairs windows—she had evidently shut up the top floor of the house—like the carven torso of an idol in a niche, looking or not looking at us, we could never tell which.

Thus she passed from generation to generation—dear, inescapable, impervious, tranquil, and perverse.

And so she died. Fell ill in the house filled with dust and shadows, with only a doddering Negro man to wait on her. We did not even know she was sick; we had long since given up trying to get any information from the Negro. He talked to no one, probably not even to her, for his voice had grown harsh and rusty, as if from disuse.

She died in one of the downstairs rooms, in a heavy walnut bed with a curtain, her gray head propped on a pillow yellow and moldy with age and lack of sunlight.

V

The Negro met the first of the ladies at the front door and let them in, with their hushed, sibilant voices and their quick, curious glances, and then he disappeared. He walked right through the house and out the back and was not seen again.

The two female cousins came at once. They held the funeral on the second day, with the town coming to look at Miss Emily beneath a mass of bought flowers, with the crayon face of her father musing profoundly above the bier and the ladies sibilant and macabre; and the very old men—some in their brushed Confederate uniforms—on the porch and the lawn, talking of Miss Emily as if she had been a contemporary of theirs, believing that they had danced with her and courted her perhaps, confusing time with its mathematical progression, as the old do, to whom all the past is not a diminishing road but, instead, a huge meadow which no winter ever quite touches, divided from them now by the narrow bottleneck of the most recent decade of years.

Already we knew that there was one room in that region above stairs which no one had seen in forty years, and which would have to be forced. They waited until Miss Emily was decently in the ground before they opened it.

The violence of breaking down the door seemed to fill this room with pervading dust. A thin, acrid pall as of the tomb seemed to lie everywhere upon this room decked and furnished as for a bridal: upon the valance curtains of faded rose color, upon the rose-shaded lights, upon the dressing table, upon the delicate array of crystal and the man's toilet things backed with tarnished silver, silver so tarnished that the monogram was obscured. Among them lay a collar and tie, as if they had just been removed, which, lifted, left upon the surface a pale crescent in the dust. Upon a chair hung the suit, carefully folded; beneath it the two mute shoes and the discarded socks.

The man himself lay in the bed.

For a long while we just stood there, looking down at the profound and fleshless grin. The body had apparently once lain in the attitude of an embrace, but now the long sleep that outlasts love, that conquers even the grimace of love, had cuckolded him. What was left of him, rotted beneath what was left of the nightshirt, had become inextricable from the bed in which he lay; and upon him and upon the pillow beside him lay that even coating of the patient and biding dust.

Then we noticed that in the second pillow was the indentation of a head. One of us lifted something from it, and leaning forward, that faint and invisible dust dry and acrid in the nostrils, we saw a long strand of iron-gray hair.

FROM
Shiloh

SHELBY FOOTE

WHEN I WENT to sleep the stars were out and there was even a moon, thin like a sickle and clear against the night, but when I woke up there was only the blackness and the wind sighing high in the treetops. That was what roused me I believe, because for a minute I disremembered where I was. I thought I was back home, woke up early and laying in bed waiting for pa to come with the lantern to turn me out to milk (that was the best thing about the army: no cows) and ma was in the kitchen humming a hymn while she shook up the stove. But then I realized part of the sound was the breathing and snoring of the men all around me, with maybe a whimper or a moan every now and again when the bad dreams came, and I remembered. We had laid down to sleep in what they call Line of Battle and now the night was nearly over. And when I remembered I wished I'd stayed asleep: because that was the worst part, to lie there alone, feeling lonely, and no one to tell you he was feeling the same.

But it was warm under the blanket and my clothes had dried and I could feel my new rifle through the cloth where I had laid it to be safe from the dew when I wrapped the covers round me. Then it was the same as if theyd all gone away, or *I* had; I was back home with my brothers and sisters again, myself the oldest by over a year, and they were gathered around to tell me goodbye the way they did a month ago when I left to join up in Corinth after General Beauregard sent word that all true men were needed to save the country. That was the way he said it. I was just going to tell them I would be back with a Yankee sword for the fireplace, like pa did with the Mexican one, when I heard somebody talking in a hard clear voice not like any of *my* folks, and when I looked up it was Sergeant Tyree.

"Roll out there," he said. "Roll out to fight."

89

I had gone to sleep and dreamed of home, but here I was, away up in Tennessee, further from Ithaca and Jordan County than I'd ever been in all my life before. It was Sunday already and we were fixing to hit them where they had their backs to the river, the way it was explained while we were waiting for our marching orders three days ago. I sat up.

From then on everything moved fast with a sort of mixed-up jerkiness, like Punch and Judy. Every face had a kind of drawn look, the way it would be if a man was picking up on something heavy. Late ones like myself were pulling on their shoes or rolling their blankets. Others were already fixed. They squatted with their rifles across their thighs, sitting there in the darkness munching biscuits, those that had saved any, and not doing much talking. They nodded their heads with quick flicky motions, like birds, and nursed their rifles, keeping them out of the dirt. I had gotten to know them all in a month and a few of them were even from the same end of the county I was, but now it was like I was seeing them for the first time, different. All the put-on had gone out of their faces—they were left with what God gave them at the beginning.

We lined up. And while Sergeant Tyree passed among us, checking us one by one to make sure everything was where it was supposed to be, dawn began to come through, faint and high. While we were answering roll-call the sun rose big and red through the trees and all up and down the company front they begun to get excited and jabber at one another: "The sun of oyster itch," whatever that meant. I was glad to see the sun again, no matter what they called it.

One minute we were standing there, shifting from leg to leg, not saying much and more or less avoiding each other's eyes: then we were going forward. It happened that sudden. There was no bugle or drum or anything like that. The men on our right started moving and we moved too, lurching forward through the underbrush and trying to keep the line straight the way we had been warned to do, but we couldnt. Captain Plummer was cussing. "Dwess it up," he kept saying, cussing a blue streak; "Dwess it up, dod dam it, dwess it up," all the way through the woods. So after a while, when the trees thinned, we stopped to straighten the line.

There was someone on a tall claybank horse out front, a fine-looking man in a new uniform with chicken guts on the sleeves all the way to his elbows, spruce and sprang as a game-cock. He had on a stiff red cap, round and flat on top like a sawed-off dice box, and he was making a speech. "Soldiers of the South!" he shouted in a fine proud voice, a little husky, and everybody cheered. All I could hear was the cheering and yipping all around me, but I could see his eyes light up and his mouth moving the way it will do when a man is using big words. I thought I heard something about defenders and liberty and even something about the women back home but I couldn't be sure; there was so much racket. When he was through he stood in the stirrups, raising his cap to us as we went by, and I recognized him. It was General Beauregard, the man I'd come to fight for, and I hadnt hardly heard a word he said.

We stayed lined up better now because we were through the worst of the briers and vines, but just as we got going good there was a terrible clatter off to the right, the sound of firecrackers mixed with a roaring and yapping like a barn full of folks at a Fourth of July dogfight or a gouging match. The line begun to crook and weave because some of the men had stopped to listen, and Captain Plummer was cussing them, tongue-tied. Joe Marsh was next to me—he was nearly thirty, middle-aged, and had seen some battle up near Bowling Green. "There you are," he said, slow and calm and proud of himself. "Some outfit has met the elephant." That was what the ones who had been in action always called it: the elephant.

They had told us how it would be. They said we would march two days and on the third day we would hit them where they were camped between two creeks with their backs to the Tennes-see River. We would drive them, the colonel told us, and when they were pushed against the river we would kill or capture the whole she-bang. I didnt understand it much because what the colonel said was full of tactics talk. Later the captain explained it, and that was better but not much. So then Sergeant Tyree showed it to us by drawing lines on the ground with a stick. That way it was clear as could be.

It sounded fine, the way he told it; it sounded simple and easy. Maybe it was too simple, or something. Anyhow things didnt turn out so good when it came to doing them. On the third day we were still marching, all day, and here it was the fourth day and we were still just marching, stop and go but mostly stop—the only real difference was that the column was moving sideways now, through the woods instead of on the road. From all that racket over on the right I thought maybe the other outfits would have the Yankees pushed back and captured before we even got to see it. The noise had died down for a minute, but as we went forward it swelled up again, rolling toward the left where we were, rifles popping and popping and the soldiers yelling crazy in the distance. It didnt sound like any elephant to me.

We came clear of the woods where they ended on a ridge overlooking a valley with a little creek running through it. The ground was open all across the valley, except where the creek bottom was overgrown, and mounted to another ridge on the other side where the woods began again. There were white spots in the fringe of trees—these were tents, I made out. We were the left brigade of the whole army. The 15th Arkansas, big men mostly, with bowie knives and rolled-up sleeves, was spread across the front for skirmishers, advanced a little way in the open. There was a Tennessee regiment on our right and two more on our left and still another at the left rear with flankers out. Then we were all in the open, lined up with our flags riffling in the breeze. Colonel Thornton was out front, between us and the skirmishers. His saber flashed in the sun. Looking down the line I saw the other regimental commanders, and all their sabers were flashing sunlight too. It was like a parade just before it begins.

This is going to be what they promised us, I said to myself. This is going to be the charge.

That was when General Johnston rode up. He came right past where I was standing, a fine big man on a bay stallion. He had on a broad-brim hat and a cape and thigh boots with gold spurs that twinkled like sparks of fire. I watched him ride by, his mustache flaring out from his mouth and his eyes set deep under his forehead. He was certainly the handsomest man I ever saw, bar none; he made the other officers on his staff look small. There was a little blond-headed lieutenant bringing up the rear, the one who would go all red in the face when the men guyed him back on the march. He looked about my age, but that was the only thing about us that was alike. He had on a natty uniform: bobtail jacket, red silk neckerchief, fire-gilt buttons, and all. I said to myself, I bet his ma would have a fit if she could see him now.

General Johnston rode between our regiment and the Tennessee boys on our right, going forward to where the skirmish line was waiting. When the colonel in charge had reported, General Johnston spoke to the skirmishers: "Men of Arkansas, they say you boast of your prowess with the bowie knife. Today you wield a nobler weapon: the bayonet. Employ it well." They stood there holding their rifles and looking up at him, shifting their feet a little and looking sort of embarrassed. He was the only man I ever saw who wasnt a preacher and yet could make that high-flown way of talking sound right. Then he turned his horse and rode back through our line, and as he passed he leaned sideways in the saddle and spoke to us: "Look along your guns, and fire low." It made us ready and anxious for what was coming.

Captain Plummer walked up and down the company front. He was short, inclined to fat, and walked with a limp from the blisters he developed on the march. "Stay dwessed on me, wherever I go," he said. "And shoot low. Aim for their knees." All up and down the line the flags were flapping and other officers were speaking to their men.

I was watching toward the front, where we would go, but all I could see was that empty valley with the little creek running through it and the rising ground beyond with the trees on top. While I was looking, trying hard to see was anybody up there, all of a sudden there was a Boom! Boom! Boom! directly in the rear and it scared me so bad I almost broke for cover. But when I looked around I saw they had brought up the artillery and it was shooting over our heads toward the left in a shallow swale. I felt real sheepish from having jumped but when I looked around I saw that the others had jumped as much as I had, and now they were joking at one another about who had been the most scared, carrying it off all brave-like but looking kind of hang-dog about it too. I was still trying to see whatever it was out front that the artillery was shooting at, but all I could see was that valley with the creek in it and the dark trees on the flanks.

I was still mixed up, wondering what it all meant, when we begun to go forward, carrying our rifles at right shoulder shift the way we had been taught to do on parade. Colonel Thornton was still out front, flashing his saber and calling back over his shoulder: "Close up, men. Close up. Guiiide centerrrrr!" The skirmishers went out of sight in the swale, the same as if they had marched into the ground. When we got to where they had gone down, we saw them again, but closer now, kneeling and popping little white puffs of smoke from their rifles. The rattle of firing rolled across the line and back again, and then it broke into just general firing. I still couldnt see what they were shooting at, specially not now that the smoke was banking up and drifting back against us with a stink like burning feathers.

Then, for the first time since we left Corinth, bugles begun to blare and it passed to the double. The line wavered like a shaken rope, gaining in places and lagging in others and all around me they were yelling those wild crazy yells. General Cleburne was on his mare to our left, between us and the 5th Tennessee. He was waving his sword and the mare was plunging and tossing her mane. I could hear him hollering the same as he would when we did wrong on the drill field—he had that thick, Irish way of speaking that came on him when he got mad. We were trotting by then.

As we went forward we caught up with the skirmishers. They had given around a place where the ground was flat and dark green and there was water in the grass, sparkling like silver. It was a bog. We gave to the right to stay on hard ground and the 5th Tennessee gave to the left; the point of swampland was between us, growing wider as we went. General Cleburne rode straight ahead, waving his sword and bawling at us to close the gap, close the gap, and before he knew what had separated us, the mare was pastern-deep in it, floundering and bucking to get rid of the general's weight. He was waving his sword with one hand and shaking his fist at us with the other, so that when the mare gave an extra hard buck General Cleburne went flying off her nigh side and landed on his hands and knees in the mud. We could hear him cussing across two hundred yards of bog. The last I saw of him he was walking out, still waving the sword, picking his knees high and sinking almost to his boottops every step. His face was red as fire.

The brigade was split, two regiments on the right and four on the left, with a swamp between us; we would have to charge the high ground from two sides. By this time we had passed around where the other slope came out to a point leading down to the bog and we couldnt even see the other regiments. When we hit the rise we begun to run. I could hear Colonel Thornton puffing like a switch engine and I thought to myself, He's too old for this. Nobody was shooting yet because we didn't see anything to shoot at; we were so busy trying to keep up, we didn't have a chance to see anything at all. The line was crooked as a ram's horn. Some men were pushing out front and others were beginning to breathe hard and lag behind. My heart was hammering at my throat—it seemed like every breath would bust my lungs. I passed a fat fellow holding his side and groaning. At first I thought he was shot, but then I realized he just had a stitch. It was Burt Tapley, the one everybody jibed about how much he ate; he was a great one for the sutlers. Now all that fine food, canned peaches and suchlike, was staring him in the face.

When we were halfway up the rise I begun to see black shapes against the rim where it sloped off sharp. At first I thought they were scarecrows—they looked like scarecrows. That didnt make sense, except they looked so black and stick-like. Then I saw they were moving, wiggling, and the rim broke out with smoke, some of it going straight up and some jetting toward our line, rolling and jumping with spits of fire mixed in and a humming like wasps past my ears. I thought: *Lord to God, theyre shooting; theyre shooting at me!* And it surprised me so, I stopped to look. The smoke kept rolling up and out, rolling and rolling, still with the stabs of fire mixed in, and some of the men passed me, bent forward like they were running into a high wind, rifles held crossways so that the bayonets glinted and snapped in the sunlight, and their faces were all out of shape from the yelling.

When I stopped I begun to hear all sorts of things I hadnt heard while I was running. It was like being born again, coming into a new world. There was a great crash and clatter of firing, and over all this I could hear them all around me, screaming and yelping like on a foxhunt except there was something crazy mixed up in it too, like horses trapped in a burning barn. I thought theyd all gone crazy—they looked it, for a fact. Their faces were split wide open with screaming, mouths twisted every which way, and this wild lunatic yelping coming out. It wasnt like they were yelling with their mouths: it was more like the yelling was something pent up inside them and they were opening their mouths to let it out. That was the first time I really knew how scared I was.

If I'd stood there another minute, hearing all this, I would have gone back. I thought: Luther, you got no business mixed up in all this ruckus. This is all crazy, I thought. But a big fellow I never saw before ran into me full tilt, knocking me forward so hard I nearly went sprawling. He looked at me sort of desperate, like I was a post or something that got in the way, and went by, yelling. By the time I got my balance I was stumbling forward, so I just kept going. And that was better. I found that as long as I was moving I was all right, because then I didn't hear so much or even see so much. Moving, it was more like I was off to myself, with just my own particular worries.

I kept passing men lying on the ground, and at first I thought they were winded, like the fat one—that was the way they looked to me. But directly I saw a corporal with the front of his head mostly gone, what had been under his skull spilling over his face, and I knew they were down because they were hurt. Every now and then there would be one just sitting there holding an arm or leg and groaning. Some of them would reach out at us and even call us by name, but we stayed clear. For some reason we didnt like them, not even the sight of them. I saw Lonny Parker that I grew up with; he was holding his stomach, bawling like a baby, his face all twisted and big tears on his cheeks. But it wasnt any different with Lonny—I stayed clear of him too, just like I'd never known him, much less grown up with him back in Jordan County. It wasnt a question of luck, the way some folks will tell you; they will tell you it's bad luck to be near the wounded. It was just that we didnt want to be close to them any longer than it took to run past, the way you wouldnt want to be near someone who had something catching, like smallpox.

We were almost to the rim by then and I saw clear enough that they werent scarecrows—that was a foolish thing to think anyhow. They were men, with faces and thick blue uniforms. It was only a glimpse, though, because then we gave them a volley and smoke rolled out between us. When we came through the smoke they were gone except the ones who were on the ground. They lay in every position, like a man I saw once that had been drug out on bank after he was run over by a steamboat and the paddles hit him. We were running and yelling, charging across the flat ground where white canvas tents stretched out in an even row. The racket was louder now, and then I knew why. It was because I was yelling too, crazy and blood-curdled as the rest of them.

I passed one end of the row of tents. That must have been where their officers stayed, for breakfast was laid on a table there with a white cloth nice as a church picnic. When I saw the white-flour biscuits and the coffee I understood why people called them the Feds and us the Corn-feds. I got two of the biscuits (I had to grab quick; everybody was snatching at them) and while I was stuffing one in my mouth and the other in my pocket, I saw Burt Tapley. He'd caught up when we stopped to give them that volley, I reckon, and he was holding the coffee pot like a loving-cup, drinking scalding coffee in big gulps. It ran from both corners of his mouth, down onto the breast of his uniform.

Officers were running around waving their swords and hollering. "Form!" they yelled at us. "Form for attack!" But nobody paid them much mind—we were too busy rummaging the tents. So they begun to lay about with the flats of their swords, driving us away from the plunder. It didnt take long. When we were formed in line again, reloading our guns, squads and companies mixed every which way, they led us through the row of tents at a run. All around me, men were tripping on the ropes and cussing and barking their shins on the stakes. Then we got through and I saw why the officers had been yelling for us to form.

There was a gang of Federal soldiers standing shoulder to shoulder in the field beyond the tents. I thought it was the whole Yankee army, lined up waiting for us. Those in front were kneeling under the guns of the men in the second line, a great bank of blue uniforms and rifle barrels and white faces like rows of eggs, one above another. When they fired, the smoke came at us in a solid wall. Things plucked at my clothes and twitched my hat, and when I looked around I saw men all over the ground, in the same ugly positions as the men back on the slope, moaning and whimpering, clawing at the grass. Some were gut-shot, making high yelping sounds like a turpentined dog.

Smoke was still thick when the second volley came. For a minute I thought I was the only one left alive. Then I saw the others through the smoke, making for the rear, and I ran too, back toward the tents and the slope where we'd come up. They gave us another volley as we ran but it was high; I could hear the balls screech over my head. I cleared the ridge on the run, and when I came over I saw them stopping. I pulled up within twenty yards or so and lay flat on the ground, panting.

No bullets were falling here but everybody laid low because they were crackling and snapping in the air over our heads on a line with the rim where our men were still coming over. They would come over prepared to run another mile, and then they would see us lying there and they would try to stop, stumbling and sliding downhill.

I saw one man come over, running sort of straddle-legged, and just as he cleared the rim I saw the front of his coat jump where the shots came through. He was running down the slope, stone dead already, the way a deer will do when it's shot after picking up speed. This man kept going for nearly fifty yards downhill before his legs stopped pumping and he crashed into the ground on his stomach. I could see his face as he ran, and there was no doubt about it, no doubt at all: he was dead and I could see it in his face.

That scared me worse than anything up to then. It wasn't really all that bad, looking back on it: it was just that he'd been running when they shot him and his drive kept him going down the slope. But it seemed so wrong, so scandalous, somehow so un*religious* for a dead man to have to keep on fighting—or running, anyhow— that it made me sick to my stomach. I didnt want to have any more to do with the war if this was the way it was going to be.

They had told us we would push them back to the river. Push, they said; that was the word they used. I really thought we were going to push them—with bullets and bayonets of course, and of course I knew there were going to be men killed: I even thought I might get killed myself; it crossed my mind a number of times. But it wasnt the way they said. It wasnt that way at all. Because even the dead and dying didn't have any decency about them— first the Yankees back on the slope, crumpled and muddy where their own men had overrun them, then the men in the field beyond the tents, yelping like gut-shot dogs while they died, and now this one, this big fellow running straddle-legged and stone cold dead in the face, that wouldnt stop running even after he'd been killed.

I was what you might call unnerved, for they may warn you there's going to be bleeding in battle but you don't believe it till you see the blood. What happened from then on was all mixed up in the smoke. We formed again and went back through the tents. But the same thing happened: they were there, just as before, and when they threw that wall of smoke and humming bullets at us, we came running back down the slope. Three times we went through and it was the same every time. Finally a fresh brigade came up from the reserve and we went through together.

This trip was different—we could tell it even before we got started. We went through the smoke and the bullets, and that was the first time we used bayonets. For a minute it was jab and slash, everyone yelling enough to curdle your blood just with the shrillness. I was running, bent low with the rifle held out front, the way they taught me, and all of a sudden I saw I was going to have it with a big Yank wearing his coat unbuttoned halfway, showing a red flannel undershirt. I was running and he was waiting, braced, and it occurred to me, the words shooting through my mind: What kind of a man is this, would wear a red wool undershirt in April?

I saw his face from below, but he had bent down and his eyebrows were drawn in a straight line like a black bar over his eyes. He was full-grown, with a wide brown mustache; I could see the individual hairs on each side of the shaved line down the middle. I'd have had to say Sir to him back home. Then something hit my arm a jar—I stumbled against him, lifting my rifle and falling sideways. Ee! I'm killed! I thought. He turned with me and we were falling, first a slow fall the way it is in dreams, then sudden, and the ground came up and hit me: ho! We were two feet apart, looking at each other. He seemed even bigger now, up close, and there was something wrong with the way he looked. Then I saw why.

My bayonet had gone in under his jaw, the handguard tight against the bottom of his chin, and the point must have stuck in his head bone because he appeared to be trying to open his mouth but couldnt. It was like he had a mouthful of something bitter and couldnt spit—his eyes were screwed up, staring at me and blinking a bit from the strain. All I could do was look at him; I couldnt look away, no matter how I tried. A man will look at something that is making him sick but he cant stop looking until he begins to vomit—something holds him. That was the way it was with me. Then, while I was watching him, this fellow reached up and touched the handle of the bayonet under his chin. He touched it easy, using the tips of his fingers, tender-like. I could see he wanted to grab and pull it out but he was worried about how much it would hurt and he didnt dare.

I let go of the rifle and rolled away. There were bluecoats running across the field and through the woods beyond. All around me men were kneeling and shooting at them like rabbits as they ran. Captain Plummer and two lieutenants were the only officers left on their feet. Two men were bent over Colonel Thornton where they had propped him against a tree with one of his legs laid crooked. Captain Plummer wasnt limping now—he'd forgotten his blisters, I reckon. He wasnt even hurt, so far as I could see, but the skirt of his coat was ripped where somebody had taken a swipe at him with a bayonet or a saber.

He went out into the open with a man carrying the colors, and then begun to wave his sword and call in a high voice: "6th Mississippi, wally here! 6th Mississippi, wally here!"

Men begun straggling over, collecting round the flag, so I got up and went over with them. We were a sorry lot. My feet were so heavy I could barely lift them, and I had to carry my left arm with my right, the way a baby would cradle a doll. The captain kept calling, "Wally here! 6th Mississippi, wally here!" but after a while he saw there werent any more to rally so he gave it up. There were a little over a hundred of us, all that were left out of the four hundred and twenty-five that went in an hour before.

Our faces were gray, the color of ashes. Some had powder burns red on their cheeks and foreheads and running back into singed patches in their hair. Mouths were rimmed with grime from biting cartridges, mostly a long smear down one corner, and hands were blackened with burnt powder off the ramrods. We'd aged a lifetime since the sun came up. Captain Plummer was calling us to rally, rally here, but there wasnt much rally left in us.

There wasnt much left in me, anyhow. I felt so tired it was all I could do to make it to where the flag was. I was worried, too, about not having my rifle. I remembered what Sergeant Tyree was always saying: "Your rifle is your best friend. Take care of it." But if that meant pulling it out of the man with the mustache, it would just have to stay there. Then I looked down and be durn if there wasnt one just like it at my feet. I picked it up, stooping and nursing my bad arm, and stood there with it.

Joe Marsh was next to me. At first I didnt know him. He didnt seem bad hurt, but he had a terrible look around the eyes and there was a knot on his forehead the size of a walnut where some Yank had bopped him with a rifle butt. I thought to ask him how the Tennessee breed of elephant compared with the Kentucky breed, but I didnt. He looked at me, first in the face till he finally recognized me, then down at my arm.

"You better get that tended to."

"It dont hurt much," I said.

"All right. Have it your way."

He didnt pay me any mind after that. He had lorded it over me for a month about being a greenhorn, yet here I was, just gone through meeting as big an elephant as any he had met, and he was still trying the same high-and-mightiness. He was mad now because he wasnt the only one who had seen some battle. He'd had his big secret to throw up to us, but not any more. We all had it now.

We were milling around like ants when their hill is upset, trying to fall-in the usual way, by platoons and squads, but some were all the way gone and others had only a couple of men. So we gave that up and just fell-in in three ranks, not even making a good-sized company. Captain Plummer went down the line, looking to see who was worst hurt. He looked at the way I was holding my arm. "Bayonet?"

"Yes sir."

"Cut you bad?"

"It don't hurt much, captain. I just cant lift it no higher than this."

He looked me in the face, and I was afraid he thought I was lying to keep from fighting any more. "All wight," he said. "Fall out and join the others under that twee."

There were about two dozen of us under it when he got through, including some that hadnt been able to get in ranks in the first place. They were hacked up all kinds of ways. One had lost an ear and he was the worst worried man of the lot; "Does it look bad?" he kept asking, wanting to know how it would seem to the folks back home. We sat under the tree and watched Captain Plummer march what was left of the regiment away. They were a straggly lot. We were supposed to wait there under the tree till the doctor came.

We waited, hearing rifles clattering and cannons booming and men yelling further and further in the woods, and the sun climbed up and it got burning hot. I could look back over the valley where we had charged. It wasnt as wide as it had been before. There were men left all along the way, lying like bundles of dirty clothes. I had a warm, lazy feeling, like on a summer Sunday in the scuppernong arbor back home; next thing I knew I was sound asleep. Now that was strange. I was never one for sleeping in the daytime, not even in that quiet hour after dinner when all the others were taking their naps.

When I woke up the sun was past the overhead and only a dozen or so of the wounded were still there. The fellow next to me (he was hurt in the leg) said they had drifted off to find a doctor. "Aint no doctor coming here," he said. "They aint studying us now we're no more good to them." He had a flushed look, like a man in a fever, and he was mad at the whole army, from General Johnston down to me.

My arm was stiff and the blood had dried on my sleeve. There was just a slit where the bayonet blade went in. It felt itchy, tingling in all directions from the cut, like the spokes of a wheel, but I still hadnt looked at it and I wasnt going to. All except two of the men under the tree were leg wounds, not counting myself, and those two were shot up bad around the head. One was singing a song about the bells of Tennessee but it didnt make much sense.

"Which way did they go?"

"Ever which way," one said.

"Yonder ways, mostly," another said, and pointed over to the right. The shooting was a long way off now, loudest toward the right front. It seemed reasonable that the doctors would be near the loudest shooting.

I thought I would be dizzy when I stood up but I felt fine, light on my feet and tingly from not having moved for so long. I walked away nursing my arm. When I reached the edge of the field I looked back. They were spread around the tree trunk, sprawled out favoring their wounds. I could hear that crazy one singing the Tennessee song.

I walked on, getting more and more light-headed, till finally it felt like I was walking about six inches off the ground. I thought I was still asleep, dreaming, except for the ache in my arm. And I saw things no man would want to see twice. There were dead men all around, Confederate and Union, some lying where they fell and others up under bushes where theyd crawled to keep from getting trampled. There were wounded men too, lots of them, wandering around like myself, their faces dazed and pale from losing blood and being scared.

I told myself: You better lay down before you fall down. Then I said: No, youre not bad hurt; keep going. It was like an argument, two voices inside my head and neither one of them mine:

You better lay down.

—No: you feel fine.

Youll fall and theyll never find you.

—Thats not true. Youre just a little light-headed. Youll be all right.

No you wont. Youre hurt. Youre hurt worse than you think. Lay down.

They went on like that, arguing, and I followed the road, heading south by the sun until I came to a log cabin with a cross on its ridgepole and a little wooden signboard, hand-lettered: Shiloh Meeting House. It must have been some kind of headquarters now because there were officers inside, bending over maps, and messengers kept galloping up with papers.

I took a left where the road forked, and just beyond the fork there was a sergeant standing with the reins of two horses going back over his shoulder. When I came up he looked at me without saying anything.

"Where is a doctor?" I asked him. My voice sounded strange from not having used it for so long.

"I dont know, bud," he said. But he jerked his thumb down the road toward the sound of the guns. "Should be some of them up there, back of where the fighting is." He was a Texan, by the sound of his voice; it came partly through his nose.

So I went on down the road. It had been a line of battle that morning, the dead scattered thick on both sides. I was in a fever by then, thinking crazy, and it seemed to me that all the dead men got there this way:

God was making men and every now and then He would do a bad job on one, and He would look at it and say, "This one wont do," and He would toss it in a tub He kept there, maybe not even finished with it. And finally, 6 April 1862, the tub got full and God emptied it right out of heaven and they landed here, along this road, tumbled down in all positions, some without arms and legs, some with their heads and bodies split open where they hit the ground so hard.

I was in a fever bad, to think a thing like that. So there's no telling how long I walked or how far, but I know I came near covering that battlefield from flank to flank. It must have been a couple of hours and maybe three miles, but far as I was concerned it could have been a year and a thousand miles. At first all I wanted was a doctor. Finally I didnt even want that. All I wanted was to keep moving. I had an idea if I stopped I wouldnt be able to start again. That kept me going.

I didnt notice much along the way, but once I passed an open space with a ten-acre peach orchard in bloom at the far end and cannons puffing smoke up through the blossoms. Great crowds of men were trying to reach the orchard—they would march up in long lines and melt away; there would be a pause and then other lines would march up and melt away. Then I was past all this, in the woods again, and I came to a little gully where things were still and peaceful, like in another world almost; the guns seemed far away. That was the place for me to stop, if any place was. I sat down, leaning back against a stump, and all the weariness came down on me at once. I knew I wouldnt get up then, not even if I could, but I didnt mind.

I didnt mind anything. It was like I was somewhere outside myself, looking back. I had reached the stage where a voice can tell you it is over, youre going to die, and that is all right too.

Dying is as good as living, maybe better. The main thing is to be left alone, and if it takes dying to be let alone, a man thinks: All right, let me die. He thinks: Let me die, then.

This gully was narrow and deep, really a little valley, less than a hundred yards from ridge to ridge. The trees were thick but I could see up to the crest in each direction. There were some dead men and some wounded scattered along the stream that ran through, but I think they must have crawled in after water—there hadnt been any fighting here and there werent any bullets in the trees. I leaned back against the stump, holding my arm across my lap and facing the forward ridge. Then I saw two horsemen come over, side by side, riding close together, one leaning against the other. The second had his arm around the first, holding him in the saddle.

The second man was in civilian clothes, a boxback coat and a wide black hat. It was Governor Harris; I used to see him when he visited our brigade to talk to the Tennessee boys—electioneering, he called it; he was the Governor of Tennessee. The first man had his head down, reeling in the saddle, but I could see the braid on his sleeves and the wreath of stars on his collar. Then he lolled the other way, head rolling, and I saw him full in the face. It was General Johnston.

His horse was shot up, wounded in three legs, and his uniform had little rips in the cape and trouser-legs where minie balls had nicked him. One bootsole flapped loose, cut crossways almost through. In his right hand he held a tin cup, one of his fingers still hooked through the handle. I heard about the cup afterwards— he got it earlier in the day. He was riding through a captured camp and one of his lieutenants came out of a Yank colonel's tent and showed him a fine brier pipe he'd found there. General Johnston said "None of that, Sir. We are not here for plunder." Then he must have seen he'd hurt the lieutenant's feelings, for he leaned down from his horse and picked up this tin cup off a table and said, "Let this be my share of the spoils today," and used it instead of a sword to direct the battle.

They came down the ridge and stopped under a big oak at the bottom, near where I was, and Governor Harris got off between the horses and eased the general down to the ground. He began to ask questions, trying to make him answer, but he wouldnt—

couldnt. He undid the general's collar and unfastened his clothes, trying to find where he was shot, but he couldn't find it. He took out a bottle and tried to make him drink (it was brandy; I could smell it) but he wouldnt swallow, and when Governor Harris turned his head the brandy ran out of his mouth.

Then a tall man, wearing the three stars of a colonel, came hurrying down the slope, making straight for where General Johnston was laid out on the ground. He knelt down by his side, leaning forward so that their faces were close together, eye to eye, and begun to nudge him on the shoulder and speak to him in a shaky voice: "Johnston, do you know me? Johnston, do you know me?"

But the general didnt know him; the general was dead. He still looked handsome, lying there with his eyes glazing over.

Revenge

ELLEN GILCHRIST

IT WAS THE SUMMER of the Broad Jump Pit.

The Broad Jump Pit, how shall I describe it! It was a bright orange rectangle in the middle of a green pasture. It was three feet deep, filled with river sand and sawdust. A real cinder track led up to it, ending where tall poles for pole-vaulting rose forever in the still Delta air.

I am looking through the old binoculars. I am watching Bunky coming at a run down the cinder path, pausing expertly at the jump-off line, then rising into the air, heels stretched far out in front of him, landing in the sawdust. Before the dust has settled Saint John comes running with the tape, calling out measurements in his high, excitable voice.

Next comes my thirteen-year-old brother, Dudley, coming at a brisk jog down the track, the pole-vaulting pole held lightly in his delicate hands, then vaulting, high into the sky. His skinny tanned legs make a last, desperate surge, and he is clear and over.

Think how it looked from my lonely exile atop the chicken house. I was ten years old, the only girl in a house full of cousins. There were six of us, shipped to the Delta for the summer, dumped on my grandmother right in the middle of a world war.

They built this wonder in answer to a V-Mail letter from my father in Europe. The war was going well, my father wrote, within a year the Allies would triumph over the forces of evil, the world would be at peace, and the Olympic torch would again be brought down from its mountain and carried to Zurich or Amsterdam or London or Mexico City, wherever free men lived and worshiped sports. My father had been a participant in an Olympic event when he was young.

Therefore, the letter continued, Dudley and Bunky and Philip

107

and Saint John and Oliver were to begin training. The United States would need athletes now, not soldiers.

They were to train for broad jumping and pole-vaulting and discus throwing, for fifty-, one-hundred-, and four-hundred-yard dashes, for high and low hurdles. The letter included instructions for building the pit, for making pole-vaulting poles out of cane, and for converting ordinary sawhorses into hurdles. It ended with a page of tips for proper eating and admonished Dudley to take good care of me as I was my father's own dear sweet little girl.

The letter came one afternoon. Early the next morning they began construction. Around noon I wandered out to the pasture to see how they were coming along. I picked up a shovel.

"Put that down, Rhoda," Dudley said. "Don't bother us now. We're working."

"I know it," I said. "I'm going to help."

"No, you're not," Bunky said. "This is the Broad Jump Pit. We're starting our training."

"I'm going to do it too," I said. "I'm going to be in training."

"Get out of here now," Dudley said. "This is only for boys, Rhoda. This isn't a game."

"I'm going to dig it if I want to," I said, picking up a shovelful of dirt and throwing it on Philip. On second thought I picked up another shovelful and threw it on Bunky.

"Get out of here, Ratface," Philip yelled at me. "You German spy." He was referring to the initials on my Girl Scout uniform.

"You goddamn niggers," I yelled. "You niggers. I'm digging this if I want to and you can't stop me, you nasty niggers, you Japs, you Jews." I was throwing dirt on everyone now. Dudley grabbed the shovel and wrestled me to the ground. He held my arms down in the coarse grass and peered into my face.

"Rhoda, you're not having anything to do with this Broad Jump Pit. And if you set foot inside this pasture or come around here and touch anything we will break your legs and drown you in the bayou with a crowbar around your neck." He was twisting my leg until it creaked at the joints. "Do you get it, Rhoda? Do you understand me?"

"Let me up," I was screaming, my rage threatening to split open my skull. "Let me up, you goddamn nigger, you Jap, you spy. I'm telling Grannie and you're going to get the worst whipping of your life. And you better quit digging this hole for the horses to fall in. Let me up, let me up. Let me go."

"You've been ruining everything we've thought up all summer," Dudley said, "and you're not setting foot inside this pasture."

In the end they dragged me back to the house, and I ran screaming into the kitchen where Grannie and Calvin, the black man who did the cooking, tried to comfort me, feeding me pound cake and offering to let me help with the mayonnaise.

"You be a sweet girl, Rhoda," my grandmother said, "and this afternoon we'll go over to Eisenglas Plantation to play with Miss Ann Wentzel."

"I don't want to play with Miss Ann Wentzel," I screamed. "I hate Miss Ann Wentzel. She's fat and she calls me a Yankee. She said my socks were ugly."

"Why, Rhoda," my grandmother said. "I'm surprised at you. Miss Ann Wentzel is your own sweet friend. Her momma was your momma's roommate at All Saint's. How can you talk like that?"

"She's a nigger," I screamed. "She's a goddamn nigger German spy."

"Now it's coming. Here comes the temper," Calvin said, rolling his eyes back in their sockets to make me madder. I threw my second fit of the morning, beating my fists into a door frame. My grandmother seized me in soft arms. She led me to a bedroom where I sobbed myself to sleep in a sea of down pillows.

The construction went on for several weeks. As soon as they finished breakfast every morning they started out for the pasture. Wood had to be burned to make cinders, sawdust brought from the sawmill, sand hauled up from the riverbank by wheelbarrow.

When the pit was finished the savage training began. From my several vantage points I watched them. Up and down, up and down they ran, dove, flew, sprinted. Drenched with sweat they wrestled each other to the ground in bitter feuds over distances and times and fractions of inches.

Dudley was their self-appointed leader. He drove them like a demon. They began each morning by running around the edge of the pasture several times, then practicing their hurdles and dashes, then on to discus throwing and calisthenics. Then on to the Broad Jump Pit with its endless challenges.

They even pressed the old mare into service. Saint John was from New Orleans and knew the British ambassador and was thinking of being a polo player. Up and down the pasture he drove the poor old creature, leaning far out of the saddle, swatting a basketball with my grandaddy's cane.

I spied on them from the swing that went out over the bayou, and from the roof of the chicken house, and sometimes from the pasture fence itself, calling out insults or attempts to make them jealous.

"Guess what," I would yell, "I'm going to town to the Chinaman's store." "Guess what, I'm getting to go to the beauty parlor." "Doctor Biggs says you're adopted."

They ignored me. At meals they sat together at one end of the table, making jokes about my temper and my red hair, opening their mouths so I could see their half-chewed food, burping loudly in my direction.

At night they pulled their cots together on the sleeping porch, plotting against me while I slept beneath my grandmother's window, listening to the soft assurance of her snoring.

I began to pray the Japs would win the war, would come marching into Issaquena County and take them prisoners, starving and torturing them, sticking bamboo splinters under their fingernails. I saw myself in the Japanese colonel's office, turning them in, writing their names down, myself being treated like an honored guest, drinking tea from tiny blue cups like the ones the Chinaman had in his store.

They would be outside, tied up with wire. There would be Dudley, begging for mercy. What good to him now his loyal gang, his photographic memory, his trick magnet dogs, his perfect pitch, his camp shorts, his Baby Brownie camera.

I prayed they would get polio, would be consigned forever to iron lungs. I put myself to sleep at night imagining their labored breathing, their five little wheelchairs lined up by the store as I drove by in my father's Packard, my arm around the jacket of his blue uniform, on my way to Hollywood for my screen test.

Meanwhile, I practiced dancing. My grandmother had a black housekeeper named Baby Doll who was a wonderful dancer. In the mornings I followed her around while she dusted, begging for dancing lessons. She was a big woman, as tall as a man, and gave off a dark rich smell, an unforgettable incense, a combination of Evening in Paris and the sweet perfume of the cabins.

Baby Doll wore bright skirts and on her blouses a pin that said REMEMBER, then a real pearl, then HARBOR. She was engaged to a sailor and was going to California to be rich as soon as the war was over.

I would put a stack of heavy, scratched records on the record player, and Baby Doll and I would dance through the parlors to the music of Glenn Miller or Guy Lombardo or Tommy Dorsey.

Sometimes I stood on a stool in front of the fireplace and made up lyrics while Baby Doll acted them out, moving lightly across the old dark rugs, turning and swooping and shaking and gliding.

Outside the summer sun beat down on the Delta, beating down a million volts a minute, feeding the soybeans and cotton and clover, sucking Steele's Bayou up into the clouds, beating down on the road and the store, on the pecans and elms and magnolias, on the men at work in the fields, on the athletes at work in the pasture.

Inside Baby Doll and I would be dancing. Or Guy Lombardo would be playing "Begin the Beguine" and I would be belting out lyrics.

> *Oh, let them begin . . . we don't care,*
> *America all . . . ways does its share,*
> *We'll be there with plenty of ammo,*
> *Allies . . . don't ever despair . . .*

Baby Doll thought I was a genius. If I was having an especially creative morning she would go running out to the kitchen and bring anyone she could find to hear me.

"Oh, let them begin any warrr . . ." I would be singing, tapping one foot against the fireplace tiles, waving my arms around like a conductor.

> *Uncle Sam will fight*
> *for the underrr . . . doggg.*
> *Never fear, Allies, never fear.*

A new record would drop. Baby Doll would swoop me into her fragrant arms, and we would break into an improvisation on Tommy Dorsey's "Boogie-Woogie."

*   *   *

But the Broad Jump Pit would not go away. It loomed in my dreams. If I walked to the store I had to pass the pasture. If I stood on the porch or looked out my grandmother's window, there it was, shimmering in the sunlight, constantly guarded by one of the Olympians.

Things went from bad to worse between me and Dudley. If we so much as passed each other in the hall a fight began. He would hold up his fists and dance around, trying to look like a fighter. When I came flailing at him he would reach underneath my arms and punch me in the stomach.

I considered poisoning him. There was a box of white powder in the toolshed with a skull and crossbones above the label. Several times I took it down and held it in my hands, shuddering at the power it gave me. Only the thought of the electric chair kept me from using it.

Every day Dudley gathered his troops and headed out for the pasture. Every day my hatred grew and festered. Then, just about the time I could stand it no longer, a diversion occurred.

One afternoon about four o'clock an official-looking sedan clattered across the bridge and came roaring down the road to the house.

It was my cousin, Lauralee Manning, wearing her WAVE uniform and smoking Camels in an ivory holder. Lauralee had been widowed at the beginning of the war when her young husband crashed his Navy training plane into the Pacific.

Lauralee dried her tears, joined the WAVES, and went off to avenge his death. I had not seen this paragon since I was a small child, but I had memorized the photograph Miss Onnie Maud, who was Lauralee's mother, kept on her dresser. It was a photograph of Lauralee leaning against the rail of a destroyer.

Not that Lauralee even went to sea on a destroyer. She was spending the war in Pensacola, Florida, being secretary to an admiral.

Now, out of a clear blue sky, here was Lauralee, home on leave with a two-carat diamond ring and the news that she was getting married.

"You might have called and given some warning," Miss Onnie

Maud said, turning Lauralee into a mass of wrinkles with her embraces. "You could have softened the blow with a letter."

"Who's the groom," my grandmother said. "I only hope he's not a pilot."

"Is he an admiral?" I said, "or a colonel or a major or a commander?"

"My fiancé's not in uniform, Honey," Lauralee said. "He's in real estate. He runs the war-bond effort for the whole state of Florida. Last year he collected half a million dollars."

"In real estate!" Miss Onnie Maud said, gasping. "What religion is he?"

"He's Unitarian," she said. "His name is Donald Marcus. He's best friends with Admiral Semmes, that's how I met him. And he's coming a week from Saturday, and that's all the time we have to get ready for the wedding."

"Unitarian!" Miss Onnie Maud said. "I don't think I've ever met a Unitarian."

"Why isn't he in uniform?" I insisted.

"He has flat feet," Lauralee said gaily. "But you'll love him when you see him."

Later that afternoon Lauralee took me off by myself for a ride in the sedan.

"Your mother is my favorite cousin," she said, touching my face with gentle fingers. "You'll look just like her when you grow up and get your figure."

I moved closer, admiring the brass buttons on her starched uniform and the brisk way she shifted and braked and put in the clutch and accelerated.

We drove down the river road and out to the bootlegger's shack where Lauralee bought a pint of Jack Daniel's and two Cokes. She poured out half of her Coke, filled it with whiskey, and we roared off down the road with the radio playing.

We drove along in the lengthening day. Lauralee was chain-smoking, lighting one Camel after another, tossing the butts out the window, taking sips from her bourbon and Coke. I sat beside her, pretending to smoke a piece of rolled-up paper, making little noises into the mouth of my Coke bottle.

We drove up to a picnic spot on the levee and sat under a tree to look out at the river.

"I miss this old river," she said. "When I'm sad I dream about it licking the tops of the levees."

I didn't know what to say to that. To tell the truth I was afraid to say much of anything to Lauralee. She seemed so splendid. It was enough to be allowed to sit by her on the levee.

"Now, Rhoda," she said, "your mother was matron of honor in my wedding to Buddy, and I want you, her own little daughter, to be maid of honor in my second wedding."

I could hardly believe my ears! While I was trying to think of something to say to this wonderful news I saw that Lauralee was crying, great tears were forming in her blue eyes.

"Under this very tree is where Buddy and I got engaged," she said. Now the tears were really starting to roll, falling all over the front of her uniform. "He gave me my ring right where we're sitting."

"The maid of honor?" I said, patting her on the shoulder, trying to be of some comfort. "You really mean the maid of honor?"

"Now he's gone from the world," she continued, "and I'm marrying a wonderful man, but that doesn't make it any easier. Oh, Rhoda, they never even found his body, never even found his body."

I was patting her on the head now, afraid she would forget her offer in the midst of her sorrow.

"You mean I get to be the real maid of honor?"

"Oh, yes, Rhoda, Honey," she said. "The maid of honor, my only attendant." She blew her nose on a lace-trimmed handkerchief and sat up straighter, taking a drink from the Coke bottle.

"Not only that, but I have decided to let you pick out your own dress. We'll go to Greenville and you can try on every dress at Nell's and Blum's and you can have the one you like the most."

I threw my arms around her, burning with happiness, smelling her whiskey and Camels and the dark Tabu perfume that was her signature. Over her shoulder and through the low branches of the trees the afternoon sun was going down in an orgy of reds and blues and purples and violets, falling from sight, going all the way to China.

Let them keep their nasty Broad Jump Pit, I thought. Wait till they hear about this. Wait till they find out I'm maid of honor in a military wedding.

*   *   *

Finding the dress was another matter. Early the next morning Miss Onnie Maud and my grandmother and Lauralee and I set out for Greenville.

As we passed the pasture I hung out the back window making faces at the athletes. This time they only pretended to ignore me. They couldn't ignore this wedding. It was going to be in the parlor instead of the church so they wouldn't even get to be altar boys. They wouldn't get to light a candle.

"I don't know why you care what's going on in that pasture," my grandmother said. "Even if they let you play with them all it would do is make you a lot of ugly muscles."

"Then you'd have big old ugly arms like Weegie Toler," Miss Onnie Maud said. "Lauralee, you remember Weegie Toler, that was a swimmer. Her arms got so big no one would take her to a dance, much less marry her."

"Well, I don't want to get married anyway," I said. "I'm never getting married. I'm going to New York City and be a lawyer."

"Where does she get those ideas?" Miss Onnie Maud said.

"When you get older you'll want to get married," Lauralee said. "Look at how much fun you're having being in my wedding."

"Well, I'm never getting married," I said. "And I'm never having any children. I'm going to New York and be a lawyer and save people from the electric chair."

"It's the movies," Miss Onnie Maud said. "They let her watch anything she likes in Indiana."

We walked into Nell's and Blum's Department Store and took up the largest dressing room. My grandmother and Miss Onnie Maud were seated on brocade chairs and every saleslady in the store came crowding around trying to get in on the wedding.

I refused to even consider the dresses they brought from the "girls'" department.

"I told her she could wear whatever she wanted," Lauralee said, "and I'm keeping my promise."

"Well, she's not wearing green satin or I'm not coming," my grandmother said, indicating the dress I had found on a rack and was clutching against me.

"At least let her try it on," Lauralee said. "Let her see for herself." She zipped me into the green satin. It came down to my

ankles and fit around my midsection like a girdle, making my
waist seem smaller than my stomach. I admired myself in the
mirror. It was almost perfect. I looked exactly like a nightclub
singer.

"This one's fine," I said. "This is the one I want."

"It looks marvelous, Rhoda," Lauralee said, "but it's the wrong
color for the wedding. Remember I'm wearing blue."

"I believe the child's color-blind," Miss Onnie Maud said. "It
runs in her father's family."

"I am not color-blind," I said, reaching behind me and unzipping
the dress. "I have twenty-twenty vision."

"Let her try on some more," Lauralee said. "Let her try on
everything in the store."

I proceeded to do just that, with the salesladies getting grumpier and grumpier. I tried on a gold gabardine dress with a
rhinestone-studded cummerbund. I tried on a pink ballerina-
length formal and a lavender voile tea dress and several silk suits.
Somehow nothing looked right.

"Maybe we'll have to make her something," my grandmother
said.

"But there's no time," Miss Onnie Maud said. "Besides first
we'd have to find out what she wants. Rhoda, please tell us what
you're looking for."

Their faces all turned to mine, waiting for an answer. But I
didn't know the answer.

The dress I wanted was a secret. The dress I wanted was dark
and tall and thin as a reed. There was a word for what I wanted, a
word I had seen in magazines. But what was that word? I could
not remember.

"I want something dark," I said at last. "Something dark and
silky."

"Wait right there," the saleslady said. "Wait just a minute."
Then, from out of a prewar storage closet she brought a black-
watch plaid recital dress with spaghetti straps and a white piqué
jacket. It was made of taffeta and rustled when I touched it. There
was a label sewn into the collar of the jacket. *Little Miss Sophisticate*,
it said. *Sophisticate*, that was the word I was seeking.

I put on the dress and stood triumphant in a sea of ladies and
dresses and hangers.

"This is the dress," I said. "This is the dress I'm wearing."

"It's perfect," Lauralee said. "Start hemming it up. She'll be the prettiest maid of honor in the whole world."

All the way home I held the box on my lap thinking about how I would look in the dress. Wait till they see me like this, I was thinking. Wait till they see what I really look like.

I fell in love with the groom. The moment I laid eyes on him I forgot he was flat-footed. He arrived bearing gifts of music and perfume and candy, a warm dark-skinned man with eyes the color of walnuts.

He laughed out loud when he saw me, standing on the porch with my hands on my hips.

"This must be Rhoda," he exclaimed, "the famous red-haired maid of honor." He came running up the steps, gave me a slow, exciting hug, and presented me with a whole album of Xavier Cugat records. I had never owned a record of my own, much less an album.

Before the evening was over I put on a red formal I found in a trunk and did a South American dance for him to Xavier Cugat's "Poinciana." He said he had never seen anything like it in his whole life.

The wedding itself was a disappointment. No one came but the immediate family and there was no aisle to march down and the only music was Onnie Maud playing "Liebestraum."

Dudley and Philip and Saint John and Oliver and Bunky were dressed in long pants and white shirts and ties. They had fresh military crew cuts and looked like a nest of new birds, huddled together on the blue velvet sofa, trying to keep their hands to themselves, trying to figure out how to act at a wedding.

The elderly Episcopal priest read out the ceremony in a gravelly smoker's voice, ruining all the good parts by coughing. He was in a bad mood because Lauralee and Mr. Marcus hadn't found time to come to him for marriage instruction.

Still, I got to hold the bride's flowers while he gave her the ring and stood so close to her during the ceremony I could hear her breathing.

*   *   *

The reception was better. People came from all over the Delta. There were tables with candles set up around the porches and sprays of greenery in every corner. There were gentlemen sweating in linen suits and the record player playing every minute. In the back hall Calvin had set up a real professional bar with tall, permanently frosted glasses and ice and mint and lemons and every kind of whiskey and liqueur in the world.

I stood in the receiving line getting compliments on my dress, then wandered around the rooms eating cake and letting people hug me. After a while I got bored with that and went out to the back hall and began to fix myself a drink at the bar.

I took one of the frosted glasses and began filling it from different bottles, tasting as I went along. I used plenty of crème de menthe and soon had something that tasted heavenly. I filled the glass with crushed ice, added three straws, and went out to sit on the back steps and cool off.

I was feeling wonderful. A full moon was caught like a kite in the pecan trees across the river. I sipped along on my drink. Then, without planning it, I did something I had never dreamed of doing. I left the porch alone at night. Usually I was in terror of the dark. My grandmother had told me that alligators come out of the bayou to eat children who wander alone at night.

I walked out across the yard, the huge moon giving so much light I almost cast a shadow. When I was nearly to the water's edge I turned and looked back toward the house. It shimmered in the moonlight like a jukebox alive in a meadow, seemed to pulsate with music and laughter and people, beautiful and foreign, not a part of me.

I looked out at the water, then down the road to the pasture. The Broad Jump Pit! There it was, perfect and unguarded. Why had I never thought of doing this before?

I began to run toward the road. I ran as fast as my Mary Jane pumps would allow me. I pulled my dress up around my waist and climbed the fence in one motion, dropping lightly down on the other side. I was sweating heavily, alone with the moon and my wonderful courage.

I knew exactly what to do first. I picked up the pole and hoisted it over my head. I felt solid and balanced and alive. I hoisted it up and down a few times as I had seen Dudley do, getting the feel of it.

Then I laid it ceremoniously down on the ground, reached behind me, and unhooked the plaid formal. I left it lying in a heap on the ground. There I stood, in my cotton underpants, ready to take up pole-vaulting.

I lifted the pole and carried it back to the end of the cinder path. I ran slowly down the path, stuck the pole in the wooden cup, and attempted throwing my body into the air, using it as a lever.

Something was wrong. It was more difficult than it appeared from a distance. I tried again. Nothing happened. I sat down with the pole across my legs to think things over.

Then I remembered something I had watched Dudley doing through the binoculars. He measured down from the end of the pole with his fingers spread wide. That was it, I had to hold it closer to the end.

I tried it again. This time the pole lifted me several feet off the ground. My body sailed across the grass in a neat arc and I landed on my toes. I was a natural!

I do not know how long I was out there, running up and down the cinder path, thrusting my body further and further through space, tossing myself into the pit like a mussel shell thrown across the bayou.

At last I decided I was ready for the real test. I had to vault over a cane barrier. I examined the pegs on the wooden poles and chose one that came up to my shoulder.

I put the barrier pole in place, spit over my left shoulder, and marched back to the end of the path. Suck up your guts, I told myself. It's only a pole. It won't get stuck in your stomach and tear out your insides. It won't kill you.

I stood at the end of the path eyeballing the barrier. Then, above the incessant racket of the crickets, I heard my name being called. Rhoda...the voices were calling. Rhoda...Rhoda... Rhoda...Rhoda.

I turned toward the house and saw them coming. Mr. Marcus and Dudley and Bunky and Calvin and Lauralee and what looked like half the wedding. They were climbing the fence, calling my name, and coming to get me. Rhoda...they called out. Where on earth have you been? What on earth are you doing?

I hoisted the pole up to my shoulders and began to run down the path, running into the light from the moon. I picked up speed, thrust the pole into the cup, and threw myself into the sky, into the still Delta night. I sailed up and was clear and over the barrier.

I let go of the pole and began my fall, which seemed to last a long, long time. It was like falling through clear water. I dropped into the sawdust and lay very still, waiting for them to reach me.

Sometimes I think whatever has happened since has been of no real interest to me.

Testimony of Pilot

BARRY HANNAH

WHEN I WAS TEN, eleven and twelve, I did a good bit of my play in the backyard of a three-story wooden house my father had bought and rented out, his first venture into real estate. We lived right across the street from it, but over here was the place to do your real play. Here there was a harrowed but overgrown garden, a vine-swallowed fence at the back end, and beyond the fence a cornfield which belonged to someone else. This was not the country. This was the town, Clinton, Mississippi, between Jackson on the east and Vicksburg on the west. On this lot stood a few water oaks, a few plum bushes, and much overgrowth of honeysuckle vine. At the very back end, at the fence, stood three strong nude chinaberry trees.

In Mississippi it is difficult to achieve a vista. But my friends and I had one here at the back corner of the garden. We could see across the cornfield, see the one lone tin-roofed house this side of the railroad tracks, then on across the tracks many other bleaker houses with rustier tin roofs, smoke coming out of the chimneys in the late fall. This was niggertown. We had binoculars and could see the colored children hustling about and perhaps a hopeless sow or two with her brood enclosed in a tiny boarded-up area. Through the binoculars one afternoon in October we watched some men corner and beat a large hog on the brain. They used an ax and the thing kept running around, head leaning toward the ground, for several minutes before it lay down. I thought I saw the men laughing when it finally did. One of them was staggering, plainly drunk to my sight from three hundred yards away. He had the long knife. Because of that scene I considered Negroes savage cowards for a good five more years of my life. Our maid brought some sausage to my mother and when it was put in the pan to fry, I made a point of running out of the house.

121

I went directly across the street and to the back end of the garden behind the apartment house we owned, without my breakfast. That was Saturday. Eventually, Radcleve saw me. His parents had him mowing the yard that ran alongside my dad's property. He clicked off the power mower and I went over to his fence, which was storm wire. His mother maintained handsome flowery grounds at all costs; she had a leafmold bin and St. Augustine grass as solid as a rug.

Radcleve himself was a violent experimental chemist. When Radcleve was eight, he threw a whole package of .22 shells against the sidewalk in front of his house until one of them went off, driving lead fragments into his calf, most of them still deep in there where the surgeons never dared tamper. Radcleve knew about the sulfur, potassium nitrate and charcoal mixture for gunpowder when he was ten. He bought things through the mail when he ran out of ingredients in his chemistry sets. When he was an infant, his father, a quiet man who owned the Chevrolet agency in town, bought an entire bankrupt sporting-goods store, and in the middle of their backyard he built a house, plain-painted and neat, one room and a heater, where Radcleve's redundant toys forevermore were kept—all the possible toys he would need for boyhood. There were things in there that Radcleve and I were not mature enough for and did not know the real use of. When we were eleven, we uncrated the new Dunlop golf balls and went on up a shelf for the tennis rackets, went out in the middle of his yard, and served new golf ball after new golf ball with blasts of the rackets over into the cornfield, out of sight. When the strings busted we just went in and got another racket. We were absorbed by how a good smack would set the heavy little pills on an endless flight. Then Radcleve's father came down. He simply dismissed me. He took Radcleve into the house and covered his whole body with a belt. But within the week Radcleve had invented the mortar. It was a steel pipe into which a flashlight battery fit perfectly, like a bullet into a muzzle. He had drilled a hole for the fuse of an M-80 firecracker at the base, for the charge. It was a grand cannon, set up on a stack of bricks at the back of my dad's property, which was the free place to play. When it shot, it would back up violently with thick smoke and you could hear the flashlight battery whistling off. So that morning when I

ran out of the house protesting the hog sausage, I told Radcleve
to bring over the mortar. His ma and dad were in Jackson for the
day, and he came right over with the pipe, the batteries and the
M-80 explosives. He had two gross of them.

Before, we'd shot off toward the woods to the right of niggertown. I
turned the bricks to the left; I made us a very fine cannon
carriage pointing toward niggertown. When Radcleve appeared,
he had two pairs of binoculars around his neck, one pair a newly
plundered German unit as big as a brace of whiskey bottles. I told
him I wanted to shoot for that house where we saw them killing
the pig. Radcleve loved the idea. We singled out the house with
heavy use of the binoculars.

There were children in the yard. Then they all went in. Two
men came out of the back door. I thought I recognized the
drunkard from the other afternoon. I helped Radcleve fix the
direction of the cannon. We estimated the altitude we needed to
get down there. Radcleve put the M-80 in the breech with its fuse
standing out of the hole. I dropped the flashlight battery in. I lit
the fuse. We backed off. The M-80 blasted off deafeningly, smoke
rose, but my concentration was on that particular house over
there. I brought the binoculars up. We waited six or seven
seconds. I heard a great joyful wallop on tin. "We've hit him on
the first try, the first try!" I yelled. Radcleve was ecstatic. "Right
on his roof!" We bolstered up the brick carriage. Radcleve
remembered the correct height of the cannon exactly. So we fixed
it, loaded it, lit it and backed off. The battery landed on the roof,
blat, again, louder. I looked to see if there wasn't a great dent or
hole in the roof. I could not understand why niggers weren't
pouring out distraught from that house. We shot the mortar again
and again, and always our battery hit the tin roof. Sometimes
there was only a dull thud, but other times there was a wild
distress of tin. I was still looking through the binoculars, amazed
that the niggers wouldn't even come out of their house to see
what was hitting their roof. Radcleve was on to it better than me.
I looked over at him and he had the huge German binocs much
lower than I did. He was looking straight through the cornfield,
which was all bare and open, with nothing left but rotten stalks.
"What we've been hitting is the roof of the house just this side of
the tracks. White people live in there," he said.

I took up my binoculars again. I looked around the yard of that white wooden house on this side of the tracks, almost next to the railroad. When I found the tin roof, I saw four significant dents in it. I saw one of our batteries lying in the middle of a sort of crater. I took the binoculars down into the yard and saw a blond middle-aged woman looking our way.

"Somebody's coming up toward us. He's from that house and he's got, I think, some sort of fancy gun with him. It might be an automatic weapon."

I ran my binoculars all over the cornfield. Then, in a line with the house, I saw him. He was coming our way but having some trouble with the rows and dead stalks of the cornfield.

"That is just a boy like us. All he's got is a saxophone with him," I told Radcleve. I had recently got in the school band, playing drums, and had seen all the weird horns that made up a band.

I watched this boy with the saxophone through the binoculars until he was ten feet from us. This was Quadberry. His name was Ard, short for Arden. His shoes were foot-square wads of mud from the cornfield. When he saw us across the fence and above him, he stuck out his arm in my direction.

"My dad says stop it!"

"We weren't doing anything," says Radcleve.

"Mother saw the smoke puff up from here. Dad has a hangover."

"A what?"

"It's a headache from indiscretion. You're lucky he does. He's picked up the poker to rap on you, but he can't move further the way his head is."

"What's your name? You're not in the band," I said, focusing on the saxophone.

"It's Ard Quadberry. Why do you keep looking at me through the binoculars?"

It was because he was odd, with his hair and its white ends, and his Arab nose, and now his name. Add to that the saxophone.

"My dad's a doctor at the college. Mother's a musician. You better quit what you're doing. . . . I was out practicing in the garage. I saw one of those flashlight batteries roll off the roof. Could I see what you shoot 'em with?"

"No," said Radcleve. Then he said: "If you'll play that horn."

Quadberry stood out there ten feet below us in the field, skinny, feet and pants booted with black mud, and at his chest the slung-on, very complex, radiant horn.

Quadberry began sucking and licking the reed. I didn't care much for this act, and there was too much desperate oralness in his face when he began playing. That was why I chose the drums. One had to engage himself like suck's revenge with a horn. But what Quadberry was playing was pleasant and intricate. I was sure it was advanced, and there was no squawking, as from the other eleven-year-olds on sax in the band room. He made the end with a clean upward riff, holding the final note high, pure and unwavering.

"Good!" I called to him.

Quadberry was trying to move out of the sunken row toward us, but his heavy shoes were impeding him.

"Sounded like a duck. Sounded like a girl duck," said Radcleve, who was kneeling down and packing a mudball around one of the M-80s. I saw and I was an accomplice, because I did nothing. Radcleve lit the fuse and heaved the mudball over the fence. An M-80 is a very serious firecracker; it is like the charge they use to shoot up those sprays six hundred feet on July Fourth at country clubs. It went off, this one, even bigger than most M-80s.

When we looked over the fence, we saw Quadberry all muck specks and fragments of stalks. He was covering the mouthpiece of his horn with both hands. Then I saw there was blood pouring out of, it seemed, his right eye. I thought he was bleeding directly out of his eye.

"Quadberry?" I called.

He turned around and never said a word to me until I was eighteen. He walked back holding his eye and staggering through the cornstalks. Radcleve had him in the binoculars. Radcleve was trembling . . . but intrigued.

"His mother just screamed. She's running out in the field to get him."

I thought we'd blinded him, but we hadn't. I thought the Quadberrys would get the police or call my father, but they didn't. The upshot of this is that Quadberry had a permanent white space next to his right eye, a spot that looked like a tiny upset crown.

* * *

I went from sixth through half of twelfth grade ignoring him and that wound. I was coming on as a drummer and a lover, but if Quadberry happened to appear within fifty feet of me and my most tender, intimate sweetheart, I would duck out. Quadberry grew up just like the rest of us. His father was still a doctor— professor of history—at the town college; his mother was still blond, and a musician. She was organist at an Episcopalian church in Jackson, the big capital city ten miles east of us.

As for Radcleve, he still had no ear for music, but he was there, my buddy. He was repentant about Quadberry, although not so much as I. He'd thrown the mud grenade over the fence only to see what would happen. He had not really wanted to maim. Quadberry had played his tune on the sax, Radcleve had played his tune on the mud grenade. It was just a shame they happened to cross talents.

Radcleve went into a long period of nearly nothing after he gave up violent explosives. Then he trained himself to copy the comic strips, *Steve Canyon* to *Major Hoople,* until he became quite a versatile cartoonist with some very provocative new faces and bodies that were gesturing intriguingly. He could never fill in the speech balloons with the smart words they needed. Sometimes he would pencil in "Err" or "What?" in the empty speech places. I saw him a great deal. Radcleve was not spooked by Quadberry. He even once asked Quadberry what his opinion was of his future as a cartoonist. Quadberry told Radcleve that if he took all his cartoons and stuffed himself with them, he would make an interesting dead man. After that, Radcleve was shy of him too.

When I was a senior we had an extraordinary band. Word was we had outplayed all the big A.A.A. division bands last April in the state contest. Then came news that a new blazing saxophone player was coming into the band as first chair. This person had spent summers in Vermont in music camps, and he was coming in with us for the concert season. Our director, a lovable aesthete named Richard Prender, announced to us in a proud silent moment that the boy was joining us tomorrow night. The effect was that everybody should push over a seat or two and make room for this boy and his talent. I was annoyed. Here I'd been with the band and had kept hold of the taste among the whole percussion section. I could play rock and jazz drum and didn't even really need to be here. I could be in Vermont too, give me a piano and a bass. I looked at the kid on first sax, who was going to be supplanted tomorrow. For two years he had thought he was the star, then suddenly enters this boy who's three times better.

The new boy was Quadberry. He came in, but he was meek, and when he tuned up he put his head almost on the floor, bending over trying to be inconspicuous. The girls in the band had wanted him to be handsome, but Quadberry refused and kept himself in such hiding among the sax section that he was neither handsome, ugly, cute or anything. What he was was pretty near invisible, except for the bell of his horn, the all-but-closed eyes, the Arabian nose, the brown hair with its halo of white ends, the desperate oralness, the giant reed punched into his face, and hazy Quadberry, loving the wound in a private dignified ecstasy.

I say dignified because of what came out of the end of his horn. He was more than what Prender had told us he would be. Because of Quadberry, we could take the band arrangement of Ravel's *Bolero* with us to the state contest. Quadberry would do the saxophone solo. He would switch to alto sax, he would do the sly Moorish ride. When he played, I heard the sweetness, I heard the horn which finally brought human *talk* into the realm of music. It could sound like the mutterings of a field nigger, and then it could get up into inhumanly careless beauty, it could get among mutinous helium bursts around Saturn. I already loved *Bolero* for the constant drum part. The percussion was always there, driving along with the subtly increasing triplets, insistent, insistent, at last outraged and trying to steal the whole show from the horns and the others. I knew a large boy with dirty blond hair, name of Wyatt, who played viola in the Jackson Symphony and sousaphone in our band—one of the rare closet transmutations of my time—who was forever claiming to have discovered the central *Bolero* one Sunday afternoon over FM radio as he had seven distinct sexual moments with a certain B., girl flutist with black bangs and skin like mayonnaise, while the drums of Ravel carried them on and on in a ceremony of Spanish sex. It was agreed by all the canny in the band that *Bolero* was exactly the piece to make the band soar—now especially as we had Quadberry, who made his walk into the piece like an actual lean Spanish bandit. This boy could blow his horn. He was, as I had suspected, a genius. His solo was not quite the same as the New York Phil's saxophonist's, but it was better. It came in and was with us. It entered my spine and, I am sure, went up the skirts of the girls. I had almost deafened myself playing drums in the most famous rock and jazz band in the state, but I could hear the voice that went through and out that horn. It sounded like a very troubled forty-year-old man, a man who had had his brow in his hands a long time.

The next time I saw Quadberry up close, in fact the first time I had seen him up close since we were eleven and he was bleeding in the cornfield, was in late February. I had only three classes this last semester, and went up to the band room often, to loaf and complain and keep up my touch on the drums. Prender let me keep my set in one of the instrument rooms, with a tarpaulin thrown over it, and I would drag it out to the practice room and whale away. Sometimes a group of sophomores would come up and I would make them marvel, whaling away as if not only deaf but blind to them, although I wasn't at all. If I saw a sophomore girl with exceptional bod or face, I would do miracles of technique I never knew were in me. I would amaze myself. I would be threatening Buddy Rich and Sam Morello. But this time when I went into the instrument room, there was Quadberry on one side, and, back in a dark corner, a small ninth-grade euphonium player whose face was all red. The little boy was weeping and grinning at the same time.

"Queerberry," the boy said softly.

Quadberry flew upon him like a demon. He grabbed the boy's collar, slapped his face, and yanked his arm behind him in a merciless wrestler's grip, the one that made them bawl on TV. Then the boy broke it and slugged Quadberry in the lips and ran across to my side of the room. He said "Queerberry" softly again and jumped for the door. Quadberry plunged across the room and tackled him on the threshold. Now that the boy was under him, Quadberry pounded the top of his head with his fist like a mallet. The boy kept calling him "Queerberry" throughout this. He had not learned his lesson. The boy seemed to be going into concussion, so I stepped over and touched Quadberry, telling him to quit. Quadberry obeyed and stood up off the boy, who crawled on out into the band room. But once more the boy looked back with a bruised grin, saying "Queerberry." Quadberry made a move toward him, but I blocked it.

"Why are you beating up on this little guy?" I said. Quadberry was sweating and his eyes were wild with hate; he was a big fellow now, though lean. He was, at six feet tall, bigger than me.

"He kept calling me Queerberry."

"What do you care?" I asked.

"I care," Quadberry said, and left me standing there.

We were to play at Millsaps College Auditorium for the concert. It was April. We got on the buses, a few took their cars, and were a big tense crowd getting over there. To Jackson was only a twenty-minute trip. The director, Prender, followed the bus in his Volkswagen. There was a thick fog. A flashing ambulance, snaking the lanes, piled into him head on. Prender, who I would imagine was thinking of *Bolero* and hearing the young horn voices in his band—perhaps he was dwelling on Quadberry's spectacular gypsy entrance, or perhaps he was meditating on the percussion section, of which I was the king—passed into the airs of band-director heaven. We were told by the student director as we set up on the stage. The student director was a senior from the town college, very much afflicted, almost to the point of drooling, by a love and respect for Dick Prender, and now afflicted by a heart-breaking esteem for his ghost. As were we all.

I loved the tough and tender director awesomely and never knew it until I found myself bawling along with all the rest of the boys of the percussion. I told them to keep setting up, keep tuning, keep screwing the stands together, keep hauling in the kettledrums. To just quit and bawl seemed a betrayal to Prender. I caught some girl clarinetists trying to flee the stage and go have their cry. I told them to get the hell back to their section. They obeyed me. Then I found the student director. I had to have my say.

"Look. I say we just play *Bolero* and junk the rest. That's our horse. We can't play *Brighton Beach* and *Neptune's Daughter.* We'll never make it through them. And they're too happy."

"We aren't going to play anything," he said. "Man, to play is filthy. Did you ever hear Prender play piano? Do you know what a cool man he was in all things?"

"We play. He got us ready, and we play."

"Man, you can't play any more than I can direct. You're bawling your face off. Look out there at the rest of them. Man, it's a herd, it's a weeping herd."

"What's wrong? Why aren't you pulling this crowd together?" This was Quadberry, who had come up urgently. "I got those little brats in my section sitting down, but we've got people abandoning the stage, tearful little finks throwing their horns on the floor."

"I'm not directing," said the mustached college man.

"Then get out of here. You're weak, weak!"

"Man, we've got teen-agers in ruin here, we got sorrowville. Nobody can—"

"Go ahead. Do your number. Weak out on us."

"Man, I—"

Quadberry was already up on the podium, shaking his arms.

"We're right here! The band is right here! Tell your friends to get back in their seats. We're doing *Bolero*. Just put *Bolero* up and start tuning. *I'm* directing. I'll be right here in front of you. You look at *me*! Don't you dare quit on Prender. Don't you dare quit on me. You've got to be heard. *I've* got to be heard. Prender wanted me to be heard. I am the star, and I say we sit down and blow."

And so we did. We all tuned and were burning low for the advent into *Bolero*, though we couldn't believe that Quadberry was going to remain with his saxophone strapped to him and conduct us as well as play his solo. The judges, who apparently hadn't heard about Prender's death, walked down to their balcony desks.

One of them called out "Ready" and Quadberry's hand was instantly up in the air, his fingers hard as if around the stem of something like a torch. This was not Prender's way, but it had to do. We went into the number cleanly and Quadberry one-armed it in the conducting. He kept his face, this look of hostility, at the reeds and the trumpets. I was glad he did not look toward me and the percussion boys like that. But he must have known we would be constant and tasteful because I was the king there. As for the others, the soloists especially, he was scaring them into excellence. Prender had never got quite this from them. Boys became men and girls became women as Quadberry directed us through *Bolero*. I even became a bit better of a man myself, though Quadberry did not look my way. When he turned around toward the people in the auditorium to enter on his solo, I knew it was my baby. I and the drums were the metronome. That was no trouble. It was talent to keep the metronome ticking amidst any given chaos of sound.

But this keeps one's mind occupied and I have no idea what Quadberry sounded like on his sax ride. All I know is that he looked grief-stricken and pale, and small. Sweat had popped out on his forehead. He bent over extremely. He was wearing the red brass-button jacket and black pants, black bow tie at the throat, just like the rest of us. In this outfit he bent over his horn almost out of sight. For a moment, before I caught the glint of his horn through the music stands, I thought he had pitched forward off the stage. He went down so far to do his deep oral thing, his conducting arm had disappeared so quickly, I didn't know but what he was having a seizure.

When *Bolero* was over, the audience stood up and made meat out of their hands applauding. The judges themselves applauded. The band stood up, bawling again, for Prender and because we had done so well. The student director rushed out crying to embrace Quadberry, who eluded him with his dipping shoulders. The crowd was still clapping insanely. I wanted to see Quadberry myself. I waded through the red backs, through the bow ties, over the white bucks. Here was the first-chair clarinetist, who had done his bit like an angel; he sat close to the podium and could hear Quadberry.

"Was Quadberry good?" I asked him.

"Are you kidding? These tears in my eyes, they're for how good he was. He was too good. I'll never touch my clarinet again." The clarinetist slung the pieces of his horn into their case like underwear and a toothbrush.

I found Quadberry fitting the sections of his alto in the velvet holds of his case.

"Hooray," I said. "Hip damn horray for you."

Arden was smiling too, showing a lot of teeth I had never seen. His smile was sly. He knew he had pulled off a monster unlikelihood.

"Hip hip hooray for me," he said. "Look at her. I had the bell of the horn almost smack in her face."

There was a woman of about thirty sitting in the front row of the auditorium. She wore a sundress with a drastic cleavage up front; looked like something that hung around New Orleans and kneaded your heart to death with her feet. She was still mesmerized by Quadberry. She bore on him with a stare and there was moisture in her cleavage.

"You played well."

"Well? Play well? Yes."

He was trying not to look at her directly. Look at *me*, I beckoned to her with full face: I was the *drums*. She arose and left.

"I was walking downhill in a valley, is all I was doing," said Quadberry. "Another man, a wizard, was playing my horn." He locked his sax case. "I feel nasty for not being able to cry like the rest of them. Look at them. Look at them crying."

True, the children of the band were still weeping, standing around the stage. Several moms and dads had come up among them, and they were misty-eyed too. The mixture of grief and superb music had been unbearable.

A girl in tears appeared next to Quadberry. She was a majorette in football season and played third-chair sax during the concert season. Not even her violent sorrow could take the beauty out of the face of this girl. I had watched her for a number of years—her alertness to her own beauty, the pride of her legs in the majorette outfit—and had taken out her younger sister, a second-rate version of her and a wayward overcompensating nymphomaniac whom several of us made a hobby out of pitying. Well, here was Lilian herself crying in Quadberry's face. She told him that she'd run off the stage when she heard about Prender, dropped her horn and everything, and had thrown herself into a tavern across the street and drunk two beers quickly for some kind of relief. But she had come back through the front doors of the auditorium and sat down, dizzy with beer, and seen Quadberry, the miraculous way he had gone on with *Bolero*. And now she was eaten up by feelings of guilt, weakness, cowardice.

"We didn't miss you," said Quadberry.

"Please forgive me. Tell me to do something to make up for it."

"Don't breathe my way, then. You've got beer all over your breath."

"I want to talk to you."

"Take my horn case and go out, get in my car, and wait for me. It's the ugly Plymouth in front of the school bus."

"I know," she said.

Lilian Field, this lovely teary thing, with the rather pious grace of her carriage, with the voice of imminent swoon, picked up Quadberry's horn case and her own and walked off the stage.

I told the percussion boys to wrap up the packing. Into my suitcase I put my own gear and also managed to steal drum keys, two pairs of brushes, a twenty-inch Turkish cymbal, a Gretsch snare drum that I desired for my collection, a wood block, kettledrum mallets, a tuning harp and a score sheet of *Bolero* full of marginal notes I'd written down straight from the mouth of Dick Prender, thinking I might want to look at the score sheet sometime in the future when I was having a fit of nostalgia such as I am having right now as I write this. I had never done any serious stealing before, and I was stealing for my art. Prender was dead, the band had done its last thing of the year, I was a senior. Things were finished at the high school. I was just looting a sinking ship. I could hardly lift the suitcase. As I was pushing it across the stage, Quadberry was there again.

"You can ride back with me if you want to."

"But you've got Lilian."

"Please ride back with me...us. Please."

"Why?"

"To help me get rid of her. Her breath is full of beer. My father always had that breath. Every time he was friendly, he had that breath. And she looks a great deal like my mother." We were interrupted by the Tupelo band director. He put his baton against Quadberry's arm.

"You were big with *Bolero*, son, but that doesn't mean you own the stage."

Quadberry caught the end of the suitcase and helped me with it out to the steps behind the auditorium. The buses were gone. There sat his ugly ocher Plymouth; it was a failed, gay, experimental shade from the Chrysler people. Lilian was sitting in the front seat wearing her shirt and bow tie, her coat off.

"Are you going to ride back with me?" Quadberry said to me.

"I think I would spoil something. You never saw her when she was a majorette. She's not stupid, either. She likes to show off a little, but she's not stupid. She's in the History Club."

"My father has a doctorate in history. She smells of beer."

I said, "She drank two cans of beer when she heard about Prender."

"There are a lot of other things to do when you hear about death. What I did, for example. She ran away. She fell to pieces."

"She's waiting for us," I said.

"One damned thing I am never going to do is drink."

"I've never seen your mother up close, but Lilian doesn't look like your mother. She doesn't look like anybody's mother."

I rode with them silently to Clinton. Lilian made no bones about being disappointed I was in the car, though she said nothing. I knew it would be like this and I hated it. Other girls in town would not be so unhappy that I was in the car with them. I looked for flaws in Lilian's face and neck and hair, but there weren't any. Couldn't there be a mole, an enlarged pore, too much gum on a tooth, a single awkward hair around the ear? No. Memory, the whole lying opera of it, is killing me now. Lilian was faultless beauty, even sweating, even and especially in the white man's shirt and the bow tie clamping together her collar, when one knew her uncomfortable bosoms, her poor nipples. . . .

"Don't take me back to the band room. Turn off here and let me off at my house," I said to Quadberry. He didn't turn off.

"Don't tell Arden what to do. He can do what he wants to," said Lilian, ignoring me and speaking to me at the same time. I couldn't bear her hatred. I asked Quadberry to please just stop the car and let me out here, wherever he was: this front yard of the mobile home would do. I was so earnest that he stopped the car. He handed back the keys and I dragged my suitcase out of the trunk, then flung the keys back at him and kicked the car to get it going again.

My band came together in the summer. We were the Bop Fiends . . . that was our name. Two of them were from Ole Miss, our bass player was from Memphis State, but when we got together this time, I didn't call the tenor sax, who went to

Mississippi Southern, because Quadberry wanted to play with us. During the school year the college boys and I fell into minor groups to pick up twenty dollars on a weekend, playing dances for the Moose Lodge, medical-student fraternities in Jackson, teen-age recreation centers in Greenwood, and such as that. But come summer we were the Bop Fiends again, and the price for us went up to $1,200 a gig. Where they wanted the best rock and bop and they had some bread, we were called. The summer after I was a senior, we played in Alabama, Louisiana and Arkansas. Our fame was getting out there on the interstate route.

This was the summer that I made myself deaf.

Years ago Prender had invited down an old friend from a high school in Michigan. He asked me over to meet the friend, who had been a drummer with Stan Kenton at one time and was now a band director just like Prender. This fellow was almost totally deaf and he warned me very sincerely about deafing myself. He said there would come a point when you had to lean over and concentrate all your hearing on what the band was doing and that was the time to quit for a while, because if you didn't you would be irrevocably deaf like him in a month or two. I listened to him but could not take him seriously. Here was an oldish man who had his problems. My ears had ages of hearing left. Not so. I played the drums so loud the summer after I graduated from high school that I made myself, eventually, stone deaf.

We were at, say, the National Guard Armory in Lake Village Arkansas, Quadberry out in front of us on the stage they'd built. Down on the floor were hundreds of sweaty teen-agers. Four girls in sundresses, showing what they could, were leaning on the stage with broad ignorant lust on their minds. I'd play so loud for one particular chick, I'd get absolutely out of control. The guitar boys would have to turn the volume up full blast to compensate. Thus I went deaf. Anyhow, the dramatic idea was to release Quadberry on a very soft sweet ballad right in the middle of a long ear-piercing run of rock-and-roll tunes. I'd get out the brushes and we would astonish the crowd with our tenderness. By August, I was so deaf I had to watch Quadberry's fingers changing notes on the saxophone, had to use my eyes to keep time. The other members of the Bop Fiends told me I was hitting out of time. I pretended I was trying to do experimental things

with rhythm when the truth was I simply could no longer hear. I
was no longer a tasteful drummer, either. I had become deaf
through lack of taste.

Which was—taste—exactly the quality that made Quadberry
wicked on the saxophone. During the howling, during the churning, Quadberry had taste. The noise did not affect his personality;
he was solid as a brick. He could blend. Oh, he could hoot
through his horn when the right time came, but he could do
supporting roles for an hour. Then, when we brought him out
front for his solo on something like "Take Five," he would play
with such light blissful technique that he even eclipsed Paul
Desmond. The girls around the stage did not cause him to enter
into excessive loudness or vibrato.

Quadberry had his own girl friend now, Lilian back at Clinton,
who put all the sundressed things around the stage in the shade.
In my mind I had congratulated him for getting up next to this
beauty, but in June and July, when I was still hearing things a
little, he never said a word about her. It was one night in August,
when I could hear nothing and was driving him to his house, that
he asked me to turn on the inside light and spoke in a retarded
deliberate way. He knew I was deaf and counted on my being
able to read lips.

"Don't . . . make . . . fun . . . of her . . . or me . . . . We . . . think . . .
she . . . is . . . in trouble."

I wagged my head. Never would I make fun of him or her. She
detested me because I had taken out her helpless little sister for a
few weeks, but I would never think there was anything funny
about Lilian, for all her haughtiness. I only thought of this event
as monumentally curious.

"No one except you knows," he said.

"Why did you tell me?"

"Because I'm going away and you have to take care of her. I
wouldn't trust her with anybody but you."

"She hates the sight of my face. Where are you going?"

"Annapolis."

"You aren't going to any damned Annapolis."

"That was the only school that wanted me."

"You're going to play your saxophone on a boat?"

"I don't know what I'm going to do."

"How ... how can you just leave her?"

"She wants me to. She's very excited about me at Annapolis. William [this is my name], there is no girl I could imagine who has more inner sweetness than Lilian."

I entered the town college, as did Lilian. She was in the same chemistry class I was. But she was rows away. It was difficult to learn anything, being deaf. The professor wasn't a pantomimer— but finally he went to the blackboard with the formulas and the algebra of problems, to my happiness. I hung in and made a B. At the end of the semester I was swaggering around the grade sheet he'd posted. I happened to see Lilian's grade. She'd only made a C. Beautiful Lilian got only a C while I, with my handicap, had made a B.

It had been a very difficult chemistry class. I had watched Lilian's stomach the whole way through. It was not growing. I wanted to see her look like a watermelon, make herself an amazing mother shape.

When I made the B and Lilian made the C, I got up my courage and finally went by to see her. She answered the door. Her parents weren't home. I'd never wanted this office of watching over her as Quadberry wanted me to, and this is what I told her. She asked me into the house. The rooms smelled of nail polish and pipe smoke. I was hoping her little sister wasn't in the house, and my wish came true. We were alone.

"You can quit watching over me."

"Are you pregnant?"

"No." Then she started crying. "I wanted to be. But I'm not."

"What do you hear from Quadberry?"

She said something, but she had her back to me. She looked to me for an answer, but I had nothing to say. I knew she'd said something, but I hadn't heard it.

"He doesn't play the saxophone anymore," she said.

This made me angry.

"Why not?"

"Too much math and science and navigation. He wants to fly. That's what his dream is now. He wants to get into an F-something jet."

I asked her to say this over and she did. Lilian really was full of inner sweetness, as Quadberry had said. She understood that I was deaf. Perhaps Quadberry had told her.

The rest of the time in her house I simply witnessed her beauty and her mouth moving.

I went through college. To me it is interesting that I kept a B average and did it all deaf, though I know this isn't interesting to people who aren't deaf. I loved music, and never heard it. I loved poetry, and never heard a word that came out of the mouths of the visiting poets who read at the campus. I loved my mother and dad, but never heard a sound they made. One Christmas Eve, Radcleve was back from Ole Miss and threw an M-80 out in the street for old times' sake. I saw it explode, but there was only a pressure in my ears. I was at parties when lusts were raging and I went home with two girls (I am medium handsome) who lived in apartments of the old two-story 1920 vintage, and I took my shirt off and made love to them. But I have no real idea what their reaction was. They were stunned and all smiles when I got up, but I have no idea whether I gave them the last pleasure or not. I hope I did. I've always been partial to women and have always wanted to see them satisfied till their eyes popped out.

Through Lilian I got the word that Quadberry was out of Annapolis and now flying jets off the *Bonhomme Richard*, an aircraft carrier headed for Vietnam. He telegrammed her that he would set down at the Jackson airport at ten o'clock one night. So Lilian and I were out there waiting. It was a familiar place to her. She was a stewardess and her loops were mainly in the South. She wore a beige raincoat, had red sandals on her feet; I was in a black turtleneck and corduroy jacket, feeling significant, so significant I could barely stand it. I'd already made myself the lead writer at Gordon-Marx Advertising in Jackson. I hadn't seen Lilian in a year. Her eyes were strained, no longer the bright blue things they were when she was a pious beauty. We drank coffee together. I loved her. As far as I knew, she'd been faithful to Quadberry.

He came down in an F-something Navy jet right on the dot of ten. She ran out on the airport pavement to meet him. I saw her crawl up the ladder. Quadberry never got out of the plane. I could see him in his blue helmet. Lilian backed down the ladder. Then Quadberry had the cockpit cover him again. He turned the plane around so its flaming red end was at us. He took it down the runway. We saw him leap out into the night at the middle of the runway going west, toward San Diego and the *Bonhomme Richard*. Lilian was crying.

"What did he say?" I asked.

"He said, 'I am a dragon. America the beautiful, like you will never know.' He wanted to give you a message. He was glad you were here."

"What was the message?"

"The same thing. 'I am a dragon. America the beautiful, like you will never know.'"

"Did he say anything else?"

"Not a thing."

"Did he express any love toward you?"

"He wasn't Ard. He was somebody with a sneer in a helmet."

"He's going to war, Lilian."

"I asked him to kiss me and he told me to get off the plane, he was firing up and it was dangerous."

"Arden is going to war. He's just on his way to Vietnam and he wanted us to know that. It wasn't just him he wanted us to see. It was him in the jet he wanted us to see. He *is* that black jet. You can't kiss an airplane."

"And what are we supposed to do?" cried sweet Lilian.

"We've just got to hang around. He didn't have to lift off and disappear straight up like that. That was to tell us how he isn't with us anymore."

Lilian asked me what she was supposed to do now. I told her she was supposed to come with me to my apartment in the old 1920 Clinton place where I was. I was supposed to take care of her. Quadberry had said so. His six-year-old directive was still working.

She slept on the fold-out bed of the sofa for a while. This was the only bed in my place. I stood in the dark in the kitchen and drank a quarter bottle of gin on ice. I would not turn on the light and spoil her sleep. The prospect of Lilian asleep in my apartment made me feel like a chaplain on a visit to the Holy Land; I stood there getting drunk, biting my tongue when dreams of lust burst on me. That black jet Quadberry wanted us to see him in, its flaming rear end, his blasting straight up into the night at mid-runway—what precisely was he wanting to say in this stunt? Was he saying remember him forever or forget him forever? But I had my own life and was neither going to mother-hen it over his memory nor his old sweetheart. What did he mean, *America the beautiful, like you will never know?* I, William Howly, knew a goddamn good bit about America the beautiful, even as a deaf man. Being deaf had brought me closer to people. There were only about five I knew, but I knew their mouth movements, the perspiration under their noses, their tongues moving over the crowns of their teeth, their fingers on their lips. Quadberry, I said, you don't have to get up next to the stars in your black jet to see America the beautiful.

I was deciding to lie down on the kitchen floor and sleep the night, when Lilian turned on the light and appeared in her panties and bra. Her body was perfect except for a tiny bit of fat on her upper thighs. She'd sunbathed herself so her limbs were brown, and her stomach, and the instinct was to rip off the white underwear and lick, suck, say something terrific into the flesh that you discovered.

She was moving her mouth.

"Say it again slowly."

"I'm lonely. When he took off in his jet, I think it meant he wasn't ever going to see me again. I think it meant he was laughing at both of us. He's an astronaut and he spits on us."

"You want me on the bed with you?" I asked.

"I know you're an intellectual. We could keep on the lights so you'd know what I said."

"You want to say things? This isn't going to be just sex?"

"It could never be just sex."

"I agree. Go to sleep. Let me make up my mind whether to come in there. Turn out the lights."

Again the dark, and I thought I would cheat not only Quadberry but the entire Quadberry family if I did what was natural.

I fell asleep.

Quadberry escorted B-52s on bombing missions into North Vietnam. He was catapulted off the *Bonhomme Richard* in his suit at 100 degrees temperature, often at night, and put the F-8 on all it could get—the tiny cockpit, the immense long two-million-dollar fuselage, wings, tail and jet engine, Quadberry, the genius master of his dragon, going up to twenty thousand feet to be cool. He'd meet with the B-52 turtle of the air and get in a position, his cockpit glowing with green and orange lights, and turn on his transistor radio. There was only one really good band, never mind the old American rock-and-roll from Cambodia, and that was Red Chinese opera. Quadberry loved it. He loved the nasal horde in the finale, when the peasants won over the old fat dilettante mayor. Then he'd turn the jet around when he saw the squatty abrupt little fires way down there after the B-52s had dropped their diet. It was a seven-hour trip. Sometimes he slept, but his body knew when to wake up. Another thirty minutes and there was his ship waiting for him out in the waves.

All his trips weren't this easy. He'd have to blast out in daytime and get with the B-52s, and a SAM missile would come up among them. Two of his mates were taken down by these missiles. But Quadberry, as on saxophone, had endless learned technique. He'd put his jet perpendicular in the air and make the SAMs look silly. He even shot down two of them. Then, one day in daylight, a MIG came floating up level with him and his squadron. Quadberry couldn't believe it. Others in the squadron were shy, but Quadberry knew where and how the MIG could shoot. He flew below the cannons and then came in behind it. He knew the MIG wanted one of the B-52s and not mainly him. The MIG was so concentrated on the fat B-52 that he forgot about Quadberry. It was really an amateur suicide pilot in the MIG. Quadberry got on top of him and let down a missile, rising out of the way of it. The missile blew off the tail of the MIG. But then Quadberry wanted to see if the man got safely out of the cockpit. He thought it would be pleasant if the fellow got out with his parachute working. Then Quadberry saw that the fellow wanted to collide his wreckage with the B-52, so Quadberry turned himself over and cannoned, evaporated the pilot and cockpit. It was the first man he'd killed.

The next trip out, Quadberry was hit by a ground missile. But his jet kept flying. He flew it a hundred miles and got to the sea. There was the *Bonhomme Richard*, so he ejected. His back was snapped but, by God, he landed right on the deck. His mates caught him in their arms and cut the parachute off him. His back hurt for weeks, but he was all right. He rested and recuperated in Hawaii for a month.

Then he went off the front of the ship. Just like that, his F-6 plopped in the ocean and sank like a rock. Quadberry saw the ship go over him. He knew he shouldn't eject just yet. If he ejected now he'd knock his head on the bottom and get chewed up in the motor blades. So Quadberry waited. His plane was sinking in the green and he could see the hull of the aircraft carrier getting smaller, but he had oxygen through his mask and it didn't seem that urgent a decision. Just let the big ship get over. Down what later proved to be sixty feet, he pushed the ejection button. It fired him away, bless it, and he woke up ten feet under the surface swimming against an almost overwhelming body of underwater parachute. But two of his mates were in a helicopter, one of them on the ladder to lift him out.

Now Quadberry's back was really hurt. He was out of this war and all wars for good.

Lilian, the stewardess, was killed in a crash. Her jet exploded with a hijacker's bomb, an inept bomb which wasn't supposed to go off, fifteen miles out of Havana; the poor pilot, the poor passengers, the poor stewardesses were all splattered like flesh sparklers over the water just out of Cuba. A fisherman found one seat of the airplane. Castro expressed regrets.

Quadberry came back to Clinton two weeks after Lilian and the others bound for Tampa were dead. He hadn't heard about her. So I told him Lilian was dead when I met him at the airport. Quadberry was thin and rather meek in his civvies—a gray suit and an out-of-style tie. The white ends of his hair were not there—the halo had disappeared—because his hair was cut short. The Arab nose seemed a pitiable defect in an ash-whiskered face that was beyond anemic now. He looked shorter, stooped. The truth was he was sick, his back was killing him. His breath was heavy-laden with airplane martinis and in his limp right hand he held a wet cigar. I told him about Lilian. He mumbled something sideways that I could not possibly make out.

"You've got to speak right at me, remember? Remember me, Quadberry?"

"Mom and Dad of course aren't here."

"No. Why aren't they?"

"He wrote me a letter after we bombed Hué. Said he hadn't sent me to Annapolis to bomb the architecture of Hué. He had been there once and had some important experience—French-kissed the queen of Hué or the like. Anyway, he said I'd have to do a hell of a lot of repentance for that. But he and Mom are separate people. Why isn't *she* here?"

"I don't know."

"I'm not asking you the question. The question is to God."

He shook his head. Then he sat down on the floor of the terminal. People had to walk around. I asked him to get up.

"No. How is old Clinton?"

"Horrible. Aluminum subdivisions, cigar boxes with four thin columns in front, thick as a hive. We got a turquoise water tank; got a shopping center, a monster Jitney Jungle, fifth-rate teeny-boppers covering the place like ants." Why was I being so frank just now, as Quadberry sat on the floor downcast, drooped over like a long weak candle? "It's not our town anymore, Ard. It's going to hurt to drive back into it. Hurts me every day. Please get up."

"And Lilian's not even over there now."

"No. She's a cloud over the Gulf of Mexico. You flew out of Pensacola once. You know what beauty those pink and blue clouds are. That's how I think of her."

"Was there a funeral?"

"Oh, yes. Her Methodist preacher and a big crowd over at Wright Ferguson funeral home. Your mother and father were there. Your father shouldn't have come. He could barely walk. Please get up."

"Why? What am I going to do, where am I going?"

"You've got a saxophone."

"Was there a coffin? Did you all go by and see the pink or blue cloud in it?" He was sneering now as he had done when he was eleven and fourteen and seventeen.

"Yes, they had a very ornate coffin."

"Lilian was the Unknown Stewardess. I'm not getting up."

"I said you still have your saxophone."

"No, I don't. I tried to play it on the ship after the last time I hurt my back. No go. I can't bend my neck or spine to play it. The pain kills me."

"Well, *don't* get up, then. Why am I asking you to get up? I'm just a deaf drummer, too vain to buy a hearing aid. Can't stand to write the ad copy I do. Wasn't I a good drummer?"

"Superb."

"But we can't be in this condition forever. The police are going to come and make you get up if we do it much longer."

The police didn't come. It was Quadberry's mother who came. She looked me in the face and grabbed my shoulders before she saw Ard on the floor. When she saw him she yanked him off the floor, hugging him passionately. She was shaking with sobs. Quadberry was gathered to her as if he were a rope she was trying to wrap around herself. Her mouth was all over him. Quadberry's mother was a good-looking woman of fifty. I simply held her purse. He cried out that his back was hurting. At last she let him go.

"So now we walk," I said.

"Dad's in the car trying to quit crying," said his mother.

"This is nice," Quadberry said. "I thought everything and everybody was dead around here." He put his arms around his mother. "Let's all go off and kill some time together." His mother's hair was on his lips. "You?" he asked me.

"Murder the devil out of it," I said.

I pretended to follow their car back to their house in Clinton. But when we were going through Jackson, I took the North 55 exit and disappeared from them, exhibiting a great amount of taste, I thought. I would get in their way in this reunion. I had an unimprovable apartment on Old Canton Road in a huge plaster house, Spanish style, with a terrace and ferns and yucca plants, and a green door where I went in. When I woke up I didn't have to make my coffee or fry my egg. The girl who slept in my bed did that. She was Lilian's little sister, Esther Field. Esther was pretty in a minor way and I was proud how I had tamed her to clean and cook around the place. The Field family would appreciate how I lived with her. I showed her the broom and the skillet, and she loved them. She also learned to speak very slowly when she had to say something.

* * *

Esther answered the phone when Quadberry called me seven months later. She gave me his message. He wanted to know my opinion on a decision he had to make. There was this Dr. Gordon, a surgeon at Emory Hospital in Atlanta, who said he could cure Quadberry's back problem. Quadberry's back was killing him. He was in torture even holding up the phone to say this. The surgeon said there was a seventy-five/twenty-five chance. Seventy-five that it would be successful, twenty-five that it would be fatal. Esther waited for my opinion. I told her to tell Quadberry to go over to Emory. He'd got through with luck in Vietnam, and now he should ride it out in this petty back operation.

Esther delivered the message and hung up.

"He said the surgeon's just his age; he's some genius from Johns Hopkins Hospital. He said this Gordon guy has published a lot of articles on spinal operations," said Esther.

"Fine and good. All is happy. Come to bed."

I felt her mouth and her voice in my ears, but I could hear only a sort of loud pulse from the girl. All I could do was move toward moisture and nipples and hair.

Quadberry lost his gamble at Emory Hospital in Atlanta. The brilliant surgeon his age lost him. Quadberry died. He died with his Arabian nose up in the air.

That is why I told this story and will never tell another.

Good Old Boy

WILLIE MORRIS

WHEN I WAS FIVE my mother took me by the hand into the two-story brick schoolhouse on Main Street, and left me in the care of Miss Bass, a stern old lady who looked as if she would bite. Bubba Barrier was in my room. Someone was supposed to get me after the first day was out, but failed to come. Bubba and I were frightened, but finally we walked hand in hand away from the school, along the bayou, up Grand Avenue and home. Such adventure befitted a boy's stature as a first grader in the Free Public School System of Yazoo County, Mississippi.

The school was a big old structure with white columns, iron fire escapes, and tall old-fashioned windows. It was set in a large plot of three or four acres; the public library was at one end of the lot, and at the other, in the farthest corner of the grounds, the gray Confederate monument. On top of the monument about thirty feet from the ground were two statues: a lady holding a Confederate flag in front of her, and a soldier with a rifle in one hand, his other hand slightly raised to accept the flag—but a little shyly, as if he did not want to go around all day holding both a flag and a gun, particularly with a ten-inch bayonet attached.

Inside, the school building was all long, shadowy halls, smelling always of wax. On the wall near the front door were portraits of George Washington and Jefferson Davis. Downstairs was a large basement, where we met to wait for the morning bell to ring on rainy days and where, at noon, we took our lunch. It was a dark, eerie place; I was to have a nightmare of those years. I am trying to climb out of the sunless basement through a small, narrow window to the playground outside. The window is not big enough. My trouser legs are caught in it, nothing can budge me. The bell rings, everyone goes upstairs, and I am left alone. Some rainy gray mornings, waiting in that concrete chamber with its one light bulb in the peeled ceiling casting strange shadows, I could hardly bear the time until the bell rang. The room was attached to the boys' toilet, and from it came the echoes of the toilets flushing. Off to the side, in a kind of wired-in room, was the lunch hall, where lunches sold for a dime apiece and where the teachers, with shouts and sometimes slaps, would make us finish all our wieners and sauerkraut or bologna and black-eyed peas. It was our small contribution to the "war effort," eating everything on our plate. It might have been easier to lose the war.

All this was in the early 1940s, and the Second World War was on to defend democracy, as our teachers told us. They told us we were in school to help democracy, to strengthen our country and our God, and to learn enough so we could make good money for ourselves. In the assembly hall upstairs, where we marched in every Friday with the music teacher playing the March from *Aida* on the spinet piano, the American flag on the right of the stage and the Confederate flag on the left, the speaker would tell us of the man he once knew who could have been President of the United States, except that when the time came for him to be chosen, some of his friends felt honorbound to tell everybody that he had been lazy, lied a great deal, and had taken to liquor when he was young; so he never got the chance to be President. Quite frankly, I did not believe this story, and neither did Bubba Barrier.

I had a friend named Spit McGee who lived far out in the country. Spit was something of a lone wolf. He wore khaki clothes and did not come to school except when the mood was upon him. He was long and skinny, with a red face and a nose that should have belonged with somebody else's face. His given name was Clarence, but he concealed that fact; he could spit farther than anyone else, and with unusual accuracy.

Spit lived in the swamps, and he was a hunter and fisherman. Foxie Tompkins might bring an apple to school for the teacher, but not Spit. If he brought her anything it would be a catfish, or a dead squirrel for frying. Rivers Applewhite was often the recipient of the most beautiful wild swamp flowers, which Spit brought into town in the spring. One day he brought the teacher a dead chicken snake in a burlap sack, and a chicken was still inside the snake's belly (or whatever snakes call bellies); but the teacher made him bury it behind the Confederate monument. Later she caught him chewing tobacco near the snake's grave and gave him an F in Conduct. When she caught him smoking a Camel two weeks later she sent a note to Spit's mother, but Spit told me he wasn't worried because his mother couldn't read.

One day during recess Spit reached into his pockets and pulled out a dead grubworm, a live boll weevil, a wad of chewed-up bubble gum, four leaves of poison ivy which he said he was not allergic to, two shotgun shells, a small turtle, a rusty fish hook, the feather from a wild turkey, a minnow, the shrunken head of a chipmunk, and a slice of bacon. Spit may not have been smart in the ways of books, but he was diligent and resourceful, with a wisdom that came straight from the swamps. He claimed that he had taken an old useless .12 gauge shotgun and made it into a pellet gun, manufacturing his own bullets from rusty tin cans and soaking them in a mixture of frog's blood, burnt moss, dust from rattlesnake rattles, cypress juice, and mashed black widow spiders. When a victim was hit by one of these pellets, he said, it would not kill him, but knock him completely unconscious for three hours. He even said he had tried it once on his father, who was drunk in a willow tree, and that his father, not knowing what hit him, had not only been knocked out for six hours but once he did awaken gave up whiskey for three months.

We were envious of him not merely because of the bounty he carried in his pockets, but because he came to school barefooted whenever he felt like it, while we had to wear shoes that pinched our big toes and made our feet itch. He also claimed he could predict when it would rain from an ache he got in his arm, which he had broken falling out of a chinaberry tree. To my knowledge he was not wrong on a single rainfall. He further claimed that he was the great-great-nephew of Joe Bob Duggett—the boy who had discovered the witch in 1884—that he had once spent the night sleeping on an old blanket on the witch's grave in the cemetery, that he had dug up a grave in a Baptist cemetery on a plantation near the River, and that he had not taken a bath since the previous Easter. On the first three points we felt he was lying, but we believed him on the fourth.

At noon recess one day, when we were in third grade, Spit said he was going to play a prank on our teacher. Then he took off mysteriously for the bayou with a big box under his arm. When the bell rang half an hour later and we filed into our room, I saw a sight such as I will never forget. About three dozen crawdads, in all postures and movements, were crawling around the room. Five or six of them were on the teacher's desk, and one had gotten into her purse. The teacher was in a state of considerable anger, and she demanded to know who had done this horrible deed. For a while there was silence, and then Foxie Tompkins and Edith Stillwater, the teacher's pets, shouted almost at once. "It was Spit McGee!" Poor Spit got three paddlings: one from the teacher, one from the principal, and one from the superintendent of city schools, the last one being the worst because the superintendent had a paddle with air holes in it to make bigger blisters.

The next day there was revenge on a massive scale. Since I had taken Edith Stillwater to two war movies at the Dixie Theater (*Guadalcanal Diary* and *Flying Leathernecks*), spending ten cents each on her, I demanded the return of my twenty cents. (She only gave me back a dime.) She was giving a piano recital at the Baptist Church that afternoon before about fifty proud and cooing relatives and friends; we sneaked into the church early and got the piano out of tune, scraped some fresh cow manure onto the piano pedals, and placed a stray alley cat inside the piano and put the top back down. Then, led by Spit, we cornered Foxie Tompkins and marched him off to our official meeting place, the chicken shed behind Henjie Henick's house. After borrowing a rope from Henjie, Spit tied one end to the rafter and made a hangman's noose with the other. Then we put Foxie on a wooden box, tightened the noose around his neck, and told him to apologize fifty times in a row, but that he had better do it quickly because the box was shaky and if it fell over, that would be the end of Foxie's fine career, both in school and otherwise. We retired from the chicken coop and closed the door. From outside we heard Foxie apologizing rapidly, in a determined but squeaky voice. Just at that moment a funeral came by on Grand Avenue, and we went over to watch it. We forgot about Foxie. Luckily for his career, Henjie Henick's mother went back to feed the chickens and found Foxie balancing on his toes just as the box was beginning to fall over.

At the Baptist Church, we were told later, the cat squealed as Edith Stillwater started her off-key étude, ruining the recital. All that remained was to take the crawdads, which the teacher had returned to Spit, back to the bayou. As a celebration, Spit led us to the chicken snake's grave and we dug it up, to find that the snake had rotted but the chicken was still there.

This list of my schooltime favorites, Bubba, Spit, and all the rest, would not be complete without the one I think of the most: Rivers. Rivers Applewhite. She was without doubt the most beautiful girl in our class, but she was not a demure kind of beauty. Not at all. She wore her dark brown hair short (sometimes the way the models did in *Harper's Bazaar*) to offset her fine willowy grace, and she had deep green eyes, and in spring and summer she was always brown as a berry from all the time she spent in the sun. I am also pleased to say that she was not a tomboy; who in his proper senses would want a girl to kick a football farther than he could, or outrun him in the 50-yard dash? She was smart as could be—much smarter than Edith Stillwater, even though Edith got better grades—and she got Spit McGee through final exams in the third grade by bribing him, with the lemon pies she always was baking, to practice his long division and memorize poems. (Spit McGee once recited Browning: "Oh to be in April, Now that England's here.") She was also partial to Old Skip, my dog, and would bring him bones and cotton candy, so Skip was a regular old fool over Rivers Applewhite, sidling up to her with his tail wagging, putting his wet black nose against the palm of her hand, jumping and gyrating in her presence like the craziest creature alive. Unlike some of the other girls, especially Edith Stillwater, she would never so much as consider telling the teacher on anybody, and to this day I cannot recall a traitorous or deceitful act on her part. Kind, beautiful, a fount of good fun and cheer, she was the best of all feminine symbols to the wild and unregenerate boys of Yazoo. All of us, dogs and boys alike, were a little bit in love with Rivers Applewhite.

I remember her in a white summer dress, one day shortly before Christmas in Yazoo, walking up a sidewalk of Main Street under the bright holiday tinsel. As always, we were riding in Bubba's old red Ford, and we saw her from a half a block away, recognizing her from behind by the way she walked, half on her toes and half on her heels. As we got up close behind her near Kuhn's Nickel and Dime Store, I noticed that she *rippled* along that sidewalk, and that when she passed by people coming her way, just smiling calmly and being her jaunty self, they got a smile on their faces too.

There was terror for me in that school. Miss Abbott was my fourth grade teacher, and for the first time my grades were bad and my conduct report worse.

Miss Abbott had a pink nose and came from a small town in South Mississippi. The only book she ever read through and through, she told us, was the Bible, and you lived to believe her, and to feel bad about the day she got hold of that book. I myself liked the Bible. I had my own private friendship with God, which included the good old hymns and quiet mumbled prayers and holy vengeance when it was really deserved, and in that town and in that age you took God so much for granted that you knew he was keeping a separate book on you as part of His day's work.

But Miss Abbott's religion was one of fear and terror—it got you by the hind end and never let go. It was a thing of long, crazy speeches; she wanted you to believe she herself was in telephone contact with the Lord, and had hung the moon for Him on day number four. She played a little plastic flute which she had bought at Woolworth's for a quarter, and she would play us rousing hymns and marches, paying no attention to the saliva trickling down the instrument to the floor. She would not drink Coca-Cola, she said, because of the liquor hidden in it. She would preach to us every day: if God ever caught us doing something wrong, she said, we would surely go to hell before the next sunrise.

Twice a day, early in the morning and in the afternoon after lunch, she would call on each of us to pray. We would all begin by blessing our soldiers and then ripping into the Germans and the Japs. Once Spit began his prayer by saying, "Dear Lord, thank you for the bombs that ain't fallin' on us," and then stopped. "What's wrong?" the teacher asked, and he said, "I just can't think of nuthin' else to say." Then would come the Bible verses. For two hours each morning she would make us recite the verses she had assigned us to learn by heart. When we forgot a verse, she would rap our palms with a twelve-inch ruler. Then out would come that flute again, and if she caught you drowsing while she piped away on some song, or scratching your weary tail, she would go to her conduct book, and with a slight little flourish write down a "5."

I made the mistake of correcting her one day, during one of the rare hours in which we were doing schoolwork. The capital of Missouri, she said, was St. Louis. I held up my hand.

"What is it, Willie?" she said.

"Miss Abbott, the capital of Missouri is Jefferson City."

"No, it's St. Louis."

"I bet it's Jefferson City," I said, and then immediately wished I hadn't said it because the Bible was against gambling.

"Kay King," she snapped, "look in the book and show him it's St. Louis."

The girl looked in the book and turned red. "Well," she said, "it says here Jefferson City," but frightened, like everyone else in that ill-fated class, she added, "But Miss Abbott ought to—"

"We'll see," Miss Abbott growled, and changed the subject. Later, during "silent study," I caught her glowering at me. Why couldn't those wretched people in Missouri have settled on St. Louis? Then Rivers Applewhite sent a note over to me that said: "I'm proud of you. Someday you will be Governor of Mississippi."

At noon recess that spring, while the teacher sat on the grass with a group of fawning little girls around her who fetched things for her and scratched her back when it itched, gave her little compliments and practiced their Bible verses, held her hand and looked for four-leaf clovers to put behind her red ears, we were playing softball nearby. Honest Ed Upton hit a lazy foul that went high into the air behind third base. From shortstop I watched it come down with mounting interest, with an almost fanatic regard, as the ball drifted earthward and smacked Miss Abbott on the head. She sprawled on the ground, with a moo like a milk cow's—out cold. *Oh joy of joys!* The other teachers picked her up and carried her away in a car. In our room later, with the principal looking out for us, all the little girls cried—silent little bawls—and even Honest Ed Upton shed tears. The boys scratched their heads and fiddled with their pencils; such was the fear in that room, they dared not look into one another's eyes. All except Spit McGee. He caught a glance of mine and puckered up his lips, and before long a note in pencil came over from him—*i wich she got hit with a hardbal insted.* I prayed that she would die.

But back she came, risen on the third day. One Friday afternoon, when she had stepped out of the room, I made a spitball and threw it over two rows at Kay King. *"Willie!"* The sound of Miss Abbott's voice sent terror to my soul. Each afternoon during that wonderful spring I had to stay in, two hours a day for six weeks, working long division. Miss Abbott would sit at her desk, reading the Bible or *Reader's Digest,* while the shadows got longer and the sound of the boys' voices wafted in through the open window. And when that year ended, with a C on my report card in math, I had crossed, waded, swum the Sea of Galilee, and joyously entered the city limits of old Jerusalem.

FROM
The Moviegoer

WALKER PERCY

MY HALF BROTHERS and sisters are eating crabs at a sawbuck table on the screened porch. The carcasses mount toward a naked light bulb.

They blink at me and at each other. Suddenly they feel the need of a grown-up. A grown-up must certify that they are correct in thinking that they see me. They all, every last one, look frantically for their mother. Thèrése runs to the kitchen doorway.

"Mother! Jack is here!" She holds her breath and watches her mother's face. She is rewarded. "Yes, Jack!"

"Jean-Paul ate some lungs." Mathilde looks up from directly under my chin.

My half brother Jean-Paul, the son of my mother, is a big fat yellow baby piled up like a buddha in his baby chair, smeared with crab paste and brandishing a scarlet claw. The twins goggle at us but do not leave off eating.

Lonnie has gone into a fit of excitement in his wheelchair. His hand curls upon itself. I kiss him first and his smile starts his head turning away in a long trembling torticollis. He is fourteen and small for his age, smaller than Clare and Donice, the ten year old twins. But since last summer when Duval, the oldest son, was drowned, he has been the "big boy." His dark red hair is nearly always combed wet and his face is handsome and pure when it is not contorted. He is my favorite, to tell the truth. Like me, he is a moviegoer. He will go see anything. But we are good friends because he knows I do not feel sorry for him. For one thing, he has the gift of believing that he can offer his sufferings in reparation for men's indifference to the pierced heart of Jesus Christ. For another thing, I would not mind so much trading places with him. His life is a serene business.

154

My mother is drying her hands on a dishcloth.

"Well well, look who's here," she says but does not look.

Her hands dry, she rubs her nose vigorously with her three middle fingers held straight up. She has hay fever and crabs make it worse. It is a sound too well known to me to be remembered, this quick jiggle up and down and the little wet wringing noises under her fingers.

We give each other a kiss or rather we press our cheeks together, Mother embracing my head with her wrist as if her hands were still wet. Sometimes I feel a son's love for her, or something like this, and try to give her a special greeting, but at these times she avoids my eye and gives me her cheek and calls on me to notice this about Mathilde or that about Thérèse.

"Mother, I want you to meet Sharon Kincaid."

"Well now!" cried Mother, turning away and inserting herself among the children, not because she has anything against Sharon but because she feels threatened by the role of hostess. "There is nobody here but us children," she is saying.

Sharon is in the best of humors, rounding her eyes and laughing so infectiously that I wonder if she is not laughing at me. From the beginning she is natural with the children. Linda, I remember, was nervous and shifted from one foot to the other and looked over their heads, her face gone heavy as a pudding. Marcia made too much over them, squatting down and hugging her knees like Joan Fontaine visiting an orphanage.

Mother does not ask how I happen to be here or give a sign that my appearance is in any way remarkable—though I have not seen them for six months. "Tessie, tell Jack about your class's bus trip."—and she makes her escape to the kitchen. After a while her domesticity will begin to get on my nerves. By the surest of instincts she steers clear of all that is exceptional or "stimulating." Any event or idea which does not fall within the household regimen, she stamps at once with her own brand of the familiar. If, as a student, I happened to get excited about Jackson's Valley Campaign or Freud's *Interpretation of Dreams*, it was not her way to oppose me. She approved it as a kind of wondrous Rover boy eccentricity: "Those? Oh those are Jack's books. The stacks and stacks of books that boy brings home! Jack, do you know everything in those books?" "No'm." Nevertheless I became Dick Rover, the serious-minded Rover boy.

It is good to see the Smiths at their fishing camp. But not at their home in Biloxi. Five minutes in that narrow old house and dreariness sets into the marrow of my bones. The gas logs strike against the eyeballs, the smell of two thousand Sunday dinners clings to the curtains, voices echo round and round the bare stairwell, a dismal Sacred Heart forever points to itself above the chipped enamel mantelpiece. Everything is white and chipped. The floors, worn powdery, tickle the nostrils like a schoolroom. But here on Bayou des Allemands everybody feels the difference. Water laps against the piling. The splintered boards have secret memories of winter, the long dreaming nights and days when no one came and the fish jumped out of the black water and not a soul in sight in the whole savannah; secrets the children must find out and so after supper they are back at their exploring, running in a gang from one corner to another. Donice shows me a muskrat trap he had left last August and wonder of wonders found again. They only came down this morning, Mother explains, such a fine day it was, and since the children have a holiday Monday, will stay through Mardi Gras if the weather holds. With Roy away, Mother is a member of the gang. Ten minutes she will spend in the kitchen working with her swift cat-efficiency, then out and away with the children, surging to and fro in their light inconstant play, her eyes fading in a fond infected look.

Thérése is telling about her plans to write her Congressman about the Rivers and Harbors bill. Thérése and Mathilde are something like Joan and Jane in the Civics reader.

"Isn't that Tessie a *case?*" my mother cries as she disappears into the kitchen, signifying that Tessie is smart but also that there is something funny about her precocity.

"Where's Roy? We didn't see a car. We almost didn't walk over."

"Playing poker!" they all cry. This seems funny and everybody laughs. Lonnie's hand curls. If our arrival had caused any confusion, we are carried quickly past by the strong current of family life.

"Do you have any more crabs, Mother?"

"Any more crabs! Ask Lonnie if we weren't just wondering what to do with the rest. You haven't had your supper?"

"No'm."

Mother folds up the thick layer of newspapers under the crab carcasses, making a neat bundle with her strong white hands. The whole mess comes away leaving the table dry and clean. Thèrése spreads fresh paper and Mathilde fetches two cold bottles of beer and two empty bottles for hammering the claws and presently we have a tray apiece, two small armies of scarlet crabs marching in neat rows. Sharon looks queer but she pitches in anyhow and soon everybody is making fun of her. Mathilde shows her how to pry off the belly plate and break the corner at the great claw so that the snowy flesh pops out in a fascicle. Sharon affects to be amazed and immediately the twins must show her how to suck the claws.

Outside in the special close blackness of night over water. Bugs dive into the tight new screen and bounce off with a guitar thrum. The children stand in close, feeling the mystery of the swamp and the secrecy of our cone of light. Clairain presses his stomach against the arm of my chair. Lonnie tries to tune his transistor radio; he holds it in the crook of his wrist, his hands bent back upon it. Once his lip falls open in the most ferocious leer. This upsets Sharon. It seems to her that a crisis is at hand, that Lonnie has at least reached the limit of his endurance. When no one pays any attention to him, she grows fidgety—why doesn't somebody help him?—then, after an eternity, Mathilde leans over carelessly and tunes in a station loud and clear. Lonnie turns his head, weaving, to see her, but not quite far enough.

Lonnie is dressed up, I notice. It turns out that Aunt Ethel, Roy's sister, was supposed to take him and the girls to a movie. It was not a real date, Mother reminds him, but Lonnie looks disappointed.

"What is the movie?" I ask him.

"*Fort Dobbs.*" His speech is crooning but not hard to understand.

"Where is it?"

"At the Moonlite."

"Let's go."

Lonnie's head teeters and falls back like a dead man's.

"I mean it. I want to see it."

He believes me.

*   *   *

I corner my mother in the kitchen.

"What's the matter with Lonnie?"

"Why nothing."

"He looks terrible."

"That child won't drink his milk!" sings out my mother.

"Has he had pneumonia again?"

"He had the five day virus. And it was bad bad bad bad bad. Did you ever hear of anyone with virus receiving extreme unction?"

"Why didn't you call me?"

"He wasn't in danger of death. The extreme unction was his idea. He said it would strengthen him physically as well as spiritually. Have you ever heard of that?"

"Yes. But is he all right now?"

She shrugs. My mother speaks of such matters in a light allusive way, with the overtones neither of belief nor disbelief but rather of a general receptivity to lore.

"Dr Murtag said he'd never seen anything like it. Lonnie got out of bed in half an hour."

Sometimes when she mentions God, it strikes me that my mother uses him as but one of the devices that come to hand in an outrageous man's world, to be put to work like all the rest in the one enterprise she has any use for: the canny management of the shocks of life. It is a bargain struck at the very beginning in which she settled for a general belittlement of everything, the good and the bad. She is as wary of good fortune as she is immured against the bad, and sometimes I seem to catch sight of it in her eyes, this radical mistrust: an old knowledgeable gleam, as old and sly as Eve herself. Losing Duval, her favorite, confirmed her in her election of the ordinary. No more heart's desire for her, thank you. After Duval's death she has wanted everything colloquial and easy, even God.

"But now do you know what he wants to do? Fast and abstain during Lent." Her eyes narrow. Here is the outrage. "He weighs eighty pounds and he has one foot in the grave and he wants to fast." She tells it as a malignant joke on Lonnie and God. For a second she is old Eve herself.

*   *   *

Fort Dobbs is good. The Moonlite Drive-In is itself very fine. It does not seem too successful and has the look of the lonesome pine country behind the Coast. Gnats swim in the projection light and the screen shimmers in the sweet heavy air. But in the movie we are in the desert. There under the black sky rides Clint Walker alone. He is a solitary sort and a wanderer. Lonnie is very happy. Thérése and Mathilde, who rode the tops of the seats, move to a bench under the projector and eat snowballs. Lonnie likes to sit on the hood and lean back against the windshield and look around at me when a part comes he knows we both like. Sharon is happy too. She thinks I am a nice fellow to take Lonnie to the movies like this. She thinks I am being unselfish. By heaven she is just like the girls in the movies who won't put out until you prove to them what a nice unselfish fellow you are, a lover of children and dogs. She holds my hand on her knee and gives it a squeeze from time to time.

Clint Walker rides over the badlands, up a butte, and stops. He dismounts, squats, sucks a piece of mesquite and studies the terrain. A few decrepit buildings huddle down there in the canyon. We know nothing of him, where he comes from or where he goes.

A good night: Lonnie happy (he looks around at me with the liveliest sense of the secret between us; the secret is that Sharon is not and never will be onto the little touches we see in the movie and, in the seeing, know that the other sees—as when Clint Walker tells the saddle tramp in the softest easiest old Virginian voice: "Mister, I don't believe I'd do that if I was you"—Lonnie is beside himself, doesn't know whether to watch Clint Walker or me), this ghost of a theater, a warm Southern night, the Western Desert and this fine big sweet piece, Sharon.

A good rotation. A rotation I define as the experiencing of the new beyond the expectation of the experiencing of the new. For example, taking one's first trip to Taxco would not be a rotation, or no more than a very ordinary rotation; but getting lost on the way and discovering a hidden valley would be.

The only other rotation I can recall which was possibly superior was a movie I saw before the war called *Dark Waters*. I saw it in Lafitte down on Bayou Barataria. In the movie Thomas Mitchell and Merle Oberon live in a decaying mansion in a Louisiana swamp. One night they drive into the village—to see a movie! A repetition within a rotation. I was nearly beside myself with rotatory emotion. But *Fort Dobbs* is as good as can be. My heart sings like Octavian and there is great happiness between me and Lonnie and this noble girl and they both know it and have the sense to say nothing.

The Day Before

Elizabeth Spencer

WHEN I STARTED to school, my grandfather and the old maid next door and her two old bachelor brothers took a great interest in the event, so important in my life, and tried to do everything they could think of for me. One bought me a lunch basket; another planned just what should be put in it, and Miss Charlene Thomas, the old maid, made me a book satchel out of green linen with my initial embroidered on it in gold thread. Somebody even went uptown to the drugstore where the school books were sold and got me a new primer to replace an old one, still perfectly good, which had belonged to my cousin. And there was a pencil box, also green, with gilt lettering saying PENCILS, containing: three long yellow Ticonderoga pencils, an eraser—one end for ink, the other for lead—a pen staff, two nibs, and a tiny steel pencil sharpener. My grandfather laid the oblong box across his knees, unsnapped the cover, and carefully using the sharpener he began to sharpen the pencils. After doing one of them and dusting off his trousers, he took out his pen knife, which had a bone handle, and sharpened the other two in the manner which he preferred. Then he closed up the box and handed it to me. I put it in the satchel along with the primer.

Mr. Dave Thomas, one of the two bachelor brothers of Miss Charlene, having made a special trip uptown in the August heat, came in to say that copy books were not yet on sale as they had not arrived, but could be bought for a nickel from the teachers on opening day. "Here's a nickel right now," said Mr. Dave, digging in his trousers' pocket. "*I'll* give her one," said my grandfather. I was spoiled to death, but I did not know it. Miss Charlene was baking ginger cakes to go in my lunch basket. I went around saying that I hated to go to school because I would have to put

161

shoes on, but everybody including the cook laughed at such a flagrant lie. I had been dying to start to school for over a year.

My grandfather said that the entire family was smart and that I would make good grades, too. My mother said she did not think I would have any trouble the first year because I already knew how to read a little (I had, in fact, already read through the primer). "After that, I don't know," she said. I wondered if she meant that I would fail the second grade. This did not fill me with any alarm, any more than hearing that somebody had died, but made me feel rather cautious. Mr. Ed, Mr. Dave's brother, called me all the way over across the calf lot to his house to show me how to open a new book. I stood by his chair, one bare foot on top the other, watching him while he spread the pages out flat, first from the center, then taking up a few at a time on either side and smoothing them out in a steady firm way, slowly, so as not to crack the spine, and so on until all were done. It was a matter, he said (so they all said), of having respect for books. He said that I should do it a second time, now that he had showed me how. "Make sure your hands are clean," he said, "then we can go eat some cold watermelon." I remember still the smell of that particular book, the new pages, the binding, the glue, and the print as combining to make a book smell—a particular thing. The pencil box had another smell altogether, as did the new linen of the satchel. My brown shoes were new also, a brand called Buster Brown. I did not like the name, for it was invariably printed above a picture of a little round-faced boy with straight bangs and square-cut hair who was smiling as though he was never anything but cheerful. I did not know what I looked like especially, but I knew I did not look like that, nor did I want to. I asked to be allowed to wear new tennis shoes to school, and if not new ones, then old ones. My mother said I could not wear tennis shoes of any description to school and when I said I wanted to go barefoot then, she said I was crazy. I told my grandfather but he only said I had to mind her. I felt that he would have let me do as I liked and was only saying what he had to. I felt that my parents were never as intelligent as my grandfather, Mr. Dave, Mr. Ed, and Miss Charlene.

After dinner that day it was very hot and when everybody lay down and quit fanning themselves with funeral parlor fans because they had fallen sound asleep, some with the fans laid across their chests or stomachs and some snoring, the two Airedales that belonged to Mr. Dave had running fits. If a relative was visiting, or any stranger to our road, which was a street that didn't go anywhere except to us and the Thomas house, they were liable to get scared to death by those Airedales because the way they sometimes tore around in hot weather it looked as if they had gone mad. It was something about the heat that affected their brains and made them start running. It all happened silently; they would just come boiling out of nowhere, frothing at the mouth, going like two balls of fire, first around Miss Charlene's house, then up and down the calf lot between their house and ours, then all around our house, finally tearing out toward the field in front of the house, where, down among the cotton and the corn, they would wear it all out like the tail of a tornado. Eventually the foliage would stop shaking and after a long while they would come dragging themselves out again, heads down and tongues lolling, going back to where they belonged. They would crawl under the house and sleep for hours. We had got used to their acting this way, and though it was best, we agreed, to keep out of their way, they did not scare us. The Negro children used to watch them more closely than anybody did, saying "Hoo, boy, look a-yonder." White people had sunstrokes or heatstrokes or heat exhaustion—I did not ever learn quite what the difference in these conditions was, and don't know yet. Dogs had running fits instead.

The Airedales were named Pet and Beauty, and only Mr. Dave, who owned them, could tell them apart. He took their fits as being a sort of illness, and as he loved them, he worried about them. He gave them buttermilk out of dishes on the floor and got them to take cobalt blue medicine out of a spoon, holding their jaws wide with his thumb, pouring in the medicine, then clamping the jaws shut tight. It must have tasted awful, for the dogs always resisted swallowing and tried to fight free, their paws clawing the ground, head lashing around to get away and eyes rolling white and terrible. They could jump straight up and fight like wild ponies, but he always brought them down, holding on like a vise and finally, just when it seemed they weren't ever going to, they would give up and swallow. Then it was all over. I never knew if the medicine did them any good or not.

They had one of their fits that very afternoon, the day before school started. We had a friend of my aunt's from out in the country who had stopped by and been persuaded to stay for dinner and she saw them out her window and woke everybody up out of their nap. "Those dogs!" she cried. "Just look at those dogs!" "It's all right!" my father hollered from down the hall. "They've just got running fits, Miss Fannie," my mother cried. "It's not rabies," she added. "At least they don't bark," said my grandfather, who was angry because she had waked him up. He didn't care much for her anyway and said she had Indian blood.

I don't know what I thought school was going to be like. It was right up the road, only about twenty minutes' walk, just a little too far to come home for dinner, and I had passed the building and campus all my life, since I could remember. My brother had gone there, and all my cousins, and still were recognizable when they returned home from it. But to me, in my imagination beforehand, it was a blur, in the atmosphere of which my mind faltered, went blank, and came to with no clear picture whatsoever.

After I got there it was all clear enough, but strange to the last degree. I might as well have been in another state or even among Yankees, whom I had heard about but never seen. I could see our house from the edge of the campus, but it seemed to me I was observing it from the moon. There were many children there, playing on the seesaws, sliding down the sliding board, drinking at the water fountains, talking and running and lining up to file inside to the classrooms. All of them seemed to know each other. I myself did not recognize any of them except occasionally one of the older ones who went to our tiny Sunday School. They stopped and said, "Hey," and I said, "Hey." One said, "I didn't know you were starting to school." And I said, "Yes I am." I went up to a child in my grade and said that I lived down that street there and pointed. "I know it," she answered. She had white-blonde hair, pale blue eyes and very fair skin, and did not look at me when she spoke. The way she said "I know it" gave me to understand that she probably knew just about everything. I have seen sophisticated people since, and at that time I did not, of course, know the word, but she was, and always remained in my mind, its definition. I did not want to go away and stand by myself again, so I said, "I live next door to Miss Charlene Thomas and Mr. Dave and Mr. Ed Thomas." "I know it," she said again, still not looking at me. After a time she said, "They feed their old dogs out of Havilland china." It was my turn to say I know it, because I certainly had seen it happen often enough. But I said nothing at all.

I had often lingered for long minutes before the glass-front china cabinet on its tiny carved bowed legs, the glass, not flat, but swelling smoothly forward like a sheet in the wind, and marveled to see all the odd-shaped matching dishes—"Syllabub cups," Miss Charlene said, when I asked her. "Bone dishes," she said, "for when you eat fish." There were tiny cups and large cups, sauce bowls and gravy boats, and even a set of salt holders, no bigger than a man's thumb, each as carefully painted as a platter. It was known to me that this china, like the house itself and all the fine things in it, the rosewood my mother admired, the rose taffeta draperies and gilt mirrors, had belonged to the aunt of the three Thomases, a certain Miss Bedford, dead before I was born, who had been highly educated, brilliant in conversation, and whose parrot could quote Shakespeare. I did not find the words to tell any of this to the girl who knew everything. The reason I did not was because, no more than I knew how to do what she so easily accomplished in regard to the dogs' being fed out of Havilland china—which had often been held up to the light for me and shown to be transparent as an eggshell—I did not know what value to give to what I knew, what my ears had heard, eyes had seen, hands had handled, nor was there anything I could say about it. I did not think the child was what my grandfather meant by being smart, but I did know that she made me feel dumb. I retreated and was alone again, but a day is a long time when you are six and you cannot sit opening and closing your new pencil box forever. So I went up to other children and things of the same sort continued to happen. In the classroom I did as I was told, and it was easy. I must have realized by the end of the week that I would never fail the second or any other grade. So everything would be all right.

From then on, life changed in a certain way I could not define, and at home in the afternoons and on weekends I did not feel the same. I missed something but did not know what it was. I knew if I lived to be a thousand I would never do anything but accept it if an old man fed his dogs out of the best china or if a parrot could quote Shakespeare. At home when I looked up, I saw the same faces; even the dogs were the same, named the same, though they, as was usual, had stopped having fits once the nights got cooler. Everybody, every single person, was just the same. Yet I was losing them; they were fading before my eyes. You can go somewhere, anywhere you want—any day now you can go to the moon—but you can't ever quite come back. Having gone up a road and entered a building at an appointed hour, there was no way to come back out of it and feel the same about my grandfather, ginger cakes, or a new book satchel. This was the big surprise, and I had no power over it.

Life is important right down to the last crevice and corner. The tumult of a tree limb against the stormy early morning February sky will tell you forever about the poetry, the tough non-sad, non-guilty struggle of nature. It is important the way ants go one behind the other, hurrying to get there, up and down the white-painted front-porch post. The nasty flash and crack of lightning, striking a tall young tree, is something you have got to see to know about. Nothing can change it; it is just itself.

So nothing changed, nothing and nobody, and yet having once started to lose them a little, I couldn't make the stream run backward, I lost them completely in the end. The little guilt, the little sadness I felt sometimes: was it because I hadn't really wanted them enough, held on tightly enough, had not, in other words, loved them?

They are, by now, nearly every one dead and buried—dogs, parrot, people, and all. The furniture was all either given away or inherited by cousins from far away, the house bought by somebody and chopped up into apartments; none of this can really be dwelt on or thought of as grievous: that is an easy way out.

For long before anybody died, or any animal, I was walking in a separate world; our questions and answers, visits and exchanges no more communicated what they had once than if we were already spirits and flesh and could walk right through each other without knowing it.

Years later, only a few months ago, when home for a visit, I was invited to play bridge with some friends and on the coffee table saw a box of blue milk glass, carved with a golden dragon across the lid, quite beautiful. "That came out of the old Thomas house," my friend said. She had got it in a devious way, which she related, but had never been able to open it. I picked it up, not remembering it, and without even thinking my finger moved at once to the hidden catch, and the box flew open. It wasn't chance; I must have once been shown how it worked, and something in me was keeping an instinctive faith with what it knew. Had they never been lost then at all? I wondered. A great hidden world shimmered for a moment, grew almost visible, just beyond the breaking point of knowledge. Had nothing perhaps ever been lost by that great silent guardian within?

Weep No More, My Lady

JAMES STREET

THE MOONLIGHT SYMPHONY of swamp creatures hushed abruptly, and the dismal bog was as peaceful as unborn time and seemed to brood in its silence. The gaunt man glanced back at the boy and motioned for him to be quiet, but it was too late. Their presence was discovered. A jumbo frog rumbled a warning and the swamp squirmed into life as its denizens scuttled to safety.

Fox fire was glowing to the west and the bayou was slapping the cypress knees when suddenly a haunting laugh echoed through the wilderness, a strange chuckling yodel ending in a weird "gro-o-o."

The boy's eyes were wide and staring. "That's it, Uncle Jess. Come on! Let's catch it!"

"Uh, oh." The man gripped his shotgun. "That ain't no animal. That's a thing."

They hurried noiselessly in the direction of the sound that Skeeter had been hearing for several nights. Swamp born and reared, they feared nothing they could shoot or outwit, so they slipped out of the morass and to the side of a ridge. Suddenly, Jesse put out his hand and stopped the child, then pointed up the slope. The animal, clearly visible in the moonlight, was sitting on its haunches, its head cocked sideways as it chuckled. It was a merry and rather melodious little chuckle.

Skeeter grinned in spite of his surprise, then said, "Sh-h-h. It'll smell us."

Jesse said, "Can't nothing smell that far. Wonder what the durn thing is?" He peered up the ridge, studying the creature. He had no intention of shooting unless attacked, for Jesse Tolliver and his nephew never killed wantonly.

The animal, however, did smell them and whipped her nose into the wind, crouched and braced. She was about sixteen inches high and weighed twenty-two pounds. Her coat was red and silky and there was a blaze of white down her chest and a circle of white around her throat. Her face was wrinkled and sad, like a wise old man's.

Jesse shook his head. "Looks som'n like a mixture of blood-hound and terrier from here," he whispered. "It beats me—"

"It's a dog, all right," Skeeter said.

"Can't no dog laugh."

"That dog can." The boy began walking toward the animal, his right hand outstretched. "Heah, heah. I ain't gonna hurt you."

The dog, for she was a dog, cocked her head from one side to the other and watched Skeeter. She was trembling, but she didn't run. And when Skeeter knelt by her, she stopped trembling, for the ways of a boy with a dog are mysterious. He stroked her, and the trim little creature looked up at him and blinked her big hazel eyes. Then she turned over and Skeeter scratched her. She closed her eyes, stretched and chuckled, a happy mixture of chortle and yodel. Jesse ambled up and the dog leaped to her feet and sprang between the boy and the man.

Skeeter calmed her. "That's just Uncle Jess."

Jesse, still bewildered, shook his head again. "I still say that ain't no dog. She don't smell and she don't bark. Ain't natural. And look at her! Licking herself like a cat."

"Well, I'll be a catty wampus," Skeeter said. "Never saw a dog do that before." However, he was quick to defend any mannerism of his friend and said, "She likes to keep herself clean. She's a lady and I'm gonna name her that, and she's mind 'cause I found her."

"Lady, huh?"

"No, sir. My Lady. If I name her just plain Lady, how folks gonna know she's mine?" He began stroking his dog again. "Gee m'netty, Uncle Jess, I ain't never had nothing like this before."

"It still don't make sense to me," Jesse said. But he didn't care, for he was happy because the child was happy.

Like most mysteries, there was no mystery at all about My Lady. She was a lady, all right, an aristocratic Basenji, one of those strange barkless dogs of Africa. Her ancestors were pets of the Pharaohs and her line was well established when the now proud races of men were wandering about Europe, begging handouts from Nature. A bundle of nerves and muscles, she would fight anything, and could scent game up to eighty yards. She had the gait of an antelope and was odorless, washing herself before and after meals. However, the only noises she could make were a piercing cry that sounded almost human and that chuckling little chortle. She could chuckle only when happy and she had been happy in the woods. Now she was happy again.

As most men judge values, she was worth more than all the possessions of Jesse and his nephew. Several of the dogs had been shipped to New Orleans to avoid the dangerous upper route, thence by motor to a northern kennel. While crossing Mississippi, My Lady had escaped from the station wagon. Her keeper had advertised in several papers, but Jesse and Skeeter never saw papers.

Skeeter said, "Come on, M'Lady. Let's go home."

The dog didn't hesitate, but walked proudly at the boy's side to a cabin on the bank of the bayou. Skeeter crumbled corn bread, wet it with pot likker and put it before her. She sniffed the food disdainfully at first, then ate it only when she saw the boy fix a bowl for his uncle. She licked herself clean and explored the cabin, sniffing the brush brooms, the piles of wild pecans and hickory nuts, and then the cots. Satisfied at last, she jumped on Skeeter's bed, tucked her nose under her paws and went to sleep.

"Acts like she owns the place," Jesse said.

"Where you reckon she came from?" The boy slipped his overall straps from his shoulders, flexed his stringy muscles and yawned.

"Lord knows. Circus maybe." He looked at M'Lady quickly. "Say, maybe she's a freak and run off from some show. But they'd give us two dollars for her."

Skeeter's face got long. "You don't aim to get rid of her?"

The old man put his shotgun over the mantel and lit his pipe. "Skeets, if you want that thing, I wouldn't get shed of her for a piece of bottom land a mile long. Already plowed and planted."

"I reckoned you wouldn't, 'cause you like me so much. And I know how you like dogs, 'cause I saw you cry when yours got killed. But you can have part of mine."

Jesse sat down and leaned back, blowing smoke into the air to drive away mosquitoes. The boy got a brick and hammer and began cracking nuts, pounding the meat to a pulp so his uncle could chew it. Skeeter's yellow hair hadn't been cut for months and was tangled. He had freckles too. And his real name was Jonathan. His mother was Jesse's only sister and died when the child was born. No one thereabouts ever knew what happened to his father. Jesse, a leathery, toothless old man with faded blue eyes, took him to bring up and called him Skeeter because he was so little.

In the village, where Jesse seldom visited, folks wondered if he were fit'n to rear a little boy. They considered him shiftless and no-count. Jesse had lived all of his sixty years in the swamp and his way of life was a torment to folks who believed life must be lived by rules. He earned a few dollars selling jumbo frogs and pelts, but mostly he just paddled around the swamp, watching things and teaching Skeeter about life.

The villagers might have tried to send Skeeter to an orphanage, but for Joe (Cash) Watson, the storekeeper. Cash was a hard man, but fair. He often hunted with Jesse, and the old man had trained Cash's dogs. When there was talk of sending Skeeter away, Cash said, "You ain't agonna do it. You just don't take young'uns away from their folks." And that's all there was to it.

Jesse never coveted the "frills and furbelows of damn-fool folks" and yearned for only two things—a twenty-gauge shotgun for Skeeter and a set of Roebuckers for himself, as he called store-bought teeth. Cash had promised him the gun and the best false teeth in the catalogue for forty-six dollars. Jesse had saved $9.37.

"Someday I'm gonna get them Roebuckers," he often told Skeeter. "Then I'm gonna eat me enough roastin' ears to kill a goat. Maybe I can get a set with a couple of gold teeth in 'em. I seen a man once with six gold teeth."

Once Skeeter asked him, "Why don't you get a job with the W.P. and A. and make enough money to buy them Roebuckers?"

"I don't want 'em that bad," Jesse said.

So he was happy for Skeeter to have M'Lady, thinking the dog would sort of make up for the shotgun.

The boy cracked as many nuts as his uncle wanted, then put the hammer away. He was undressing when he glanced over at his dog. "Gosh, Uncle Jess. I'm scared somebody'll come get her."

"I ain't heard of nobody losing no things around here. If'n they had, they'd been to me 'fo' now, being's I know all about dogs and the swamp."

"That's so," Skeeter said. "But you don't reckon she belonged to another fellow like me, do you? I know how I'd feel if I had a dog like her and she got lost."

Jesse said, "She didn't belong to another fellow like you. If'n she had, she wouldn't be so happy here."

Skeeter fed M'Lady biscuits and molasses for breakfast, and although the Basenji ate it, she still was hungry when she went into the swamp with the boy. He was hoping he could find a bee tree or signs of wild hogs. They were at the edge of a clearing when M'Lady's chokebore nose suddenly tilted and she froze to a flash point, pausing only long enough to get set. Then she darted to the bayou, at least sixty yards away, dived into a clump of reeds and snatched a water rat. She was eating it when Skeeter ran up.

"Don't do that," he scolded. "Ain't you got no more sense than run into water after things? A snake or a gator might snatch you."

The Basenji dropped the rat and tucked her head. She knew the boy was displeased, and when she looked up at him her eyes were filled and a woebegone expression was on her face.

Skeeter tried to explain, "I didn't mean to hurt your feelings. Don't cry." He stepped back quickly and stared at her, at the tears in her eyes. "She is crying! Be John Brown!" Skeeter called her and ran toward the cabin, where Jesse was cutting splinters.

"Uncle Jess! Guess what else my dog can do!"

"Whistle?" the old man laughed.

"She can cry! I declare to goodness! Not out loud, but she can cry just the same."

Jesse knew that most dogs will get watery-eyed on occasion, but, not wanting to ridicule M'Lady's accomplishments, asked, "What made her cry?"

"Well, sir, we were walking along and all of a sudden she got a scent and flash pointed and then—" Skeeter remembered something.

"Then what?"

Skeeter sat on the steps. "Uncle Jess," he said slowly, "we must have been fifty or sixty yards from that rat when she smelled it."

"What rat? What's eating you?"

The child told him the story and Jesse couldn't believe it. For a dog to pick up the scent of a water rat at sixty yards simply isn't credible. Jesse reckoned Skeeter's love for M'Lady had led him to exaggerate.

Skeeter knew Jesse didn't believe the story, so he said, "Come on. I'll show you." He whistled for M'Lady.

The dog came up. "Hey," Jesse said. "That thing knows what a whistle means. Shows she's been around folks." He caught the dog's eye and commanded, "Heel!"

But M'Lady cocked her head quizzically. Then she turned to the boy and chuckled softly. She'd never heard the order before. That was obvious. Her nose came up into the breeze and she wheeled.

Her curved tail suddenly was still and her head was poised.

"Flash pointing," Jesse said. "Well, I'll be a monkey's uncle!"

M'Lady held the strange point only for a second, though, then dashed toward a corn patch about eighty yards from the cabin.

Halfway to the patch, she broke her gait and began creeping. A whir of feathered lightning sounded in the corn and a covey of quail exploded almost under her nose. She sprang and snatched a bird.

"Partridges!" Jesse's jaw dropped.

The child was as motionless as stone, his face white and his eyes wide in amazement. Finally he found his voice, "She was right here when she smelled them birds. A good eighty yards."

"I know she ain't no dog now," Jesse said. "Can't no dog do that."

"She's fast as greased lightning and ain't scared of nothing." Skeeter still was under the spell of the adventure. "She's a hunting dog from way back."

"She ain't no dog a-tall, I'm telling you. It ain't human." Jesse walked toward M'Lady and told her to fetch the bird, but the dog didn't understand. Instead, she pawed it. "Well," Jesse said. "One thing's certain. She ain't no bird hunter."

"She can do anything," Skeeter said. "Even hunt birds. Maybe I can make a bird dog out'n her. Wouldn't that be som'n?"

"You're batty. Maybe a coon dog, but not a bird dog. I know 'bout dogs."

"Me too," said Skeeter. And he did. He'd seen Jesse train many dogs, even pointers, and had helped him train Big Boy, Cash Watson's prize gun dog.

Jesse eyed Skeeter and read his mind.

"It can't be done, Skeets."

"Maybe not, but I aim to try. Any dog can run coons and rabbits, but it takes a pure D humdinger to hunt birds. Ain't no sin in trying, is it?"

"Naw," Jesse said slowly. "But she'll flush birds."

"I'll learn her not to."

"She won't hold no point. Any dog'll flash point. And she'll hunt rats."

"I'm gonna learn her just to hunt birds. And I'm starting right now," Skeeter said. He started walking away, then turned. "I seen a man once train a razorback hawg to point birds. You know as good as me that if a dog's got pure D hoss sense and a fellow's got bat brains, he can train the dog to hunt birds."

"Wanta bet?" Jesse issued the challenge in an effort to keep Skeeter's enthusiasm and determination at the high-water mark.

"Yes, sir. If I don't train my dog, then I'll cut all the splinters for a year. If I do, you cut 'em."

"It's a go," Jesse said.

Skeeter ran to the bayou and recovered the rat M'Lady had killed. He tied it around his dog's neck. The Basenji was indignant and tried to claw off the hateful burden. Failing, she ran into the house and under a bed, but Skeeter made her come out. M'Lady filled up then and her face assumed that don't-nobody-love-me look. The boy steeled himself, tapped M'Lady's nose with the rat, and left it around her neck.

"You done whittled out a job for yourself," Jesse said. "If'n you get her trained, you'll lose her in the brush. She's too fast and too little to keep up with."

"I'll bell her," Skeeter said. "I'm gonna learn her ever'thing. I got us a gun dog, Uncle Jess."

The old man sat on the porch and propped against the wall. "Bud, I don't know what that thing is. But you're a thoroughbred. John dog my hide!"

If Skeeter had loved M'Lady one bit less, his patience would have exploded during the ordeal of training the Basenji. It takes judgment and infinite patience to train a bird dog properly, but to train a Basenji, that'll hunt anything, to concentrate only on quail took something more than discipline and patience. It never could have been done except for that strange affinity between a boy and a dog, and the blind faith of a child.

M'Lady's devotion to Skeeter was so complete that she was anxious to do anything to earn a pat. It wasn't difficult to teach her to heel and follow at Skeeter's feet regardless of the urge to dash away and chase rabbits. The boy used a clothesline as a guide rope and made M'Lady follow him. The first time the dog tried to chase an animal, Skeeter pinched the rope around her neck just a bit and commanded, "Heel!" And when she obeyed, Skeeter released the noose. It took M'Lady only a few hours to associate disobedience with disfavor.

The dog learned that when she chased and killed a rat or rabbit, the thing would be tied around her neck. The only things she could hunt without being disciplined were quail. Of course, she often mistook the scent of game chickens for quail and hunted them, but Skeeter punished her by scolding. He never switched his dog, but to M'Lady a harsh word from the boy hurt more than a hickory limb.

Jesse watched the dog's progress and pretended not to be impressed. He never volunteered suggestions. M'Lady learned quickly, but the task of teaching her to point birds seemed hopeless. Skeeter knew she'd never point as pointers do, so he worked out his own system. He taught her to stand motionless when he shouted "Hup!" One day she got a scent of birds, paused or pointed for a moment as most animals will, and was ready to spring away when Skeeter said "Hup!"

M'Lady was confused. Every instinct urged her to chase the birds, but her master had said stand still. She broke, however, and Skeeter scolded her. She pouted at first, then filled up, but the boy ignored her until she obeyed the next command, then he patted her and she chuckled.

The lessons continued for days and weeks, and slowly and surely M'Lady learned her chores. She learned that the second she smelled birds she must stop and stand still until Skeeter flushed them. That she must not quiver when he shot.

Teaching her to fetch was easy, but teaching her to retrieve

dead birds without damaging them was another matter. M'Lady
had a hard mouth—that is, she sank her teeth into the birds.
Skeeter used one of the oldest hunting tricks of the backwoods to
break her.

He got a stick and wrapped it with wire and taught his dog to
fetch it. Only once did M'Lady bite hard on the stick, and then
the wire hurt her sensitive mouth. Soon she developed a habit of
carrying the stick on her tongue and supporting it lightly with her
teeth. Skeeter tied quail feathers on the stick, and soon M'Lady's
education was complete.

Skeeter led Jesse into a field one day and turned his dog loose.
She flashed to a point almost immediately. It was a funny point
and Jesse almost laughed. The dog's curved tail poked up over
her back, she spraddled her front legs and sort of squatted, her
nose pointing the birds, more than forty yards away. She remained
rigid until the boy flushed and shot, then she leaped away,
seeking and fetching dead birds.

Jesse was mighty proud. "Well, Skeets, looks like you got
yourself a bird hunter."

"Yes, sir," Skeeter said. "And you got yourself a job." He
pointed toward the kindling pile.

The swamp was dressing for winter when Cash Watson drove
down that day to give his Big Boy a workout in the wild brush.

He fetched Jesse a couple of cans of smoking tobacco and
Skeeter a bag of peppermint jawbreakers. He locked his fine
pointer in the corncrib for the night and was warming himself in
the cabin when he noticed M'Lady for the first time. She was
sleeping in front of the fire.

"What's that?" he asked.

"My dog," said Skeeter. "Ain't she a beaut?"

"She sure is," Cash grinned at Jesse. Skeeter went out to the
well and Cash asked his old friend, "What the devil kind of mutt
is that?"

"Search me," Jesse said. "Skeets found her in the swamp. I
reckon she's got a trace of bloodhound in her and some terrier
and a heap of just plain dog."

M'Lady cocked one ear and got up and stretched; then, apparently
not liking the company, turned her tail toward Cash and strutted
out, looking for Skeeter.

The men laughed. "Som'n wrong with her throat," Jesse said. "She can't bark. When she tries, she makes a funny sound, sort of a cackling, chuckling yodel. Sounds like she's laughing."

"Well," Cash said, "trust a young'un to love the orner'st dog he can find."

"Wait a minute," Jesse said. "She ain't no-count. She's a bird-hunting fool."

Just then Skeeter entered and Cash jestingly said, "Hear you got yourself a bird dog, son."

The boy clasped his hands behind him and rocked on the balls of his feet as he had seen the men do. "Well, now, I'll tell you, Mr. Cash. M'Lady does ever'thing except tote the gun."

"She must be fair to middling. Why not take her out with Big Boy tomorrow? Do my dog good to hunt in a brace."

"Me and my dog don't want to show Big Boy up. He's a pretty good ol' dog."

"Whoa!" Cash was every inch a bird-dog man and nobody could challenge him without a showdown. Besides, Skeeter was shooting up and should be learning a few things about life. "Any old boiler can pop off steam." Cash winked at Jesse.

"Well, now, sir, if you're itching for a run, I'll just double-dog dare you to run your dog against mine. And anybody who'll take a dare will pull up young cotton and push a widow woman's ducks in the water."

Cash admired the boy's confidence. "All right, son. It's a deal. What are the stakes?"

Skeeter started to mention the twenty-gauge gun he wanted, but changed his mind quickly. He reached down and patted M'Lady, then looked up. "If my dog beats yours, then you get them Roebuckers for Uncle Jess."

Jesse's chest suddenly was tight. Cash glanced from the boy to the man and he, too, was proud of Skeeter. "I wasn't aiming to go that high. But all right. What do I get if I win?"

"I'll cut you ten cords of stove-wood."

"And a stack of splinters?"

"Yes, sir."

Cash offered his hand and Skeeter took it. "It's a race," Cash said. "Jesse will be the judge."

The wind was rustling the sage and there was a nip in the

early-morning air when they took the dogs to a clearing and set
them down. Skeeter snapped a belt around M'Lady's neck and, at
word from Jesse, the dogs were released.

Big Boy bounded away and began circling, ranging into the
brush. M'Lady tilted her nose into the wind and ripped away
toward the sage, her bell tinkling. Cash said, "She sure covers
ground." Skeeter made no effort to keep up with her, but waited
until he couldn't hear the bell, then ran for a clearing where he
had last heard it. And there was M'Lady on a point.

Cash almost laughed out loud. "That ain't no point, son. That's
a squat."

"She's got birds."

"Where?"

Jesse leaned against a tree and watched the fun.

Skeeter pointed toward a clump of sage. "She's pointing birds
in that sage."

Cash couldn't restrain his mirth. "Boy, now that's what I call
some pointing. Why, Skeeter, it's sixty or seventy yards to that
sage."

Just then Big Boy flashed by M'Lady, his head high. He raced
to the edge of the sage, caught the wind, then whipped around,
freezing to a point. Cash called Jesse's attention to the point.

"That's M'Lady's point," Skeeter said. "She's got the same
birds Big Boy has."

Jesse sauntered up. "The boy's right, Cash. I aimed to keep my
mouth out'n this race, but M'Lady is pointing them birds. She
can catch scents up to eighty yards."

Cash said, "Aw, go on. You're crazy." He walked over and
flushed the birds.

Skeeter picked one off and ordered M'Lady to fetch. When she
returned with the bird, the boy patted her and she began
chuckling.

Cash really studied her then for the first time. "Hey!" he said
suddenly. "A Basenji! That's a Basenji!"

"A what?" Jesse asked.

"I should have known." Cash was very excited. "That's the dog
that was lost by them rich Yankees. I saw about it in the paper."
He happened to look at Skeeter than and wished he had cut out
his tongue.

The boy's lips were compressed and his face was drawn and white. Jesse had closed his eyes and was rubbing his forehead.

Cash, trying to dismiss the subject, said, "Just 'cause it was in the paper don't make it so. I don't believe that's the same dog, come to think of it."

"Do you aim to tell 'em where the dog is?" Skeeter asked.

Cash looked at Jesse, then at the ground. "It ain't none of my business."

"How 'bout you, Uncle Jess?"

"I ain't telling nobody nothin'."

"I know she's the same dog," Skeeter said. "On account of I just know it. But she's mine now." His voice rose and trembled. "And ain't nobody gonna take her away from me." He ran into the swamp. M'Lady was at his heels.

Cash said, "Durn my lip. I'm sorry, Jesse. If I'd kept my big mouth shut he'd never known the difference."

"It can't be helped now," Jesse said.

"'Course she beat Big Boy. Them's the best hunting dogs in the world. And she's worth a mint of money."

They didn't feel up to hunting and returned to the cabin and sat on the porch. Neither had much to say, but kept glancing toward the swamp where Skeeter and M'Lady were walking along the bayou. "Don't you worry," he said tenderly. "Ain't nobody gonna bother you."

He sat on a stump and M'Lady put her head on his knee. She wasn't worrying. Nothing could have been more contented than she was.

"I don't care if the sheriff comes down." Skeeter pulled her onto his lap and held her. "I don't give a whoop if the governor comes down. Even the President of the United States! The whole shebang can come, but ain't nobody gonna mess with you."

His words gave him courage and he felt better, but for only a minute. Then the tug-of-war between him and his conscience started.

"Once I found a Barlow knife and kept it and it was all right," he mumbled.

But that is different.

"Finders, keepers; losers, weepers."

No, Skeeter.

"Well, I don't care. She's mine."

Remember what your Uncle Jess said.

"He said a heap of things."

Yes, but you remember one thing more than the rest. He said, "Certain things are right and certain things are wrong. And nothing ain't gonna ever change that. When you learn that, then you're fit'n to be a man." Remember, Skeeter?

A feeling of despair and loneliness almost overwhelmed him. He fought off the tears as long as he could, but finally he gave in, and his sobs caused M'Lady to peer into his face and wonder why he was acting that way when she was so happy. He put his arms around her neck and pulled her to him.

"My li'l' old puppy dog. Poor li'l' old puppy dog. But I got to do it."

He sniffed back his tears and got up and walked to the cabin. M'Lady curled up by the fire and the boy sat down, watching the logs splutter for several minutes. The he said, almost in a whisper, "Uncle Jess, if you keep som'n that ain't yours, it's the same as stealing, ain't it?"

Cash leaned against the mantel and stared into the fire.

Jesse puffed his pipe slowly. "Son, that's som'n you got to settle with yourself."

Skeeter stood and turned his back to the flames, warming his hands.

"Mr. Cash," he said slowly, "when you get back to your store, please let them folks know their dog is here."

"If that's how it is—"

"That's how it is," Skeeter said.

The firelight dancing on Jesse's face revealed the old man's dejection, and Skeeter, seeing it, said quickly, "It's best for M'Lady. She's too good for the swamp. They'll give her a good home."

Jesse flinched, and Cash, catching the hurt look in his friend's eyes, said, "Your dog outhunted mine, Skeets. You win them Roebuckers for your uncle."

"I don't want 'em," Jesse said, rather childishly. "I don't care if'n I never eat no roastin' ears." He got up quickly and hurried outside. Cash reckoned he'd better be going, and left Skeeter by the fire, rubbing his dog.

Jesse came back in directly and pulled up a chair. Skeeter started to speak, but Jesse spoke first. "I been doing a heap of thinking lately. You're sprouting up. The swamp ain't no place for you."

Skeeter forgot about his dog and faced his uncle, bewildered.

"I reckon you're too good for the swamp too," Jesse said. "I'm aiming to send you into town for a spell. I can make enough to keep you in fit'n clothes and all." He dared not look at the boy.

"Uncle Jess!" Skeeter said reproachfully. "You don't mean that. You're just saying that on account of what I said about M'Lady. I said it just to keep you from feeling so bad about our dog going away. Gee m'netty, Uncle Jess. I ain't ever gonna leave you." He buried his face in his uncle's shoulder. M'Lady put her head on Jesse's knee and he patted the boy and rubbed the dog.

"Reckon I'll take them Roebuckers," he said at last. "I been wanting some for a long, long time."

Several days later Cash drove down and told them the man from the kennels was at his store. Skeeter didn't say a word, but called M'Lady and they got in Cash's car. All the way to town, the boy was silent. He held his dog's head in his lap.

The keeper took just one look at M'Lady and said, "That's she, all right. Miss Congo III." He turned to speak to Skeeter, but the boy was walking away. He got a glance at Skeeter's face, however. "Hell," he muttered. "I wish you fellows hadn't told me. I hate to take a dog away from a kid."

"He wanted you to know," Cash said.

"Mister"—Jesse closed his left eye and struck his swapping pose—"I'd like to swap you out'n that hound. Now, course she ain't much 'count—"

The keeper smiled in spite of himself. "If she was mine, I'd give her to the kid. But she's not for sale. The owner wants to breed her and establish her line in this country. And if she was for sale, she'd cost more money than any of us will ever see." He called Skeeter and offered his hand. Skeeter shook it.

"You're a good kid. There's a reward for this dog."

"I don't want no reward." The boy's words tumbled out. "I don't want nothing, except to be left alone. You've got your dog, mister. Take her and go on. Please." He walked away again, fearing he would cry.

Cash said, "I'll take the reward and keep it for him. Someday he'll want it."

Jesse went out to the store porch to be with Skeeter. The keeper handed Cash the money. "It's tough, but the kid'll get over it. The dog never will."

"Is that a fact?"

"Yep. I know the breed. They never forget. That dog'll never laugh again. They never laugh unless they're happy."

He walked to the post where Skeeter had tied M'Lady. He untied the leash and started toward his station wagon. M'Lady braced her front feet and looked around for the boy. Seeing him on the porch, she jerked away from the keeper and ran to her master.

She rubbed against his legs. Skeeter tried to ignore her. The keeper reached for the leash again and M'Lady crouched, baring her fangs. The keeper shrugged, a helpless gesture.

"Wild elephants couldn't pull that dog away from that boy," he said.

"That's all right, mister." Skeeter unsnapped the leash and tossed it to the keeper. Then he walked to the station wagon, opened the door of a cage and called, "Heah, M'Lady!" She bounded to him. "Up!" he commanded. She didn't hesitate, but leaped into the cage. The keeper locked the door.

M'Lady, having obeyed a command, poked her nose between the bars, expecting a pat. The boy rubbed her head. She tried to move closer to him, but the bars held her. She looked quizzically at the bars, then tried to nudge them aside. Then she clawed them. A look of fear suddenly came to her eyes and she fastened them on Skeeter, wistfully at first, then pleadingly. She couldn't make a sound, for her unhappiness had sealed her throat. Slowly her eyes filled up.

"Don't cry no more, M'Lady. Ever'thing's gonna be all right." He reached out to pat her, but the station wagon moved off, leaving him standing there in the dust.

Back on the porch, Jesse lit his pipe and said to his friend, "Cash, the boy has lost his dog and I've lost a boy."

"Aw, Jesse, Skeeter wouldn't leave you."

"That ain't what I mean. He's growned up, Cash. He don't look no older, but he is. He growed up that day in the swamp."

Skeeter walked into the store and Cash followed him. "I've got that reward for you, Jonathan."

It was the first time anyone ever had called him that and it sounded like man talk.

"And that twenty-gauge is waiting for you," Cash said. "I'm gonna give it to you."

"Thank you, Mr. Cash." The boy bit his lower lip. "But I don't aim to do no more hunting. I don't never want no more dogs."

"Know how you feel. But if you change your mind, the gun's here for you."

Skeeter looked back toward the porch where Jesse was waiting, and said, "Tell you what, though. When you get them Roebuckers, get some with a couple of gold teeth in 'em. Take it out of the reward money."

"Sure, Jonathan."

Jesse joined them, and Skeeter said, "We better be getting back toward the house."

"I'll drive you down," Cash said. "But first I aim to treat you to some lemon pop and sardines."

"That's mighty nice of you," Jesse said, "but we better be gettin' on."

"What's the hurry?" Cash opened the pop.

"It's my time to cut splinters," Jesse said. "That's what I get for betting with a good man."

Roll of Thunder, Hear My Cry

MILDRED D. TAYLOR

"LITTLE MAN, would you come on? You keep it up and you're gonna make us late."

My youngest brother paid no attention to me. Grasping more firmly his newspaper-wrapped notebook and his tin-can lunch of cornbread and oil sausages, he continued to concentrate on the dusty road. He lagged several feet behind my other brothers, Stacey and Christopher-John, and me, attempting to keep the rusty Mississippi dust from swelling with each step and drifting back upon his shiny black shoes and the cuffs of his corduroy pants by lifting each foot high before setting it gently down again. Always meticulously neat, six-year-old Little Man never allowed dirt or tears or stains to mar anything he owned. Today was no exception.

"You keep it up and make us late for school, Mama's gonna wear you out," I threatened, pulling with exasperation at the high collar of the Sunday dress Mama had made me wear for the first day of school—as if that event were something special. It seemed to me that showing up at school at all on a bright August-like October morning made for running the cool forest trails and wading barefoot in the forest pond was concession enough; Sunday clothing was asking too much. Christopher-John and Stacey were not too pleased about the clothing or school either. Only Little Man, just beginning his school career, found the prospects of both intriguing.

"Y'all go ahead and get dirty if y'all wanna," he replied without even looking up from his studied steps. "Me, I'm gonna stay clean."

"I betcha Mama's gonna 'clean' you, you keep it up," I grumbled.

"Ah, Cassie, leave him be," Stacey admonished, frowning and kicking testily at the road.

184

"I ain't said nothing but—"

Stacey cut me a wicked look and I grew silent. His disposition had been irritatingly sour lately. If I hadn't known the cause of it, I could have forgotten very easily that he was, at twelve, bigger than I, and that I had promised Mama to arrive at school looking clean and ladylike. "Shoot," I mumbled finally, unable to restrain myself from further comment, "it ain't my fault you gotta be in Mama's class this year."

Stacey's frown deepened and he jammed his fists into his pockets, but said nothing.

Christopher-John, walking between Stacey and me, glanced uneasily at both of us but did not interfere. A short. round boy of seven, he took little interest in troublesome things, preferring to remain on good terms with everyone. Yet he was always sensitive to others and now, shifting the handle of his lunch can from his right hand to his right wrist and his smudged notebook from his left hand to his left armpit, he stuffed his free hands into his pockets and attempted to make his face as moody as Stacey's and as cranky as mine. But after a few moments he seemed to forget that he was supposed to be grouchy and began whistling cheerfully. There was little that could make Christopher-John unhappy for very long, not even the thought of school.

I tugged again at my collar and dragged my feet in the dust, allowing it to sift back onto my socks and shoes like gritty red snow. I hated the dress. And the shoes. There was little I could do in a dress, and as for shoes, they imprisoned freedom-loving feet accustomed to the feel of the warm earth.

"Cassie, stop that," Stacey snapped as the dust billowed in swirling clouds around my feet. I looked up sharply, ready to protest. Christopher-John's whistling increased to a raucous, nervous shrill, and grudgingly I let the matter drop and trudged along in moody silence, my brothers growing as pensively quiet as I.

Before us the narrow, sun-splotched road wound like a lazy red serpent dividing the high forest bank of quiet, old trees on the left from the cotton field, forested by giant green-and-purple stalks, on the right. A barbed-wire fence ran the length of the deep field, stretching eastward for over a quarter of a mile until it met the sloping green pasture that signaled the end of our family's four hundred acres. An ancient oak tree on the slope, visible even now, was the official dividing mark between Logan land and the beginning of a dense forest. Beyond the protective fencing of the forest, vast farming fields, worked by a multitude of share-cropping families, covered two thirds of a ten-square-mile planta-tion. That was Harlan Granger land.

Once our land had been Granger land too, but the Grangers had sold it during Reconstruction to a Yankee for tax money. In 1887, when the land was up for sale again, Grandpa had bought two hundred acres of it, and in 1918, after the first two hundred acres had been paid off, he had bought another two hundred. It was good rich land, much of it still virgin forest, and there was no debt on half of it. But there was a mortgage on the two hundred acres bought in 1918 and there were taxes on the full four hundred, and for the past three years there had not been enough money from the cotton to pay both and live on too.

That was why Papa had gone to work on the railroad.

In 1930 the price of cotton dropped. And so, in the spring of 1931, Papa set out looking for work, going as far north as Memphis and as far south as the Delta country. He had gone west too, into Louisiana. It was there he found work laying track for the railroad. He worked the remainder of the year away from us, not returning until the deep winter when the ground was cold and barren. The following spring after the planting was finished, he did the same. Now it was 1933, and Papa was again in Louisiana laying track.

I asked him once why he had to go away, why the land was so important. He took my hand and said in his quiet way: "Look out there, Cassie girl. All that belongs to you. You ain't never had to live on nobody's place but your own and long as I live and the family survives, you'll never have to. That's important. You may not understand that now, but one day you will. Then you'll see."

I looked at Papa strangely when he said that, for I knew that all the land did not belong to me. Some of it belonged to Stacey, Christopher-John, and Little Man, not to mention the part that belonged to Big Ma, Mama, and Uncle Hammer, Papa's older brother who lived in Chicago. But Papa never divided the land in his mind; it was simply Logan land. For it he would work the long, hot summer pounding steel; Mama would teach and run the farm; Big Ma, in her sixties, would work like a woman of twenty in the fields and keep the house; and the boys and I would wear threadbare clothing washed to dishwater color; but always, the taxes and the mortgage would be paid. Papa said that one day I would understand.

I wondered.

When the fields ended and the Granger forest fanned both sides of the road with long overhanging branches, a tall, emaciated-looking boy popped suddenly from a forest trail and swung a thin arm around Stacey. It was T. J. Avery. His younger brother Claude emerged a moment later, smiling weakly as if it pained him to do so. Neither boy had on shoes, and their Sunday clothing, patched and worn, hung loosely upon their frail frames. The Avery family sharecropped on Granger land.

"Well," said T.J., jauntily swinging into step with Stacey, "here we go again startin' another school year."

"Yeah," sighed Stacey.

"Ah, man, don't look so down," T.J. said cheerfully. "Your mama's really one great teacher. I should know." He certainly should. He had failed Mama's class last year and was now returning for a second try.

"Shoot! You can say that," exclaimed Stacey. "You don't have to spend all day in a classroom with your mama."

"Look on the bright side," said T.J. "Jus' think of the advantage you've got. You'll be learnin' all sorts of stuff 'fore the rest of us. . . ." He smiled slyly. "Like what's on all them tests."

Stacey thrust T.J.'s arm from his shoulders. "If that's what you think, you don't know Mama."

"Ain't no need gettin' mad," T.J. replied undaunted. 'Jus' an idea." He was quiet for a moment, then announced, "I betcha I could give y'all an earful 'bout that burnin' last night."

"Burning? What burning?" asked Stacey.

"Man, don't y'all know nothin'? The Berrys' burning'. I thought y'all's grandmother went over there last night to see 'bout 'em."

Of course we knew that Big Ma had gone to a sick house last night. She was good at medicines and people often called her instead of a doctor when they were sick. But we didn't know anything about any burnings, and I certainly didn't know anything about any Berrys either.

"What Berrys he talking 'bout, Stacey?" I asked. "I don't know no Berrys."

"They live way over on the other side of Smellings Creek. They come up to church sometimes," said Stacey absently. Then he turned back to T.J. "Mr. Lanier come by real late and got Big Ma. Said Mr. Berry was low sick and needed her to help nurse him, but he ain't said nothing 'bout no burning."

"He's low sick all right—'cause he got burnt near to death. Him and his two nephews. And you know who done it?"

"Who?" Stacey and I asked together.

"Well, since y'all don't seem to know nothin'," said T.J., in his usual sickening way of nursing a tidbit of information to death, "maybe I ought not tell y'all. It might hurt y'all's little ears."

"Ah, boy," I said, "don't start that mess again." I didn't like T.J. very much and his stalling around didn't help.

"Come on T.J.," said Stacey, "out with it."

"Well . . ." T.J. murmured, then grew silent as if considering whether or not he should talk.

We reached the first of two crossroads and turned north; another mile and we would approach the second crossroads and turn east again.

Finally T.J. said, "Okay. See, them Berrys' burnin' wasn't no accident. Some white men took a match to 'em."

"Y-you mean just lit 'em up like a piece of wood?" stammered Christopher-John, his eyes growing big with disbelief.

"But why?" asked Stacey.

T.J. shrugged. "Don't know why. Jus' know they done it, that's all."

"How you know?" I questioned suspiciously.

He smiled smugly. "'Cause your mama come down on her way to school and talked to my mama 'bout it."

"She did?"

"Yeah, and you should've seen the way she looked when she come outa that house."

"How'd she look?" inquired Little Man, interested enough to glance up from the road for the first time.

T.J. looked around grimly and whispered, "Like . . . death." He waited a moment for his words to be appropriately shocking, but the effect was spoiled by Little Man, who asked lightly, "What does death look like?"

T.J. turned in annoyance. "Don't he know nothin'?"

"Well, what does it look like?" Little Man demanded to know. He didn't like T.J. either.

"Like my grandfather looked jus' 'fore they buried him," T.J. described all-knowingly.

"Oh," replied Little Man, losing interest and concentrating on the road again.

"I tell ya, Stacey, man," said T.J. morosely, shaking his head, "sometimes I jus' don't know 'bout that family of yours."

Stacey pulled back, considering whether or not T.J.'s words were offensive, but T.J. immediately erased the question by continuing amiably. "Don't get me wrong, Stacey. They some real swell kids, but that Cassie 'bout got me whipped this morning'."

"Good!" I said.

"Now how'd she do that?" Stacey laughed.

"You wouldn't be laughin' if it'd've happened to you. She up and told your mama 'bout me goin' up to that Wallace store dancin' room and Miz Logan told Mama." He eyed me disdainfully then went on. "But don't worry, I got out of it though. When Mama asked me 'bout it, I jus' said old Claude was always sneakin' up there to get some of that free candy Mr. Kaleb give out sometimes and I had to go and get him 'cause I knowed good and well she didn't want us up there. Boy, did he get it!" T.J. laughed. "Mama 'bout wore him out."

I stared at quiet Claude. "You let him do that?" I exclaimed. But Claude only smiled in that sickly way of his and I knew that he had. He was more afraid of T.J. than of his mother.

Again Little Man glanced up and I could see his dislike for T.J. growing. Friendly Christopher-John glared at T.J., and putting his short arm around Claude's shoulder said, "Come on, Claude, let's go on ahead." Then he and Claude hurried up the road, away from T.J.

Stacey, who generally overlooked T.J.'s underhanded stunts, shook his head. "That was dirty."

"Well, what'd ya expect me to do? I couldn't let her think I was goin' up there 'cause I like to, could I? She'd've killed me!"

"And good riddance," I thought, promising myself that if he ever pulled anything like that on me, I'd knock his block off.

We were nearing the second crossroads, where deep gullies lined both sides of the road and the dense forest crept to the very edges of high, jagged, clay-walled banks. Suddenly, Stacey turned. "Quick!" he cried. "Off the road!" Without another word, all of us but Little Man scrambled up the steep right bank into the forest.

"Get up here, Man," Stacey ordered, but Little Man only gazed at the ragged red bank sparsely covered with scraggly brown briars and kept on walking. "Come on, do like I say."

"But I'll get my clothes dirty!" protested Little Man.

"You're gonna get them a whole lot dirtier you stay down there. Look!"

Little Man turned around and watched saucer-eyed as a bus bore down on him spewing clouds of red dust like a huge yellow dragon breathing fire. Little Man headed toward the bank, but it was too steep. He ran frantically along the road looking for a foothold and, finding one, hopped onto the bank, but not before the bus had sped past enveloping him in a scarlet haze while laughing white faces pressed against the bus windows.

Little Man shook a threatening fist into the thick air, then looked dismally down at himself.

"Well, ole Little Man done got his Sunday clothes dirty," T.J. laughed as we jumped down from the bank. Angry tears welled in Little Man's eyes but he quickly brushed them away before T.J. could see them.

"Ah, shut up, T.J.," Stacey snapped.

"Yeah, shut up, T.J.," I echoed.

"Come on, Man," Stacey said, "and next time do like I tell ya."

Little Man hopped down from the bank. "How's come they did that, Stacey, huh?" he asked, dusting himself off. "How's come they didn't even stop for us?"

"'Cause they like to see us run and it ain't our bus," Stacey said, balling his fists and jamming them tightly into his pockets.

"Well, where's our bus?" demanded Little Man.

"We ain't got one."

"Well, why not?"

"Ask Mama," Stacey replied as a towheaded boy, barefooted and pale, came running down a forest path toward us. The boy quickly caught up and fell in stride with Stacey and T.J.

"Hey, Stacey," he said shyly.

"Hey, Jeremy," Stacey said.

There was an awkward silence.

"Y'all jus' startin school today?"

"Yeah," replied Stacey.

"I wishin' ours was jus' startin'," sighed Jeremy. "Ours been goin' since the end of August." Jeremy's eyes were a whitewashed blue and they seemed to weep when he spoke.

"Yeah," said Stacey again.

Jeremy kicked the dust briskly and looked toward the north. He was a strange boy. Ever since I had begun school, he had walked with us as far as the crossroads in the morning, and met us there in the afternoon. He was often ridiculed by the other children at his school and had shown up more than once with wide red welts on his arms which Lillian Jean, his older sister, had revealed with satisfaction were the result of his associating with us. Still, Jeremy continued to meet us.

When we reached the crossroads, three more children, a girl of twelve or thirteen and two boys, all looking very much like Jeremy, rushed past. The girl was Lillian Jean. "Jeremy, come on," she said without a backward glance, and Jeremy, smiling sheepishly, waved a timid good-bye and slowly followed her.

We stood in the crossing gazing after them. Jeremy looked back once but then Lillian Jean yelled shrilly at him and he did not look back again. They were headed for the Jefferson Davis County School, a long white wooden building looming in the distance. Behind the building was a wide sports field around which were scattered rows of tiered gray-looking benches. In front of it were two yellow buses, our own tormentor and one that brought students from the other direction, and loitering students awaiting the knell of the morning bell. In the very center of the expansive front lawn, waving red, white, and blue with the emblem of the Confederacy emblazoned in its upper left-hand corner, was the Mississippi flag. Directly below it was the American flag. As Jeremy and his sister and brothers hurried toward those transposed flags, we turned eastward toward our own school.

* * *

The Great Faith Elementary and Secondary School, one of the largest black schools in the county, was a dismal end to an hour's journey. Consisting of four weather-beaten wooden houses on stilts of brick, 320 students, seven teachers, a principal, a caretaker, and the caretaker's cow, which kept the wide crabgrass lawn sufficiently clipped in spring and summer, the school was located near three plantations, the largest and closest by far being the Granger plantation. Most of the students were from families that sharecropped on Granger land, and the others mainly from Montier and Harrison plantation families. Because the students were needed in the fields from early spring when the cotton was planted until after most of the cotton had been picked in the fall, the school adjusted its terms accordingly, beginning in October and dismissing in March. But even so, after today a number of the older students would not be seen again for a month or two, not until the last puff of cotton had been gleaned from the fields, and eventually most would drop out of school altogether. Because of this the classes in the higher grades grew smaller with each passing year.

The class buildings, with their backs practically against the forest wall, formed a semicircle facing a small one-room church at the opposite edge of the compound. It was to this church that many of the school's students and their parents belonged. As we arrived, the enormous iron bell in the church belfry was ringing vigorously, warning the milling students that only five minutes of freedom remained.

Little Man immediately pushed his way across the lawn to the well. Stacey and T.J., ignoring the rest of us now that they were on the school grounds, wandered off to be with the other seventh-grade boys, and Christopher-John and Claude rushed to reunite with their classmates of last year. Left alone, I dragged slowly to the building that held the first four grades and sat on the bottom step. Plopping my pencils and notebook into the dirt, I propped my elbows on my knees and rested my chin in the palms of my hands.

"Hey, Cassie," said Mary Lou Wellever, the principal's daughter, as she flounced by in a new yellow dress.

"Hey, yourself," I said, scowling so ferociously that she kept on walking. I stared after her a moment noting that she *would* have on a new dress. Certainly no one else did. Patches on faded pants and dresses abounded on boys and girls come so recently from the heat of the cotton fields. Girls stood awkwardly, afraid to sit, and boys pulled restlessly at starched, high-buttoned collars. Those students fortunate enough to have shoes hopped from one pinched foot to the other. Tonight the Sunday clothes would be wrapped in newspaper and hung for Sunday and the shoes would be packed away to be brought out again only when the weather turned so cold that bare feet could no longer traverse the frozen roads; but for today we all suffered.

On the far side of the lawn I spied Moe Turner speeding toward the seventh-grade-class building, and wondered at his energy. Moe was one of Stacey's friends. He lived on the Montier plantation, a three-and-a-half-hour walk from the school. Because of the distance, many children from the Montier plantation did not come to Great Faith after they had finished the four-year school near Smellings Creek. But there were some girls and boys like Moe who made the trek daily, leaving their homes while the sky was black and not returning until all was blackness again. I for one was certainly glad that I didn't live that far away. I don't think my feet would have wanted that badly for me to be educated.

The chiming of the second bell began. I stood up dusting my bottom as the first, second, third, and fourth graders crowded up the stairs into the hallway. Little Man flashed proudly past, his face and hands clean and his black shoes shining again. I glanced down at my own shoes powdered red and, raising my right foot, rubbed it against the back of my left leg, then reversed the procedure. As the last gong of the bell reverberated across the compound, I swooped up my pencils and notebook and ran inside.

A hallway extended from the front to the back door of the building. On either side of the hallway were two doorways, both leading into the same large room which was divided into two classrooms by a heavy canvas curtain. The second and third grades were on the left, the first and fourth grades on the right. I hurried to the rear of the building, turned to the right, and slid into a third-row bench occupied by Gracey Pearson and Alma Scott.

"You can't sit here," objected Gracey. "I'm saving it for Mary Lou."

I glanced back at Mary Lou Wellever depositing her lunch pail on a shelf in the back of the room and said, "Not any more you ain't."

Miss Daisy Crocker, yellow and buckeyed, glared down at me from the middle of the room with a look that said, "Sooooooooo, it's you, Cassie Logan." Then she pursed her lips and drew the curtain along the rusted iron rod and tucked it into a wide loop in the back wall. With the curtain drawn back, the first graders gazed quizzically at us. Little Man sat by a window, his hands folded, patiently waiting for Miss Crocker to speak.

Mary Lou nudged me. "That's my seat, Cassie Logan."

"Mary Lou Wellever," Miss Crocker called primly, "have a seat."

"Yes, ma'am," said Mary Lou, eyeing me with a look of pure hate before turning away.

Miss Crocker walked stiffly to her desk, which was set on a tiny platform and piled high with bulky objects covered by a tarpaulin. She rapped the desk with a ruler, although the room was perfectly still, and said, "Welcome, children, to Great Faith Elementary School." Turning slightly so that she stared squarely at the left side of the room, she continued, "To all of you fourth graders, it's good to have you in my class. I'll be expecting many good and wonderful things from you." Then addressing the right side of the room, she said, "And to all our little first grade friends only today starting on the road to knowledge and education, may your tiny feet find the pathways of learning steady and forever before you."

Already bored, I stretched my right arm on the desk and rested my head in my upraised hand.

Miss Crocker smiled mechanically, then rapped on her desk again. "Now, little ones," she said, still talking to the first grade, "your teacher, Miss Davis, has been held up in Jackson for a few days so I'll have the pleasure of sprinkling your little minds with the first rays of knowledge." She beamed down upon them as if she expected to be applauded for this bit of news, then with a swoop of her large eyes to include the fourth graders, she went on.

"Now since there's only one of me, we shall have to sacrifice for

the next few days. We shall work, work, work, but we shall have
to work like little Christian boys and girls and share, share, share.
Now are we willing to do that?"

"YES'M, MIZ CROCKER," the children chorused.

But I remained silent. I never did approve of group responses.
Adjusting my head in my hand, I sighed heavily, my mind on the
burning of the Berrys.

"Cassie Logan?"

I looked up, startled.

"Cassie Logan!"

"Yes, ma'am?" I jumped up quickly to face Miss Crocker.

"Aren't you willing to work and share?"

"Yes'm."

"Then say so!"

"Yes'm," I murmured, sliding back into my seat as Mary Lou,
Gracey, and Alma giggled. Here it was only five minutes into the
new school year and already I was in trouble.

By ten o'clock, Miss Crocker had rearranged our seating and
written our names on her seating chart. I was still sitting beside
Gracey and Alma but we had been moved from the third to the
first row in front of a small potbellied stove. Although being
eyeball to eyeball with Miss Crocker was nothing to look forward
to, the prospect of being warm once the cold weather set in was
nothing to be sneezed at either, so I resolved to make the best of
my rather dubious position.

Now Miss Crocker made a startling announcement: This year
we would all have books.

Everyone gasped, for most of the students had never handled a
book at all besides the family Bible. I admit that even I was
somewhat excited. Although Mama had several books, I had
never had one of my very own.

"Now we're very fortunate to get these readers," Miss Crocker
explained while we eagerly awaited the unveiling. "The county
superintendent of schools himself brought these books down here
for our use and we must take extra-good care of them." She
moved toward her desk. "So let's all promise that we'll take the
best care possible of these new books." She stared down, expecting
our response. "All right, all together, let's repeat, 'We promise to

take good care of our new books.'" She looked sharply at me as she spoke.

"WE PROMISE TO TAKE GOOD CARE OF OUR NEW BOOKS!"

"Fine," Miss Crocker beamed, then proudly threw back the tarpaulin.

Sitting so close to the desk, I could see that the covers of the books, a motley red, were badly worn and that the gray edges of the pages had been marred by pencils, crayons, and ink. My anticipation at having my own book ebbed to a sinking disappointment. But Miss Crocker continued to beam as she called each fourth grader to her desk and, recording a number in her roll book, handed him or her a book.

As I returned from my trip to her desk, I noticed the first graders anxiously watching the disappearing pile. Miss Crocker must have noticed them too, for as I sat down she said, "Don't worry, little ones, there are plenty of readers for you too. See there on Miss Davis's desk." Wide eyes turned to the covered teacher's platform directly in front of them and an audible sigh of relief swelled in the room.

I glanced across at Little Man, his face lit in eager excitement. I knew that he could not see the soiled covers or the marred pages from where he sat, and even though his penchant for cleanliness was often annoying, I did not like to think of his disappointment when he saw the books as they really were. But there was nothing that I could do about it, so I opened my book to its center and began browsing through the spotted pages. Girls with blond braids and boys with blue eyes stared up at me. I found a story about a boy and his dog lost in a cave and began reading while Miss Crocker's voice droned on monotonously.

Suddenly I grew conscious of a break in that monotonous tone and I looked up. Miss Crocker was sitting at Miss Davis's desk with the first-grade books stacked before her, staring fiercely down at Little Man, who was pushing a book back upon the desk.

"What's that you said, Clayton Chester Logan?" she asked.

The room became gravely silent. Everyone knew that Little Man was in big trouble for no one, but no one, ever called Little Man "Clayton Chester" unless she or he meant serious business.

Little Man knew this too. His lips parted slightly as he took his hands from the book. He quivered, but he did not take his eyes from Miss Crocker. "I—I said may I have another book please, ma'am," he squeaked. "That one's dirty."

"Dirty!" Miss Crocker echoed, appalled by such temerity. She stood up, gazing down upon Little Man like a bony giant, but Little Man raised his head and continued to look into her eyes. "Dirty! And just who do you think you are, Clayton Chester! Here the county is giving us these wonderful books during these hard times and you're going to stand there and tell me that the book's too dirty? Now you take that book or get nothing at all!"

Little Man lowered his eyes and said nothing as he stared at the book. For several moments he stood there, his face barely visible above the desk, then he turned and looked at the few remaining books and, seeming to realize that they were as badly soiled as the one Miss Crocker had given him, he looked across the room at me. I nodded and Little Man, glancing up again at Miss Crocker, slid the book from the edge of the desk, and with his back straight and his head up returned to his seat.

Miss Crocker sat down again. "Some people around here seem to be giving themselves airs. I'll tolerate no more of that," she scowled. "Sharon Lake, come get your book."

I watched Little Man as he scooted into his seat beside two other little boys. He sat for a while with a stony face looking out the window; then, evidently accepting the fact that the book in front of him was the best that he could expect, he turned and opened it. But as he stared at the book's inside cover, his face clouded, changing from sulky acceptance to puzzlement. His brows furrowed. Then his eyes grew wide, and suddenly he sucked in his breath and sprang from his chair like a wounded animal, flinging the book onto the floor and stomping madly upon it.

Miss Crocker rushed to Little Man and grabbed him up in powerful hands. She shook him vigorously, then set him on the floor again. "Now, just what's gotten into you, Clayton Chester?"

But Little Man said nothing. He just stood staring down at the open book, shivering with indignant anger.

"Pick it up," she ordered.

"No!" defied Little Man.

"No? I'll give you ten seconds to pick up that book, boy, or I'm going to get my switch."

Little Man bit his lower lip, and I knew that he was not going to pick up the book. Rapidly, I turned to the inside cover of my own book and saw immediately what had made Little Man so furious. Stamped on the inside cover was a chart which read:

PROPERTY OF THE BOARD OF EDUCATION
Spokane County, Mississippi
September, 1922

CHRONOLOGICAL ISSUANCE	DATE OF ISSUANCE	CONDITION OF BOOK	RACE OF STUDENT
1	September 1922	New	White
2	September 1923	Excellent	White
3	September 1924	Excellent	White
4	September 1925	Very Good	White
5	September 1926	Good	White
6	September 1927	Good	White
7	September 1928	Average	White
8	September 1929	Average	White
9	September 1930	Average	White
10	September 1931	Poor	White
11	September 1932	Poor	White
12	September 1933	Very Poor	nigra
13			

The blank lines continued down to line 20 and I knew that they had all been reserved for black students. A knot of anger swelled in my throat and held there. But as Miss Crocker directed Little Man to bend over the "whipping" chair, I put aside my anger and jumped up.

"Miz Crocker, don't, please!" I cried. Miss Crocker's dark eyes warned me not to say another word. "I know why he done it!"

"You want part of this switch, Cassie?"

"No'm," I said hastily. "I just wanna tell you how come Little Man done what he done."

"Sit down!" she ordered as I hurried toward her with the open book in my hand.

Holding the book up to her, I said, "See, Miz Crocker, see what it says. They give us these ole books when they didn't want 'em no more."

She regarded me impatiently, but did not look at the book. "Now how could he know what it says? He can't read."

"Yes'm, he can. He been reading since he was four. He can't read all them big words, but he can read them columns. See what's in the last row. Please look, Miz Crocker."

This time Miss Crocker did look, but her face did not change. Then, holding up her head, she gazed unblinkingly down at me.

"S-see what they called us," I said, afraid she had not seen.

"That's what you are," she said coldly. "Now go sit down."

I shook my head, realizing now that Miss Crocker did not even know what I was talking about. She had looked at the page and had understood nothing.

"I said sit down, Cassie!"

I started slowly toward my desk, but as the hickory stick sliced the tense air, I turned back around. "Miz Crocker," I said, "I don't want my book neither."

The switch landed hard upon Little Man's upturned bottom. Miss Crocker looked questioningly at me as I reached up to her desk and placed the book upon it. Then she swung the switch five more times and discovering that Little Man had no intention of crying, ordered him up.

"All right, Cassie," she sighed, turning to me, "come on and get yours."

By the end of the school day I had decided that I would tell Mama everything before Miss Crocker had a chance to do so. From nine years of trial and error, I had learned that punishment was always less severe when I poured out the whole truth to Mama on my own before she had heard anything from anyone else. I knew that Miss Crocker had not spoken to Mama during the lunch period, for she had spent the whole hour in the classroom preparing for the afternoon session.

As soon as class was dismissed I sped from the room, weaving a path through throngs of students happy to be free. But before I could reach the seventh-grade-class building, I had the misfortune to collide with Mary Lou's father. Mr. Wellever looked down on me with surprise that I would actually bump into him, then proceeded to lecture me on the virtues of watching where one was going. Meanwhile Miss Crocker briskly crossed the lawn to Mama's class building. By the time I escaped Mr. Wellever, she had already disappeared into the darkness of the hallway.

Mama's classroom was in the back. I crept silently along the quiet hall and peeped cautiously into the open doorway. Mama, pushing a strand of her long, crinkly hair back into the chignon at the base of her slender neck, was seated at her desk watching Miss Crocker thrust a book before her. "Just look at that, Mary," Miss Crocker said, thumping the book twice with her forefinger. "A perfectly good book ruined. Look at that broken binding and those foot marks all over it."

Mama did not speak as she studied the book.

"And here's the one Cassie wouldn't take," she said, placing a second book on Mama's desk with an outraged slam. "At least she didn't have a tantrum and stomp all over hers. I tell you, Mary, I just don't know what got into those children today. I always knew Cassie was rather high-strung, but Little Man! He's always such a perfect little gentleman."

Mama glanced at the book I had rejected and opened the front cover so that the offensive pages of both books faced her. "You say Cassie said it was because of this front page that she and Little Man didn't want the books?" Mama asked quietly.

"Yes, ain't that something?" Miss Crocker said, forgetting her teacher-training-school diction in her indignation. "The very idea! That's on all the books, and why they got so upset about it I'll never know."

"You punish them?" asked Mama, glancing up at Miss Crocker.

"Well, I certainly did! Whipped both of them good with my hickory stick. Wouldn't you have?" When Mama did not reply, she added defensively, "I had a perfect right to."

"Of course you did, Daisy," Mama said, turning back to the books again. "They disobeyed you." But her tone was so quiet and noncommittal that I knew Miss Crocker was not satisfied with her reaction.

"Well, I thought you would've wanted to know, Mary, in case you wanted to give them a piece of your mind also."

Mama smiled up at Miss Crocker and said rather absently, "Yes, of course, Daisy. Thank you." Then she opened her desk drawer and pulled out some paper, a pair of scissors, and a small brown bottle.

Miss Crocker, dismayed by Mama's seeming unconcern for the seriousness of the matter, thrust her shoulders back and began moving away from the desk. "You understand that if they don't have those books to study from, I'll have to fail them in both reading and composition, since I plan to base all my lessons around—" She stopped abruptly and stared in amazement at Mama. "Mary, what in the world are you doing?"

Mama did not answer. She had trimmed the paper to the size of the books and was now dipping a gray-looking glue from the brown bottle onto the inside cover of one of the books. Then she took the paper and placed it over the glue.

"Mary Logan, do you know what you're doing? That book belongs to the county. If somebody from the superintendent's office ever comes down here and sees that book, you'll be in real trouble."

Mama laughed and picked up the other book. "In the first place no one cares enough to come down here, and in the second place if anyone should come, maybe he could see all the things we need—current books for all of our subjects, not just somebody's old throwaways, desks, paper, blackboards, erasers, maps, chalk..." Her voice trailed off as she glued the second book.

"Biting the hand that feeds you. That's what you're doing, Mary Logan, biting the hand that feeds you."

Again, Mama laughed. "If that's the case, Daisy, I don't think I need that little bit of food." With the second book finished, she stared at a small pile of seventh-grade books on her desk.

"Well, I just think you're spoiling those children, Mary. They've got to learn how things are sometime."

"Maybe so," said Mama, "but that doesn't mean they have to accept them... and maybe we don't either."

Miss Crocker gazed suspiciously at Mama. Although Mama had

been a teacher at Great Faith for fourteen years, ever since she had graduated from the Crandon Teacher Training School at nineteen, she was still considered by many of the other teachers as a disrupting maverick. Her ideas were always a bit too radical and her statements a bit too pointed. The fact that she had not grown up in Spokane County but in the Delta made her even more suspect, and the more traditional thinkers like Miss Crocker were wary of her. "Well, if anyone ever does come from the county and sees Cassie's and Little Man's books messed up like that," she said, "I certainly won't accept the responsibility for them."

"It will be easy enough for anyone to see whose responsibility it is, Daisy, by opening any seventh-grade book. Because tomorrow I'm going to 'mess them up' too."

Miss Crocker, finding nothing else to say, turned imperiously and headed for the door. I dashed across the hall and awaited her exit, then crept back.

Mama remained at her desk, sitting very still. For a long time she did not move. When she did, she picked up one of the seventh-grade books and began to glue again. I wanted to go and help her, but something warned me that now was not the time to make my presence known, and I left.

I would wait until the evening to talk to her; there was no rush now. She understood.

Jubilee

MARGARET WALKER

When Israel was in Egypt's land—
Let my people go.
Oppressed so hard they could not stand—
Let my people go.

"VYRY, WAKE UP CHILD, wake up so's we can make haste and git along."

Mammy Sukey shook the sleeping child and she stirred in her sleep.

"Wake up, wake up! Sun's up, and us got a far ways to travel. Git up, now, git up and make haste, I says."

Vyry was seven, and the old crone, Mammy Sukey, was all the mother she had ever known or could remember. Today was special. When Vyry remembered, she jumped up from her pallet, rubbing her eyes with her fists and nudging her legs and feet together.

"Today I'm going to the Big House to stay!" she thought to herself.

"What you gone say when you sees Big Missy?" and Mammy Sukey's words shook her out of her reverie. Vyry bowed herself and crossed her legs in an elaborate curtsey, and with a solemn face and soft voice said, "I'm gone say, 'Morning to yall, Missy.'"

"What you gone say to Marster?"

"Morning to yall, Marster."

"And the young Missy Lillyum?"

"Morning, Missy!"

"And young Marster John?"

"Morning, Marster!"

After the slow and serious rehearsal Mammy Sukey nodded approval.

"That's good. That's good. That's just like I showed you. Mind your manners good, and be real nice and polite. You a big gal now, but you ain't gone be no field hand and no yard nigger. You

203

is gone wait on Quality and you got to act like Quality. Go to now—eat your vittles."

While she talked she fixed their breakfast, pulling out of a flour sack two tin plates. She went outside her cabin and from the smoldering fire, dying away into ashes, she brought a hoecake of bread and scraps of fried salt meat. Together they ate, after Mammy Sukey muttered a blessing over the food. The child mixed the bread and the sweet thick syrup with her fingers as she had long watched the toothless old woman do, and together they washed down the food with a gourd dipper of cold water, Mammy Sukey drinking first, and then Vyry.

When they started down the Big Road toward Marse John's Big House, nearly five miles away as the crow flies, dew was still on the grass, but the rising sun was already beaming down on Vyry's bonnet and on Mammy Sukey's head rag. At first the cool, damp grass and the moist earth felt squishy under Vyry's bare feet, but soon they were on a hot dusty clay road. Occasionally she felt pebbles and roots roughen her way so that she stubbed her toes, and sometimes she stumbled.

Ever since she could remember Mammy Sukey had been bringing her along this dirt road, taking her to the Big House many times. Sometimes they picked a pail of blackberries early in the morning before the sun was high. Sometimes they went fishing and caught catfish for their supper. Most times they ambled along just enjoying the summer and the Georgia countryside—butterflies and will-o'-the-wisps, and pretty pink flowers with deep cups of gold pollen that grew along the wayside, or scarlet-colored cardinals and blue jays chattering and screeching and flying over their heads.

But today was different. Today they were in a big hurry, and Mammy Sukey held her hand so tightly it felt hot and sweaty, and her fingers felt cramped. The old woman muttered to herself, and sometimes she seemed to forget the little girl who was trudging along beside her.

"Ain't make a speck of difference nohow. Politeness and cleanness and sweet ways ain't make no difference nohow. She gone stomp her and tromp her and beat her and mighty nigh kill her anyhow." And the child listening was puzzled and troubled, but she did not question Mammy Sukey.

She had been to the Big House many times and she knew what to expect. Marse John was always kind to her when he was around. He would tell the little Missy to share when he brought bananas and oranges and other goodies. "Give Vyry some, too," he would tell her and Miss Lillian would do as her father said. The two little girls often played together making mud pies, or running over the hillside playing hide-and-go-seek and playhouse under the big live oaks and shouting and laughing in fun. On a hot summer's day Vyry had sometimes seen inside the Big House and stood in awe at the dark coolness inside and the richness of the lavish furnishings. In Big Missy's bedroom there was a great oaken bed whose headboard nearly touched the high ceiling and the high mountain of feather mattresses always was covered with a snow-white counterpane. In young Missy Lillian's there was a tester bed with a canopy of sprigged pink and white cotton while the Marster and young Marster had rooms with massive dark furniture with silk furnishing in dark greens and reds and blues. Vyry would go from room to room, tiptoeing in awe and not daring to touch all the wonderful things she saw and the beauty of the rooms that seemed endless. Now, when she thought about it, she wondered why she did not feel happy about going to the Big House to stay.

She vaguely felt, however, that neither young Marster John nor his mother, Big Missy Salina, liked her very much. They were never kind and Mammy Sukey was always trying to keep her out of their way. Why this was true Vyry did not understand, and she did not ask. It was not her place to ask and Mammy Sukey taught her never to get out of her place.

There was that time when Big Missy had company from Savannah and Vyry was at the Big House playing in the yard with Miss Lillian. She heard the lady ask Big Missy, "My, but those children look so much alike, are they twins?" Vyry jumped when she heard the question and dared not turn her burning face in Big Missy's direction. Big Missy's cold angry voice hastened to correct the mistake. "Of course not. Vyry's Lillian's nigger maid. John brought her here to be a playmate to Lillian because they're around the same age, and Lillian has nobody else to play with. I must say they're near the same size, but I never have seen where they look alike at all."

The woman must have realized what a terrible mistake she had made, for she fumbled with the ivory fan that hung around her neck, at the same time changing color and muttering incoherent phrases in half-apologetic and half-frightened tones. But Vyry had a staunch champion in Miss Lillian. In those early years the little Missy did not mind saying to anyone, "Yes, Vyry's my sister, and I love her dearly, and she loves me, too, now don't you, Vyry?" And Vyry would mumble, "Yes, Missy, I reckon I does." But that was child's talk and had nothing to do with their elders, Big Missy and Marse John.

Marse John was forty years of age and slowly settling into a man of serious purpose. At this time of morning he was just getting out of bed. His little daughter, Lillian, still in her long white batiste nightdress with insertions of pink ribbon and lace, ran in to kiss him good morning and confide happily. "Vyry's coming today!"

"Oh, is she? I guess that means making mud pies all day?"

"Oh, no, she's coming to stay. She's going to be my own individual maid all the time, isn't she, Mama?" And Lillian clapped her hands in happy anticipation. Marse John dropped one of the heavy riding boots he was about to put on and turned a questioning look to his wife, Salina, who was standing before a large and ornate mirror arranging her hair.

"What the devil is the child talking about?"

"What she said. The nigger Vyry starts working today as Lillian's maid. Run along now, Lillian, and let Caline get you dressed and comb your hair. Breakfast ought to be ready in a little while."

He put on his boot and then stood fully dressed except for his riding coat. As soon as the child was out of earshot he turned on his wife, "What in hell is going on around here? Why the devil wasn't I told about what's happening in my own house?" His voice was pitched low and well controlled to keep the slaves in the upstairs hall from hearing him, but his face bespoke his deep hostility and anger.

"Because you were either not here when I made the decision, what with all your new political notions and hunting all night in the swamps—if that is what you are really doing all night—or else you were too drunk to notice. And anyway, the house is my affair. I run things here as I please. Unless you change your ways overnight, which isn't likely, I'll have to run the whole plantation. Everything's going to rack and ruin, what with all your nigger-loving ways. You were going to bring her in here anyhow when you got good and ready, just like you've brought all your other bastards. I just beat you to it, and you've got the nerve to be angry."

For a full moment they eyed each other without speaking, and then in an oddly controlled voice he said, "I'm riding over to the Smith Barrow and Crenshaw plantations. They've got some horses and dogs for sale that I want to see."

"You going before breakfast?"

"I don't want any breakfast."

"Humph, well remind them about the dinner party, will you?"

"I will not. That is really your affair, so you attend to it yourself." And grabbing up his riding cap he rushed out of the room slamming the door behind him.

Downstairs, out of the house, and on his way to the stables his mind was busy with a half-dozen things, the confusion of the morning, his abrupt leave of Salina, Vyry and Lillian, and the dead girl, Hetta, and his growing political ambitions. Already it was a warm August morning and the sun was hot. Sweat popped out on him and he mopped his face and brow more than once before spying Grandpa Tom.

"Morning, Tom. Saddle my horse and be quick about it. I'm riding over to the Barrow and Crenshaw plantations, and I'm in a powerful big hurry."

"Yassah, Marster, morning to yall. Ain't you riding kind of early, suh?"

"Not early enough. This blasted sun'll cook me before I get halfway there."

"Yassah, yassah, I reckon so. Hope you'll find it cooler before you starts back home."

John Morris Dutton, sitting astride his chestnut bay horse, threw his head back and laughed. "Now, how'd you know I won't be home soon? Evening or cooler weather, hanh?"

"Nice to see you then, Marster. Nice to see you then."

And as the horse and his rider went trotting down the path to the Big Road, old Grandpa Tom laughed to himself and scratched the bald top of his head.

When Marse John rode away from his house, Vyry and Mammy Sukey were well on their way toward the Big House. At the same time the slave driver, Grimes, who was Marse John's overseer on the plantation, was returning home with six new slaves he had purchased two days before at the slave market in Louisville. They were all field hands, or supposed to be, and they had brought a high price in the market. But Grimes was a little uneasy. He had been on his way since sunup, and since he was already in the swamp bottoms near Marse John's place he hoped to be home soon after breakfast or close around breakfast time. But the youngest of his chattel purchases, a boy in his early teens who was supposedly seventeen but who acted and looked more like fourteen, kept slowing down the journey by falling on the ground and tugging at the line of rope on which the six were strung. Grimes prodded him on with his horse whip by hitting him a lick or two. Both times the boy got up and staggered forward only to drop again in a half-hour or three-quarters of an hour's time. The sun was hot, and they had not had much water, but Grimes was beginning to suspect that the boy was not just suffering from heat and fatigue, he was sick. The auctioneer had cheated him and sold him a sick slave in the lot. He swore softly under his breath, and then yelled, "Hey you, there! Move along there now! You act like you got lice falling off you. We ain't got all day."

Uneasy as he was, he rode along lazily on his old gray nag not wanting to push the horse too hard. He was tired sitting in the saddle, and the butts of his pistols rubbed against his flesh uncomfortably. The Negroes were glum. When they first started out they talked among themselves. Each night when they stopped to make camp, they had sung their mournful songs while sitting in the darkness before lying down to sleep. Grimes kept them tied together even at night for fear of a runaway, and he hardly dared doze despite the loaded pistols he was wearing. In the morning light the boy's eyes looked glazed and sick. Jack, the big brawny slave standing six feet in his bare feet, put his hand on the boy's forehead as it to determine whether he had fever. Two of the others, Ben and Rizzer, gave the child their water, and he drank thirstily, but he would not eat anything. He vomited once and cried out during the night in his sleep.

Grimes looked up at the early morning sky where buzzards

circled high above the trees, and he wished he were already home.

The six slaves, all male, were naked to the waist. Their one piece of clothing was a pair of ragged and faded cotton breeches cut off at the knees and tied around their waists with small ropecord. To this was attached the long piece of rope stringing them together in single file. Their bare legs and feet moved carefully through the swampy ground and the thickets of briers and weeds, heedless of scratches or cuts, while their quick eyes were ever watchful for snakes. Around their faces and feet buzzed flies, gnats, and mosquitoes, which they constantly tried to brush away with their manacled hands. Sweat glistened on all the bodies but the boy's. He looked dry and parched and his thin body was bony. Across his face was a long scar like a cut, and across his back and shoulders a huge welt, which had healed, still stood out prominently. The boy groaned constantly, making a wheezing and delirious sound that was first a moan then a whine mixed with a high-pitched, babbling, sing-song cry. Annoyed by this, Grimes started to hit him again, and thought better of it. They couldn't have much farther to go.

Grimes was a short, thick-set man, his shoulders big and round like a barrel and his heavy thighs like the broad flanks of a big boar with short, stocky legs and short but powerful arms. His watery blue eyes were as small as pig eyes, and when he was angry they turned a fiery red, though not exactly the same red as his thin carrot-colored hair and the dull red freckles that peppered his face and mottled his neck and arms. Even his upper lip and stubby chin were covered with a day's growth of red bristles which also stuck out of his nostrils and ears. His squinting eyes darted right and left, watching carefully for every turn of the road, and keeping the Negroes well in front of him. He was chewing tobacco and when he spat he stained the creases around his mouth and dropped dabs of the brown juice on his blue cotton-linsey shirt. His collar was open enough to show the red bristles on his chest, for the perspiration rolled off him, and where his cotton breeches were stuck in his fine leather boots they were soaking wet to the skin. He used his boots to nudge his nag and urge the beast along. When a horse has trotted nearly a hundred miles without much fancy attention a little easy nudge is in order. Of course, he never did have a good horse. John Morris Dutton kept all the fine thoroughbreds for hunting and carriage pulling and riding, while he gave Grimes all the nags and mules for work horses. Grimes did not think this was exactly right, but then what can you expect from a nigger-loving man like Dutton when it comes to treating poor white people right?

Now his wife's different. She's a lady, Missy Salina Dutton is, a fine, good lady. She nurses the sick far and wide, white and black. She knows how to handle niggers and keep a big establishment; how to set a fine table, and act morally decent like a first-class lady. She's a real Christian woman, a Bible-reading, honest-dealing, high-quality lady who knows and acts the difference between niggers and white people. She ain't no nigger-loving namby-pamby like that s.o.b. pretty boy she's married to. She knows how to lay the law down to niggers and keep her business to herself. Deep down in their hearts, a lot of people might feel sorry for the way her husband mistreats her, carrying on with nigger wenches, and even stooping so low as to raise whole families by them, shaming a good wife and a decent white woman of Quality. Not that she never gives a sign like she knows about his goings-on. She is always strictly business-like and matter-of-fact. She acts so unconcerned you have to admire her for her guts. Of course people know and folks can't help talking about it, anyhow. Then too, it wouldn't be so bad if she wasn't so all-fired good-looking, but she is a beautiful woman. He sometimes wished his Jane Ellen had the kind of quality looks Miss Salina Dutton had. Of course Janey has had a hard time. She come from the pine barrens and her folks is awful poor, so poor they eat dirt, and sometimes, like right now while Janey is expecting (this'll be number eight), she craves dirt like her Maw done before her and that's why she eats so much snuff. But Janey was once real nice-looking too, before all these younguns, and when her blonde hair was real light colored and not so stringy as it is now, and she wasn't so careless, like walking around in a dirty dress with her feet stomp barefooted like she come in the world. But they is one sure thing, by God, she is a true, good wife and she don't have no nigger-loving husband like that trashy John Morris Dutton.

Most folks would never guess how he longed some day to have a farm of his own. He knew darn well how to run a farm, and he wouldn't be running off all the time leaving the work to somebody else. A lot of people think running a farm and handling nigras is nothing, but that ain't so, it's hard work. Managing a farm and keeping a pack of evil, black slaves in line ain't no child's play, but he knew how to do it. That's what he told Mister Dutton when he hired him, and he, Ed Grimes, was tough and hard enough a man to prove it. Of course you got a lot of things against you, things to contend with like the weather, for an instance. Rain slows the work down and niggers always hollering, "more rain, more rest." You got to keep a firm hand on niggers, else they won't hit a lick of the snake. Half the time they make out like they sick and got the rheumatiz or the whooping cough or just plain misery, and half the time they is just putting on. You can't pay them no mind, because they are the biggest liars God ever made—that is, if God made them. Sometimes it seems like a fact for certain that niggers is the work of the devil, and cursed by God. They is evil, and they is ignorant, and the blacker they is the more evil; lazy, trifling liars, every one of them. The Marster, Mister Dutton, indulges niggers cause he thinks they are helpless and childish, and they ain't got no mind, but the truth is they is just plain evil and stubborn and hardheaded. Best thing to keep a nigger working and jumping is a good bull whip. All you got to do is flick that whip, and believe you me, they jumps. I ought to know. And Missy Salina knows, too, you can't give niggers no rope, do and they'll hang you, give em an inch and they'll take a mile. You can't let up on a niggah if you wanta be a good driver, and that's what I am, a first class A-number-one good driver.

Vyry and Mammy Sukey walked into the back yard of the Big House just in time to see a big commotion. All the house servants and yard hands were crowded around Mister Grimes, the overseer, who had brought six slaves into the back yard and was cutting the rope and unlocking the chains holding them together. Big Missy Salina was standing in the back door of the Big House. Mammy Sukey turned to Vyry and said, "Go ask Aunt Sally for a washpan so's you can wash your footses fore you goes inside." And just at that moment when Vyry ran to obey, the sick black boy fell sprawling face down in the dust. Mammy Sukey pushed forward into the group around Grimes, and then her eyes widened in horror. She yelled, "Lord, have mercy, all you niggers get back! Send for Granny Ticey fast and tell Missy get the doctor quick. I clare fore God this nigger's got the plague."

Vyry pushed open the back door to the one-room, lean-to kitchen-house and saw Aunt Sally bending over the brick oven in the large fireplace chimney where she did all of Marster's cooking. For a minute Vyry stood there in the hot kitchen inhaling the smell of biscuits still baking, of fried ham with the smell still hanging on the air, and bubbling coffee. It seemed a long time since she and Mammy Sukey had eaten.

"Shucks, child, you scared me so I like to blistered myself with this here coffeepot. What you doing here?"

"I come to stay in the Big House with Miss Lillyum, and Mammy Sukey say give me a pot, please ma'am, so I can wash my footses fore I mess up Big Missy's pretty clean house, and they's a nigger outen there laying on the ground, Mammy say he got the plague . . ."

All her words came out in the rush of one breath. Aunt Sally stood looking through her for another long minute before she seemed to understand about the washpan the child was seeking.

"Got the plague? Oh, my Lord have mercy! Look-a-yonder hanging on the back porch and get that water bucket. You can set out there and wash yourself. I gotta see what's going on outside."

Vyry took the wooden bucket and went to the rain barrel to get water. But all that first day she could scarcely understand what was going on outside or inside. First, Big Ben and Rizzer moved the sick boy to one of the empty slave cabins where Big Missy kept all her medicines and where sick slaves went when they were bad off enough to need the doctor or stay on their pallets and need nursing, and then, as Mammy Sukey said, they had better be sick enough to die and prove it. Granny Ticey and Mammy Sukey took charge because Big Missy said she wasn't fooling with no niggers who had the plague, and she shooed all the rest of the slaves, including Aunt Sally, back to their work. When Big Ben and Rizzer saw that the sick boy was dying they stayed to help the two old women. Twenty-four hours later Ben and Rizzer dug a fresh grave. By their second evening that first new grave was filled. The dead boy was put naked into a feed sack, and then into a pine box in which he was hastily buried. Lime was spread liberally inside the grave, over, and around it.

That first night away from Mammy Sukey, lying on a strange pallet at the foot of Miss Lillian's bed, Vyry trembled for a long time before she could go to sleep. All day long she had gone back and forth from the kitchen to the springhouse, back to pull the dinner bell, then to gather eggs, to help feed the chickens, to fetch Miss Lillian a glass of water, and everything she had done and said was wrong. Twice Big Missy slapped her in the mouth with the back of her hand, and once Vyry barely escaped the foot of her mistress kicking her. Once she yelled to the startled child, "You stupid bastard, if you break airy one of my china dishes, I'll break your face."

If Vyry's first day was confusing, because Mammy Sukey was too busy to get her off to a good start in the Big House, it was increasingly confusing in the days that followed. Big Missy, Aunt Sally, and Caline kept explaining what to do next, and before many hours had passed Vyry sensed that her days here were not going to be what she had thought. There was no more time for mud pies. Miss Lillian was studying book lessons after breakfast. While Caline combed and brushed Miss Lillian's hair into curls Vyry stood by and she said, "Can I have curls, too?"

But Miss Lillian laughingly said, "Niggers don't wear curls, do they Caline?" And Caline watching Vyry's stricken face said, "Naw Missy, they sure don't."

Toward the end of the third day Vyry slipped away from the Big House twice to find Mammy Sukey, and twice she was sent back to her work and threatened with a whipping. Vyry told Aunt Sally she would rather die than catch a whipping. But the next day, fearing something she could only sense, she could not stay away, and she tried again to speak through the barred door of the cabin where Mammy Sukey still was. But the old woman's voice was now tired and troubled and she spoke a final admonition to the child:

"Gone back to the Big House, child, don't come here no more unlessen Aunt Sally sends you. Be good, and mind your manners like I told you and let Aunt Sally see after you . . ." and the familiar voice the child loved trailed off weakly.

That was the day Vyry forgot to empty Miss Lillian's chamber pot. Every morning when Caline and Jim, the houseboy, emptied slop jars, Vyry was told to empty Miss Lillian's little china chamber pot and see that it was washed outdoors and dried in the sun and brought in before bedtime and put under Miss Lillian's bed, but in her distress over being separated from Mammy Sukey, whom she dared not believe was sick, she forgot the chamber pot. That night when she heard Big Missy calling her from her supper in the kitchen with Aunt Sally she jumped up like she was shot. Trembling with fear of the whipping she knew she was going to get she stood before Big Missy, who was standing in the doorway of the kitchen and holding the pot of stale pee in her hand. Instead of whipping her, she threw the acrid contents of the pot in Vyry's face and said, "There, you lazy nigger, that'll teach you to keep your mind on what you're doing. Don't you let me have to tell you another time about this pot or I'll half-kill you, do you hear me?"

"Yas'm."

Early the next morning Vyry started toward the forbidden cabin again. When she saw them bringing out the stiff dead body of Mammy Sukey she began screaming and crying as if she could never stop. She cried all day, but after that evening when she knew Mammy Sukey would never take her down the Big Road any more she hushed her tears and determined not to cry any more.

For five days there was a new grave every day. But Vyry bent her back to Big Missy's hatred and struggled hard to please her. She lost track of the days and she could not know she had been there two weeks when she broke one of Missy's china dishes. This time she knew Big Missy was going to whip her. Vyry saw Big Missy standing with the leather strap in her hands, and she looked up impassive and resigned, then she clasped her hands tightly, bowed her head and closed her eyes, tensely waiting for the first terrible lick, but Missy Salina laughed and said, "Do you think I'm going to hurt myself whipping you? Open your eyes and come here to me." Too startled to feel relieved, Vyry looked up and saw her mistress holding a closet door open. She hooked the strap to a nail, then, snatching up Vyry, she crossed her hands and caught them securely with the strap. Vyry's toes barely touched the floor of the closet. Suddenly Big Missy slammed the door behind her and left Vyry hanging by her hands there in the darkness. Terribly frightened, the child did not whimper. At first she was terrified in the dark, but after such a long time, with her arm-pits hurting so bad, she lost consciousness of everything and did not know how long she hung there in torture.

Two weeks after his early morning encounter with his wife, Marse John was returning home. Riding along the edge of his vast home properties he was savoring the pleasant air of a bright September morning. His mind was not on the pedigreed hunting hounds he bought from Barrow, nor the good whiskey he drank with Crenshaw. His neighbors were coming to his house for a hunting party as soon as the weather was cold enough. That would mark the beginning of his political campaign. Things ought to stack up in his favor as a candidate from Terrell County for the legislature. He expected to win hands down since he owned Terrell County and most of what was left of Lee County, too. His drivers were already his deputy sheriffs. Law and order in the county was gradually taking shape under his hands with political organization as his ultimate goal. He owned enough slaves to give him a large number of votes. For every five slaves he could count three votes. The only trouble was it took so much time, and he needed more time to spend covering the state. Rural traveling wasn't fun, and the weather determined everything. This trip had not been extended enough to visit his lands in Bainbridge and Newton counties for these bordered the Alabama line on one side, and the Florida line on another end. He would like to go more often traveling out of the state, but Salina never wanted to go anywhere except Augusta and Savannah. Once, before he was married, he spent a carnival season in New Orleans; pretty nearly spent the winter there. He surely enjoyed the lavish balls and gay social affairs in that exotic city. He even toyed with the idea of setting up one of those colored gals who had taken his fancy at the Quadroon balls. My God, but they were pretty! Only very rich white men were sought for them; they were bred only for the purpose of being some white man's mistress. But he decided it was foolish, a waste of good money, and too far from home to be convenient. Besides, at that time, he still had Hetta. Anyway, when he came home to Georgia, he came to God's country, and no other place on earth could be half so fine.

Here on his plantation between the Flint and Chattahoochee rivers was the land he remembered as a boy, where he had grown to manhood. What good times he had in these very woods when he was just a slip of a lad and his father took him coon hunting at night with the hounds, slaves, patter-rollers, and all! He laughed loudly just remembering.

Once they were coming along this same stretch of swampland with a pack of dogs hot on the scent of a possum or coon or something, and they ran smack-dab through the tangled briars and sticky thickets of vines following the yelping dogs who were barking up a helluva lot of noise. His father, excited, kept edging the dogs on, calling them by name, Queenie and Bessie, while they moaned and hollered, leading them into the thickest and deepest part of the woods. There the dogs barked like bedlam, the hunters hollered, "She's treed him." And they gathered around a big live oak tree. It was midnight and no moon, and they almost ran into the tree before his father flashed his lantern, and he, a young boy, stood gaping with the rest of the party, a tattered and tired bunch, with his father still breathing hard from running, when suddenly there was a dead hush. The light flickered at the base of the huge tree. The dogs tucked their tails, whined, and drew back. Against the dark bark of the tree stood a very large and glittering rooster. He appeared to be all of two feet high. His red and green and black feathers were gleaming like satin. His coxcomb was a bright, bristling red. But his eyes were fantastic. They looked like the eyes of a human being. He was wide-eyed and unblinking, and stared back at them unruffled, calm, and steadily. Finally his father said in a tired voice, "Call off your dogs, boys, let's go home." Disappointed, he said, "But why, Poppa? Where's our game? We ain't got no coon yet."

"Ain't no game, son, leastwise not tonight. When did you ever see a chicken this far from roost this time of night?"

And the wide-eyed slave boys shook their heads and whispered among themselves.

"Sho ain't no coon!"

". . . and sho ain't no possum!"

". . . and it sho ain't no rooster neither."

Yes, this was his land, and this was home. His mother's holdings and his father's father's land had become his. They made him one of the seven richest planters in the center of Georgia. They kept him on the go so much he had to trust most of the running of the plantations to his drivers, even though Salina accused him of leaving the home place in her hands. He couldn't be in two or three places at the same time. On one plantation alone, the last time he had it surveyed, he owned three thousand acres. In addition to the rivers, his broad fertile lands in the river valleys were also watered by the Kinchafoonee and the Muckalee creeks. It was here in the marshy thickets and lush swamps of many meandering streams and treacherous bogs that a number of slaves had tried to run away to freedom. Most of them were caught by the patter-rollers and brought back for a flogging, in order to teach them a lesson and set an example for the others. Once when he was a half-grown boy he had gone on a searching party after a runaway slave. They gave the hounds the scent of his clothes. It sickened him now to remember. Flogging wasn't necessary that time because the dogs tore the fellow to pieces. Even now he could see the hideous bloody sight. His father was fighting mad. Runaway or no runaway, slaves cost money and mangled expensive property didn't please him one little bit, no sir-ee!

Sometimes Grimes overstepped his authority now, but they really had to depend upon him. He had a reputation of knowing how to handle nigras. Perhaps Salina was correct when she accused her husband of being a weak disciplinarian and not firm enough with his slaves. He preferred to leave the stern punishing of all his black labor in Grimes's hands as long as he didn't go too far.

Like an ancient lord in a great feudal, medieval castle surrounded by water and inaccessible except by a drawbridge over a moat (before one entered the fortified dwelling), he lived in a most inaccessible section of Georgia—deep in the forest, miles from the cities, and impossible distances to travel on foot. It was fully a half-day's journey from the old Wagon Road, where the stage coaches once traveled the Big Road, to the long oak-lined avenues leading up to the stately white manor of his own Shady Oaks. When he turned off the Wagon Road he had to travel ten or twelve miles on this narrow road that was overhung with great live oaks and towering virgin pine trees that touched the sky. From the live oak trees hung the weird gray veils of Spanish moss waving wildly in the wind, and trailing like gray tresses of an old woman's hair, lost from the head of some ghost in the wilderness. Often during daylight hours the sky was completely obscured by an archway of these trees. Here in the stillness of the forest one was cut off from reality and lost in a fantastic world of jungle. In this world of half-darkness and half-light he had often felt as though eyes were watching him.

After the twelve miles the road led along the path of the Kinchafoonee Creek where the swampy woods were full of cypress, so dense and dank and dark that it seemed as if the sky were overcast and a shadow hung over the day, sending a shiver creeping along his spine in the eerie atmosphere. Though the summer was waning, the air was fragrant with exotic sub-tropical flowers mingling with the pungent smell of pine. The colorful pink and orange bougainvillea and the royal purple wisteria hung in thick grape-like and trumpeting clusters. They grew in wild profusion, while the undergrowth was tangled with blue morning glory vines and running bushes of the climbing Cherokee rose. Yellow flickers, blue jays, thrashers, kildeers, brown wrens, speckled field larks, and scissor tails darted back and forth through the brush and through the trees, screeching with merriment, while here and there a chattering school of crows made their caw-caw noise. Gradually the swampy woods disappeared and Marse John came at last to his broad fields which were under cultivation on both sides of the road. Now the cotton was white with harvest, and as always his slaves were working in the fields, filling long croker sacks with the fluffy yield.

On his way to the house he passed the cemetery, the family plot where his parents and his grandparents were buried, where he too, in time, would be laid beside them. Fresh mounds of earth drew his quick attention and he got down off his horse to investigate. Six new graves in two short weeks? Name of God, who could they be? The rough wooden boards told him they were slaves but only two bore names, Granny Ticey and Mammy Sukey! From the plentiful sprinkling of lime he knew very well the deaths were due to something contagious.

Sorrowful now, he remounted and went to the house where such a stillness seemed unnatural. Chickens pecking around the back kitchen house and well were a familiar sight. Curtains were drawn against the heat and he was relieved to have his daughter Lillian run to meet him. She whispered in his ear, "Oh, Poppa, come quick, Vyry's hanging by her thumbs in the closet and I do believe she's dead."

He lost no time running up the stairs where Salina sat in her room with a basket of mending in her lap as though nothing were unusual, but when she saw him bound for the closet she jumped up. Quickly he caught the child, Vyry, whose feet barely touched the floor, and he saw she was only in a dead faint.

"What you trying to do, Salina, kill her?"

"Yes. I reckon that's what I oughta do. Kill her and all other yellow bastards like her. Killing's too good for her."

"Well, don't you try it again, d'ye hear me? Don't you dare try it again! She's nothing but a child, but someday she'll be grown-up and worth much as a slave. Then you'll be sorry."

"Humph! Are you talking to me? I'll never be sorry. Never, d'ye hear? How much do you expect me to put up with? Here in this very house with my own dear little children. And my friends mortifying me with shame! Telling me she looks like Lillian's twin. Don't you dare threaten me, John Morris Dutton, don't you dare threaten me. So far as killing her, I ain't even hurt her. I oughta kill her, but I ain't got the strength to kill a tough nigra bastard like her."

A Memory

EUDORA WELTY

ONE SUMMER MORNING when I was a child I lay on the sand
after swimming in the small lake in the park. The sun beat
down—it was almost noon. The water shone like steel, motionless
except for the feathery curl behind a distant swimmer. From my
position I was looking at a rectangle brightly lit, actually
glaring at me, with sun, sand, water, a little pavilion, a few
solitary people in fixed attitudes, and around it all a border of
dark rounded oak trees, like the engraved thunderclouds sur-
rounding illustrations in the Bible. Ever since I had begun
taking painting lessons, I had made small frames with my
fingers, to look out at everything.

Since this was a weekday morning, the only persons who were
at liberty to be in the park were either children, who had nothing
to occupy them, or those older people whose lives are obscure,
irregular, and consciously of no worth to anything: this I put down
as my observation at that time. I was at an age when I formed a
judgment upon every person and every event which came under
my eye, although I was easily frightened. When a person, or a
happening, seemed to me not in keeping with my opinion, or
even my hope or expectation, I was terrified by a vision of
abandonment and wildness which tore my heart with a kind of
sorrow. My father and mother, who believed that I saw nothing in
the world which was not strictly coaxed into place like a vine on
our garden trellis to be presented to my eyes, would have been
badly concerned if they had guessed how frequently the weak and
inferior and strangely turned examples of what was to come
showed themselves to me.

I do not know even now what it was that I was waiting to see,
but in those days I was convinced that I almost saw it at every
turn. To watch everything about me I regarded grimly and

possessively as a *need*. All through this summer I had lain on the sand beside the small lake, with my hands squared over my eyes, finger tips touching, looking out by this device to see everything: which appeared as a kind of projection. It did not matter to me what I looked at; from any observation I would conclude that a secret of life had been nearly revealed to me—for I was obsessed with notions about concealment, and from the smallest gesture of a stranger I would wrest what was to me a communication or a presentiment.

This state of exaltation was heightened, or even brought about, by the fact that I was in love then for the first time: I had identified love at once. The truth is that never since has any passion I have felt remained so hopelessly unexpressed within me or appeared so grotesquely altered in the outward world. It is strange that sometimes, even now, I remember unadulteratedly a certain morning when I touched my friend's wrist (as if by accident, and he pretended not to notice) as we passed on the stairs in school. I must add, and this is not so strange, that the child was not actually my friend. We had never exchanged a word or even a nod of recognition; but it was possible during that entire year for me to think endlessly on this minute and brief encounter which we endured on the stairs, until it would swell with a sudden and overwhelming beauty, like a rose forced into premature bloom for a great occasion.

My love had somehow made me doubly austere in my observations of what went on about me. Through some intensity I had come almost into a dual life, as observer and dreamer. I felt a necessity for absolute conformity to my ideas in any happening I witnessed. As a result, all day long in school I sat perpetually alert, fearing for the untoward to happen. The dreariness and regularity of the school day were a protection for me, but I remember with exact clarity the day in Latin class when the boy I loved (whom I watched constantly) bent suddenly over and brought his handkerchief to his face. I saw red—vermilion—blood flow over the handkerchief and his square-shaped hand; his nose had begun to bleed. I remember the very moment: several of the older girls laughed at the confusion and distraction; the boy rushed from the room; the teacher spoke sharply in warning. But this small happening which had closed in upon my friend was a tremendous shock to me; it was unforeseen, but at the same time dreaded; I recognized it, and suddenly I leaned heavily on my arm and fainted. Does this explain why, ever since that day, I have been unable to bear the sight of blood?

I never knew where this boy lived, or who his parents were. This occasioned during the year of my love a constant uneasiness in me. It was unbearable to think that his house might be slovenly and unpainted, hidden by tall trees, that his mother and father might be shabby—dishonest—crippled—dead. I speculated endlessly on the dangers of his home. Sometimes I imagined that his house might catch on fire in the night and that he might die. When he would walk into the schoolroom the next morning, a look of unconcern and even stupidity on his face would dissipate my dream; but my fears were increased through his unconsciousness of them, for I felt a mystery deeper than danger which hung about him. I watched everything he did, trying to learn and translate and verify. I could reproduce for you now the clumsy weave, the exact shade of faded blue in his sweater. I remember how he used to swing his foot as he sat at his desk—softly, barely not touching the floor. Even now it does not seem trivial.

As I lay on the beach that sunny morning, I was thinking of my friend and remembering in a retarded, dilated, timeless fashion the incident of my hand brushing his wrist. It made a very long story. But like a needle going in and out among my thoughts were the children running on the sand, the upthrust oak trees growing over the clean pointed roof of the white pavilion, and the slowly changing attitudes of the grown-up people who had avoided the city and were lying prone and laughing on the water's edge. I still would not care to say which was more real—the dream I could make blossom at will, or the sight of the bathers. I am presenting them, you see, only as simultaneous.

I did not notice how the bathers got there, so close to me. Perhaps I actually fell asleep, and they came out then. Sprawled close to where I was lying, at any rate, appeared a group of loud, squirming, ill-assorted people who seemed thrown together only by the most confused accident, and who seemed driven by foolish intent to insult each other, all of which they enjoyed with a hilarity which astonished my heart. There were a man, two women, two young boys. They were brown and roughened, but not foreigners; when I was a child such people were called "common." They wore old and faded bathing suits which did not hide either the energy or the fatigue of their bodies, but showed it exactly.

The boys must have been brothers, because they both had very white straight hair, which shone like thistles in the red sunlight. The older boy was greatly overgrown—he protruded from his costume at every turn. His cheeks were ballooned outward and hid his eyes, but it was easy for me to follow his darting, sly glances as he ran clumsily around the others, inflicting pinches, kicks, and idiotic sounds upon them. The smaller boy was thin and defiant; his white bangs were plastered down where he had thrown himself time after time headfirst into the lake when the older child chased him to persecute him.

Lying in leglike confusion together were the rest of the group, the man and the two women. The man seemed completely given over to the heat and glare of the sun; his relaxed eyes sometimes squinted with faint amusement over the brilliant water and the hot sand. His arms were flabby and at rest. He lay turned on his side, now and then scooping sand in a loose pile about the legs of the older woman.

She herself stared fixedly at his slow, undeliberate movements, and held her body perfectly still. She was unnaturally white and fatly aware, in a bathing suit which had no relation to the shape of her body. Fat hung upon her upper arms like an arrested earthslide on a hill. With the first motion she might make, I was afraid that she would slide down upon herself into a terrifying heap. Her breasts hung heavy and widening like pears into her bathing suit. Her legs lay prone one on the other like shadowed bulwarks, uneven and deserted, upon which, from the man's hand, the sand piled higher like the teasing threat of oblivion. A slow, repetitious sound I had been hearing for a long time unconsciously, I identified as a continuous laugh which came through the motionless open pouched mouth of the woman.

The younger girl, who was lying at the man's feet, was curled tensely upon herself. She wore a bright green bathing suit like a bottle from which she might, I felt, burst in a rage of churning smoke. I could feel the genie-like rage in her narrowed figure as she seemed both to crawl and to lie still, watching the man heap the sand in his careless way about the larger legs of the older woman. The two little boys were running in wobbly ellipses about the others, pinching them indiscriminately and pitching sand into the man's roughened hair as though they were not afraid of him. The woman continued to laugh, almost as she would hum an annoying song. I saw that they were all resigned to each other's daring and ugliness.

There had been no words spoken among these people, but I began to comprehend a progression, a circle of answers, which they were flinging toward one another in their own way, in the confusion of vulgarity and hatred which twined among them all like a wreath of steam rising from the wet sand. I saw the man lift his hand filled with crumbling sand, shaking it as the woman laughed, and pour it down inside her bathing suit between her bulbous descending breasts. There it hung, brown and shapeless, making them all laugh. Even the angry girl laughed, with an insistent hilarity which flung her to her feet and tossed her about the beach, her stiff, cramped legs jumping and tottering. The little boys pointed and howled. The man smiled, the way panting dogs seem to be smiling, and gazed about carelessly at them all and out over the water. He even looked at me, and included me. Looking back, stunned, I wished that they all were dead.

But at that moment the girl in the green bathing suit suddenly whirled all the way around. She reached rigid arms toward the screaming children and joined them in a senseless chase. The small boy dashed headfirst into the water, and the larger boy churned his overgrown body through the blue air onto a little bench, which I had not even known was there! Jeeringly he called to the others, who laughed as he jumped, heavy and ridiculous, over the back of the bench and tumbled exaggeratedly in the sand below. The fat woman leaned over the man to smirk, and the child pointed at her, screaming. The girl in green then came running toward the bench as though she would destroy it, and with a fierceness which took my breath away, she dragged herself through the air and jumped over the bench. But no one seemed to notice, except the smaller boy, who flew out of the water to dig his fingers into her side, in mixed congratulation and derision; she pushed him angrily down into the sand.

I closed my eyes upon them and their struggles but I could see them still, large and almost metallic, with painted smiles, in the sun. I lay there with my eyes pressed shut, listening to their moans and their frantic squeals. It seemed to me that I could hear also the thud and the fat impact of all their ugly bodies upon one another. I tried to withdraw to my most inner dream, that of touching the wrist of the boy I loved on the stair; I felt the shudder of my wish shaking the darkness like leaves where I had closed my eyes; I felt the heavy weight of sweetness which always accompanied this memory; but the memory itself did not come to me.

I lay there, opening and closing my eyes. The brilliance and then the blackness were like some alternate experiences of night and day. The sweetness of my love seemed to bring the dark and to swing me gently in its suspended wind; I sank into familiarity; but the story of my love, the long narrative of the incident on the stairs, had vanished. I did not know, any longer, the meaning of my happiness; it held me unexplained.

Once when I looked up, the fat woman was standing opposite the smiling man. She bent over and in a condescending way pulled down the front of her bathing suit, turning it outward, so that the lumps of mashed and folded sand came emptying out. I felt a peak of horror, as though her breasts themselves had turned to sand, as though they were of no importance at all and she did not care.

When finally I emerged again from the protection of my dream, the undefined austerity of my love, I opened my eyes onto the blur of an empty beach. The group of strangers had gone. Still I lay there, feeling victimized by the sight of the unfinished bulwark where they had piled and shaped the wet sand around their bodies, which changed the appearance of the beach like the ravages of a storm. I looked away, and for the object which met my eye, the small worn white pavilion, I felt pity suddenly overtake me, and I burst into tears.

That was my last morning on the beach. I remember continuing to lie there, squaring my vision with my hands, trying to think ahead to the time of my return to school in winter. I could imagine the boy I loved walking into a classroom, where I would watch him with this hour on the beach accompanying my recovered dream and added to my love. I could even foresee the way he would stare back, speechless and innocent, a medium-sized boy with blond hair, his unconscious eyes looking beyond me and out the window, solitary and unprotected.

Why I Live at the P.O.

Eudora Welty

I WAS GETTING ALONG fine with Mama, Papa-Daddy and Uncle Rondo until my sister Stella-Rondo just separated from her husband and came back home again. Mr. Whitaker! Of course I went with Mr. Whitaker first, when he first appeared here in China Grove, taking "Pose Yourself" photos, and Stella-Rondo broke us up. Told him I was one-sided. Bigger on one side than the other, which is a deliberate, calculated falsehood: I'm the same. Stella-Rondo is exactly twelve months to the day younger than I am and for that reason she's spoiled.

She's always had anything in the world she wanted and then she'd throw it away. Papa-Daddy gave her this gorgeous Add-a-Pearl necklace when she was eight years old and she threw it away playing baseball when she was nine, with only two pearls.

So as soon as she got married and moved away from home the first thing she did was separate! From Mr. Whitaker! This photographer with the popeyes she said she trusted. Came home from one of those towns up in Illinois and to our complete surprise brought this child of two.

Mama said she like to made her drop dead for a second. "Here you had this marvelous blonde child and never so much as wrote your mother a word about it," says Mama. "I'm thoroughly ashamed of you." But of course she wasn't.

Stella-Rondo just calmly takes off this *hat*, I wish you could see it. She says, "Why, Mama, Shirley-T.'s adopted, I can prove it."

"How?" says Mama, but all I says was, "H'm!" There I was over the hot stove, trying to stretch two chickens over five people and a completely unexpected child into the bargain, without one moment's notice.

"What do you mean—'H'm!'?" says Stella-Rondo, and Mama says, "I heard that, Sister."

I said that oh, I didn't mean a thing, only that whoever
Shirley-T. was, she was the spit-image of Papa-Daddy if he'd cut
off his beard, which of course he'd never do in the world.
Papa-Daddy's Mama's papa and sulks.

Stella-Rondo got furious! She said, "Sister, I don't need to tell
you you got a lot of nerve and always did have and I'll thank you
to make no future reference to my adopted child whatsoever."

"Very well," I said. "Very well, very well. Of course I noticed at
once she looks like Mr. Whitaker's side too. That frown. She looks
like a cross between Mr. Whitaker and Papa-Daddy."

"Well, all I can say is she isn't."

"She looks exactly like Shirley Temple to me," says Mama, but
Shirley-T. just ran away from her.

So the first thing Stella-Rondo did at the table was turn
Papa-Daddy against me.

"Papa-Daddy," she says. He was trying to cut up his meat.
"Papa-Daddy!" I was taken completely by surprise. Papa-Daddy
is about a million years old and's got this long-long beard.
"Papa-Daddy, Sister says she fails to understand why you don't cut
off your beard."

So Papa-Daddy l-a-y-s down his knife and fork! He's real rich.
Mama says he is, he says he isn't. So he says, "Have I heard
correctly? You don't understand why I don't cut off my beard?"

"Why," I says, "Papa-Daddy, of course I understand, I did not
say any such of a thing, the idea!"

He says, "Hussy!"

I says, "Papa-Daddy, you know I wouldn't any more want you
to cut off your beard than the man in the moon. It was the
farthest thing from my mind! Stella-Rondo sat there and made
that up while she was eating breast of chicken."

But he says, "So the postmistress fails to understand why I
don't cut off my beard. Which job I got you through my influence
with the government. 'Birds' nest'—is that what you call it?"

Not that it isn't the next to smallest P.O. in the entire state of
Mississippi.

I says, "Oh, Papa-Daddy," I says, "I didn't say any such of a
thing, I never dreamed it was a bird's nest, I have always been
grateful though this is the next to smallest P.O. in the state of

Mississippi, and I do not enjoy being referred to as a hussy by my own grandfather."

But Stella-Rondo says, "Yes, you did say it too. Anybody in the world could of heard you, that had ears."

"Stop right there," says Mama, looking at *me*.

So I pulled my napkin straight back through the napkin ring and left the table.

As soon as I was out of the room Mama says, "Call her back, or she'll starve to death," but Papa-Daddy says, "This is the beard I started growing on the Coast when I was fifteen years old." He would of gone on till nightfall if Shirley-T. hadn't lost the Milky Way she ate in Cairo.

So Papa-Daddy says, "I am going out and lie in the hammock, and you can all sit here and remember my words: I'll never cut off my beard as long as I live, even one inch, and I don't appreciate it in you at all." Passed right by me in the hall and went straight out and got in the hammock.

It would be a holiday. It wasn't five minutes before Uncle Rondo suddenly appeared in the hall in one of Stella-Rondo's flesh-colored kimonos, all cut on the bias, like something Mr. Whitaker probably thought was gorgeous.

"Uncle Rondo!" I says. "I didn't know who that was! Where are you going?"

"Sister," he says, "get out of my way, I'm poisoned."

"If you're poisoned stay away from Papa-Daddy," I says. "Keep out of the hammock. Papa-Daddy will certainly beat you on the head if you come within forty miles of him. He thinks I deliberately said he ought to cut off his beard after he got me the P.O., and I've told him and told him and told him, and he acts like he just don't hear me. Papa-Daddy must of gone stone deaf."

"He picked a fine day to do it then," says Uncle Rondo, and before you could say "Jack Robinson" flew out in the yard.

What he'd really done, he'd drunk another bottle of that prescription. He does it every single Fourth of July as sure as shooting, and it's horribly expensive. Then he falls over in the hammock and snores. So he insisted on zigzagging right on out to the hammock, looking like a half-wit.

Papa-Daddy woke up with this horrible yell and right there without moving an inch he tried to turn Uncle Rondo against me.

I heard every word he said. Oh, he told Uncle Rondo I didn't learn to read till I was eight years old and he didn't see how in the world I ever got the mail put up at the P.O., much less read it all, and he said if Uncle Rondo could only fathom the lengths he had gone to to get me that job! And he said on the other hand he thought Stella-Rondo had a brilliant mind and deserved credit for getting out of town. All the time he was just lying there swinging as pretty as you please and looping out his beard, and poor Uncle Rondo was *pleading* with him to slow down the hammock, it was making him as dizzy as a witch to watch it. But that's what Papa-Daddy likes about a hammock. So Uncle Rondo was too dizzy to get turned against me for the time being. He's Mama's only brother and is a good case of a one-track mind. Ask anybody. A certified pharmacist.

Just then I heard Stella-Rondo raising the upstairs window. While she was married she got this peculiar idea that it's cooler with the windows shut and locked. So she has to raise the window before she can make a soul hear her outdoors.

So she raises the window and says, "*Oh!*" You would have thought she was mortally wounded.

Uncle Rondo and Papa-Daddy didn't even look up, but kept right on with what they were doing. I had to laugh.

I flew up the stairs and threw the door open! I says, "What in the wide world's the matter, Stella-Rondo? You mortally wounded?"

"No," she says, "I'm not mortally wounded but I wish you would do me the favor of looking out that window there and telling me what you see."

So I shade my eyes and look out the window.

"I see the front yard," I says.

"Don't you see any human beings?" she says.

"I see Uncle Rondo trying to run Papa-Daddy out of the hammock," I says. "Nothing more. Naturally, it's so suffocating-hot in the house, with all the windows shut and locked, everybody who cares to stay in their right mind will have to go out and get in the hammock before the Fourth of July is over."

"Don't you notice anything different about Uncle Rondo?" asks Stella-Rondo.

"Why, no, except he's got on some terrible-looking flesh-colored contraption I wouldn't be found dead in, is all I can see," I says.

"Never mind, you won't be found dead in it, because it happens to be part of my trousseau, and Mr. Whitaker took several dozen photographs of me in it," says Stella-Rondo. "What on earth could Uncle Rondo *mean* by wearing part of my trousseau out in the broad open daylight without saying so much as 'Kiss my foot,' *knowing* I only got home this morning after my separation and hung my negligee up on the bathroom door, just as nervous as I could be?"

"I'm sure I don't know, and what do you expect me to do about it?" I says. "Jump out the window?"

"No, I expect nothing of the kind. I simply declare that Uncle Rondo looks like a fool in it, that's all," she says. "It makes me sick to my stomach."

"Well, he looks as good as he can," I says. "As good as anybody in reason could." I stood up for Uncle Rondo, please remember. And I said to Stella-Rondo, "I think I would do well not to criticize so freely if I were you and came home with a two-year-old child I had never said a word about, and no explanation whatever about my separation."

"I asked you the instant I entered this house not to refer one more time to my adopted child, and you gave me your word of honor you would not," was all Stella-Rondo would say, and started pulling out every one of her eyebrows with some cheap Kress tweezers.

So I merely slammed the door behind me and went down and made some green-tomato pickle. Somebody had to do it. Of course Mama had turned both the Negroes loose; she always said no earthly power could hold one anyway on the Fourth of July, so she wouldn't even try. It turned out that Jaypan fell in the lake and came within a very narrow limit of drowning.

So Mama trots in. Lifts up the lid and says, "H'm! Not very good for your Uncle Rondo in his precarious condition, I must say. Or poor little adopted Shirley-T. Shame on you!"

That made me tired. I says, "Well, Stella-Rondo had better thank her lucky stars it was her instead of me came trotting in with that very peculiar-looking child. Now if it had been me that trotted in from Illinois and brought a peculiar-looking child of two, I shudder to think of the reception I'd of got, much less controlled the diet of an entire family."

"But you must remember, Sister, that you were never married to Mr. Whitaker in the first place and didn't go up to Illinois to live," says Mama, shaking a spoon in my face. "If you had I would of been just as overjoyed to see you and your little adopted girl as I was to see Stella-Rondo, when you wound up with your separation and came on back home."

"You would not," I says.

"Don't contradict me, I would," says Mama.

But I said she couldn't convince me though she talked till she was blue in the face. Then I said, "Besides, you know as well as I do that that child is not adopted."

"She most certainly is adopted," says Mama, stiff as a poker.

I says, "Why, Mama, Stella-Rondo had her just as sure as anything in this world, and just too stuck up to admit it."

"Why, Sister," said Mama. "Here I thought we were going to have a pleasant Fourth of July, and you start right out not believing a word your own baby sister tells you!"

"Just like Cousin Annie Flo. Went to her grave denying the facts of life," I remind Mama.

"I told you if you ever mentioned Annie Flo's name I'd slap your face," says Mama, and slaps my face.

"All right, you wait and see," I says.

"I," says Mama, "*I* prefer to take my children's word for anything when it's humanly possible." You ought to see Mama, she weighs two hundred pounds and has real tiny feet.

Just then something perfectly horrible occurred to me.

"Mama," I says, "can that child talk?" I simply had to whisper! "Mama, I wonder if that child can be—you know—in any way? Do you realize," I says, "that she hasn't spoken one single, solitary word to a human being up to this minute? This is the way she looks," I says, and I looked like this.

Well, Mama and I just stood there and stared at each other. It was horrible!

"I remember well that Joe Whitaker frequently drank like a fish," says Mama. "I believed to my soul he drank *chemicals*." And without another word she marches to the foot of the stairs and calls Stella-Rondo.

"Stella-Rondo? O-o-o-o-o! Stella-Rondo!"

"What?" says Stella-Rondo from upstairs. Not even the grace to get up off the bed.

"Can that child of yours talk?" asks Mama.

Stella-Rondo says, "Can she what?"

"Talk! Talk!" says Mama. "Burdyburdyburdyburdy!"

So Stella-Rondo yells back, "Who says she can't talk?"

"Sister says so," says Mama.

"You didn't have to tell me, I know whose word of honor don't mean a thing in this house," says Stella-Rondo.

And in a minute the loudest Yankee voice I ever heard in my life yells out, "OE'm Pop-OE the Sailor-r-r-r Ma-a-an!" and then somebody jumps up and down the upstairs hall. In another second the house would of fallen down.

"Not only talks she can tap-dance!" calls Stella-Rondo. "Which is more than some people I won't name can do."

"Why, the little precious darling thing!" Mama says, so surprised. "Just as smart as she can be!" Starts talking baby talk right there. Then she turns on me. "Sister, you ought to be thoroughly ashamed! Run upstairs this instant and apologize to Stella-Rondo and Shirley-T."

"Apologize for what?" I says. "I merely wondered if the child was normal, that's all. Now that she's proved she is, why, I have nothing further to say."

But Mama just turned on her heel and flew out, furious. She ran right upstairs and hugged the baby. She believed it was adopted. Stella-Rondo hadn't done a thing but turn her against me from upstairs while I stood there helpless over the hot stove. So that made Mama, Papa-Daddy and the baby all on Stella-Rondo's side.

Next, Uncle Rondo.

I must say that Uncle Rondo has been marvelous to me at various times in the past and I was completely unprepared to be made to jump out of my skin, the way it turned out. Once Stella-Rondo did something perfectly horrible to him—broke a chain letter from Flanders Field—and he took the radio back he had given her and gave it to me. Stella-Rondo was furious! For six months we all had to call her Stella instead of Stella-Rondo, or she wouldn't answer. I always thought Uncle Rondo had all the brains of the entire family. Another time he sent me to Mammoth Cave, with all expenses paid.

But this would be the day he was drinking that prescription, the Fourth of July.

So at supper Stella-Rondo speaks up and says she thinks Uncle Rondo ought to try to eat a little something. So finally Uncle Rondo said he would try a little cold biscuits and ketchup, but that was all. So *she* brought it to him.

"Do you think it wise to disport with ketchup in Stella-Rondo's flesh-colored kimono?" I says. Trying to be considerate! If Stella-Rondo couldn't watch out for her trousseau, somebody had to.

"Any objections?" asks Uncle Rondo, just about to pour out all the ketchup.

"Don't mind what she says, Uncle Rondo," says Stella-Rondo. "Sister has been devoting this solid afternoon to sneering out my bedroom window at the way you look."

"What's that?" says Uncle Rondo. Uncle Rondo has got the most terrible temper in the world. Anything is liable to make him tear the house down if it comes at the wrong time.

So Stella-Rondo says, "Sister says, 'Uncle Rondo certainly does look like a fool in that pink kimono!'"

Do you remember who it was really said that?

Uncle Rondo spills out all the ketchup and jumps out of his chair and tears off the kimono and throws it down on the dirty floor and puts his foot on it. It had to be sent all the way to Jackson to the cleaners and re-pleated.

"So that's your opinion of your Uncle Rondo, is it?" he says. "I look like a fool, do I? Well, that's the last straw. A whole day in this house with nothing to do, and then to hear you come out with a remark like that behind my back!"

"I didn't say any such of a thing, Uncle Rondo," I says, "and I'm not saying who did, either. Why, I think you look all right. Just try to take care of yourself and not talk and eat at the same time," I says. "I think you better go lie down."

"Lie down my foot," says Uncle Rondo. I ought to of known by that he was fixing to do something perfectly horrible.

So he didn't do anything that night in the precarious state he was in—just played Casino with Mama and Stella-Rondo and Shirley-T. and gave Shirley-T. a nickel with a head on both sides.

It tickled her nearly to death, and she called him "Papa." But at 6:30 A.M. the next morning, he threw a whole five-cent package of some unsold one-inch firecrackers from the store as hard as he could into my bedroom and they every one went off. Not one bad one in the string. Anybody else, there'd be one that wouldn't go off.

Well, I'm just terribly susceptible to noise of any kind, the doctor has always told me I was the most sensitive person he had ever seen in his whole life, and I was simply prostrated. I couldn't eat! People tell me they heard it as far as the cemetery, and old Aunt Jep Patterson, that had been holding her own so good, thought it was Judgment Day and she was going to meet her whole family. It's usually so quiet here.

And I'll tell you it didn't take me any longer than a minute to make up my mind what to do. There I was with the whole entire house on Stella-Rondo's side and turned against me. If I have anything at all I have pride.

So I just decided I'd go straight down to the P.O. There's plenty of room there in the back, I says to myself.

Well! I made no bones about letting the family catch on to what I was up to. I didn't try to conceal it.

The first thing they knew, I marched in where they were all playing Old Maid and pulled the electric oscillating fan out by the plug, and everything got real hot. Next I snatched the pillow I'd done the needlepoint on right off the davenport from behind Papa-Daddy. He went "Ugh!" I beat Stella-Rondo up the stairs and finally found my charm bracelet in her bureau drawer under a picture of Nelson Eddy.

"So that's the way the land lies," says Uncle Rondo. There he was, piecing on the ham. "Well, Sister, I'll be glad to donate my army cot if you got any place to set it up, providing you'll leave right this minute and let me get some peace." Uncle Rondo was in France.

"Thank you kindly for the cot and 'peace' is hardly the word I would select if I had to resort to firecrackers at 6:30 A.M. in a young girl's bedroom," I says back to him. "And as to where I intend to go, you seem to forget my position as postmistress of China Grove, Mississippi," I says. "I've always got the P.O."

Well, that made them all sit up and take notice.

I went out front and started digging up some four-o'clocks to plant around the P.O.

"Ah-ah-ah!" says Mama, raising the window. "Those happen to be my four-o'clocks. Everything planted in that star is mine. I've never known you to make anything grow in your life."

"Very well," I says. "But I take the fern. Even you, Mama, can't stand there and deny that I'm the one watered that fern. And I happen to know where I can send in a box top and get a packet of one thousand mixed seeds, no two the same kind, free."

"Oh, where?" Mama wants to know.

But I says, "Too late. You 'tend to your house, and I'll 'tend to mine. You hear things like that all the time if you know how to listen to the radio. Perfectly marvelous offers. Get anything you want free."

So I hope to tell you I marched in and got that radio, and they could of all bit a nail in two, especially Stella-Rondo, that it used to belong to, and she well knew she couldn't get it back, I'd sue for it like a shot. And I very politely took the sewing-machine motor I helped pay the most on to give Mama for Christmas back in 1929, and a good big calendar, with the first-aid remedies on it. The thermometer and the Hawaiian ukulele certainly were rightfully mine, and I stood on the step-ladder and got all my watermelon-rind preserves and every fruit and vegetable I'd put up, every jar. Then I began to pull the tacks out of the bluebird wall vases on the archway to the dining room.

"Who told you you could have those, Miss Priss?" says Mama, fanning as hard as she could.

"I bought 'em and I'll keep track of 'em," I says. "I'll tack 'em up one on each side the post-office window, and you can see 'em when you come to ask me for your mail, if you're so dead to see 'em."

"Not I! I'll never darken the door to that post office again if I live to be a hundred," Mama says. "Ungrateful child! After all the money we spent on you at the Normal."

"Me either," says Stella-Rondo. "You can just let my mail lie there and *rot*, for all I care. I'll never come and relieve you of a single, solitary piece."

"I should worry," I says. "And who you think's going to sit down and write you all those big fat letters and postcards, by the way?

Mr. Whitaker? Just because he was the only man ever dropped down in China Grove and you got him—unfairly—is he going to sit down and write you a lengthy correspondence after you come home giving no rhyme nor reason whatsoever for your separation and no explanation of the presence of that child? I may not have your brilliant mind, but I fail to see it."

So Mama says, "Sister, I've told you a thousand times that Stella-Rondo simply got homesick, and this child is far too big to be hers," and she says, "Now, why don't you all just sit down and play Casino?"

Then Shirley-T. sticks out her tongue at me in this perfectly horrible way. She has no more manners than the man in the moon. I told her she was going to cross her eyes like that some day and they'd stick.

"It's too late to stop me now," I says. "You should have tried that yesterday. I'm going to the P.O. and the only way you can possibly see me is to visit me there."

So Papa-Daddy says, "You'll never catch me setting foot in that post office, even if I should take a notion into my head to write a letter some place." He says, "I won't have you reachin' out of that little old window with a pair of shears and cuttin' off any beard of mine. I'm too smart for you!"

"We all are," says Stella-Rondo.

But I said, "If you're so smart, where's Mr. Whitaker?"

So then Uncle Rondo says, "I'll thank you from now on to stop reading all the orders I get on postcards and telling everybody in China Grove what you think is the matter with them," but I says, "I draw my own conclusions and will continue in the future to draw them." I says, "If people want to write their inmost secrets on penny postcards, there's nothing in the wide world you can do about it, Uncle Rondo."

"And if you think we'll ever *write* another postcard you're sadly mistaken," says Mama.

"Cutting off your nose to spite your face then," I says."But if you're all determined to have no more to do with the U.S. mail, think of this: What will Stella-Rondo do now, if she wants to tell Mr. Whitaker to come after her?"

"Wah!" says Stella-Rondo. I knew she'd cry. She had a conniption fit right there in the kitchen.

"It will be interesting to see how long she holds out," I says. "And now—I am leaving."

"Good-bye," says Uncle Rondo.

"Oh, I declare," says Mama, "to think that a family of mine should quarrel on the Fourth of July, or the day after, over Stella-Rondo leaving old Mr. Whitaker and having the sweetest little adopted child! It looks like we'd all be glad!"

"Wah!" says Stella-Rondo, and has a fresh conniption fit.

"*He* left *her*—you mark my words," I says. "That's Mr. Whitaker. I know Mr. Whitaker. After all, I knew him first. I said from the beginning he'd up and leave her. I foretold every single thing that's happened."

"Where did he go?" asks Mama.

"Probably to the North Pole, if he knows what's good for him," I says.

But Stella-Rondo just bawled and wouldn't say another word. She flew to her room and slammed the door.

"Now look what you've gone and done, Sister," says Mama. "You go apologize."

"I haven't got time, I'm leaving," I says.

"Well, what are you waiting around for?" asks Uncle Rondo.

So I just picked up the kitchen clock and marched off, without saying "Kiss my foot" or anything, and never did tell Stella-Rondo good-bye.

There was a girl going along on a little wagon right in front.

"Girl," I says, "come help me haul these things down the hill, I'm going to live in the post office."

Took her nine trips in her express wagon. Uncle Rondo came out on the porch and threw her a nickel.

And that's the last I've laid eyes on any of my family or my family laid eyes on me for five solid days and nights. Stella-Rondo may be telling the most horrible tales in the world about Mr. Whitaker, but I haven't heard them. As I tell everybody, I draw my own conclusions.

But oh, I like it here. It's ideal, as I've been saying. You see, I've got everything cater-cornered, the way I like it. Hear the radio? All the war news. Radio, sewing machine, book ends, ironing board and that great big piano lamp—peace, that's what I like. Butterbean vines planted all along the front where the strings are.

Of course, there's not much mail. My family are naturally the main people in China Grove, and if they prefer to vanish from the face of the earth, for all the mail they get or the mail they write, why, I'm not going to open my mouth. Some of the folks here in town are taking up for me and some turned against me. I know which is which. There are always people who will quit buying stamps just to get on the right side of Papa-Daddy.

But here I am, and here I'll stay. I want the world to know I'm happy.

And if Stella-Rondo should come to me this minute, on bended knees, and *attempt* to explain the incidents of her life with Mr. Whitaker, I'd simply put my fingers in both my ears and refuse to listen.

Almos' a Man

RICHARD WRIGHT

DAVE STRUCK OUT across the fields, looking homeward through paling light. Whut's the usa talkin wid em niggers in the field? Anyhow, his mother was putting supper on the table. Them niggers can't understan nothing. One of these days he was going to get a gun and practice shooting, then they can't talk to him as though he was a little boy. He slowed, looking at the ground. Shucks, Ah ain scareda them even ef they are biggern me! Aw, Ah know whut Ahma do. . . . Ahm going by ol Joe's sto n git that Sears Roebuck catlog n look at them guns. Mabbe Ma will lemme buy one when she gits mah pay from ol man Hawkins. Ahma beg her t gimme some money. Ahm ol ernough to hava gun. Ahm seventeen. Almos a man. He strode, feeling his long, loose-jointed limbs. Shucks, a man oughta hava little gun aftah he done worked hard all day. . . .

He came in sight of Joe's store. A yellow lantern glowed on the front porch. He mounted steps and went through the screen door, hearing it bang behind him. There was a strong smell of coal oil and mackerel fish. He felt very confident until he saw fat Joe walk in through the rear door, then his courage began to ooze.

"Howdy, Dave! Whatcha want?"

"How yuh, Mistah Joe? Aw, Ah don wanna buy nothing. Ah jus wanted t see ef yuhd lemme look at tha ol catlog erwhile."

"Sure! You wanna see it here?"

"Nawsuh. Ah wans t take it home wid me. Ahll bring it back termorrow when Ah come in from the fiels."

"You plannin on buyin something?"

"Yessuh."

"Your ma letting you have your own money now?"

"Shucks. Mistah Joe, Ahm gittin t be a man like anybody else!"

240

Joe laughed and wiped his greasy white face with a red bandanna.

"Whut you plannin on buyin?"

Dave looked at the floor, scratched his head, scratched his thigh, and smiled. Then he looked up shyly.

"Ahll tell yuh, Mistah Joe, ef yuh promise yuh won't tell."

"I promise."

"Waal, Ahma buy a gun."

"A gun? Whut you want with a gun?"

"Ah wanna keep it."

"You ain't nothing but a boy. You don't need a gun."

"Aw, lemme have the catlog, Mistah Joe. Ahll bring it back."

Joe walked through the rear door. Dave was elated. He looked around at barrels of sugar and flour. He heard Joe coming back. He craned his neck to see if he were bringing the book. Yeah, he's got it! Gawddog, he's got it!

"Here, but be sure you bring it back. It's the only one I got."

"Sho, Mistah Joe."

"Say, if you wanna buy a gun, why don't you buy one from me? I gotta gun to sell."

"Will it shoot?"

"Sure it'll shoot."

"Whut kind is it?"

"Oh, it's kinda old. . . . A lefthand Wheeler. A pistol. A big one."

"Is it got bullets in it?"

"It's loaded."

"Kin Ah see it?"

"Where's your money?"

"Whut yuh wan fer it?"

"I'll let you have it for two dollars."

"Just two dollahs? Shucis, Ah could buy tha when Ah git mah pay."

"I'll have it here when you want it."

"Awright, suh. Ah be in fer it."

He went through the door, hearing it slam again behind him. Ahma git some money from Ma n buy me a gun! Only two dollahs! He tucked the thick catalogue under his arm and hurried.

"Where yuh been, boy?" His mother held a steaming dish of black-eyed peas.

"Aw, Ma, Ah jus stopped down the road t talk wid th boys."

"Yuh know bettah than t keep suppah waitin."

He sat down, resting the catalogue on the edge of the table.

"Yuh git up from there and git to the well n wash yosef! Ah ain feedin no hogs in mah house!"

She grabbed his shoulder and pushed him. He stumbled out of the room, then came back to get the catalogue.

"Whut this?"

"Aw, Ma, it's jusa catlog."

"Who yuh git it from?"

"From Joe, down at the sto."

"Waal, thas good. We kin use it around the house."

"Naw, Ma." He grabbed for it. "Gimme mah catlog, Ma." She held onto it and glared at him.

"Quit hollerin at me! Whut's wrong wid yuh? Yuh crazy?"

"But Ma, please. It ain mine! It's Joe's! He tol me t bring it back t im termorrow."

She gave up the book. He stumbled down the back steps, hugging the thick book under his arm. When he had splashed water on his face and hands, he groped back to the kitchen and fumbled in a corner for the towel. He bumped into a chair; it clattered to the floor. The catalogue sprawled at his feet. When he had dried his eyes, he snatched up the book and held it again under his arm. His mother stood watching him.

"Now, ef yuh gonna acka fool over that ol book, Ahll take it n burn it up."

"Naw, Ma, please."

"Waal, set down n be still!"

He sat down and drew the oil lamp close. He thumbed page after page, unaware of the food his mother set on the table. His father came in. Then his small brother.

"Whutcha got there, Dave?" his father asked.

"Jusa catlog," he answered, not looking up.

"Yawh, here they is!" His eyes glowed at blue and black revolvers. He glanced up, feeling sudden guilt. His father was watching him. He eased the book under the table and rested it on his knees. After the blessing was asked, he ate. He scooped up

peas and swallowed fat meat without chewing. Buttermilk helped
to wash it down. He did not want to mention money before his
father. He would do much better by cornering his mother when
she was alone. He looked at his father uneasily out of the edge of
his eye.

"Boy, how come yuh don quit foolin wid tha book n eat yo
suppah."

"Yessuh."

"How yuh n ol man Hawkins gittin erlong?"

"Shuh?"

"Can't yuh hear. Why don yuh listen? Ah ast yuh how wuz yuh
n ol man Hawkins gittin erlong?"

"Oh, swell, Pa. Ah plows mo lan than anybody over there."

"Waal, yuh oughta keep yo min on whut yuh doin."

"Yessuh."

He poured his plate full of molasses and sopped at it slowly
with a chunk of cornbread. When all but his mother had left the
kitchen he still sat and looked again at the guns in the catalogue.
Lawd, ef Ah only had the pretty one! He could almost feel the
slickness of the weapon with his fingers. If he had a gun like that
he would polish it and keep it shining so it would never rust. N
Ahd keep it loaded, by Gawd!

"Ma?"

"Hunh?"

"Ol man Hawkins give yuh mah money yit?"

"Yeah, but ain no usa yuh thinin bout thowin nona it erway.
Ahm keepin tha money sos yuh kin have cloes t go to school this
winter."

He rose and went to her side with the open catalogue in his
palms. She was washing dishes, her head bent low over a pan.
Shyly he raised the open book. When he spoke his voice was
husky, faint.

"Ma, Gawd knows Ah wans one of these."

"One of whut?" she asked, not raising her eyes.

"One of these," he said again, not daring even to point. She
glanced up at the page, then at him with wide eyes.

"Nigger, is yuh gone plum crazy?"

"Aw, Ma—"

"Git outta here! Don't yuh talk t me bout no gun! Yuh a fool!"

"Ma, Ah kin buy one fer two dollahs."

"Not ef Ah knows it yuh ain!"

"But yuh promised me one—"

"Ah don care whut Ah promised! Yuh ain nothing but a boy yit!"

"Ma, ef yuh lemme buy one Ahll never ast yuh fer nothing no mo."

"Ah tol yuh t git outta here! Yuh ain gonna toucha penny of tha money fer no gun! Thas how come Ah has Mistah Hawkins pay yo wages t me, cause Ah knows yuh ain got no sense."

"But Ma, we needa gun. Pa ain got no gun. We needa gun in the house. Yuh kin never tell whut might happen."

"Now don yuh try to maka fool outta me, boy! Ef we did hava gun yuh wouldn't have it!"

He laid the catalogue down and slipped his arm around her waist. "Aw, Ma, Ah done worked hard alls summer n ain ast yuh fer nothing, is Ah, now?"

"Thas whut yuh spose t do!"

"But Ma. Ah wants a gun. Yuh kin lemme have two dollah outa mah money. Please Ma. I kin give it to Pa. . . . Please, Ma! Ah loves yuh, Ma."

When she spoke her voice came soft and low.

"What yuh wan wida gun, Dave? Yuh don need no gun. Yuhll git in trouble. N ef yo Pa jus thought Ah letyuh have money t buy a gun he'd hava fit."

"Ahll hide it, Ma. It ain't but two dollahs."

"Lawd, chil, whuts wrong wid yuh?"

"Ain nothing wrong, Ma. Ahm almos a man now. Ah wants a gun."

"Who gonna sell yuh a gun?"

"Ol Joe at the sto."

"N it don cos but two dollahs?"

"Thas all, Ma. Just two dollahs. Please, Ma."

She was stacking the plates away; her hands moved slowly, reflectively. Dave kept an anxious silence. Finally she turned to him.

"Ahll let yuh git the gun ef yuh promise me one thing."

"Whuts tha, Ma?"

"Yuh bring it straight back t me, yuh hear? It'll be fer Pa."

"Yessum! Lemme go now, Ma."

She stooped, turned slightly to one side, raised the hem of her dress, rolled down the top of her stocking, and came up with a slender wad of bills.

"Here," she said. "Lawd knows yuh don need no gun. But yer Pa does. Yuh bring it right back t me, yuh hear. Ahma put it up. Now ef yuh don, Ahma have yuh Pa lick yuh so hard yuh won ferget it."

"Yessum."

He took the money, ran down the steps, and across the yard.

"Dave! Yuuuuuuh Daaaaaave!"

He heard, but he was not going to stop now. "Naw, Lawd!"

The first movement he made the following morning was to reach under his pillow for the gun. In the gray light of dawn he held it loosely, feeling a sense of power. Could killa man wida gun like this. Kill anybody, black or white. And if he were holding this gun in his hand nobody could run over him; they would have to respect him. It was a big gun, with a long barrel and a heavy handle. He raised and lowered it in his hand, marveling at its weight.

He had not come straight home with it as his mother had asked; instead he had stayed out in the fields, holding the weapon in his hand, aiming it now and then at some imaginary foe. But he had not fired it; he had been afraid that his father might hear. Also he was not sure he knew how to fire it.

To avoid surrendering the pistol he had not come into the house until he knew that all were asleep. When his mother had tiptoed to his bedside late that night and demanded the gun, he had first played 'possum; then he had told her that the gun was hidden outdoors, that he would bring it to her in the morning. Now he lay turning it slowly in his hands. He broke it, took out the cartridges, felt them, and then put them back.

He slid out of bed, got a long strip of old flannel from a trunk, wrapped the gun in it, and tied it to his naked thigh while it was still loaded. He did not go in to breakfast. Even though it was not yet daylight, he started for Jim Hawkins's plantation. Just as the sun was rising he reached the barns where the mules and plows were kept.

"Hey! That you, Dave?"

He turned. Jim Hawkins stood eyeing him suspiciously.

"What're yuh doing here so early?"

"Ah didn't know Ah wuz gettin up so early, Mistah Hawkins. Ah wuz fixin t hitch up ol Jenny n take her t the fiels."

"Good. Since you're here so early, how about plowing that stretch down by the woods?"

"Suits me, Mistah Hawkins."

"O.K. Go to it!"

He hitched Jenny to a plow and started across the fields. Hot dog! This was just what he wanted. If he could get down by the woods, he could shoot his gun and nobody would hear. He walked behind the plow, hearing the traces creaking, feeling the gun tied tight to his thigh.

When he reached the woods, he plowed two whole rows before he decided to take out the gun. Finally he stopped, looked in all directions, then untied the gun and held it in his hand. He turned to the mule and smiled.

"Know whut this is, Jenny? Naw, yuh wouldn't know! Yuhs jusa ol mule! Anyhow, this is a gun, n it kin shoot, by Gawd!"

He held the gun at arm's length. Whut t hell, Ahma shoot this thing! He looked at Jenny again.

"Lissen here, Jenny! When Ah pull this ol trigger Ah don wan yuh t run n acka fool now."

Jenny stood with head down, her short ears pricked straight. Dave walked off about twenty feet, held the gun far out from him, at arm's length, and turned his head. Hell, he told himself, Ah ain afraid. The gun felt loose in his fingers; he waved it wildly for a moment. Then he shut his eyes and tightened his forefinger. Bloom! The report half-deafened him and he thought his right hand was torn from his arm. He heard Jenny whinnying and galloping over the field, and he found himself on his knees squeezing his fingers hard between his legs. His hand was numb; he jammed it into his mouth, trying to warm it, trying to stop the pain. The gun lay at his feet. He did not quite know what had happened. He stood up and stared at the gun as though it were a living thing. He gritted his teeth and kicked the gun. Yuh almos broke mah arm! He turned to look for Jenny; she was far over the fields, tossing her head and kicking wildly.

"Hol on there, ol mule!"

When he caught up with her she stood trembling, walling her

big white eyes at him. The plow was far away; the traces had broken. Then Dave stopped short, looking, not believing. Jenny was bleeding. Her left side was red and wet with blood. He went closer. Lawd, have mercy! Wondah did Ah shoot this mule? He grabbed for Jenny's mane. She flinched, snorted, whirled, tossing her head.

"Hol on now! Hol on."

Then he saw the hole in Jenny's side, right between the ribs. It was round, wet, red. A crimson stream streaked down the front leg, flowing fast. Good Gawd! Ah wuzn't shooting at tha mule. He felt panic. He knew he had to stop that blood, or Jenny would bleed to death. He had never seen so much blood in all his life. He chased the mule for half a mile, trying to catch her. Finally she stopped, breathing hard, stumpy tail half arched. He caught her mane and led her back to where the plow and gun lay. Then he stooped and grabbed handfuls of damp black earth and tried to plug the bullet hole. Jenny shuddered, whinnied, and broke from him.

"Hol on! Hol on now!"

He tried to plug it again, but blood came anyhow. His fingers were hot and sticky. He rubbed dirt into his palms, trying to dry them. Then again he attempted to plug the bullet hole, but Jenny shied away, kicking her heels high. He stood helpless. He had to do something. He ran at Jenny; she dodged him. He watched a red stream of blood flow down Jenny's leg and form a bright pool at her feet.

"Jenny... Jenny..." he called weakly.

His lips trembled! She's bleeding t death! He looked in the direction of home, wanting to go back, wanting to get help. But he saw the pistol lying in the damp black clay. He had a queer feeling that if he only did something, this would not be; Jenny would not be there bleeding to death.

When he went to her this time, she did not move. She stood with sleepy, dreamy eyes; and when he touched her she gave a low-pitched whinny and knelt to the ground, her front knees slopping in blood.

"Jenny... Jenny..." he whispered.

For a long time she held her neck erect; then her head sank, slowly. Her ribs swelled with a mighty heave and she went over.

Dave's stomach felt empty, very empty. He picked up the gun and held it gingerly between his thumb and forefinger. He buried it at the foot of a tree. He took a stick and tried to cover the pool of blood with dirt—but what was the use? There was Jenny lying with her mouth open and her eyes walled and glassy. He could not tell Jim Hawkins he had shot his mule. But he had to tell him something. Yeah, Ahll tell em Jenny started gittin wil n fell on the joint of the plow. . . . But that would hardly happen to a mule. He walked across the field slowly, head down.

It was sunset. Two of Jim Hawkins's men were over near the edge of the woods digging a hole in which to bury Jenny. Dave was surrounded by a knot of people; all of them were looking down at the dead mule.

"I don't see how in the world it happened," said Jim Hawkins for the tenth time.

The crowd parted and Dave's mother, father, and small brother pushed into the center.

"Where Dave?" his mother called.

"There he is," said Jim Hawkins.

His mother grabbed him.

"Whut happened, Dave? Whut yuh done?"

"Nothing."

"C'mon, boy, talk," his father said.

Dave took a deep breath and told the story he knew nobody believed.

"Waal," he drawled. "Ah brung ol Jenny down here sos Ah could do mah plowin. Ah plowed bout two rows, just like yuh see." He stopped and pointed at the long rows of upturned earth. "Then something musta been wrong wid ol Jenny. She wouldn't ack right a-tall. She started snortin n kickin her heels. An tried to hol her, but she pulled erway, rearin n goin on. Then when the point of the plow was stickin up in the air, she swung erroun n twisted herself back on it. . . . She stuck herself n started t bleed. N fo Ah could do anything, she wuz dead."

"Did you ever hear of anything like that in all your life?" asked Jim Hawkins.

There were white and black standing in the crowd. They murmured. Dave's mother came close to him and looked hard into his face.

"Tell the truth, Dave," she said.

"Looks like a bullet hole ter me," said one man.

"Dave, whut yuh do wid tha gun?" his mother asked.

The crowd surged in, looking at him. He jammed his hands into his pockets, shook his head slowly from left to right, and backed away. His eyes were wide and painful.

"Did he hava gun?" asked Jim Hawkins.

"By Gawd, Ah tol yuh tha wuz a gunwound," said a man, slapping his thigh.

His father caught his shoulders and shook him till his teeth rattled.

"Tell whut happened, yuh rascal! Tell whut..."

Dave looked at Jenny's stiff legs and began to cry.

"Whut yuh do wid tha gun?" his mother asked.

"Come on and tell the truth," said Hawkins. "Ain't nobody going to hurt you...."

His mother crowded close to him.

"Did yuh shoot tha mule, Dave?"

Dave cried, seeing blurred white and black faces.

"Ahh ddinnt gggo tt sshoooot hher.... Ah ssswear ffo Gawd Ahh ddint.... Ah wuz a-tryin t sssee ef the old gggun would sshoot—"

"Where yuh git the gun from?" his father asked.

"Ah got it from Joe, at the sto."

"Where yuh git the money?"

"Ma give it t me."

"He kept worryin me, Bob.... Ah had t.... Ah tol im t bring the gun right back t me.... It was fer yuh, the gun."

"But how yuh happen to shoot that mule?" asked Jim Hawkins.

"Ah wuznt shootin at the mule, Mistah Hawkins. The gun jumped when Ah pulled the trigger... N fo Ah knowed anything Jenny wuz there a-bleedin."

Somebody in the crowd laughed. Jim Hawkins walked close to Dave and looked into his face.

"Well, looks like you have bought you a mule, Dave."

"Ah swear fo Gawd, Ah didn't go t kill the mule, Mistah Hawkins!"

"But you killed her!"

All the crowd was laughing now. They stood on tiptoe and poked heads over one another's shoulders.

"Well, boy, looks like yuh done bought a dead mule! Hahaha!"

"Ain tha ershame."

"Hohohohoho."

Dave stood, head down, twisting his feet in the dirt.

"Well, you needn't worry about it, Bob," said Jim Hawkins to Dave's father. "Just let the boy keep on working and pay me two dollars a month."

"Whut yuh wan fer yo mule, Mistah Hawkins?"

Jim Hawkins screwed up his eyes.

"Fifty dollars."

"Whut yuh do wid tha gun?" Dave's father demanded.

Dave said nothing.

"Yuh wan me t take a tree lim n beat yuh till yuh talk!"

"Nawsuh!"

"Whut yuh do wid it?"

"Ah thowed it erway."

"Where?"

"Ah . . . Ah thowed it in the creek."

"Waal, c mon home. N firs thing in the mawnin git to tha creek n fin tha gun."

"Yessuh."

"Whut yuh pay fer it?"

"Two dollahs."

"Take tha gun n git yo money back n carry it t Mistah Hawkins, yuh hear? N don fergit Ahma lam you black bottom good fer this! Now march yosef on home, suh!"

Dave turned and walked slowly. He heard people laughing. Dave glared, his eyes welling with tears. Hot anger bubbled in him. Then he swallowed and stumbled on.

That night Dave did not sleep. He was glad that he had gotten out of killing the mule so easily, but he was hurt. Something hot seemed to turn over inside him each time he remembered how they had laughed. He tossed on his bed, feeling his hard pillow. N Pa says he's gonna beat me. . . . He remembered other beatings, and his back quivered. Naw, naw, Ah sho don wan im t beat me tha way no mo. . . . Dam em all! Nobody ever gave him anything. All he did was work. They treat me lika mule. . . . N then they beat me. . . . He gritted his teeth. N Ma had t tell on me.

Well, if he had to, he would take old man Hawkins that two

dollars. But that meant selling the gun. And he wanted to keep that gun. Fifty dollahs fer a dead mule.

He turned over, thinking how he had fired the gun. He had an itch to fire it again. Ef other men kin shoota gun, by Gawd, Ah kin! He was still listening. Mebbe they all sleepin now. . . . The house was still. He heard the soft breathing of his brother. Yes, now! He would go down an get that gun and see if he could fire it! He eased out of bed and slipped into overalls.

The moon was bright. He ran almost all the way to the edge of the woods. He stumbled over the ground, looking for the spot where he had buried the gun. Yeah, here it is. Like a hungry dog scratching for a bone he pawed it up. He puffed his black cheeks and blew dirt from the trigger and barrel. He broke it and found four cartridges unshot. He looked around; the fields were filled with silence and moonlight. He clutched the gun stiff and hard in his fingers. But as soon as he wanted to pull the trigger, he shut his eyes and turned his head. Naw, Ah can't shoot wid mah eyes closed n mah head turned. With effort he held his eyes open; then he squeezed. Blooooom! He was stiff, not breathing. The gun was still in his hands. Dammit, he'd done it! He fired again. Bloooom! He smiled. Bloooom! Blooooom! Click, click. There! It was empty. If anybody could shoot a gun, he could. He put the gun into his hip pocket and started across the fields.

When he reached the top of a ridge he stood straight and proud in the moonlight, looking at Jim Hawkins's big white house, feeling the gun sagging in his pocket. Lawd, ef Ah had jus one mo bullet Ahd taka shot at tha house. Ahd like t scare ol man Hawkins jussa little. . . . Jussa enough t let im know Dave Sanders is a man.

To his left the road curved, running to the tracks of the Illinois Central. He jerked his head, listening. From far off came a faint hoooof-hoooof; hoooof-hoooof; hoooof-hoooof. . . . That's number eight. He took a swift look at Jim Hawkins's white house; he thought of Pa, of Ma, of his little brother, and the boys. He thought of the dead mule and heard hooof-hooof; hooof-hooof; hooof-hooof. . . . He stood rigid. Two dollahs a mont. Les see now . . . Tha means itll take bout two years. Shucks! Ahll be dam! He started down the road, toward the tracks. Yeah, here she comes! He stood beside the track and held himself stiffly. Here she comes, erroun the ben. . . . C mon, yuh slow poke! C mon! He had his hand on his gun; something quivered in his stomach. Then the train thundered past, the gray and brown boxcars rumbling and clinking. He gripped the gun tightly; then he jerked his hand out of his pocket. Ah betcha Bill wouldn't do it! Ah betcha. . . . The cars slid past, steel grinding upon steel. Ahm riding yuh ternight so hep me Gawd! He was hot all over. He hesitated just a moment; then he grabbed, pulled atop of a car, and lay flat. He felt his pocket; the gun was still there. Ahead the long rails were glinting in moonlight, stretching away, away to somewhere, somewhere where he could be a man. . . .

Two

NONFICTION

Have We Overcome?

LERONE BENNETT, JR.

I HAVE BEEN AWAY from this state for a long time, and I hope you will permit me a personal remark or two. I grew up in this state in the thirties and forties when this institution was closed to me, and to my people, and when Mississippi occupied a position in the western world roughly equivalent to the position of South Africa today. And as I stand here tonight,* I am reminded of Richard Wright and the other great sons and daughters of Mississippi who were lost to this state and this region because of that situation. And I am reminded also of other great sons and daughters of Mississippi—the James Merediths, the Fannie Lou Hamers, the Aaron Henrys, the Margaret Walker Alexanders, the brave children of SNCC—who stayed here and fought the good fight in the hope that Mississippi would one day come into its own and recognize its own. And it seems to me that whatever the difficulties of the moment, or the magnitude of the obstacles, that we should always remember the brave and beautiful few who brought us thus far along the way. For if it was possible for them to change what they changed in Mississippi, then there is absolutely no limit to what we can dream and hope.

It is in this connection, and in the context of what has been done, and what remains to be done, that I am reminded of the story of a group of people who sought a great prize that was across a deep river, up a steep mountain, on the far side of an uncharted sea. The task before them was almost impossible, but they were a brave people, and history had given them big hearts. And so they embarked, in the white of the night, and reached the middle of the river, where a great storm arose. The storm lashed their little

*Paper presented at the 1978 Chancellor's Symposium on Southern History at the University of Mississippi

boat and washed many overboard, but they managed somehow to reach the other side, losing many of their friends on the way. When the boat touched dry land, they held a symposium of sorts, and a select group went to the captain and said: "We did a great thing in crossing that river, and we believe we will dig in and rest for a while in this new and desegregated place." And the captain said: "This thing that you did in crossing the river was splendidly done, and deserves praise. But there is no rest for us, or safety, short of the grail freedom. So sing, shout, and rap tonight, for tomorrow the journey continues. *We crossed a river, and now we've got to cross a sea.*"

The words speak to us all. They speak to white Americans, who crossed many rivers in the last two hundred years, and now face the necessary task of reinventing themselves in a world that is overwhelmingly red, brown, and black.

We crossed a river, and now we've got to cross a sea.

The words speak to black Americans, who crossed ten thousand Jordans in the years of the movement and who now face the necessity of dealing with the gravest crisis we have faced as a people since the end of slavery time.

We crossed a river, and now we've got to cross a sea.

The words speak to us all, and define us all. And it is within the context of these words that I approach the topic assigned me tonight:

"Have we overcome?"

I could, and should, say no and sit down and save your time. But this is a scholarly setting, and a scholarly no requires—I am told—at least one hour of disputation and on-the-other-handing. Let me try then to earn my keep, and let me begin by questioning the question.

The question is have we overcome?

And my question is how are we to understand that dangerous word *we?*

And what does it mean *to overcome?*

Well, in the context of the song and the struggle, *we* means black people and—watch this interpretation—white people who are committed to and involved in the struggle for equality and racial justice. And *to overcome*, again in the context of the song and the struggle, means the act of transcending and destroying all racial barriers and creating a new land of freedom and equality for all men, all women, and all children.

"Oh, deep in my heart I do believe we shall overcome," we shall overpass, triumph over mean sheriffs, robed riders, assassins of the spirit, segregation, discrimination, hunger, poverty, and humiliation.

Have we done it? No, a thousand times no.

We were there, some of us, and we sang the song, some of us, and saw the blood, some of us. And we know—deep in our hearts—that what the singers and dreamers and victims hoped for . . . what they struggled and died for . . . has not happened yet. Because of the passion and the pain of the singers and victims and dreamers, we have, in the past twenty-four years, crossed many barriers . . . but we are nowhere near the end of our journey, and we have miles to go before we sleep.

And so, it is necessary to say here, in the name of the dreamers and victims, that we have not yet started the process of grappling with the depth and the height of the dream. As a matter of fact, we haven't even defined what we must do in order to overcome. To city only one point, the admission of a handful of gifted black students and athletes to a white university in which all the lines of authority and power are still controlled by whites is not—repeat—*not* integration. It is at best desegregation and a prelude, perhaps a necessary prelude, to that great American dream which was written down on pieces of paper, which was promised, and which has never existed anywhere in America, except in the hearts of a handful of men and women.

By any reasonable standard, then, we have failed to meet the goal. And to understand the magnitude of our failure, and the dangers that failure poses to all Americans, it would be helpful, I think, to go back for a moment to the beginning, to Monday, May 17, 1954, when some man believed the millennium was around the next turning.

According to news reports of that day, the Supreme Court decision was immediately hailed by a wide variety of black voices as "a second emancipation proclamation," which was, in the words of the *Chicago Defender,* "more important to our democracy than the atom bomb or the hydrogen bomb." In Farmville,

Virginia, for example, a sixteen-year-old student named Barbara Trent burst into tears when her teacher interrupted class to announce the decision. "Our teacher told us," she told a reporter, "it may cost her her job... we went on studying history, but things weren't the same and will never be the same again."

There were, of course, cynics and dissenters, most notably Langston Hughes, who put the following words in the mouth of his fictional character, Simple:

White folks are proud, but I don't see nothing for them to be proud of just doing what they ought to do. If they was doing something extra, yes, then be proud. But Negroes have a right to go to decent schools just like everybody else. So what's there to be proud of in that they are just now letting us in. They ought to be ashamed of themselves for keeping us out so long. I might have had a good education myself had it not been for white folks. If they want something to be proud of let them pay me for the education I ain't got.

Simple's views were shared apparently by many blacks, but in the first flush of victory most people focused on the silver lining in the cloud. The most widely quoted man of the day was the architect of the victory, NAACP counsel Thurgood Marshall. Here is an excerpt from an interview with Marshall that appeared in the *New York Times* on Tuesday, May 18, 1954: "Mr. Marshall, asked how long he thought it would be before segregation in education was eliminated, replied it might be 'up to five years' for the entire country. He predicted that, by the time the 100th anniversary of the emancipation was observed in 1963, segregation in all its forms would have been eliminated from the nation."

Not only Marshall but significant sectors of the white population said the struggle would soon be over. Earl Warren recalled later that it was suggested at the Supreme Court that the processes set in motion on this day would be completed by the centennial of the Fourteenth Amendment—1966.

Thus America, thus the petitioners and dreamers, on a day of hope and triumph and innocence!

How remote, how unimaginably distant and remote that May day seems in this October of our years. The events of the intervening years—Montgomery, the sit-ins, the freedom rides, the marches, and urban rebellions—came so suddenly, so dramatically, that our sense of time has been distorted and incidents and personalities of only a few years ago have been pushed into the distant past.

For this reason, among others, it is difficult to put this period into proper perspective. For this reason, among others, it is difficult to orient and situate the young. It is a fact, worthy of long thought, that there is a whole generation of young blacks and whites who have never seen a Jim Crow sign and who express astonishment when told that they once existed.

The Jim Crow signs are gone now. There are black mayors in Alabama and black representatives in the Mississippi legislature, and there are children, and even some adults, who seem to believe that it has always been this way. But it hasn't always been this way, and it would be well for us to remember tonight that this October and the Octobers of yesterday are linked and separated by a great crossing and a great hope. During that crossing, a revolution . . . it is not too strong a word . . . in the courts and a rebellion in the streets destroyed the legal foundations of segregation and moved the racial dialogue to a new level.

The internal and external changes flowing from this event have been profound and dramatic. So have the costs. Martin Luther King, Jr., is dead; Malcolm X is dead. Whitney Young, Medgar Evers, Fred Hampton, James Earl Chaney, Viola Liuzzo, Fannie Lou Hamer, the four Birmingham girls: they are all dead. And the movement they led and symbolized has foundered on new realities.

What makes this all the more disconcerting is that the gains for which they died are threatened by a new mood of "backism" and reaction in white America. And there is the further fact that the gains of the green years, important as they were, did not go to the root of the matter, the neocolonial relations between the black and white communities of America and the institutionalized unfavorable balance of trade of black America.

It is true, and important, that blacks are going places today they couldn't go twenty-four years ago. *Everything, in fact, has changed in Mississippi and America, and yet, paradoxically, nothing has changed.*

Despite the court orders and civil rights laws, blacks are still the last hired and the first fired. They are still systematically exploited as consumers and citizens. To come right out with it, the full privileges and immunities of the U.S. Constitution do not apply to blacks tonight, in Mississippi or in Massachusetts, and they never have. You want to know how bad things are? Listen to the facts cited by Robert B. Hill of the National Urban League in a recent booklet, entitled *The Illusion of Black Progress*.

Contrary to popular belief, the economic gap between blacks and whites is widening. Between 1975 and 1976, the black to white family income ratio fell sharply from 62 to 59 percent.

Not only is black unemployment at its highest level today, but the jobless gap between blacks and whites is the widest it has ever been. . . .

The proportion of middle-income black families has not significantly increased. In fact, the proportion of black families with incomes above the labor department's intermediate budget level has remained at about one-fourth since 1972.

The proportion of upper-income black families has steadily declined. Between 1972 and 1976, the proportion of black families above the government's higher budget level dropped from 12 to 9 percent.

The two black societies thesis of a widening cleavage between middle-income and low-income blacks is not supported by national income data. The proportion of black families with incomes under $7,000, as well as those with incomes over $15,000, has remained relatively constant in recent years.

The statistical evidence strongly contradicts the popular belief that high unemployment among black youth is primarily due to their educational or skill deficiencies—when job opportunities are greater for white youth with lower educational attainment. White high school dropouts have lower unemployment rates (22.3%) than black youth with college education (27.2%).

These figures are terrible, and the reality is worse. How did this happen? How is it possible for black America to be in so much trouble after all the demonstrations, and marches, and court orders? What is the meaning of this terrible indictment?

The short answer to these questions is that we stopped marching too soon. The long . . . and scholarly . . . answer is embedded in the history of our journey.

We started out, twenty-four years ago, in the white of night. We crossed large bodies of water, marched day and night, were pushed back and advanced again, singing and shouting and stepping over the bodies of our brothers and sisters. By these methods . . . and others . . . we arrived, after indescribable anguish and pain, at this place.

But where precisely are we? What have we gained and lost? Did we go wrong somewhere? Or is this a necessary historical detour leading to a higher level of development. What, in short, is the meaning, the sense, the signification, of the twenty-four years of the great crossing struggle?

There can be no easy answer to that question, for we are too close to that event to situate it globally. But it is possible, indeed likely, that the post-*Brown* struggle, despite its limitations, was a necessary stage in the social maturation of black people. And there can be little doubt that it created black America's finest hours and one of the finest hours in the history of the republic.

It is fashionable nowadays to heap scorn on the old civil rights movement and the so-called "Hamburger War." But this is a misreading of the historical process that advances on the crest of succeeding waves, which rise and fall, over and over again, with the ebbing and flowing of the energies of the people. From this vantage point, history is a dialogue, and the movement of the last twenty-four years was a vast and leaping wave in a continuous flow of energy that started with the first revolt on the first slave ship and will not end until America deals with the revolutionary mandate of its birth.

Because of that struggle, we have made significant gains on the political front and in the middle sectors. The movement changed, destroyed, wiped out the visible and dramatic signs of racism, but it did not and perhaps could not at that time deal with the subtle forms of institutional racism. Nor did it change or even make a dent in the economic inequities of a society that can make work for black men inside prisons after they commit crimes but cannot find work for black men outside prisons before they commit crimes.

And so, as a result of the failure of the movement to make a total breakthrough on the racial front, we find ourselves tonight in the postrevolutionary phase of a revolution that never happened, the postrevolutionary phase of a revolution that turned sour because it could not be accomplished historically at that particular time under the prevailing ratio of forces.

Does this mean that the movement was a failure? By no means. As a result of that struggle, one-third of this nation—the South— was changed, perhaps forever, and the rest of the nation made its first tentative steps toward democracy. Beyond all that, the movement created the foundations for future departures, which will depend on the maturation of social forces and the courage, vision, and perseverance of black people.

The important point here, as elsewhere, is that the movement was historical. It had historical roots, its direction and limitations were historically determined. It rose and fell according to the laws of motion . . . I almost said . . . the laws of being of the political economy of blackness.

One way to avoid the implications of this fact is to focus, as so many people do, on ephemeral aspects of the movement, such as the personalities. And so we find people saying almost everywhere that the main problem was leadership. Or we find them saying—and you've heard them say it—that the movement failed because the leaders were integrationists or separationists or because they didn't brush with Crest. This is a Walt Disney approach to the historical process. The leaders didn't start the Montgomery boycott: the people started it. The leaders didn't start Watts: the people started it. And when the energy of the people ran out, when they had tried everything, or almost everything, when they had demonstrated, petitioned, rioted, prayed, and consulted astrologers, and when every new advance revealed a new all, the people withdrew to retool and rethink. And what we've got to understand tonight is that this temporary withdrawal was and is natural under the circumstances. The law of history is that people cannot live forever on the heights. The law of history is that a people advance and retreat, advance and retreat, advance and retreat, until they reach a collective decision to go for broke.

Since 1900, the black movement in America has been characterized by this rhythm of advances and withdrawals. And this entitles us to say, I think, that if the sun continues to shine and the wind continues to blow, the movement of the sixties will reemerge in America on a higher level of development.

And the task we face tonight is the task of consolidating our gains and preparing the ground for the next departure which will come, as surely as night follows day, if we stop cursing history and learn from history how to make history.

One of our problems in the sixties—certainly one of my problems—was that we underestimated the resiliency of the system. For a moment there, we thought we had the cat. For a moment there, we thought the promised land was around the next turning. But that was an illusion, and the mandate we have tonight from the dreamers and victims is to learn from our illusions and prepare ourselves for a long-range struggle for the transformation of this society.

This, in my opinion, was one of the four great lessons of the sixties, which taught us, in many a hard classroom, that the struggle to overcome is not a hundred-yard dash but a long-distance run involving phases and characteristics that have no precedent and cannot be predicted. We must prepare, therefore, for the long haul. We must prepare for a struggle of five, ten, fifteen, or even fifty years.

The second lesson, growing out of the first, is that people change only when they have to change, and that it is the task of the oppressed to do whatever is required to force change. The lesson of the sixties, and of this hour, was anticipated more than one hundred years ago by Frederick Douglass, who said:

Let me give you a word of the philosophy of reform. The whole history of the progress of human liberty shows that all concessions yet made to her august claims, have been born of earnest struggle. If there is no struggle, there is no progress. Those who profess to favor freedom and yet deprecate agitation, are men who want crops without plowing up the ground, they want rain without thunder and lightning. They want the ocean without the awful roar of its many waters.

This struggle may be a moral one, or it may be a physical one, and it may be both moral and physical, but it must be a struggle. Power concedes nothing without demand. It never did and it never will. . . . Men may not get all they pay for in this world, but they must certainly pay for all they get.

Struggle: that's the second lesson, and the third is that we cannot overcome and the gains of the post-*Brown* years cannot be preserved without a total struggle for a fundamental transformation of institutional structures. It should be clear by now, to almost everyone, that the white problem cannot be solved and black America cannot be saved without a total struggle for a fundamental transformation of American society, without real changes in the tax structure and the relations between the private and public sectors, without a redefinition of values, and a redistribution of income.

This need is particularly acute in the South. In my travels through the land of my birth, I have been struck repeatedly by the gains white southerners have made in the areas of personal relations. I have also been struck repeatedly by the same structural faults that led to the failure of the First Reconstruction. It is admitted now, by almost everyone, that the First Reconstruction was doomed from the start by the failure to provide blacks with economic as well as political votes. If we hope and intend to overcome, and if there is still time, somebody, somewhere is going to have to come up with the twentieth-century equivalent of forty acres of land and a mule.

Finally, and most importantly, the white South and white North are going to have to deal with themselves. The great lesson of the sixties, a lesson heeded almost nowhere, is that there is no Negro problem in Mississippi and in America. The problem of race in Mississippi, and in America, is a white problem, and we shall not overcome until we confront that problem. Somebody, somewhere is going to have to tell poor whites the truth about their lives. Somebody, somewhere, is going to have to assume responsibility for educating white people about the political, economic, and social realities of the twentieth century.

This is the challenge, this is the danger, this is the hope. It is the next great barrier, the sea beyond that we must cross together, before we can reach a place of safety where we can speak, with truth, to our graves and say: "You did not dream or die in vain, for we have finally and at long last overcome."

The whole wide world around, the whole wide world around, the whole wide world around someday.

Sunday Has a Different Smell

ANNE CARSLEY

I DO NOT RECALL that all the Sundays of my childhood differed. To remember one is to remember them all in an endless circle of dappled light, slow moving and serene.

I woke that Sunday morning shivering in the first faint coolness of the coming fall and reached for the sunny smelling sheet on the floor where I had kicked it during the night. The chill that drifted with the early haze would melt at the first touch of sunlight; later the day would be blaring and brilliant, stapled in brass and edged with blue. I lay back for a long moment, hugging the crisp whiteness to my shoulders, and watched the flickering patterns of light and shadow on the bare, cool floorboards. Breakfast smells mingled with the chickens' cries of accomplishment from below. From the hall where it was enthroned in massive doily draped pride came the sounds of the radio mourning the sorrows of the chosen people and the triumphant glory of faith tested in the fiery furnace. I savored the sense of anticipation, late breakfast and newness that was and is ever Sunday to me—a timeless moment to hold against all the years.

The tempo increased: A pot lid clattered; the kettle sang; I heard the slap and thwack of my father's razor; the ice box door slammed repeatedly; my aunt cried daintily from the kitchen and it was breakfast time. We three ate, spreading the Sunday paper between the dishes, each to his own island of interest. My aunt sipped dark coffee, commenting on the possible circumstances of each obituary. Second only in her fascination was the wedding section. Curious, this mingling of death and beginnings. My father hunched over the same dire headlines that, he often remarked wryly, used to infuriate his own father in his day. I sprawled over peaches and cream with the funnies, half listening, sniffing the warm, dark scent of sun bleached paper and reading

265

large-eyed of the escapades of the Katzenjammer Kids and the perils of Little Orphan Annie who was to me in those days as Deirdre of the Sorrows. In the silence that sometimes fell I could hear the distant clang of a cow bell and the small birds twittering in the purple flowers at the window.

Invariably the blare of the alarm startled us and the rush to get ready for church began. My father snarled amiably over the set of his tie, I turned over the only bottle of white shoe polish, the car fought all attempts to start it. When finally I stood ready in starchy, crimped glory, my aunt eyed me dubiously between pokes at the simmering roast and remarked hopefully that at least I ought to get to church clean—to stay that way would be beyond us both. My father, half out the door, pulled uneasily at his coat and adjusted the band of his summer straw under the admonishing eye. We moved carefully, feeling the responsibility of this day. I thought that he, no less than I, was hearing again the commands of his mother. My aunt never went with us. Prayer meeting was her forte for she had not missed a Wednesday night in ten years. She preferred to rock by the radio, raising her voice with the hymns, drink innumerable cups of scalding coffee, and slowly prepare the ritualistic Sunday dinner. We envied her as we drove stiffly, itchily, up the dirt road between the sweet glimmering fields, past the slow train with its sad little hoot, to the small church of uncompromising red brick and white boards set in a clump of shade trees. Neighbors and relatives stood talking until the first authoritative organ peal summoned them into the dim interior with the slow moving overhead fans and dusty odor of velvet.

We settled into the hard pew just as the first long Bible reading began. The begats had a rhythmic swing that made my eyelids droop. It grew stickily hot as the sun poured through the yellow, green and purple glassed windows that some contended were "Popish." I glanced up at the weatherbeaten face of my father, his eyes the same faded hazel as the deepest pool of our creek on a hot day, red knuckled hands still in his lap. Starch pricked my damp legs and I reached furtively to scratch, trying to avoid his impaling glance that could cure the fiercest itch. It was a relief to rise for the hymn, the call of longing for the River Jordan flowing deep. The choir was enthusiastic and off; the voice of old Mrs.

Benton who knew everything that happened in the county—
sometimes even before the participants—rose in a penetrating
soprano that her detractors said could give the Lord himself an
earache.

Our preacher introduced a visiting brother who would "bring
the message." The people sat back as he crossed the mundane
flatlands and soared toward the theological mountains. Old ladies
nodded in the warmth, chins sinking lower and lower into lace
collars. Farmers mopped wet brows. Their wives sat upright
assessing the dress and righteousness of each other while the
roses of their hats jounced emphatically with the movements of
the fans. Small boys sat decorously under vigilant parental scruti-
ny. If that eye shifted, they made horrible faces—tight shut eyes,
mouths down, tongues out—snapping back to angel smoothness
in a trice. Teenage girls in fluffy dresses sat delicately straight
with new dignity that could melt quickly into nervous uncertainty. Here and there a big boy snatched heavy fingered at an
unfortunate fly. A baby whimpered and was quickly hushed.

Time drowsed by as the visitor rolled grandiloquently along.
Mr. Jonas, a recent and fervid convert, muttered, "Amen, Brother, amen." Across the aisle, Mrs. Simms, who had four children
under six and a mother-in-law who was all tongue, slept unabashedly
on her husband's shoulder as she did each Sunday morning. My
stomach growled; I put an elbow in it, thereby making it growl all
the more. There was a thud as Ella Mae Robbins removed the
high heels that were my envy. Her feet hurt, so the ladies in our
parlor whispered, from dancing all Saturday night out at "that
dreadful place on the highway." Portly Mr. Stevens, owner of the
biggest hardware store in town, drew out his huge gold watch and
fixed a sharp eye on the preacher. Heads inclined knowingly; Mr.
Stevens was a surpassing good Christian but he liked his dinner
on the dot of twelve thirty—two wives had been trained to that.

Sweat trickled down my back as I gazed cautiously at my
father's watch. It was twelve forty-five. My stomach snarled again
and I twisted uneasily. I caught the eye of my best friend, Ruth,
and we engaged in one of those staring contests dear to the hearts
of children. Minutes ticked away and our lips began to quirk; I
felt a horde of giggles rising. There was a click as Mr. Stevens
peered incredulously at his watch, then sharply up at the preach-

er who took it for rapt attention and boldly launched his eleventh premise. Our own preacher, who knew his congregation, stirred nervously in his chair, thinking no doubt, of his annoyed wife and the drying roast, not to mention the possible—often threatened— departure of Mr. Stevens, a generous giver, to the Methodists across the street who at least knew when to stop. They had long since left. We had heard their good-byes, swishing tires and the bell clap as one of the boys yanked the rope in passing. Beside me a little boy punched his mother, demanding in a carrying whisper, "How much longer?" Quickly, I turned from Ruth's convulsed face, trying to suppress my giggles as the pew shook and several ladies craned their necks in well bred surprise. I felt the flick of my father's birch switch look while the sonorous voice rolled over us, inexorable as Jordan. It was no use, I could not stop. My father correctly judged the situation to be hopeless; he lifted me out of the pew, propelling me toward the door, murmuring about "something she ate" to the blur of faces as we moved.

Once out in the blasting heat under the shade trees, their drying leaves rattling in the little wind, I laughed helplessly until my sides ached and the hiccups came. When the paroxysm subsided, I looked apprehensively up at my stern faced father who smiled in spite of himself. We hung suspended, the mood broke and we roared with laughter in a camaraderie not of age.

We were just about to get in the car when the limp congregation emerged and several concerned ladies rushed over to us. By this time I was so pale and shaky that they could not doubt the fact that I had been suddenly "taken." What they did doubt was the kind of ailment. But, as my father wore his most resigned look and I one of imminent regurgitation, they hovered for one last minute and wisely retreated. We took the high road for home.

The cool house was hung round with Sunday smells. Roast and gravy, dumplings floating in a blue bowl, giblet gravy with egg whites, yellow cornbread, rice, peas, tomatoes, warm cake drowning in chocolate ice cream, a moisture beaded pitcher of tea. When my father regaled my aunt with the morning's happenings, he did not mention the shared time under the trees, but she looked benignly at us and I knew that she understood. I gulped tea, curling my toes and spreading them wide over the worn linoleum, contentment deep and solid in my stomach. Meaningful words sometimes came hard with us; they were as unyielding as the steel pipe I used to "skin the cat" on. Now the air lay smooth and fair between us.

After the opulence of Sunday dinner we slept amid the morass of the paper until company time—a stylized ritual. On most Sundays we dressed in our second best and waited for them to arrive. Rich cakes and tea were served in the dim, quiet parlor where shades were drawn to protect the carpet and the ancestors glared sternly down while the visitors sat uneasily on the prickly couch or precise chairs. Conversations were balanced as precariously as the cups, as delicately as the grandfather clock which struck the quarter hours.

The Sunday afternoon before, I had been fetched down from the fig tree, thrust into a pink party dress, my hastily scrubbed ears still flaming, and coerced to recite "something pretty" for the assembled ladies of my aunt's sewing circle. My face had brightened; I knew just the thing. The ladies waited, smiling and breathless, with coos of "How sweet." My aunt, suspicious of such alacrity, viewed me darkly as it occurred to her, belatedly, that it might have been better to specify a child's poem or a short Psalm. But I had my own ear for words and sonance. I launched into a perfect rendition of several choicely explicit sentences used by my father's cronies as they sat on the porch one evening. There was total and complete silence for a full minute; then a concerted screech, a gasp or two, and a look of downright fascination on several faces as my aunt, who was nothing if not a quick thinker, jerked me away, remarking as she did so on the possible morals of old Mr. Latham across the road who had recently acquired a bride half again his age. I was, naturally, soundly spanked, but some things are worth the price.

On the third Sunday of each month, which this happened to be, we usually went to visit Cousin George and his wife, Viola, who lived on a farm not far away. They were not really cousins, but in the vast, interlocking circles of relatives where precise relationships were sometimes obscure—"second cousin twice removed on your great grandmother's side"—we tended to call people in all degrees of kinship "Cousin" or, in our soft elision, "Cun." Cousin George was a passionate hunter who thought only of guns, dogs, and hunting plans. Cousin Viola was soft and fidgety; her speech was interspersed with "Dear" and "Honey" as she reached out vaguely patting fingers.

Cousin George, lured from his gun polishing, and my father sat in the yard under the shade trees, watching the smoke from their cigars spiral on the air, sipping bourbon, talking of hunting and the war. My aunt and Cousin Viola sat in the most comfortable chairs the parlor could boast, chatting in low voices that rose magically over the rattle of the fan blades when I came near. I sat covertly listening but soon grew bored with bean staking and a whiter wash.

Finally I wandered away to tour my favorite spots. I passed the stable where the amiable old horse nickered a lazy welcome, along the path where blackberries and honeysuckle had lifted their June profusion, to the clearing in which a house had once stood. Now only a blackened chimney remained near a huge cedar. Nearby a straggling rose bush was brave with late roses. There was no air of desolation; I knew that, whoever they had been, they had been happy here. I scratched idly in the loose earth as I always did in hopes of finding something that would tell me what they had been like. Perhaps they had buried their cherished treasures during the Civil War and had been unable to return.

The wash of moist air from the creek lifted my hair. I ran past the pine grove and the little garden to sit, by ritual, on the silvery old log at the edge. My questing fingers touched the curious roughness of the gray-tendrilled moss which fell, curtainlike, from the trees. Sounds from the droning afternoon penetrated my little cave: A jay cried raucously; a fish plopped in the purling water; in the distance a dog yapped steadily. Out in the bottom the grass parted before a snake's stealthy glide. High in the blue sweep of sky a lone buzzard circled. A bright, humming quiet hung over all.

I went up to the crown of the hill which overlooked the green-gold fields, the browning corn patch, red roofed house and barn, on to the distant band of dust that was the road to home. Here were three ancient mock orange trees which grew so closely that they could have been one. I stared up into the endless caverns of twisted branches and trembling leaves that melted into secret greenness, thinking with a sense of trepidation that they might reach up to the land of giants. They were titans, those trees; several times, in tears over some small thing or large, I had clung to their rough bark, feeling a form of comfort at their height and strength in a shifting world. I stood for a long moment, looking at the panorama, then I fled down the long sweep of hill with the doleful hound dogs baying at my heels, the mad summer ecstasy upon me.

The afternoon was shading softly toward evening as I reached the house and slithered in the screen door, for once without banging it. The tea glasses sat in a neat row on the drainboard and the cake plate stood almost empty on the table. I popped a forgotten morsel in my mouth and started on noiseless bare feet for the parlor. I was stopped by the sound of Cousin Viola's voice as I had never heard it, full of tension and pain, hard at the edges, each word etched in vitriol. The fluttery manner, blurriness, genteel sweetness—all were gone.

"I told you, Edna, I've stood it just as long as I can. George doesn't even see me any more. I'm just a thing to cook, wash, iron, and feed those everlasting hound dogs. Maybe if there'd been children . . . We're getting old now. There's more tenderness in the way he pats those animals than there ever was with me, even years ago."

A palpable sense of disaster came over me as I peeped around the door in curiosity and horror. She sat in a disconsolate lump on the couch, clenched hands shaking, lips twitching. She was not crying; that would have been bearable. Her sad middle-aged face, so carefully rouged and powdered, was blotchy and streaked. She rushed on.

"It wouldn't do any good to leave. Where would I go? The awful thing is, George wouldn't know what I was talking about if I tried to tell him. When we were younger it didn't matter that we couldn't talk too much, but it matters now. God! How it matters!"

I felt cold at the long anguish in her voice. So that was what it was like to be grown up. Goosebumps stood out on my arms and my usually volatile stomach recoiled as I looked again, unable to turn away. My always positive aunt put her arms around Cousin Viola and made the sensible, soothing sounds she did so well. She had routed many a green peach stomach ache for me. But Cousin

Viola jerked away furiously and her face ran together in little lines.

"There's just nothing. Nothing." The words hung there in that dim parlor that I would hate from this time on. I have remembered that tone and have heard it but few times since—matter of fact, devoid of life and hope, paralyzing. I could bear it no longer; the world that had been so right was suddenly awry and faintly sickening in the way that it sometimes was when we played "Swing the Statue" and I whirled too long. I was afraid of that which had no name. My hand was heavy on the door knob and my voice seemed to come from a distance; it was high, trembling, with the sheen of tears on it.

"What's the matter?"

Cousin Viola was once more soft as pigeon down. "Nothing, dear. Nothing at all. Your auntie and I have just been having a nice chat. Now, honey, just run and find your daddy. I expect he'll be getting ready to go."

I stared at her, knowing that I disliked her. Her face still shook but her mouth said things were all right. Wrongness was a miasma in the air. There was desolation behind the words. I recognized it because I felt it when I woke sometimes in the depths of night when the morning is years away and saw strange shapes in my room. Cousin Viola and I seemed the same age then. But she said one thing and meant another. What was real? I issued my own defiance of fear.

"No. I don't want to. I won't."

I chewed my thumb end and dug my big toe deep in the patterned carpet. Cousin Viola sank back on the couch, her fading hair tangled in the fringed cover. My aunt stood up, slapping her knee. The birch switches swished in her eyes. Her voice was that of authority and certainty.

"Go do what Cousin Viola says. This very instant. Don't let me have to say it again."

I saw her strength and my own was renewed; the rock to which I held was still sure and steady. I ran and was glad to run. It was ridiculously good to see the tall, spare form of my father coming up the steps, draining his glass, remarking irritably that it was past time to go and what were we doing anyway?

Our goodbyes were quick. Cousin Viola handed me a jar of

plums, smoothing my hair with nervous fingers. She appeared not to see my instinctive move backward but her eyes were empty above the smile. Cousin George lifted an abstracted hand in farewell; his attention never left the gun he was readying for the morning's hunt.

Going home I lay on the back seat of the car with my head pushed down into the mustiness, letting the bumps and jerks lull me. For once I did not listen to the murmured conversation from the front. The strangely bruising afternoon had rendered me vaguely unhappy for things I could not understand and the tears ran warm and salt over my dirty fingers.

Never had home been so welcome. We sat rocking on the porch in the paling evening with the trees limned dark against the saffron sky. A cricket rasped hesitantly. The fireflies flickered on in the hedge. The old green swing creaked back and forth companionably as the dog snuffled in her sleep. Mist rose white in the hollow; a bird call came round and delicate in the twilight.

Slowly the knot in me lessened and peace settled on my shoulders. The calm and comfort of sure things was all about; even if the world appeared strange and hurting this remained. We smiled at each other in a tenderness as real as the tension had been. This day bound us in a circle all our own, in a kindness and warmth that was a seal against the inexplicable. So my world came right as we sat there in the calm of the Lord's day, in the warm coming darkness, yawning, commenting, slapping a stray mosquito, touching the velvet ears of the dog.

Sunday has a different smell.

FROM

Southern Legacy

HODDING CARTER

WHEN I WAS a brash youngster of seventeen, with a year in a Yankee college behind me, I visited my maternal grandmother in Concordia Parish, Louisiana, across the river from Natchez.

She was a dainty little lady, given to delicate scents and a hairdo that displayed her white curls to advantage; but her femininity was no more pronounced than was her domination over the conglomeration of daughters, nephews, nieces and grandchildren who surrounded her as permanent guests or occasional visitors.

There were eighteen of us thus gathered together at midday dinner on a summer day of my visit back in 1924. Grandmother presided at the head of the table. I sat midway at her left and, in the hubbub of unrelated conversation, I was learnedly holding forth to a cousin on the evils of the resurgent Ku Klux Klan. I had just said that the Klan was a rotten, no-good, and un-American organization, or words to that effect, when I became conscious of frightened signals from my cousin and a sudden, awesome hush. I looked toward the head of the table. Obviously grandmother was about to speak to us.

But grandmother's words were for no one but me. She had heard only my concluding comment on the Klan, and her failure to understand that it was not *the* Klan I was castigating, but only a spurious, latter-day imitation thereof, was my undoing.

"Stand up, young man," she said. She had a flair for the dramatic. I stood up.

"Your year up North seems to have disagreed with you," she began. "Did they teach you to say what you have just said about the Ku Klux Klan?"

It was too late to rectify her error or mine. For a long five minutes grandmother retold the warm, familiar story. With her

274

own hands she had made my grandfather's Klan robes. Practically singlehanded, though with some minor assistance from the legendary Captain Norwood—"the second most handsome man in the Confederate Army"—grandfather had saved a large section of the South through some well-timed night riding and an unerring aim. Had it not been for grandfather and a few lesser giants in the land, no man's life and no white woman's virtue would have been safe. I had heard the story since childhood, loved it, believed it, believe some part of it even today. But I had gone back on my raising. I had denounced the Klan. I was a traitor to the South, thanks to my parents' grave mistake in permitting me to go to college in Maine.

I tried once, but only once, to interrupt with an explanation. My cousins were giggling. One or two aunts were nodding ready approval of grandmother's fury. I was hopelessly lost.

"Leave the table, young man," grandmother concluded. "You may apologize to me when we have finished dinner."

Later, of course, I received a qualified pardon after grandmother finally came to understand that I meant no sacrilege. But thereafter, in her presence, I kept my thoughts on the Klan, past, present, or future, to myself.

I have told this story many times since that uncomfortable dinner hour, as an amusing anecdote of my youth. I did not understand its implications for a long time, nor, I suspect, did many who heard the tale. For it seemed to be simply one of those incomprehensible Southern incidents, having no reference to things as they are and altogether out of place in the world today.

But this interpretation is wrong.

I was born forty-two years ago, just midway between the close of the War Between the States and the present. Similarly located in meaningful time are hundreds of thousands, even millions, of white Southerners of my age and older, who represent the thinking, the political directions, the economic attitudes of our badgered South. Almost every one of us, farmer, city man, mountaineer, teacher, preacher, poor white or so-called "Bourbon," was close to some fabulous father or grandfather, some remembering grandmother, to whom, in our childhood and even our young manhood, the war and its aftermath was a personal, bitter, and sacred reality. And if, in their declining years, they embroidered fact with fancy, our inheritance was no less real, our conviction of wrongful treatment no less strong, our resultant idealization no less significant.

For, in folk history, the eighty-four years since Appomattox is a short span, especially for people who were on the losing side. I remember bicycling through Ireland once, in the mid-twenties, and stopping for a cup of water at a peasant's hut. Rebellion was unusually rife in Ireland then, and the old woman with whom I chatted had nothing good to say for the English. Just four miles up the road, she told me, the English had tied 200 God-fearing Irishmen to stakes and burned them. I was incredulous, for I had not come across this grim tale in any reports of the Black and Tan or rebel excesses.

"My God," I exclaimed, "when did they do that?"

"It was Cromwell," she said. "The dir-r-ty dog."

The South is scarcely less persevering in remembering its dirty dogs, in bedaubing some who were not dirty, and in discrediting what might be offered as the other side of the story. Did we not have our grandfathers and grandmothers as proof? Do we not remember the old men from the Confederate home, men still hale in 1916, whose rebel yells turned the first showings of *The Birth of a Nation* into emotional pandemonium and who assured the children of nine and ten that life had been just like that, only worse? It was as true as gospel itself that Ben Butler had stolen spoons and ordered his troops to despoil the women at New Orleans; that Sherman was Satan incarnate who laughed at his bummers' toll of starving women and children along his line of march, and that Thaddeus Stevens took a Negro wife, and sought to provide white Southern wives for his Negro cohorts.

Profane history has not triumphed over such articles of faith. And, as a corollary, some of the bittersweet morsels which fed our minds have not themselves been made more savory by actual history. While in school in the East, I met and liked a student of considerable means. His grandfather, who shall be nameless here, actually gave the family fortune its sizable start by dishonest trafficking in federally seized cotton. About the time this Eastern fortune was being accumulated in the immediate wake of the war, my greatgrandmother, whose husband had been mortally wounded at Shiloh, journeyed to Washington to seek a presidential pardon for herself so that she could regain her modest properties in New Orleans. We have that pardon, signed by Andrew Johnson. In it the engraved descriptive phrase, "the late traitor," was amended in ink, with the word "traitress" scrawled above the scratched-out "traitor," and her name following thereafter. And speaking of contraband-cotton fortunes, my mother's family dreamed for years of the windfall that would come our way when Congress approved the Southern cotton claims. Only Congress never did.

These unseparated truths and fantasies did strange things to those of us who stand midway in the eighty-four-year time span. They explained inertia and genteel poverty too well. My Ku Klux grandfather, I was convinced, would have left unnumbered acres to his widow had it not been for war and Reconstruction; and I still remember my shocked disbelief when my wryly humorous mother once suggested that another reason was his postwar inability to fill inside straights when the chips represented cotton land. They provided a background which gave approval to a childish game of draping ourselves in white sheets and chasing Negro children through the woods with guns. They gave sanctity to the pronouncements of our Episcopal rector's son, who would argue with the high-school history teacher and declare baldly that Abraham Lincoln was an atheist and the illegitimate brother of Jefferson Davis, and that slavery was the foreordained and natural state of Africans.

Every now and then since those earlier days, I remind myself hopefully that, after all, these determining factors were waning even in my childhood. My own three sons would not be thus conditioned by any past. We would see to it, my wife and I, that their pride in the South and its past would be balanced, as they grew up, with proper emphasis upon the new South and the nation of which it is an irrevocable and generally wholesome part. None of that ancestor-worship business for them, no sir. And this shaping would be easy, because they had lived away from the South for almost five years during the recent war: the oldest from his sixth to his eleventh year, the second from his first year to his sixth. Even the baby, born in Washington, had been almost a Northerner for a year.

I am not so sure about that now. In June, 1946, after only a year of being home in Mississippi, we started out for our annual summer in Maine. The first night's stop was at Chattanooga, and that meant a trip to the top of Lookout Mountain and considerable, if improvised, emphasis upon a long-ago battle among the clouds. The end of the second day brought us to Lexington, Virginia. We left Lee Chapel at Washington and Lee University, laden with Confederate flags, our minds past-haunted with the words of the soft-spoken curator, whose first assumption that we were "non-Southern" I had corrected hastily and almost indignantly. Later in the morning, the older boys became starry-eyed and silent at VMI before the proud canvas that depicted the charge of the boy cadets of VMI at New Market; and we left Lexington with the Stars and Bars waving wildly from the windows of the car. In the late afternoon of that day we reached Gettysburg, and that was our undoing. First, we visited the sad, majestic battlefield, and then the ghost-ridden museum, in whose amphitheater one can look down upon an electrically controlled topographical map of Gettysburg, where changing battalions of red and blue lights illustrate the lecturer's account of the bloody campaign. When the lecturer finished, the two older boys were disconsolate.

"That was a tough one for us to lose," Hodding III said moodily. "Anyhow, we killed more of them than they did of us, didn't we?"

I roused myself from inwardly cursing at Longstreet and wondering where in hell Stuart could have been all that time, to remind him that it all happened for the best, and, anyway, where would we be today if we weren't a united country?

So there it is, this persistent initial legacy. Play "America" or the "Star Spangled Banner" before a Southern audience, and it will stand at required attention. Play "Dixie" and you had better stick cotton in your ears.

Let alone, the spirit of which these stories are symbols is harmless enough; a little pathetic perhaps, and naïve and provincial. Let alone, it will, of course, wear itself out someday. Not tomorrow or next year or the next. But someday. But it is not let alone by those least worthy to capitalize upon it, the politicians who subvert the Southern legacies to confuse their constituents and perpetuate themselves, though it can be said honestly that such instruments are losing their effectiveness.

Meanwhile, let us see this stubborn legacy for what it is. A defensive thing which stiffens the spine of the colonially exploited and prideful and poor against the urban and sophisticated and economically entrenched. A rallying point for conservatism against the impact of change and of ideas. A shared past, drawing together a long-related folk against the newcomer and the alien. A shield against the constant thrusting from the outside. And a tragically employed excuse for wrongs since committed and right things left undone.

This emotional heritage is difficult of understanding for the detached, present-minded, and amiable non-Southerners to whom that war of our grandfathers is a struggle happily over, properly won by the side which should have won, and now properly relegated to the limbo of the past. It is even more difficult of understanding for those new, zealous historians who take as a starting point the assumption that the South deserved whatever it got; that, in fact, its Bourbons came off too lightly; and that the war and Reconstruction were essentially a struggle between the submerged classes—black and white in the South lumped carefully together—on the one side, and on the other, the spirit of reaction so oversimply represented by a diabolical figure, the ante- and post-bellum Southern Planter.

Nevertheless, the stories told by aging men and women to young boys persist, and there is more than legend to them. What my grandmother remembered in microcosm represented a macrocosm of disaster whose material and spiritual effects are as readily recognizable to the psychologist as to the historian. The South's wealth was as completely gone at the close of the Civil War as is that of any postwar European country today, and there was no Marshall Plan. Its banks were closed, its currency without value, its bonds and insurance worthless too. Its principal single item of wealth, two billion dollars' worth of slaves, was destroyed. The South's largest cities were ravaged by bombardment and fire, many of its smaller towns were desolated, and the scorched-earth technique had left its countryside, where the Union armies had passed, a desert. Two thirds of its railroads were in ruins. Land dropped in value from $50.00 to as low as $3.00 an acre and was sold for taxes, and at the close of 1865 an estimated 500,000 people in three states alone existed at starvation levels. Returning

Confederates, with no clothing other than their ragged uniforms, were forced to remove the military buttons—or have them forcibly removed by Negro troops. Those among them who had been veterans of earlier American wars were stricken from the pension lists. Though courts still functioned, military commissions tried defendants in cases far removed from their ordinary jurisdiction, and the longest military occupation in modern history was accompanied by a political vengefulness that healed no wounds.

These things, however vaguely identified, were in my grandmother's mind as she lectured me there at the dinner table. Secondhand, they have persisted in the memory of many others and they cannot be shrugged off.

And I am thereby reminded of another story which, better than any other I have heard, illustrates this Southern legacy of resentment over the outcome of an ancient war. The story's heroine is in her eighties, the daughter of one of Stonewall Jackson's bodyguards, and indomitably Virginian. Not so many years ago, at an age when few of us would be interested in further pursuit of learning, she enrolled in a university summer course in the history of the South. One day during the session, the lecturer made the usual comment, namely, that it was best that the war had ended with a Northern victory. Later on during his talk he made the same apologetic interjection. The smoldering little lady could stand his treason no longer. She rose from her chair and interrupted him.

"Professor," she challenged, "you keep saying that it was best that the North won the war. But how do you know? We didn't get a chance to even *try* it our way."

Address upon Receiving
the Nobel Prize for Literature

WILLIAM FAULKNER

STOCKHOLM, DECEMBER 10, 1950

I FEEL THAT this award was not made to me as a man, but to my work—a life's work in the agony and sweat of the human spirit, not for glory and least of all for profit, but to create out of the materials of the human spirit something which did not exist before. So this award is only mine in trust. It will not be difficult to find a dedication for the money part of it commensurate with the purpose and significance of its origin. But I would like to do the same with the acclaim too, by using this moment as a pinnacle from which I might be listened to by the young men and women already dedicated to the same anguish and travail, among whom is already that one who will some day stand here where I am standing.

Our tragedy today is a general and universal physical fear so long sustained by now that we can even bear it. There are no longer problems of the spirit. There is only the question: When will I be blown up? Because of this, the young man or woman writing today has forgotten the problems of the human heart in conflict with itself which alone can make good writing because only this is worth writing about, worth the agony and the sweat.

He must learn them again. He must teach himself that the basest of all things is to be afraid; and, teaching himself that, forget it forever, leaving no room in his workshop for anything but the old verities and truths of the heart, the old universal truths lacking which any story is ephemeral and doomed—love and honor and pity and pride and compassion and sacrifice. Until he does so, he labors under a curse. He writes not of love but of lust, of defeats in which nobody loses anything of value, of victories without hope and, worst of all, without pity or compassion. His

281

griefs grieve on no universal bones, leaving no scars. He writes not of the heart but of the glands.

Until he relearns these things, he will write as though he stood among and watched the end of man. I decline to accept the end of man. It is easy enough to say that man is immortal simply because he will endure: that when the last ding-dong of doom has clanged and faded from the last worthless rock hanging tideless in the last red and dying evening, that even then there will still be one more sound: that of his puny inexhaustible voice, still talking. I refuse to accept this. I believe that man will not merely endure: he will prevail. He is immortal, not because he alone among creatures has an inexhaustible voice, but because he has a soul, a spirit capable of compassion and sacrifice and endurance. The poet's, the writer's, duty is to write about these things. It is his privilege to help man endure by lifting his heart, by reminding him of the courage and honor and hope and pride and compassion and pity and sacrifice which have been the glory of his past. The poet's voice need not merely be the record of man, it can be one of the props, the pillars to help him endure and prevail.

My Mother, in Memory

RICHARD FORD

MY MOTHER'S NAME was Edna Akin, and she was born in 1910, in the far northwest corner of the state of Arkansas—Benton County—in a place whose actual location I am not sure of and never have been. Near Decatur or Centerton, or a town no longer a town. Just a rural place. That is near the Oklahoma line there, and in 1910 it was a rough country, with a frontier feel. It had only been ten years since robbers and outlaws were in the landscape. Bat Masterson was still alive and not long gone from Galina.

I remark about this not because of its possible romance, or because I think it qualifies my mother's life in any way I can relate now, but because it seems like such a long time ago and such a far-off and unknowable place. And yet my mother, whom I loved and knew quite well, links me to that foreignness, that other thing that was her life and that I really don't know so much about and never did. This is one quality of our lives with our parents that is often overlooked and so, devalued. Parents link us—closeted as we are in our lives—to a thing we're not but they are; a separateness, perhaps a mystery—so that even together we are alone.

The act and practice of considering my mother's life is, of course, an act of love. And my incomplete memory of it, my inadequate relation to the facts, should not be thought incomplete love. I loved my mother the way a happy child does, thoughtlessly and without doubts. And when I became an adult and we were adults who knew one another, we regarded each other highly; could say "I love you" when it seemed necessary to clarify our dealings, but without pausing over it. That seems perfect to me now and did then, too.

My mother's life I am forced to piece together. We were not a

283

family for whom history had much to offer. This fact must have to do with being not rich, or with being rural, or incompletely educated, or just inadequately aware of many things. For my mother there was simply little to history, no heroics or self-dramatizing—just small business, forgettable residues, some of them mean. The Depression had something to do with it, too. My mother and father were people who lived for each other and for the day. In the thirties, after they were married, they lived, in essence, on the road. They drank some. They had a good time. They felt they had little to look back on, and didn't look.

My father's family came from Ireland and were Protestants. This was in the 1870s, and an ocean divided things. But about my mother's early life I don't know much. I don't know where her father came from, or if he too was Irish, or Polish. He was a carter, and my mother spoke affectionately about him, if elliptically and without a sense of responsibility to tell anything at all. "Oh," she would say, "my daddy was a good man." And that was it. He died of cancer in the 1930s, I think, but not before my mother had been left by her mother and had lived with him a time. This was before 1920. My sense is that they lived—daughter and father—in the country, back near where she was born—rural again—and that to her it had been a good time. As good as any. I don't know what she was enthusiastic for then, what her thoughts were. I cannot hear her voice from that time long ago, though I would like to be able to.

Of her mother there is much to say—a story of a kind. She was from the country, with brothers and sisters. There was Indian blood on that side of the family, though it was never clear what tribe of Indian. I know nothing about her parents, though I have a picture of my great-grandmother and my grandmother with her new, second husband, sitting in an old cartage wagon, and my mother in the back. My great-grandmother is old then, witchy looking; my grandmother, stern and pretty in a long beaver coat; my mother young, with piercing dark eyes aimed at the camera.

At some point my grandmother had left her husband and taken up with the younger man in the picture—a boxer and roustabout. A pretty boy. Slim and quick and tricky. "Kid Richard" was his ring name. (I, oddly enough, am *his* namesake.) This was in Fort Smith now. Possibly 1922. My grandmother was older than Kid Richard, whose real name was Bennie Shelley. And to quickly marry him and keep him, she lied about her age, took a smooth eight years off, and began to dislike having her pretty daughter— my mother—around to date her.

And so for a period—everything in her life seemed to happen for a period and never for long—my mother was sent to live at the Convent School of St. Ann's, also in Fort Smith. It must've seemed like a good idea to her father up in the country, because he paid her tuition, and she was taught by nuns. I don't exactly know what her mother—whose name was Essie or Lessie or just Les—did during that time, maybe three years. She was married to Bennie Shelley, who was from Fayetteville and had family there. He worked as a waiter, and then in the dining-car service on the Rock Island. This meant living in El Reno and as far out the line as Tucumcari, New Mexico. He quit boxing, and my grandmother ruled him as strictly as she could because she felt she could go a long way with him. He was her last and best choice for something. A ticket out. To where, I'm not sure.

My mother often told me that she'd liked the sisters at St. Ann's. They were strict. Imperious. Self-certain. Dedicated. Humorous. It was there, I think, as a boarding student, that my mother earned what education she ever did—the ninth grade, where she was an average good student and was liked, though she smoked cigarettes and was punished for it. I think if she had never told me about the nuns, if that stamp on her life hadn't been made clear for me, I might never have ordered even this much of things. St. Ann's cast a shadow into later life. In her heart of hearts my mother was a secret Catholic. A forgiver. A respecter of rituals and protocols. Reverent about the trappings of faith; respecter of inner disciplines. All I think about Catholics I think because of her, who was never one at all, but who lived among them at an early age and seemingly liked what she learned and those who taught her. Later in life, when she had married my father and gone to meet his mother, she would always feel she was thought of as a Catholic, and that his family never truly took her in as they might have another girl.

But when her father, for reasons I know nothing about, stopped her tuition, her mother—now demanding they be known as sisters—took her out of St. Ann's. And that was it for school, forever. She was not a welcome addition to her mother's life, and I have never known why they took her back. It is just one of those inexplicable acts that mean everything.

They moved around. To K.C. To El Reno again. To Davenport and Des Moines—wherever the railroad took Ben Shelley, who was going forward in the dining-car service and turning himself into a go-getter. In time, he would leave the railroad and go to work as a caterer at the Arlington Hotel in Hot Springs. And there he put my mother to work in the cigar shop, where a wider world opened an inch. People from far away were here for the baths, Jews from Chicago and New York. Foreigners. Rich people. She met baseball players, became friends with Dizzy Dean and Leo Durocher. And during that time, sometime when she was seventeen, she must've met my father.

I, of course, know nothing about their courtship except that it took place—mostly in Little Rock, probably in 1927. My father was twenty-three. He worked as a produce stocker for a grocery concern there. I have a picture of him with two other young clerks in a grocery store. He is wearing a clean white apron and a tie, and is standing beside a bin of cabbages. I don't even know where this is. Little Rock. Hot Springs—one of these. It is just a glimpse. What brought him down from the country to Little Rock I'll never know, nor what he might've had on his mind then. He died in 1960, when I was only sixteen. And I had not by then thought to ask.

But I have thought of them as a young couple. My mother, black-haired, dark-eyed, curvaceous. My father, blue-eyed like me, big, gullible, honest, gentle. I can think a thought of them together. I can sense what they each must've sensed pretty fast—here was a good person, suddenly. My mother knew things. She had worked in hotels, been to boarding school and out. Lived in cities. Traveled some. But my father was a country boy who quit school in the seventh grade. The baby of three children, all raised by their mother—the sheltered son of a suicide. I can believe my mother wanted a better life than working for her ambitious stepfather and contrary mother, at jobs that went no place; that she may have believed she'd not been treated well, and thought of her life as "rough"; that she was tired of being her mother's sister; that it was a strange life; that she was in danger of losing all expectation; that she was bored. And I can believe my father simply saw my mother and wanted her. Loved her. And that was how that went.

They were married in Morrilton, Arkansas, by a justice of the peace, in 1928, and arrived at my father's home in Atkins the next morning, newlyweds. I have no correct idea what anyone thought or said about any of that. They acted independently, and my mother never felt the need to comment. Though my guess is they heard disapproval.

I think it is safe to say my parents wanted children. How many they wanted or how soon after they were married I do not know. But it was their modest boast that my father had a job throughout the Depression. And I think there was money enough. They lived in Little Rock, and for a while my father worked as a grocer, and then, in 1932, he was fired, and went to work selling starch for a company out of Kansas City. The Faultless Company. Huey Long had worked for them, too. It was a traveling job, and most of the time they just traveled together. New Orleans. Memphis. Texarkana. They lived in hotels, spent their off-hours and off-days back in Little Rock. But mostly they traveled. My father called on groceries, wholesalers, prisons, hospitals, conducted schools for newlyweds on how to starch clothes without boiling the starch. My mother, typically, never characterized that time except to say he and she had "fun" together—that was her word for it—and had begun to think they couldn't have a child. No children. I do not even know if that mattered so much. It was not their way to fight fate, but to see life as okay. This time lasted fifteen years. An entire life lived then. A loose, pick-up-and-go life. Drinking. Cars. Restaurants. Not paying much attention. There were friends they had in New Orleans, Memphis, in Little Rock, and on the road. They made friends of my grandmother and Bennie, who was not much older than my father—four years, at most. I think they were just caught up in their life, a life in the South, in the thirties, just a kind of swirling thing that didn't really have a place to go. There must've been plenty of lives like that then. It seems a period now to me. A specific time, the Depression. But to them, of course, it was just their life.

Something about that time—to my mother—must've seemed unnarratable. Unworthy of or unnecessary for telling. My father, who was not a teller of stories anyway, never got a chance to recall it. And I, who wasn't trained to want the past filled in—as some boys are—just never asked. It seemed a privacy I shouldn't invade. And I know that my mother's only fleeting references to that time, as if the thirties were just a long weekend—drinking too much, wildness, rootlessness—gave me the impression something possibly untidy had gone on, some recklessness of spirit and attitude below the level of evil, but something that a son would be better off not to think about and be worried with. In essence, it had been *their* time, for their purposes and not mine. And it was over.

But looked at from the time of my birth, 1944, all that life lived childless, unexpectant, must've come to seem an odd time to her; a life encapsulatable, possibly even remembered unclearly, pointless, maybe, in comparison to the pointedness of a life *with* a child. Still, an intimacy established between the two of them that they brought forward into more consequential life—a life they had all but abandoned any thought of because no children had come.

All first children, and certainly all only children, date the beginning of their lives as extraspecial events. For my parents my arrival came as a surprise and coincident with the end of World War II—the event that finished the thirties in this country. And it came when my mother had been married to my father fifteen years; when, in essence, their young life was over. He was thirty-nine. She was thirty-three. They, by all accounts, were happy to have me. It may have been an event that made their life together seem conventional for once, that settled them; made them think about matters their friends had thought about years ago. Staying put. The future.

They had never owned a house or a car, although my father's job gave him a company car. They had never had to choose a "home," a place to be in permanently. But now, they did. They moved from Little Rock down to Mississippi, to Jackson, which was the geographic center of my father's territory and a place he could return most weekends with ease, since my mother wouldn't be going with him now. There was going to be a baby.

They knew no one in Jackson except the jobbers my father had called on and a salesman or two he knew off the road. I'm not sure, but I think it was not an easy transition. They rented and then bought a brick duplex next to a school. They joined a church. Found a grocery. A bus stop—though you could walk to the main street in Jackson from 736 North Congress. Also to the library and the capitol building. They had neighbors—older citizens, established families hanging on to nicer, older, larger houses in a neighborhood that was itself in transition. This was life now, for them. My father went off to work Monday morning and came back Friday night. He had never exactly done that before, but he liked it, I think. One of my earliest memories is of him moving around the sunny house on Monday mornings, whistling a tune.

And so what my beginning life was was this. A life spent with my mother—a shadow in a picture of myself. Days. Afternoons. Nights. Walks. Meals. Dressing. Sidewalks. The movies. Home. Radio. And on the weekend, my father. A nice, large, sweet man who visited us. Happy to come home. Happy to leave.

Between them, I don't know what happened. But given their characters, my best belief is that nothing did. That their life changed radically, that I was there, that the future meant something different, that there was apparently no talk of other children, that they saw far less of each other now—all meant almost nothing to how they felt about each other, or how they registered how they felt. Neither of them was an inquirer. They did not take their pulse much. Psychology was not a science they practiced. They found, if they had not known it before, that they'd signed on for the full trip. They saw life going this way now and not that way. They loved each other. They loved me. Nothing much else mattered.

I don't think my mother longed for a fulfilling career or a more active public life. I don't think my father had other women on the road. I don't think the intrusion of me into their lives was anything they didn't think of as normal and all right. I know from practice that it is now my habit to seek the normal in life, to look for reasons to believe this or that is fine. In part, that is because my parents raised me that way and lived lives that portrayed a world, a private existence, that *could be* that way. I do not think even now, in the midst of my own life's concerns, that it is a bad way to see things.

So then, the part of my life that has to do with my mother.

The first eleven years—the Korean War years, Truman and Eisenhower, television, bicycles, one big snowstorm in 1949—we lived on North Congress Street, down a hill from the state capitol and across from the house where Eudora Welty had been a young girl thirty-five years before. Next door to Jefferson Davis School. I remember a neighbor stopping me on the sidewalk and asking me who I was; this was a thing that could happen to you. Maybe I was nine or seven then. But when I said my name—Richard Ford—she said, "Oh, yes. Your mother is the cute little black-haired woman up the street." And that affected me and still does. I think this was my first conception of my mother as someone else, as someone whom other people saw and considered: a cute woman, which she was not. Black-haired, which she was. She was, I know, five feet five inches tall. But I never have known if that is tall or short. I think I must have always believed it was normal. I remember this, though, as a signal moment in my life. Small but important. It alerted me to my mother's—what?—public side. To the side that other people saw and dealt with and that was there. I do not think I ever thought of her in any other way after that. As Edna Ford, a person who was my mother and also who was someone else. I do not think I ever addressed her after that except with such a knowledge—the way I would anyone I knew.

It is a good lesson to learn. And we risk never knowing our parents if we ignore it. Cute, black-haired, five-five. Some part of her was that, and it didn't harm me to know it. It may have helped, since one of the premier challenges for us all is to know our parents, assuming they survive long enough, are worth knowing, and it is physically possible. This is a part of normal life. And the more we see them fully, as the world sees them, the better all our chances are.

About my mother I do not remember more than pieces up until the time I was sixteen: 1960, a galvanizing year for us both—the year my father woke up gasping on a Saturday morning and died before he could get out of bed; me up on the bed with him, busy trying to find something to help. Shake him. Yell in his sleeping face. Breathe in his soft mouth. Turn him over onto his belly, for some reason. Feeling terror and chill. All this while she stood in the doorway to his bedroom in our new house in the suburbs of Jackson, pushing her knuckles into her temples, becoming hysterical. Eventually she just lost her control for a while.

But before that. Those pieces. They must make a difference or I wouldn't remember them so clearly. A flat tire we all three had, halfway across the Mississippi bridge at Greenville. High, up there, over the river. We stayed in the car while my father fixed it, and my mother held me so tightly to her I could barely breathe. I was six. She always said, "I smothered you when you were little. You were all we had. I'm sorry." And then she'd tell me this story. But I wasn't sorry. It seemed fine then, since we were up there. "Smothering" meant "Here is danger," "Love protects you." They are still lessons I respect. I am not comfortable on bridges now, but my guess is I never would've been.

I remember my mother having a hysterectomy and my grandfather, Ben Shelley, joking about it—to her—about what good "barbers" the nuns at St. Dominic's had been. That made her cry.

I remember once in the front yard on Congress Street something happened, something I said or did—I don't know what—but my mother began running out across the schoolyard next door. Just running away. I remember that scared me and I yelled at her, "No," and halfway across she stopped and came back. I've never known how serious she was about that, but I have understood from it that there might be reasons to run off. Alone, with a small child, knowing no one. That's enough.

There were two fights they had that I was present for. One on St. Louis Street, in the French Quarter in New Orleans. It was in front of Antoine's Restaurant, and I now think they were both drunk, though I didn't know it, or even know what drunk was. One wanted to go in the restaurant and eat. The other didn't and wanted to go back to the hotel around the corner. This was in 1955. I think we had tickets to the Sugar Bowl—Navy vs. Ole Miss. They yelled at each other, and I think my father yanked her arm, and they walked back separately. Later we all got in bed together in the Monteleone Hotel and no one stayed mad. In our family no one ever nagged or held grudges or stayed mad, though we could all get mad.

The other fight was worse. I believe it was the same year. They were drinking. My father invited friends over and my mother didn't like it. All the lights were on in the house. She swore. I remember the guests standing in the doorway outside the screen, still on the porch looking in. I remember their white faces and my mother shouting at them to get the hell out, which they did. And then my father held my mother's shoulders up against the wall by the bathroom and yelled at her while she struggled to get free. I remember how harsh the lights were. No one got hit. No one ever did except me when I was whipped. They just yelled and struggled. Fought that way. And then after a while, I remember, we were all in bed again, with me in the middle, and my father cried. "Boo hoo hoo. Boo hoo hoo." Those were the sounds he made, as if he'd read somewhere how to cry.

A long time has passed since then, and I have remembered more than I do now. I have tried to put things into novels. I have written things down and forgotten them. I have told stories. And there was more, a life's more. My mother and I rode with my father summers and sat in his hot cars in the states of Louisiana and Arkansas and Texas and waited while he worked, made his calls. We went to the coast—to Biloxi and Pensacola. To Memphis. To Little Rock almost every holiday. We *went*. That was the motif of things. We lived in Jackson, but he traveled. And every time we could we went with him. Just to be going, or when he became not so well with heart trouble we went to help him. The staying part was never stabilized. Only being with them, and mostly being with her. My mother.

And then my father died, which changed everything—many things, it's odd to say, for the better where I was concerned. But not for my mother. Where she was concerned, nothing after that would ever be quite good again. A major part of life ended for her February 20, 1960. He had been everything to her, and all that was naturally implicit became suddenly explicit in her life, and she was neither good at that nor interested in it. And in a way I see now and saw almost as clearly then, she gave up.

Not that she gave up where I was concerned. I was sixteen and had lately been in some law scrapes, and she became, I'd say, very aware of the formal features of her life. She was a widow. She was fifty. She had a son who seemed all right, but who could veer off into trouble if she didn't pay attention. And so, in her way, she paid attention.

Not long after the funeral, when I was back in school and the neighbors had stopped calling and bringing over dishes of food—when both grief and real mourning had set in, in other words—she sat me down and told me we were now going to have to be more independent. She would not be able to look after me as she had done. We agreed that I had a future, but I would have to look after me. And as we could, we would do well to look after each other. We were partners now, is what I remember thinking. My father had really never been around that much, and so his actual absence was, for me (though not for her), not felt so strongly. And a partnership seemed like a good arrangement. I was to stay out of jail because she didn't want to get me out. *Wouldn't get me out.* I was to find friends I could rely on instead. I could have a car of my own. I could go away in the summers to find a job in Little Rock with my grandparents. This, it was understood but never exactly stated (we were trying not to state too much then; we didn't want *everything* to have to be explicit, since so much was now and so little ever had been), *this* would give her time to adjust. To think about things. To become whatever she would have to become to get along from there on out.

I don't exactly remember the time scheme to things. This was 1960, '61, '62. I was a tenth-grader and on. But I did not get put in jail. I did live summers with my grandparents, who by now ran a large hotel in Little Rock. I got a black '57 Ford, which got stolen. I got beaten up and then got new friends. I did what I was told, in other words. I started to grow up in a hurry.

I think of that time—the time between my father's death and the time I left for Michigan to go to college—as a time when I didn't see my mother much. Though that is not precisely how it was. She was there. I was there. But I cannot discount my own adjustments to my father's death and absence, to my independence. I think I may have been more dazed than grieved, and it is true my new friends took me up. My mother went to work. She got a job doing something at a company that made school pictures. It required training and she did it. And it was only then, late in 1960, when she was fifty, that she first felt the effects of having quit school in 1924. But she got along, came home tired. I do not think she had trouble. And then she left that. She became a rental agent for a new apartment house, tried afterward to get the job as manager but didn't get it—who knows why? She took another job as night cashier in a hotel, the Robert E. Lee. This job she kept maybe a year. And after that she was the admitting clerk in the emergency room at the University of Mississippi Hospital, a job she liked very much.

And there was at least one boyfriend in all that time. A married man, from Tupelo, named Matt, who lived in the apartment building she worked at. He was a big, bluff man, in the furniture business, who drove a Lincoln and carried a gun strapped to the steering column. I liked him. And I liked it that my mother liked him. It didn't matter that he was married—not to me, and I guess not to my mother. I really have no idea about what was between them, what they did alone. And I don't care about that, either. He took her on drives. Flew her to Memphis in his airplane. Acted respectfully to both of us. She may have told me she was just passing time, getting her mind off her worries, letting someone be nice to her. But I didn't care. And we both knew that nothing she told me about him either did or didn't have to match the truth. I would sometimes think I wished she would marry Matt. And at other times I would be content to have them be lovers, if that's what they were. He had boys near my age, and later I would even meet them and like them. But this was after he and my mother were finished.

What finished them was brought on by me but was not really my doing, I think now. Matt had faded for a time. His business brought him in to Jackson, then out for months. She had quit talking about him, and life had receded to almost a normal level. I was having a hard time in school—getting a D in algebra (I'd already failed once) and having no ideas for how I could improve. My mother was cashiering nights at the Robert E. Lee and coming home by eleven.

But one night for some reason she simply didn't come home. I had a test the next day. Algebra. And I must've been in an agitated state of mind. I called the hotel to hear she had left on time. And for some reason this scared me. I got in my car and drove down to the neighborhood by the hotel, a fringe neighborhood near a black section of town. I rode the streets and found her car, a gray and pink '58 Oldsmobile that had been my father's pride and joy. It was parked under some sycamore trees, across from the apartments where she had worked as a rental agent and where Matt lived. And for some reason I think I panicked. It was not a time to panic but I did anyway. I'm not sure what I thought, but thinking of it now I seem to believe I wanted to ask Matt—if he was there—if he knew where my mother was. This may be right, though it's possible, too, I knew she was there and just wanted to make her leave.

I went in the building—it must've been midnight—and up the elevator and down the hall to his door. I banged on it. Hit it hard with my fists. And then I waited.

Matt himself opened the door, but my mother was there in the room behind him. She had a drink in her hand. The lights were on, and she was standing in the middle of the room. It was a nice apartment, and both of them were shocked by me. I don't blame them. I didn't blame them then and was ashamed to be there. But I was, I think, terrified. Not that she was there. Or that I was alone. But just that I didn't know what in the hell. Where was she? What else was I going to have to lose?

I remember being out of breath. I was seventeen years old. And I really can't remember what anybody said or did except me, briefly. "Where have you been?" I said to her. "I didn't know where you were. That's all."

And that *was* all. All of that. Matt said very little. My mother got her coat and we went home in two cars. She acted vaguely annoyed at me, and I *was* mad at her. We talked that night. Eventually she said she was sorry, and I told her I didn't care if she saw Matt, only that she tell me when she would be home late. And to my knowledge she never saw Matt Matthews, or any other man, again as a lover as long as she lived.

Later, years later, when she was dying, I tried to explain it all to her again—my part, what I thought, *had* thought—as if we could still open it and repair that night. All she needed to do was call me or, even years later, say she would've called me. But that was not, of course, what she did or how she saw it. She just looked a little disgusted and shook her head. "Oh that," she said. "My God. That was just silliness. You had no business coming up there. You were out of your mind. Though I just saw I couldn't be doing things like that. I had a son to raise." And here again she looked disgusted, and at everything, I think. All the cards the fates had dealt her—a no-good childhood, my father's death, me, her own inability to vault over all of this to a better life. It was another proof of something bad, the likes of which she felt, I believe, she'd had plenty.

There are only these—snapshot instances of a time lived indistinctly, a time that whirled by for us but the last times we would ever really live together as mother and son. We did not fight. We accommodated one another almost as adults would. We grew wry and humorous with each other. Cast glances, gave each other looks. Were never ironic or indirect or crafty with anger. We knew how we were supposed to act and took pleasure in acting that way.

She sold the new house my father had bought, and we moved into a high-rise. Magnolia Towers. I did better in school. She was switching jobs. I really didn't register these changes, though based on what I know now about such things they could not have been easy.

I did not and actually do not know about the money, how it was, then. My father had a little insurance. Maybe some was saved in a bank. My grandparents stepped forward with offers. They had made money. But there was no pension from his job; it was not that kind of company. I know the government paid money for me, a dependent child. But I only mean to say I don't know how much she needed to work; how much money needed to come through; if we had debts, creditors. It may have been we didn't, and that she went to work just to thrust herself in the direction life seemed to be taking her—independence. Solitariness. All that that means.

There were memorable moments. When my Ford was stolen we went one winter day at dusk out to a car dealer in the country, where good deals were supposedly available, and looked at cars. She felt we should replace mine, and so did I. But when we were there looking at cheap stationwagons, she saw a black Thunderbird and stared at it, and I knew that was what she wanted—for herself—that that would make her feel better. Getting my father's Olds out of our lives would be a help, and there was really no one there then to tell us not to. It was a kind of new though unasked-for freedom. And so I encouraged her. She stared a long time at it, got in and tilted the steering wheel, shut the door a few times, and then we left with the promise to think about it. In a few days, though, after we'd thought, the police found my old car, and she decided just to keep the Olds.

Another time, my girlfriend and I had been experimenting in one kind of sexual pleasure and another. And quite suddenly my girlfriend—a Texas girl—sensed somehow that she was definitely pregnant and that her life and mine were ruined. Mine, I know certainly, felt ruined. And there was evidence aplenty around of kids marrying at fourteen, having babies, being divorced. This was the South, after all.

I once again found myself in terror, and on a Sunday afternoon I just unburdened myself to my mother; told her *all* we'd done, all we hadn't. Spoke specifically and methodically, in terms of parts and positions, extents and degrees. All I wanted from her was to know if Louise *could* be pregnant, based upon what she knew about those things (how much could that really have been?). These were all matters a boy should take up with his father, of course. Though, really, whoever would? I know I wouldn't have. Such a conversation would've confused and embarrassed my poor father and me. We did not know each other that well at our closest moments. And in any case, he was gone.

But my mother I knew very well. At least I acted that way and she did, too. She was fifty-two. I was eighteen. She was practiced with me, knew the kind of boy I was. We were partners in my messes and hers. I sat on the couch and carefully told her what scared me, told her what I couldn't get worked out right in my thinking, went through it all; used the words *it, hers, in.* And she, stifling her dread, very carefully assured me that everything was going to be fine. Nobody got pregnant doing what we were doing, and I should forget about it. It was all a young girl's scare fantasies. Not to worry. And so I didn't.

Of course, she was wrong. Couldn't possibly have been wronger. My girlfriend didn't get pregnant, but only because a kind fate intervened. Thousands of people get pregnant doing what we were doing. Thousands more get pregnant doing much less. I guess my mother just didn't know that much, or else understood much more: that what was done was done now, and all the worry and explaining and getting-straight wouldn't matter. I should be more careful in the future if I was to have one. And that was about it. If Louise was pregnant, what anybody thought wouldn't matter. Best just not to worry.

And there is, of course, a lesson in that—one I like and have tried ever since and unsuccessfully to have direct me. Though I have never looked at the world through eyes like hers were then. Not yet. I have never exactly felt how little all you can do can really matter. Full understanding will come to me, and undoubtedly to us all. But my mother showed that to me first, and best, and I think I may have begun to understand it even then.

In the sixties after that I went away to college, in Michigan. It was a choice of mine and no one else's, and my mother neither encouraged nor discouraged me. Going to college in Mississippi didn't enter my mind. I wanted, I thought, to be a hotel manager like my grandfather, who had done well at it. And Michigan State was the place for that. I do not, in fact, remember my mother and me ever talking about college. She hadn't been and didn't know much about it. But the assumption was that I was simply going, and it would have to be my lookout. She was interested, but in a way that was not vital or supervisory. I don't think she thought that I would go away for good, even when it happened that Michigan State took me and I said I was going. I don't know what she thought exactly. She had other things on her mind then. Maybe she thought Michigan wasn't so far from Mississippi, which is true and not true, or that I wouldn't stay and would come home soon. Maybe she thought I would never go. Or maybe she thought nothing, or nothing that was clear; just noticed that I was doing this and that, sending and getting letters, setting dates, and decided she would cross that bridge when the time came.

And it did come.

In September 1962, she and I got on the Illinois Central in Jackson and rode it to Chicago (our first such trip together). We transferred crosstown to the old La Salle Street Station and the Grand Trunk Western, and rode up to Lansing. She wanted to go with me. I think she wanted just to see all that. Michigan. Illinois. Cornfields. White barns. The Middle West. Wanted to see from a train window what went on there, how that was. What it all looked like, possibly to detect how I was going to fit myself among those people, live in their buildings, eat their food, learn their lingo. Why this was where I had chosen to go. Her son. This was how she saw her duty unfolding.

And, too, the ordinary may have been what she wanted: accompanying her son to college, a send-off; to see herself and me, for a moment in time, fitted into the pattern of what other people were up to, what people in general did. If it could happen to her, to us, that way, then maybe some normal life had reconvened, since she could not have thought of her life as normal then.

So, at the end of that week, late September 1962, when I had enrolled, invaded my room, met my roomies, and she and I had spent days touring and roaming, eating motel dinners together until nothing was left to say, I stood up on a bus-stop bench beside the train tracks, there at the old GTW station in Lansing, and held up my arms in the cool, snapping air for her to see me as she pulled away back toward Chicago. And I saw her, her white face recessed behind the tinted window, one palm flat to the glass for me to see. And she was crying. Good-bye, she was saying. And I waved one arm in that cool air and said, "Good-bye. I love you," and watched the train go out of sight through the warp of that bricky old factory town. And at that moment I suppose you could say I started my own life in earnest, and whatever there was left of my childhood ended.

After that the life that would take us to the end began. A fragmented, truncated life of visits long and short. Letters. Phone calls. Telegrams. Meetings in cities away from home. Conversations in cars, in airports, train stations. Efforts to see each other. Leaving dominating everything—my growing older, and hers, observed from varying distances.

She held out alone in Mississippi for a year, moved back into the house on Congress Street. She rented out the other side, worked at the hospital, where for a time, I think, the whole new life she'd been handed worked out, came together. I am speculating, as you can believe, because I was gone. But at least she said she liked her job, liked the young interns at the hospital, liked the drama of the ER, liked working even. It may have started to seem satisfactory enough that I was away. It may have seemed to her that there was a life to lead. That under the circumstances she had done reasonably well with things; could ease up, let events happen without fearing the worst. One bad thing did finally turn into something less bad.

This, at least, is what *I* wanted to think. How a son feels about his widowed mother when he is far away becomes an involved business. But it is not oversimplifying to say that he wants good to come to her. In all these years, the years of fragmented life with my mother, I was aware (as I have said) that things would never be completely all right with her again. Partly it was a matter of her choosing; partly it was a matter of her own character—of just how she could see her life without my father, with him gone and so much life left to be lived in an unideal way. Always she was resigned somewhere down deep. I could never plumb her without coming to that stop point—a point where expectation simply ceased. This is not to say she was unhappy after enough time had passed. Or that she never laughed. Or that she didn't see life as life, didn't regain and rejoin herself. All those she did. Only, not utterly, not in a way a mother, any mother, could disguise to her only son who loved her. I always saw that. Always felt it. Always felt her—what?—discomfort at life? Her resisting it? Always wished she could relent more than she apparently could; since in most ways my own life seemed to spirit ahead, and I did not like it that hers didn't. From almost the first I felt that my father's death surrendered to me at least as much as it took away. It gave me my life to live by my own designs, gave me my own decisions. A boy could do worse than to lose his father—a good father, at that—just when the world begins to display itself all around him.

But that is not the way it was with her, even as I can't exactly say how it *was.* I can say that in all the years after my father died, twenty-one years, her life never seemed quite fully engaged. She took trips—to Mexico, to New York, to California, to Banff, to islands. She had friends who loved her and whom she spoke well of. She had an increasingly easy life as her own parents died. She had us—my wife and me—who certainly loved her and included her in all we could. But when I would say to her—and I did say this—"Mother, are you enjoying your life? Are things all right?" she would just look at me impatiently and roll her eyes. "Richard," she'd say. "I'm never going to be ecstatic. It's not in my nature. You concentrate on your life. Leave mine alone. I'll take care of me."

And that, I think, is mostly what she did after his death and my departure, when she was on her own: she maintained herself, made a goal of that. She became brisk, businesslike, more self-insistent. Her deep voice became even deeper, assumed a kind of gravity. She drank in the evenings to get a little drunk, and took up an attitude (particularly toward men, whom she began to see as liabilities). She made her situation be the custom and cornerstone of her character. Would not be taken advantage of by people, though I suspect no one wanted to. A widow had to look out, had to pay attention to all details. No one could help you. A life lived efficiently wouldn't save you, no; but it would prepare you for what you couldn't really be saved from.

Along the way she also maintained me and my wife, at a distance and as we needed it. She maintained her mother, who finally grew ill, then crippled, but never appreciative. She maintained her stepfather—moved, in fact, back to Little Rock. She sold her house, hers and my father's first house, and lived with my grandparents in the hotel, and later—after Ben died—in apartments here and there in the town. She became a daughter again at fifty-five, one who looked after her elderly mother. They had money enough. A good car. A set of friends who were widowed, too—people in their stratum. They accompanied each other. Went to eat in small groups, played canasta afternoons, spoke on the phone, watched TV, planned arguments; grew bored, impatient, furious. Had cocktails. Laughed about men. Stared. Lived a nice and comfortable life of waiting.

Our life during this time—my mother's and mine—consisted of my knowledge of what her life was like. And visits. We lived far away from each other. She in Little Rock. I, and then I and Kristina, in New York, California, Mexico, Chicago, Michigan again, New Jersey, Vermont. To us she arrived on trains and planes and in cars, ready to loan us money and to take us to dinner. To buy us this and that we needed. To have a room painted. To worry about me. To be there for a little while wherever we were and then to go home again.

It must be a feature of anyone's life to believe that particular circumstances such as these are not exactly typical of what the mass of other lives are like. Not better. Not worse. Only peculiar in some way. Our life, my mother's and mine, seemed peculiar. Or possibly it is just imperfect that it seemed. Being away. Her being alone. Our visits and departings. All this consumed twenty years of both our lives—her last twenty, my second, when whatever my life was to be was beginning. It never felt exactly right to me that during all these years I could not see my mother more, that we did not have a day-to-day life. That the repairs we made to things after my father's death could not be shared entirely. I suppose that nowhere in time was there a moment when life for us rejoined itself as it had been before he died. This imperfection underlay everything. And when she left again and again and again, she would cry. And that is what she cried about. That we would never rejoin, that that was gone. This was all there was. Not quite enough. Not a full enough repaying of all that time together lost. She told me once that in an elevator a woman had asked her, "Mrs. Ford, do you have any children?" And she had said, "No." And then thought to herself, "Well, yes, I do. There's Richard."

Our conversations over these years had much to do with television, with movies we had seen and hadn't, with books she was reading, with baseball. The subject of Johnny Bench came up often, for some reason. My wife and I took her to the World Series, where she rooted for the team we didn't like and complained about the seats we'd moved mountains to get—for her, we thought. We took her on the Universal Tour. We took her back to Antoine's. We drove her to California and to Montreal. To Maine. To Vermont. To northern Michigan. To wherever we went that we could take her. We, she and I, observed each other. She observed my wife and my marriage and liked them both. She observed my efforts to be a writer and did not fully understand them. "But when are you going to get a job and get started?" she asked me once. She observed the fact that we had no children and offered no opinion. She observed her life and ours and possibly did not completely see how one gave rise to the other.

I observed that she grew older; saw that life was not entirely to her liking and that she made the most of its surfaces—taking a job once in a while, then finally retiring. I observed that she loved me; would sometimes take me aside early on a morning when we could be alone together as two adults and say: "Richard, are *you* happy?" And when I told her I was, she would warn, "You must be happy. That's so important."

And that is the way life went on. Not quite pointlessly. But not pointedly, either. Maybe this is typical of all our lives with our parents—a feeling that some goal should be reached, then a recognition of what that goal inevitably is, and then returning attention to what's here and present today. To what's only here.

Something, some essence of life, is not coming clear through these words. There are not words enough. There are not events enough. There is not memory enough to give a life back and have it be right, exact. In one way, over these years apart, my mother and I lived toward one another the way people do who like each other and want to see each other more. Like friends. I have not even said about her that she didn't interfere. That she agreed my life with Kristina had retired a part of her motherhood. That she didn't cultivate random judgments. That she saw her visits as welcome, which they were. Indeed, she saw that what we'd made of things—she and I—was the natural result of prior events that were themselves natural. She was now, as before, not a psychologist. Not a quizzer. She played the cards she was dealt. By some strange understanding, we knew that this was life. This is what we would have. We were fatalists, mother and son. And we made the most of it.

In 1973, my mother discovered she had breast cancer. It must've been the way with such things, and with people of her background. A time of being aware that something was there. A time of worry and growing certainty. A mention to a friend, who did nothing. Finally a casual mention to me, who saw to it immediately that she visit a doctor, who advised tests and did not seem hopeful.

What I remember of that brief period, which took place in Little Rock, is that following the first doctor visit, when all the tests and contingencies were stated and planned, she and I and

Kristina took the weekend together. She would "go in" on Monday. But Saturday we drove up to the country, visited my father's family, his cousins whom she liked, his grave. She stated she was "going in for tests," and they—who were all older than she was—put a good face on it. We drove around in her Buick and just spent the time together. It was, we knew somehow, the last of the old time, the last of the period when we were just ourselves, just the selves we had made up and perfected, given all that had gone before. Something in those tests was about to change everything, and we wanted to act out our conviction that, yes, this has been a life, this adroit coming and going, this health, this humor, this affection expressed in fits and starts. This has been a thing. Nothing would change that. We could look back, and it would seem like we were alive enough.

Death starts a long time before it ever ends. And in it, in its very self, there is life that has to be lived out efficiently. And we did this. We found to none of our surprises that the life we had confirmed that weekend could carry us on. There were seven years to go, but we didn't know it. And so we carried on. We went back to being away. To visiting. To insisting on life's being life, in the conviction that it could easily be less. And to me it seems like the time that had gone on before. Not exactly. But mostly. Talking on the phone. Visits, trips, friends, occasions. A more pointed need to know about "how things were," and a will to have them be all right for now.

My mother, I think, made the very best of her bad problems. She had a breast removed. She had some radiation. She had to face going back to her solitary life. And all this she did with a minimum of apparent fear and a great deal of dignity and resignation. It seemed as if her later years had been a training for bad news. For facing down disasters. And I think she appreciated this and was sharply aware of how she was dealing with things.

This was the first time I ever thought seriously that my mother might come to live with me, which was a well-discussed subject all our life, there having been precedent for it and plenty of opportunity to take up a point of view. My mother's attitude was very clear. She was against it. It ruined lives, spoiled things, she thought, and said no in advance. She had lived with her mother, and that had eventuated in years of dry unhappiness. Bickering.

Impossibilities. Her mother had resented her, she said, hated being looked after. Turned meaner. Vicious. It was a no-win, and she herself expected nothing like that, wanted me to swear off the idea. Which I did. We laughed about how high and dry I would leave her. How she would be in the poorhouse, and I'd be someplace living it up.

But she was practical. She made arrangements. Someplace called Presbyterian Village, in Little Rock, would be her home when she was ready, she said. She'd paid money. They'd promised to do their duty. And that was that. "I don't want to have to be at anybody's mercy," she said, and meant it. And my wife and I thought that was a good arrangement all the way around.

So then it was back to regular life, or life as regular as could be. We had moved to New Jersey by then. We had a house. And there were plenty of visits, with my mother doing most of the visiting—walking out in our shady yard, afternoons, talking to our neighbors as if she knew them, digging in the flower beds. She seemed healthy. In high spirits. Illness and the possibility of illness had made her seize her life harder. She wanted to do more, it seemed. Take cruises. Visit Hawaii. Go. She had new friends, younger than she was. Loud, personable Southerners. We heard about them by name. Blanche. Herschel. Mignon. People we never met, who drank and laughed and liked her and were liked by her. I had pictures in my mind.

The year was counted from medical exam to medical exam, always these in the late winter, not long after my birthday. But every year there was good news after worrying. And every year there was a time to celebrate and feel relief. A reprieve.

I do not mean to say that any of our lives then were lived outside the expectation and prism of death. No one, I think, can lose his parent and not live out his life waiting for the other one to drop dead or begin to die. The joy of surviving is tainted by squeamish certainty that you can't survive. And I read my mother's death in almost all of her life during those days. I looked for illness. Listened to her complaints too carefully. Planned her death obscurely, along with my own abhorrence of it—treated myself to it early so that when the time came I would not, myself, go down completely.

At first there were backaches. It is hard to remember exactly when. The spring, 1981—six years since her first operation. She came to New Jersey to visit, and something had gone wrong. She was seventy, but pain had come into her life. She looked worn down, invaded by hurting. She'd seen doctors in Little Rock, but none of this had to do with her cancer, she said they said. It was back trouble. Parts were just wearing out. She went home, but in the summer she hurt more. I would call her and the phone would ring a long time, and then her answering voice would be weak, even barely audible, "I hurt, Richard," she'd tell me, wherever I was. "The doctor is giving me pills. But they don't always work." I'll come down there, I'd say. "No. I'll be fine," she'd say. "Do what you have to do." And the summer managed past that way, and the fall began.

I started a job in Massachusetts, and then one morning the phone rang. It was just at light. I don't know why anyone would call anyone at that hour unless a death was involved; but this wasn't the case. My mother had come to the hospital the night before, in an ambulance. She was in pain. And when she got there her heart had paused, briefly, though it had started again. She was better, a nurse said over the phone from Little Rock. I said I'd come that day, from Massachusetts; find people to teach my classes, drive to the airport in Albany. And that's how I did it.

In Little Rock it was still summer. A friend of my mother's, a man named Ed, met me and drove me in. We went by old buildings, over railroad tracks and across the Arkansas River. He was in a mood to comfort me: this would not turn out well, he said. My mother had been sicker than I knew; had spent days in her apartment without coming out. She had been in bed all summer. It was something I needed to prepare myself for. Her death.

But really it was more than her death. Singular life itself— hers in particular, ours—was moving into a new class of events now. These things could be understood, is what he meant to say to me. And to hold out against them was hopeless and also maybe perverse. This all was becoming a kind of thing that happens. It was inevitable after all. And it was best to see it that way.

Which, I suppose, is what I then began to do. That ride in the car, across town, to the hospital, was the demarking line for me. A man I hardly knew suggested to me how I should look at things;

how I should consider my own mother, my own life. Suggested, in essence, I begin to see *myself* in all this. Stand back. Be him or like him. It was better. And that is what I did.

My mother, it turned out, was feeling better. But something very unusual had happened to her. Her heart had stopped. There had been congestion in her lungs, the doctor told me and her. He had already performed some more tests, and the results weren't good. He was a small, curly-headed, bright-eyed young man. He was soft-spoken, and he liked my mother, remembered how she'd looked when she first came to see him. "Healthy," he said, and he was confused now by the course of a disease he supposedly knew about. I do not remember his name now. But he came into her room, sat down in the chair with some papers, and told us bad news. Just the usual bad news. The back pain was cancer, after all. She was going to die, but he didn't know when she would. Sometime in the next year, he imagined. There didn't seem to be any thought of recovering. And I know he was sorry to know it and to say it, and in a way his job may even have been harder than ours was then.

I do not really remember what we said to him. I'm sure we asked very good questions, since we were both good when the chips were down. I do not remember my mother crying. I know I did not cry. We knew, both of us, what class of events *this* was, this message. This was the message that ended one long kind of uncertainty. And I cannot believe we both, in our own ways, did not feel some relief, as if a curiosity had been satisfied and other matters begun. The real question—how serious is this?—can be answered and over with in a hurry. It is actually an odd thing. I wonder if doctors know how odd it is.

But still, in a way, it did not change things. The persuasive powers of normal life are strong, after all. To accept less than life when it is not absolutely necessary is stupid.

I think we had talks. She was getting out of the hospital again, and at least in my memory I stayed around and got out with her before I had to go back to my job. We made plans for a visit. More going. She would come to Massachusetts when she was strong enough. We could still imagine a future, and that was exactly all we asked for.

I went back to teaching, and talked to her most days, though the thought that she was getting worse, that bad things were going on there and I couldn't stop them, made me miss some days. It became an awful time, then, when life felt ruined, futureless, edging toward disappointments.

She stayed out of the hospital during that time, took blood transfusions, which seemed to make her feel better, though they were ominous. I think she went out with her friends. Had company. Lived as if life could go on. And then in early October she came north. I drove down to New York, picked her up and drove us back to my rented house in Vermont. It was misty, and most of the leaves were down. And in the house it was cold and bleak, and I took her out to dinner in Bennington just to get warm. She said she had had another transfusion for the trip and would stay with me until its benefits wore off and she was weak again.

And that was how we did that. Just another kind of regular life between us. I went to school, did my work, came home nights. She stayed in the big house with my dog. Read. Cooked lunches for herself. Watched the World Series. Watched Sadat be assassinated. Looked out the window. At night we talked. I did my school work, went out not very much. With my wife, who was working in New York and commuting up on weekends, we went on country drives, invited visitors, paid visits, lived together as we had in places far and wide all those years. I don't know what else we were supposed to do, how else that time was meant to pass.

On a sunny day in early November, when she had been with me three weeks and we were, in fact, out of things to do and talk about, she sat down beside me on the couch and said, "Richard, I'm not sure how much longer I can look out after myself. I'm sorry. But it's just the truth."

"Does that worry you?" I said.

"Well," my mother said, "yes. I'm not scheduled to go into Presbyterian Village until way next year. And I'm not quite sure what I'm going to be able to do until then."

"What would you like to do?" I said.

"I don't exactly know," she said. And she looked worried then, looked away out the window, down the hill, where the trees were bare and it was foggy.

"Maybe you'll start to feel better," I said.

"Well, yes. I could. I suppose that's not impossible," she said.

"I think it's possible," I said. "I do."

"Well. OK," my mother said.

"If you don't," I said, "if by Christmas you don't feel you can do everything for yourself, you can move in with us. We're moving back to Princeton. You can live there."

And I saw in my mother's eyes, then, a light. A *kind* of light, anyway. Recognition. Relief. Concession. Willingness.

"Are you sure about that?" she said and looked at me. My mother's eyes were very brown, I remember.

"Yes, I'm sure," I said. "You're my mother. I love you."

"Well," she said and nodded. No tears. "I'll begin to think toward that, then. I'll make some plans about my furniture."

"Well, wait," I said. And this is a sentence I wish, above all sentences in my life, I had never said. Words I wish I'd never never heard. "Don't make your plans yet," I said. "You might feel better by then. It might not be necessary to come to Princeton."

"Oh," my mother said. And whatever had suddenly put a light in her eyes suddenly went away then. And her worries resumed. Whatever lay between then and later rose again. "I see," she said. "All right."

I could've not said that. I could've said, "Yes, make the plans. In whatever way all this works out, it'll be just fine. I'll see to that." But that is what I didn't say. I deferred instead to something else, to some other future, and at least in retrospect I know what that future was. And, I think, so did she. Perhaps you could say that in that moment I witnessed her facing death, saw it take her out beyond her limits, and feared it myself, feared all that I knew; and that I clung to life, to the possibility of life and change. Perhaps I feared something more tangible. But the truth is, anything we ever could've done for each other after that passed by then and was gone. And even together we were alone.

What remains can be told quickly. In a day or two I drove her to Albany. She was cold, she said, in my house, and couldn't get warm, and would be better at home. That was our story, though there was not heat enough anywhere to get her warm. She looked pale. And when I left her at the airport gate she cried again, stood and watched me go back down the long corridor, waved a hand. I waved. It was the last time I would see her that way. On her feet. In the world. We didn't know that, of course. But we knew something was coming.

And in six weeks she was dead. There is nothing exceptional about that to tell. She never got to Princeton. Whatever was wrong with her just took her over. "My body has betrayed me" is one thing I remember her saying. Another was, "My chances now are slim and none." And that was true. I never saw her dead, didn't care to, simply took the hospital's word about it when they called. Though I saw her face death that month, over and over, and I believe because of it that seeing death faced with dignity and courage does not confer either of those, but only pity and helplessness and fear.

All the rest is just private—moments and messages the world would not be better off to know. She knew I loved her because I told her so enough. I knew she loved me. That is all that matters to me now, all that should ever matter.

And so to end.

Does one ever have a "relationship" with one's mother? No. I think not. The typical only exists in the minds of unwise people. We—my mother and I—were never bound together by guilt or embarrassment, or even by duty. Love sheltered everything. We expected it to be reliable, and it was. We were always careful to say it—"I love you"—as if a time might come, unexpectedly, when she would want to hear that, or I would, or that each of us would want to hear ourselves say it to the other, only for some reason it wouldn't be possible, and our loss would be great— confusion. Not knowing. Life lessened.

My mother and I look alike. Full, high forehead. The same chin, nose. There are pictures to show that. In myself I see her, even hear her laugh. In her life there was no particular brilliance, no celebrity. No heroics. No one crowning achievement to swell the heart. There were bad ones enough: a childhood that did not bear strict remembering; a husband she loved forever and lost; a life to follow that did not require comment. But somehow she made possible for me my truest affections, as an act of great literature would bestow upon its devoted reader. And I have known that moment with her we would all like to know, the moment of saying, "Yes. This is what it is." An act of knowing that certifies love. I have known that. I have known any number of such moments with her, known them even at the instant they occurred. And now. And, I assume, I will know them forever.

FROM
Coming of Age in Mississippi
ANNE MOODY

CHILDHOOD

THAT WHITE LADY Mama was working for worked her so hard that she always came home griping about backaches. Every night she'd have to put a red rubber bottle filled with hot water under her back. It got so bad that she finally quit. The white lady was so mad she couldn't get Mama to stay that the next day she told Mama to leave to make room for the new maid.

This time we moved two miles up the same road. Mama had another domestic job. Now she worked from breakfast to supper and still made five dollars a week. But these people didn't work Mama too hard and she wasn't as tired as before when she came home. The people she worked for were nice to us. Mrs. Johnson was a schoolteacher. Mr. Johnson was a rancher who bought and sold cattle. Mr. Johnson's mother, an old lady named Miss Ola, lived with them.

Our house, which was separated from the Johnsons' by a field of clover, was the best two-room house we had been in yet. It was made out of big new planks and it even had a new toilet. We were also once again on paved streets. We just did make those paved streets, though. A few yards past the Johnsons' house was the beginning of the old rock road we had just moved off.

We were the only Negroes in that section, which seemed like some sort of honor. All the whites living around there were well-to-do. They ranged from schoolteachers to doctors and prosperous businessmen. The white family living across the street from us owned a funeral home and the only furniture store in Centreville. They had two children, a boy and a girl. There was another white family living about a quarter of a mile in back of the Johnsons who also had a boy and a girl. The two white girls were

312

about my age and the boys a bit younger. They often rode their bikes or skated down the little hill just in front of our house. Adline, Junior and I would sit and watch them. How we wished Mama could buy us a bike or even a pair of skates to share.

There was a wide trench running from the street alongside our house. It separated our house and the Johnsons' place from a big two-story house up on the hill. A big pecan tree grew on our side of the trench, and we made our playhouse under it so we could sit in the trench and watch those white children without their knowing we were actually out there staring at them. Our playhouse consisted of two apple crates and a tin can that we sat on.

One day when the white children were riding up and down the street on their bikes, we were sitting on the apple crates making Indian noises and beating the tin can with sticks. We sounded so much like Indians that they came over to ask if that was what we were. This was the beginning of our friendship. We taught them how to make sounds and dance like Indians and they showed us how to ride their bikes and skate. Actually, I was the only one who learned. Adline and Junior were too small and too scared, although they got a kick out of watching us. I was seven, Adline five, and Junior three, and this was the first time we had ever had other children to play with. Sometimes, they would take us over to their playhouse. Katie and Bill, the children of the whites that owned the furniture store, had a model playhouse at the side of their parents' house. That little house was just like the big house, painted snow white on the outside, with real furniture in it. I envied their playhouse more than I did their bikes and skates. Here they were playing in a house that was nicer than any house I could have dreamed of living in. They had all this to offer me and I had nothing to offer them but the field of clover in summer and the apple crates under the pecan tree.

The Christmas after we moved there, I thought sure Mama would get us some skates. But she didn't. We didn't get anything but a couple of apples and oranges. I cried a week for those skates, I remember.

Every Saturday evening Mama would take us to the movies. The Negroes sat upstairs in the balcony and the whites sat downstairs. One Saturday we arrived at the movies at the same time as the white children. When we saw each other, we ran and met. Katie walked straight into the downstairs lobby and Adline, Junior, and I followed. Mama was talking to one of the white women and didn't notice that we had walked into the white lobby. I think she thought we were at the side entrance we had always used which led to the balcony. We were standing in the white lobby with our friends, when Mama came in and saw us. "C'mon! C'mon!" she yelled, pushing Adline face on into the door. "Essie Mae, um gonna try my best to kill you when I get you home. I told you 'bout running up in these stores and things like you own 'em!" she shouted, dragging me through the door. When we got outside, we stood there crying, and we could hear the white children crying inside the white lobby. After that, Mama didn't even let us stay at the movies. She carried us right home.

All the way back to our house, Mama kept telling us that we couldn't sit downstairs, we couldn't do this or that with white children. Up until that time I had never really thought about it. After all, we were playing together. I knew that we were going to separate schools and all, but I never knew why.

After the movie incident, the white children stopped playing in front of our house. For about two weeks we didn't see them at all. Then one day they were there again and we started playing. But things were not the same. I had never really thought of them as white before. Now all of a sudden they were white, and their whiteness made them better than me. I now realized that not only were they better than me because they were white, but everything they owned and everything connected with them was better than what was available to me. I hadn't realized before that downstairs in the movies was any better than upstairs. But now I saw that it was. Their whiteness provided them with a pass to downstairs in that nice section and my blackness sent me to the balcony.

Now that I was thinking about it, their schools, homes, and streets were better than mine. They had a large red brick school with nice sidewalks connecting the buildings. Their homes were large and beautiful with indoor toilets and every other convenience that I knew of at the time. Every house I had ever lived in was a one- or two-room shack with an outdoor toilet. It really bothered me that they had all these nice things and we had nothing. "There is a secret to it besides being white," I thought. Then my mind got all wrapped up in trying to uncover that secret.

One day when we were all playing in our playhouse in the ditch under the pecan tree, I got a crazy idea. I thought the secret was their "privates." I had seen everything they had but their privates and it wasn't any different than mine. So I made up a game called "The Doctor." I had never been to a doctor myself. However, Mama had told us that a doctor was the only person that could look at children's naked bodies besides their parents. Then I remembered the time my Grandma Winnie was sick. When I asked her what the doctor had done to her she said, "He examined me." Then I asked her about "examined" and she told me he looked at her teeth, in her ears, checked her heart, blood and privates. Now I was going to be the doctor. I had all of them, Katie, Bill, Sandra, and Paul plus Adline and Junior take off their clothes and stand in line as I sat on one of the apple crates and examined them. I looked in their mouths and ears, put my ear to their hearts to listen for their heartbeats. Then I had them lie down on the leaves and I looked at their privates. I examined each of them about three times, but I didn't see any differences. I still hadn't found that secret.

That night when I was taking my bath, soaping myself all over, I thought about it again. I remembered the day I had seen my two uncles Sam and Walter. They were just as white as Katie them. But Grandma Winnie was darker than Mama, so how could Sam and Walter be white? I must have been thinking about it for a long time because Mama finally called out, "Essie Mae! Stop using up all that soap! And hurry up so Adline and Junior can bathe 'fore that water gits cold."

"Mama," I said, "why ain't Sam and Walter white?"

"'Cause they mama ain't white," she answered.

"But you say a long time ago they daddy is white."

"If the daddy is white and the mama is colored, then that don't make the children white."

"But they got the same hair and color like Bill and Katie them got," I said.

"That still don't make them white! Now git out of that tub!" she snapped.

Every time I tried to talk to Mama about white people she got mad. Now I was more confused than before. If it wasn't the

straight hair and the white skin that made you white, then what
was it?

About two weeks after school opened, all my plans were in
operation. I was busy for a total of eighteen hours a day. Each day
I spent the last two periods of school on the band or on basketball. Then I would go straight to work. I was never home until
eight or nine at night and as soon as I entered the house, I'd
begin helping Adline them with their lessons so I wouldn't even
have to talk to Mama or Raymond. On Wednesday and Friday
nights I took piano lessons. On Sundays I taught Sunday school
and B.T.U.

I was so busy now that I could work for Mrs. Burke and not
think of her or her guild meetings. I would fall asleep at night
without dreaming old, embedded, recurring dreams. I had to
keep a lot of things in the back of my mind until I finished high
school.

When our mid-semester grades were released, I discovered I
had made A's in all my subjects. Everything seemed so easy now.
Sometimes I got scared because things were moving along too
smoothly. Things had always seemed hard before. But now I was
doing three times as much and I felt as if I could take on the
whole world and not be tired by it. I was even better in
basketball than I had ever been. In fact, I was the number one
girl on the team.

Mr. Hicks, our new coach, was a nut for physical fitness—
especially for girls. He hated women who were dumb about
sports and he used to practice us until we were panting like
overplowed mules. Sometimes he'd even take us out to play touch
football with the boys so that we could learn that game. All the
girls who didn't go along with his physical fitness program or who
were fat and lazy he dismissed immediately. He was determined
to have a winning team and was interested only in tall, slim girls
who were light and fast on their feet. I think I worked harder
than almost anyone else.

Shortly after mid-semester, Mr. Hicks organized a gymnastic
and tumbling team. All the basketball players were required to

participate. Running and heaving a ball on that open basketball court wasn't so bad, but falling on it when we did somersaults, handsprings, and rolls was like falling on steel.

Mr. Hicks was the most merciless person I had ever met. The first few weeks some of the girls could hardly walk, but he made them practice anyhow. "The only way to overcome that soreness and stiffness is to work it out," he would say. We all learned to like Mr. Hicks, in spite of his cruelty because in the end he was always right. After three weeks our stiffness was completely gone and we all felt good. Now I took in all the activities without even getting shortwinded. And I finished the semester with straight A's.

One Wednesday, I was ironing in Mrs. Burke's dining room as usual when she came to me looking very serious.

"Essie, I am so tired and disgusted with Wayne," she said, sitting down in one of the dining room chairs. "He almost flunked out of school last semester. At this rate he won't finish high school. I don't know what to do. He's in algebra now and he just can't manage it. I've tried to find someone to tutor him in math, but I haven't been able to. How is *your* math teacher?" she asked me.

"Oh, he is very good, but he hardly ever teaches our class. Most of the time he lets me take over," I said.

"Are you that good in algebra?" she asked.

"Yes, I make all A's in algebra, and he thinks I am one of his best students."

She looked at me for a moment as if she didn't believe me. Then she left the dining room.

"Look, Essie," she said, coming back with a book. "These are the problems Wayne is having trouble with. Can you work them?"

"Yes, we've passed these in my book. I can do them all," I said.

"See if you can work these two," Mrs. Burke said to me. "I'll press a couple of these shirts for you meanwhile."

I sat down at the dining room table and began working the two problems. I finished them before she finished the first shirt.

When I gave her the paper, she looked at me again like she didn't believe me. But after she had studied it and checked my answers against the ones given in the back of the book, she asked me if I would tutor Wayne a few evenings a week. "I'll pay you extra," she said. "And I can also help you with your piano lessons sometimes."

Within a week I was helping Wayne and a group of his white friends with their algebra every Monday, Tuesday, and Thursday night. While Mrs. Burke watched television in the living room, we would all sit around the dining room table—Wayne, Billy, Ray, Sue, Judy and me. They were all my age and also in the tenth grade. I don't think Mrs. Burke was so pleased with the even proportion of boys to girls in the group. Neither did she like the open friendship that was developing between Wayne and me. She especially didn't like that Wayne was looking up to me now as his "teacher." However, she accepted it for a while. Often Wayne would drive me home after we had finished the problems for the night.

Then, one Tuesday, she came through the dining room just as Wayne was asking me a question. "Look Essie," he said, "how do we do this one?" He asked this as he leaned over me with his arms resting on the back of my chair, his cheek next to mine.

"*Wayne!*" Mrs. Burke called to him almost shouting. Wayne and I didn't move, but the others turned and stared at her. "Listen to what Essie is saying," she said, trying to get back her normal tone of voice.

"Mother, we *were* listening," Wayne said very indignantly, still cheek to cheek with me.

The room was extremely quiet now. I felt as if I should have said something. But I couldn't think of anything to say. I knew Wayne was purposely trying to annoy his mother so I just sat there, trying to keep from brushing my cheek against his, feeling his warm breath on my face. He stared at her until she looked away and went hurriedly into the kitchen.

Wayne straightened up for a moment and looked at each of his friends as they looked to him for an explanation. His face was completely expressionless. Then he leaned over me again and asked the same question he had asked before. At that point, Mrs. Burke came back through the dining room.

"Wayne, you can take Billy them home, now," she said.

"We haven't done this problem, Mother. If you would stop interrupting maybe we could finish."

"Finish the problem then and take Billy them home, but drop Essie off first," Mrs. Burke said and left the room.

I explained the problem. But I was just talking to the paper. Everyone had lost interest now.

When we left the house Mrs. Burke watched us get into the car and drive off. Didn't anyone say a word until Wayne stopped in front of my house. Then Billy said, "See you Thursday, Essie," as cheerfully as he could. "O.K.," I said, and Wayne drove away.

The following evening when I went to work, Mrs. Burke wasn't home and neither was Wayne. Mrs. Burke had left word with Mrs. Crosby that I was to do the ironing and she had put out so many clothes for me to do that by the time I finished I was late for my piano lesson. I ran out of the house and down the front walk with my music books in my hand just as Mrs. Burke and Wayne were pulling into the driveway.

"Did you finish the ironing already, Essie?" Mrs. Burke asked me, as she got out of the car.

"I just finished," I said.

"Where are you going in such a hurry?" Wayne asked.

"I'm late for my piano lesson."

"Let me drive you then," he said.

"I'm going to use the car shortly, Wayne," Mrs. Burke snapped.

"It's not far from here. I can walk," I said, rushing down the sidewalk.

The next evening Sue and Judy didn't show up. Only the boys came. Mrs. Burke kept passing through the dining room every few minutes or so. The moment we finished doing the problems, she came in and said, "Essie, I gotta stop in and see Mrs. Fisher tonight. I'll drop you off."

I had begun to get tired of her nagging and hinting, but I didn't know what to do about it. In a way I enjoyed helping Wayne and his friends. I was learning a lot from them, just as they were from me. And I appreciated the extra money. Mrs. Burke paid me two dollars a week for helping Wayne and Wayne's friends paid me a dollar each. I was now making twelve dollars a week, and depositing eight dollars in my savings account. I decided not to do anything about Mrs. Burke. "She will soon see that I won't mess with Wayne," I thought.

The Saturday afternoon I was out in the backyard hanging clothes on the line while Wayne was practicing golf.

"Essie, you want to play me a round of golf?" he asked as I finished and headed for the back door.

"I don't know how to play," I said.

"It's easy. I'll teach you," he said. "Come, let me show you something."

He gave me the golf club and tried to show me how to stand, putting his arms around me and fixing my hands on the club.

"Essie, the washing machine stopped long ago!" Mrs. Burke suddenly yelled out of the house.

"I'll show you when you finish the wash," Wayne said as I walked away. I didn't even look back at him. Walking into the house. I felt like crying. I could feel what was happening inside Wayne. I knew that he was extremely fond of me and he wanted to do something for me because I was helping him and his friends with their algebra. But the way he wanted to do it put me up tight. By trying to keep him from doing it, Mrs. Burke only made him want to do it more. I knew Wayne respected me and wouldn't have gotten out of his place if I'd remained distant and cool. Now I wanted to tell him that he didn't have to do anything for me—but I didn't know how.

Wayne, Billy, and Ray received B's on the mid-semester exams. They were so happy about their marks they brought their test papers over for me to see. I shall never forget that night. The four of us sat around the table after we had corrected the mistakes on their papers.

"Gee, Essie, we love you," Billy said. "And just think, Wayne, we could have gotten A's, and if we make an A on the final exam we will get a B for a final grade." Wayne didn't say anything for a while. He just looked at Billy, then at me. When he looked at me he didn't have to speak.

"Boy, let's call Sue and Judy and see what they got," he finally said. He ran to the phone in the hall, followed by Billy and Ray.

When they left me sitting there, I began to wonder how it was that Wayne and his friends were so nice and their parents so nasty and distasteful.

Sue and Judy came back to me for help because they almost

flunked the exam. Mrs. Burke seemed more relaxed once the girls were back. However, they were not relaxed at all. They felt guilty for leaving in the first place. For a week or so they brought me little gifts and it made me nervous. But after that we were again one little happy family.

The dining room in Mrs. Burke's house had come to mean many things to me. It symbolized hatred, love, and fear in many variations. The hatred and the love caused me much anxiety and fear. But courage was growing in me too. Little by little it was getting harder and harder for me not to speak out. Then one Wednesday night it happened.

Mrs. Burke seemed to discuss her most intimate concerns with me whenever I was ironing. This time she came in, sat down, and asked me, "Essie, what do you think of all this talk about integrating the schools in the South?"

At first I looked at her stunned with my mouth wide open. Then Mama's words ran through my head: "Just do your work like you don't know nothin'." I changed my expression to one of stupidity.

"Haven't you heard about the Supreme Court decision, and all this talk about integrating the schools?" she asked.

I shook my head no. But I lied.

"Well, we have a lot of talk about it here and people seemingly just don't know what to do. But I am not in favor of integrating schools. We'll move to Liberty first. I am sure that they won't stand for it there. You see, Essie, I wouldn't mind Wayne going to school with *you*. But all Negroes aren't like you and your family. You wouldn't like to go to school with Wayne, would you?" She said all this with so much honesty and concern, I felt compelled to be truthful.

"I don't know, Mrs. Burke. I think we could learn a lot from each other. I like Wayne and his friends. I don't see the difference in me helping Wayne and his friends at home and setting in a classroom with them. I've learned a lot from Judy them. Just like all Negroes ain't like me, all white children I know ain't like Wayne and Judy them. I was going to the post office the other day and a group of white girls tried to force me off the sidewalk. And I have seen Judy with one of them. But I know Judy ain't like that. She wouldn't push me or any other Negro off the street."

"What I asked you, Essie, is if you wanted to go to school with Wayne," Mrs. Burke said stiffly. "I am not interested in what Judy's friends did to you. So you are telling me you want to go to school with Wayne!" She stormed out of the dining room, her face burning with anger.

After she left I stood at the ironing board waiting—waiting for her to return with my money and tell me she didn't need me any more. But she didn't. She didn't confront me at all before I left that evening. And I went home shaking with fear.

The next evening when I came to work I found a note from Mrs. Burke stating she was at a guild meeting and telling me what to do. That made things even worse. As I read the note my hand shook. My eyes lingered on "the Guild." Then when Wayne and his friends didn't show up for their little session with me, I knew something was wrong. I didn't know what to do. I waited for an hour for Wayne and Judy them to come. When they didn't, I went to Mrs. Crosby's room and knocked.

When Mrs. Crosby didn't answer my heart stopped completely. I knew she was in there. She had been very ill and hadn't been out in a month. In fact, I hadn't even seen her because Mrs. Burke had asked me not to go to her room. At last I put my hand on the knob of her door and slowly turned it. "She can't be dead, she can't be dead," I thought. I opened the door slowly.

"Mrs. Crosby," I said. She was sitting up in bed as white as a ghost. I saw that she must have been sleeping. Her long, long hair was not braided as usual. It was all over the pillow everywhere.

"How do you feel, Mrs. Crosby?" I asked, standing at the foot of her bed. She beckoned for me to come closer. Then she motioned for me to sit on her bed. As I sat on the bed, she took my hands and held them affectionately.

"How do you feel?" I repeated.

"Weak but better," she said in a very faint voice.

"I was suppose to help Wayne them with their algebra this evening, but they didn't come," I said.

"I know," she said. "I heard Wayne and his mother fighting last night. Wayne is a nice boy, Essie. He and his friends like you very much. However, his mother is a very impatient woman. You study hard in school, Essie. When you finish I am going to help you to go to college. You will be a great math teacher one day. Now you go home. Wayne and his friends aren't coming tonight." She squeezed my hands.

The way she talked scared me stiff. When it was time to go home and I walked out on the porch, it was dark. I stood there afraid to move. "I can't go through the project now," I thought. "Mrs. Burke them might have someone out there to kill me or beat me up like they beat up Jerry. Why did I have to talk to Mrs. Burke like that yesterday?" I took the long way home that went along the lighted streets. But I trembled with fear every time a car drove past. I just knew that out of any car five or six men could jump and grab me.

The following day, I didn't go to work. I didn't even go to school. I told Mama I had a terrible headache and I stayed in bed all day.

"Essie Mae, it's four o'clock. You better git up from there and go to work," Mama called.

"My head's still hurting. I ain't going to work with my head hurting this bad," I whined.

"Why is you havin' so many headaches? You been lazin' in bed all day. Miss Burke gonna fire you. Junior, go up there and tell Miss Burke Essie Mae is sick."

I lay in bed thinking I had to find some other ache because Mama was getting wise to my headaches. If I could only tell her about Mrs. Burke, I wouldn't have to lie to her all the time. I really missed Mrs. Rice. Mrs. Rice would have told me what to do. I couldn't talk to any of the other teachers. "What can I do?" I thought. "I can't just quit, because she'll fix it so I can't get another job."

When Junior came back, I called him into my room.

"What did Mrs. Burke say?" I asked him.

"She ain't said nothing but for you to come to work tomorrow, cause the house need a good cleanin'. She want me to come with you to mow the yard."

I felt a little better after Junior told me that. But I couldn't understand Mrs. Burke's actions. It worried me that she was still going to keep me on. What if she was doing that just to try and frame me with something? "I'll see how she acts tomorrow," I finally decided.

* * *

At seven o'clock on Saturday morning Junior and I headed through the project for Mrs. Burke's house. Usually I took advantage of my walk through the project to think about things and compose myself before I got to work, but today I didn't have a single thought in my head. I guess I had thought too much the day before. When I walked up on her porch and saw her standing in the hall smiling it didn't even register. I was just there. I realized at that point I was plain tired of Mrs. Burke.

I went about the housecleaning like a robot until I got to the dining room. Then I started thinking. I stood there for some time thinking about Mrs. Burke, Wayne, and his friends. It was there I realized that when I thought of Wayne my thoughts were colored by emotions. I liked him more than a friend. I stood softly looking down at the table and the chair where Wayne sat when I helped him with his lessons.

When I looked up Mrs. Burke was standing in the doorway staring at me. I saw the hatred in her eyes.

"Essie," she said, "did you see my change purse when you cleaned my room?"

"No," I answered, "I didn't see it."

"Maybe I dropped it outside in the yard when I was showing Junior what to do," she said.

"So, that's how she's trying to hurt me," I thought, following her to the back door. "She better not dare." I stood in the back door and watched her walk across the big backyard toward Junior. First she stood talking to him for a minute, then they walked over to a corner of the yard and poked around in the grass as though she was looking for her purse. After they had finished doing that, she was still talking to Junior and he stood there trembling with fear, a horrified look on his face. She shook him down and turned his pockets inside out. I opened the door and ran down the steps. I didn't realize what I was about to do until I was only a few paces away from them.

"Did you find it out here, Mrs. Burke?" I asked her very coldly, indicating that I had seen her shake Junior down.

"No, I haven't found it," she answered. She looked at Junior as if she still believed he had it.

"Did you see Mrs. Burke's purse, Junior?" I asked him.

"No, I ain't saw it." He shook his head and never took his eyes off Mrs. Burke.

"Junior hasn't seen it, Mrs. Burke. Maybe we overlooked it in the house."

"You cleaned my bedroom, Essie, and you said you didn't see it," Mrs. Burke said, but she started back to the house, and I followed her.

When we got inside, she went in the bedroom to look for her purse and I went back to housecleaning. About thirty minutes later she interrupted me again.

"I found it, Essie," she said, showing me the change purse in her hand.

"Where was it?" I asked.

"I had forgotten. Wayne and I watched TV in his room last night." She gave me a guilty smile.

"I am glad you found it." I picked up the broom and continued sweeping.

"I'll just find me another job," I thought to myself. "This is my last day working for this bitch. School will be out soon and I'll go back to Baton Rouge and get a job. Ain't no sense in me staying on here. Sooner or later something might really happen. Then I'll wish I had quit."

"Essie, I don't have enough money to pay you today," Mrs. Burke said, sitting at the big desk in the hallway. She was looking through her wallet. "I'll pay you on Monday. I'll cash a check then."

"You can give me a check, now, Mrs. Burke. I won't be back on Monday."

"Do you go to piano lessons on Monday now?" she asked.

"I am not coming back, Mrs. Burke," I said it slowly and deliberately, so she didn't misunderstand this time.

She looked at me for a while, and then said "Why?"

"I saw what you did to Junior. Junior don't steal. And I have worked for white people since I was nine. I have worked for you almost two years, and I have never stole anything from you or anybody else. We work, Mrs. Burke, so we won't have to steal."

"O.K., Essie, I'll give you a check," Mrs. Burke said angrily. She hurriedly wrote one out and gave it to me.

"Is Junior still here?" I asked.

"No, I paid him and he's gone already. Why?" she asked.

I didn't answer. I just slowly walked to the front door. When I got there, I turned around and looked down the long hallway for the last time. Mrs. Burke stood at the desk staring at me curiously as I came back toward her again.

"Did you forget something?" she asked as I passed her.

"I forgot to tell Mrs. Crosby I am leaving," I said, still walking.

"Mama doesn't pay you. I do! I do!" she called to me, as I knocked gently and opened Mrs. Crosby's door.

Mrs. Crosby was propped up on pillows in bed as usual. But she looked much better than she had the last time I was in her room.

"How are you feeling, Mrs. Crosby?" I asked, standing by the side of her bed.

"Much better, Essie," she answered. She motioned for me to sit down.

"I just came to tell you this is my last day working for Mrs. Burke, Mrs. Crosby."

"What happened? Did she fire you, Essie?" she asked.

"She didn't fire me. I just decided to leave."

"I understand, Essie," she said. "And you take care of yourself. And remember when you are ready for college let me know, and I'll help you." She squeezed my hand.

"I gotta go, Mrs. Crosby," I said. "I hope you'll be up soon."

"Thanks, Essie, and please take care of yourself," she said.

"I will, Mrs. Crosby. 'Bye."

"'Bye, Essie," she said. She squeezed my hand again and then I left her room.

When I walked out of Mrs. Crosby's room, Mrs. Burke was still standing in the hallway by the desk.

"Maybe you would like to come back tonight and say good-bye to Wayne, too," she said sarcastically.

I didn't say anything to her. I walked past her and out of that house for good. And I hoped that as time passed I could put not only Mrs. Burke but all her kind out of my life for good.

THE MOVEMENT

During my senior year at Tougaloo, my family hadn't sent me one penny. I had only the small amount of money I had earned at

Maple Hill. I couldn't afford to eat at school or live in the dorms, so I had gotten permission to move off campus. I had to prove that I could finish school, even if I had to go hungry every day. I knew Raymond and Miss Pearl were just waiting to see me drop out. But something happened to me as I got more and more involved in the Movement. It no longer seemed important to prove anything. I had found something outside myself that gave meaning to my life.

I had become very friendly with my social science professor, John Salter, who was in charge of NAACP activities on campus. All during the year, while the NAACP conducted a boycott of the downtown stores in Jackson, I had been one of Salter's most faithful canvassers and church speakers. During the last week of school, he told me that sit-in demonstrations were about to start in Jackson and that he wanted me to be the spokesman for a team that would sit-in at Woolworth's lunch counter. The two other demonstrators would be classmates of mine, Memphis and Pearlena. Pearlena was a dedicated NAACP worker, but Memphis had not been very involved in the Movement on campus. It seemed that the organization had had a rough time finding students who were in a position to go to jail. I had nothing to lose one way or the other. Around ten o'clock the morning of the demonstrations, NAACP headquarters alerted the news services. As a result, the police department was also informed, but neither the policemen nor the newsmen knew exactly where or when the demonstrations would start. They stationed themselves along Capitol Street and waited.

To divert attention from the sit-in at Woolworth's, the picketing started at J. C. Penney's a good fifteen minutes before. The pickets were allowed to walk up and down in front of the store three or four times before they were arrested. At exactly 11 A.M., Pearlena, Memphis, and I entered Woolworth's from the rear entrance. We separated as soon as we stepped into the store, and made small purchases from various counters. Pearlena had given Memphis her watch. He was to let us know when it was 11:14. At 11:14 we were to join him near the lunch counter and at exactly 11:15 we were to take seats at it.

Seconds before 11:15 we were occupying three seats at the

previously segregated Woolworth's lunch counter. In the beginning the waitresses seemed to ignore us, as if they really didn't know what was going on. Our waitress walked past us a couple of times before she noticed we had started to write our own orders down and realized we wanted service. She asked us what we wanted. We began to read to her from our order slips. She told us that we would be served at the back counter, which was for Negroes.

"We would like to be served here," I said.

The waitress started to repeat what she had said, then stopped in the middle of the sentence. She turned the lights out behind the counter, and she and the other waitresses almost ran to the back of the store, deserting all their white customers. I guess they thought that violence would start immediately after the whites at the counter realized what was going on. There were five or six other people at the counter. A couple of them just got up and walked away. A girl sitting next to me finished her banana split before leaving. A middle-aged white woman who had not yet been served rose from her seat and came over to us. "I'd like to stay here with you," she said, "but my husband is waiting."

The newsmen came in just as she was leaving. They must have discovered what was going on shortly after some of the people began to leave the store. One of the newsmen ran behind the woman who spoke to us and asked her to identify herself. She refused to give her name, but said she was a native of Vicksburg and a former resident of California. When asked why she had said what she had said to us, she replied, "I am in sympathy with the Negro movement." By this time a crowd of cameramen and reporters had gathered around us taking pictures and asking questions, such as Where were we from? Why did we sit-in? What organization sponsored it? Were we students? From what school? How were we classified?

I told them that we were all students at Tougaloo College, that we were represented by no particular organization, and that we planned to stay there even after the store closed. "All we want is service," was my reply to one of them. After they had finished probing for about twenty minutes, they were almost ready to leave.

At noon, students from a nearby white high school started

pouring in to Woolworth's. When they first saw us they were sort of surprised. They didn't know how to react. A few started to heckle and the newsmen became interested again. Then the white students started chanting all kinds of anti-Negro slogans. We were called a little bit of everything. The rest of the seats except the three we were occupying had been roped off to prevent others from sitting down. A couple of the boys took one end of the rope and made it into a hangman's noose. Several attempts were made to put it around our necks. The crowds grew as more students and adults came in for lunch.

We kept our eyes straight forward and did not look at the crowd except for occasional glances to see what was going on. All of a sudden I saw a face I remembered—the drunkard from the bus station sit-in. My eyes lingered on him just long enough for us to recognize each other. Today he was drunk too, so I don't think he remembered where he had seen me before. He took out a knife, opened it, put it in his pocket, and then began to pace the floor. At this point, I told Memphis and Pearlena what was going on. Memphis suggested that we pray. We bowed our heads, and all hell broke loose. A man rushed forward, threw Memphis from his seat, and slapped my face. Then another man who worked in the store threw me against an adjoining counter.

Down on my knees on the floor, I saw Memphis lying near the lunch counter with blood running out of the corners of his mouth. As he tried to protect his face, the man who'd thrown him down kept kicking him against the head. If he had worn hard-soled shoes instead of sneakers, the first kick probably would have killed Memphis. Finally a man dressed in plain clothes identified himself as a police officer and arrested Memphis and his attacker.

Pearlena had been thrown to the floor. She and I got back on our stools after Memphis was arrested. There were some white Tougaloo teachers in the crowd. They asked Pearlena and me if we wanted to leave. They said that things were getting too rough. We didn't know what to do. While we were trying to make up our minds, we were joined by Joan Trumpauer. Now there were three of us and we were integrated. The crowd began to chant, "Communists, Communists, Communists." Some old man in the crowd ordered the students to take us off the stools.

"Which one should I get first?" a big husky boy said.

"That white nigger," the one man said.

The boy lifted Joan from the counter by her waist and carried her out of the store. Simultaneously, I was snatched from my stool by two high school students. I was dragged about thirty feet toward the door by my hair when someone made them turn me loose. As I was getting up off the floor, I saw Joan coming back inside. We started back to the center of the counter to join Pearlena. Lois Chaffee, a white Tougaloo faculty member, was now sitting next to her. So Joan and I just climbed across the rope at the front end of the counter and sat down. There were now four of us, two whites and two Negroes, all women. The mob started smearing us with ketchup, mustard, sugar, pies, and everything on the counter. Soon Joan and I were joined by John Salter, but the moment he sat down he was hit on the jaw with what appeared to be brass knuckles. Blood gushed from his face and someone threw salt into the open wound. Ed King, Tougaloo's chaplain, rushed to him.

At the other end of the counter, Lois and Pearlena were joined by George Raymond, a CORE field worker and a student from Jackson State College. Then a Negro high school boy sat down next to me. The mob took spray paint from the counter and sprayed it on the new demonstrators. The high school student had on a white shirt; the word "nigger" was written on his back with red spray paint.

We sat there for three hours taking a beating when the manager decided to close the store because the mob had begun to go wild with stuff from the other counters. He begged and begged everyone to leave. But even after fifteen minutes of begging, no one budged. They would not leave until we did. Then Dr. Beittel, the president of Tougaloo College, came running in. He said he had just heard what was happening.

About ninety policemen were standing outside the store; they had been watching the whole thing through the windows, but had not come in to stop the mob or do anything. President Beittel went outside and asked Captain Ray to come and escort us out. The captain refused, stating the manager had to invite him in before he could enter the premises, so Dr. Beittel himself brought us out. He had told the police that they had better protect us after we were outside the store. When we got outside, the policemen formed a single line that blocked the mob from us. However, they were allowed to throw at us everything they had collected. Within ten minutes, we were picked up by Reverend King in his station wagon and taken to the NAACP headquarters on Lynch Street.

After the sit-in, all I could think of was how sick Mississippi whites were. They believed so much in the segregated Southern way of life, they would kill to preserve it. I sat there in the NAACP office and thought of how many times they had killed when this way of life was threatened. I knew that the killing had just begun. "Many more will die before it is over with," I thought. Before the sit-in, I had always hated the whites in Mississippi. Now I knew it was impossible for me to hate sickness. The whites had a disease, an incurable disease in its final stage. What were our chances against such a disease? I thought of the students, the young Negroes who had just begun to protest, as young interns. When these young interns got older, I thought, they would be the best doctors in the world for social problems.

North Toward Home

WILLIE MORRIS

LIKE MARK TWAIN and his comrades growing up a century before in another village on the other side of the Mississippi, my friends and I had but one sustaining ambition in the 1940s. Theirs in Hannibal was to be steamboatmen, ours in Yazoo was to be major-league baseball players. In the summers, we thought and talked of little else. We memorized batting averages, fielding averages, slugging averages, we knew the roster of the Cardinals and the Red Sox better than their own managers must have known them, and to hear the broadcasts from all the big-city ballparks with their memorable names—the Polo Grounds, Wrigley Field, Fenway Park, the Yankee Stadium—was to set our imagination churning for the glory and riches those faraway places would one day bring us. One of our friends went to St. Louis on his vacation to see the Cards, and when he returned with the autographs of Stan Musial, Red Schoendienst, Country Slaughter, Marty Marion, Joe Garagiola, and a dozen others, we could hardly keep down our envy. I hated that boy for a month, and secretly wished him dead, not only because he took on new airs but because I wanted those scraps of paper with their magic characters. I wished also that my own family were wealthy enough to take me to a big-league town for two weeks, but to a bigger place even than St. Louis: Chicago, maybe, with not one but two teams, or best of all to New York, with three. I had bought a baseball cap in Jackson, a real one from the Brooklyn Dodgers, and a Jackie Robinson Louisville Slugger, and one day when I could not even locate any of the others for catch or for baseball talk, I sat on a curb on Grand Avenue with the most dreadful feelings of being caught forever by time—trapped there always in my scrawny and helpless condition. *I'm ready, I'm ready,* I kept thinking to myself, but that remote future when I would wear a cap like that and be a hero for a grandstand full of people seemed so far away I knew it would never come. I must have been the most dejected-looking child you ever saw, sitting hunched up on the curb and dreaming of glory in the mythical cities of the North. I felt worse when a carload of high school boys halted right in front of where I sat, and they started reciting what they always did when they saw me alone and day-dreaming. *Wee Willie Winkie walks through the town, upstairs and downstairs in his nightgown.* Then one of them said, "Winkie, you *gettin'* much?" "You bastards!" I shouted, and they drove off laughing like wild men.

Almost every afternoon when the heat was not unbearable my father and I would go out to the old baseball field behind the armory to hit flies. I would stand far out in center field, and he would station himself with a fungo at home plate, hitting me one high fly, or Texas Leaguer, or line drive after another, sometimes for an hour or more without stopping. My dog would get out there in the outfield with me, and retrieve the inconsequential dribblers or the ones that went too far. I was light and speedy, and could make the most fantastic catches, turning completely around and forgetting the ball sometimes to head for the spot where it would descend, or tumbling head-on for a diving catch. The smell of that new-cut grass was the finest of all smells, and I could run forever and never get tired. It was a dreamy, suspended state, those late afternoons, thinking of nothing but outfield flies as the world drifted lazily by on Jackson Avenue. I learned to judge what a ball would do by instinct, heading the way it went as if I owned it, and I knew in my heart I could make the big time. Then, after all that exertion, my father would shout, "I'm whupped!" and we would quit for the day.

When I was twelve I became a part-time sportswriter for the *Yazoo Herald*, whose courtly proprietors allowed me unusual independence. I wrote up an occasional high school or Legion game in a florid prose, filled with phrases like "two-ply blow" and "circuit-ringer." My mentor was the sports editor of the *Memphis Commercial Appeal*, whose name was Walter Stewart, a man who could invest the most humdrum athletic contest with the elements of Shakespearean tragedy. I learned whole paragraphs of his by heart, and used some of his expressions for my reports on games between Yazoo and Satartia, or the other teams. That summer when I was twelve, having never seen a baseball game higher than the Jackson Senators of Class B, my father finally relented and took me to Memphis to see the Chicks, who were Double-A. It was the farthest I had ever been from home, and the largest city I had ever seen; I walked around in a state of joyousness, admiring the crowds and the big park high above the River, and best of all, the grand old lobby of the Chisca Hotel.

Staying with us at the Chisca were the Nashville Vols, who were there for a big series with the Chicks. I stayed close to the lobby to get a glimpse of them; when I discovered they spent all day, up until the very moment they left for the ballpark, playing the pinball machine, I stationed myself there too. Their names were Tookie Gilbert, Smokey Burgess, Chuck Workman, and Bobo Hollomon, the latter being the one who got as far as the St. Louis Browns, pitched a no-hitter in his first major league game, and failed to win another before being shipped down forever to obscurity; one afternoon my father and I ran into them outside the hotel on the way to the game and gave them a ride in our taxi. I could have been fit for tying, especially when Smokey Burgess tousled my hair and asked me if I batted right or left, but when I listened to them as they grumbled about having to get out to the ballpark so early, and complained about the season having two more damned months to go and about how ramshackle their team bus was, I was too disillusioned even to tell my friends when I got home.

Because back home, even among the adults, baseball was all-meaning; it was the link with the outside. A place known around town simply as The Store, down near the train depot, was the principal center of this ferment. The Store had sawdust on the floor and long shreds of flypaper hanging from the ceiling. Its most familiar staples were Rexall supplies, oysters on the half shell, legal beer, and illegal whiskey, the latter served up, Mississippi bootlegger style, by the bottle from a hidden shelf and costing not merely the price of the whiskey but the investment in gas required to go to Louisiana to fetch it. There was a long counter in the back. On one side of it, the white workingmen congregated after hours every afternoon to compare the day's scores and talk batting averages, and on the other side, also talking baseball, were the Negroes, juxtaposed in a face-to-face arrangement with the whites. The scores were chalked up on a blackboard hanging on a red and purple wall, and the conversations were carried on in fast, galloping shouts from one end of the room to the other. An intelligent white boy of twelve was even permitted, in that atmosphere of heady freedom before anyone knew the name of Justice Warren or had heard much of the United States Supreme Court, a quasi-public position favoring the Dodgers, who had Jackie Robinson, Roy Campanella, and Don Newcombe—not to mention, so it was rumored, God knows how many Chinese and mulattoes being groomed in the minor leagues. I remember my father turned to some friends at The Store one day and observed, "Well, you can say what you want to about that nigger Robinson, but he's got *guts*," and to a man the others nodded, a little reluctantly, but in agreement nonetheless. And one of them said he had read somewhere that Pee Wee Reese, a white Southern boy, was the best friend Robinson had on the team, which proved they had chosen the right one to watch after him.

There were two firehouses in town, and on hot afternoons the firemen at both establishments sat outdoors in their shirtsleeves, with the baseball broadcast turned up as loud as it would go. On his day off work my father, who had left Cities Service and was now a bookkeeper for the wholesale grocery, usually started with Firehouse No. 1 for the first few innings and then hit Number Two before ending up at The Store for the post-game conversations.

I decided not to try out for the American Legion Junior Baseball team that summer. Legion baseball was an important thing for country boys in those parts, but I was too young and skinny, and I had heard that the coach, a dirt farmer known as Gentleman Joe, made his protégés lie flat in the infield while he walked on their stomachs; he also forced them to take three-mile runs through the streets of town, talked them into going to church, and persuaded them to give up Coca-Colas. A couple of summers later, when I did go out for the team, I found out that Gentleman Joe did in fact insist on these soul-strengthening rituals; because of them, we won the Mississippi State Championship and the merchants in town took up a collection and sent us all the way to St. Louis to see the Cards play the Phillies. My main concern that earlier summer, however, lay in the more academic aspects of the game. I knew more about baseball, its technology and its ethos, than all the firemen and Store experts put together. Having read most of its literature, I could give a sizable lecture on the infield-fly rule alone, which only a thin minority of the townspeople knew existed. Gentleman Joe was held in some esteem for his strategical sense, yet he was the only man I ever knew who could call for a sacrifice bunt with two men out and not have a bad conscience about it. I remember one dismaying moment that came to me while I was watching a country semi-pro game. The home team had runners on first and third with one out, when the batter hit a ground ball to the first baseman, who stepped on first and then threw to second. The shortstop, covering second, stepped on the base but made no attempt to tag the runner. The man on third had crossed the plate, of course, but the umpire, who was not very familiar with the subtleties of the rules, signaled a double play. Sitting in the grandstand, I knew that it was not a double play at all and that the run had scored, but when I went down, out of my Christian duty, to tell the manager of the local team that he had just been done out of a run, he told me I was crazy. This was the kind of brainpower I was up against.

That summer the local radio station, the one where we broadcast our Methodist programs, started a baseball quiz program. A razor blade company offered free blades and the station chipped in a dollar, all of which went to the first listener to telephone with the right answer to the day's baseball question. If there was no winner, the next day's pot would go up a dollar. At the end of the month they had to close down the program because I was winning all the money. It got so easy, in fact, that I stopped phoning in the answers some afternoons so that the pot could build up and make my winnings more spectacular. I netted about $25 and a ten-year supply of double-edged, smooth-contact razor blades before they gave up. One day, when the jackpot was a mere two dollars, the announcer tried to confuse me. "Babe Ruth," he said, "hit sixty home runs in 1927 to set the major-league record. What man had the next-highest total?" I telephoned and said, "George Herman Ruth. He hit fifty-nine in another season." My adversary, who had developed an acute dislike of me, said that was not the correct answer. He said it should have been *Babe* Ruth. This incident angered me, and I won for the next four days, just for the hell of it.

On Sunday afternoons we sometimes drove out of town and along hot, dusty roads to baseball fields that were little more than parched red clearings, the outfield sloping out of the woods and ending in some tortuous gully full of yellowed paper, old socks, and vintage cow shit. One of the backwoods teams had a fastball pitcher named Eckert, who didn't have any teeth, and a fifty-year-old left-handed catcher named Smith. Since there were no catcher's mitts made for left-handers, Smith had to wear a mitt on his throwing hand. In his simian posture he would catch the ball and toss it lightly into the air and then whip his mitt off and catch the ball in his bare left hand before throwing it back. It was a wonderfully lazy way to spend those Sunday afternoons—my father and my friends and I sitting in the grass behind the chicken-wire backstop with eight or ten dozen farmers, watching the wrong-handed catcher go through his contorted gyrations, and listening at the same time to our portable radio, which brought us the rising inflections of a baseball announcer called the Old Scotchman. The sounds of the two games, our own and the one being broadcast from Brooklyn or Chicago, merged and rolled across the bumpy outfield and the gully into the woods; it was a combination that seemed perfectly natural to everyone there.

I can see the town now on some hot, still weekday afternoon in mid-summer: ten thousand souls and nothing doing. Even the red water truck was a diversion, coming slowly up Grand Avenue with its sprinklers on full force, the water making sizzling steam-clouds on the pavement while half-naked Negro children followed the truck up the street and played in the torrent until they got soaking wet. Over on Broadway, where the old men sat drowsily in straw chairs on the pavement near the Bon-Ton Café, whittling to make the time pass, you could laze around on the sidewalks—barefoot, if your feet were tough enough to stand the scalding concrete—watching the big cars with out-of-state plates whip by, the driver hardly knowing and certainly not caring what place this was. Way up that fantastic hill, Broadway seemed to end in a seething mist—little heat mirages that shimmered off the asphalt; on the main street itself there would be only a handful of cars parked here and there, and the merchants and the lawyers sat in the shade under their broad awnings, talking slowly, aimlessly, in the cryptic summer way. The one o'clock whistle at the sawmill would send out its loud bellow, reverberating up the streets to the bend in the Yazoo River, hardly making a ripple in the heavy somnolence.

But by two o'clock almost every radio in town was tuned in to the Old Scotchman. His rhetoric dominated the place. It hovered in the branches of the trees, bounced off the hills, and came out of the darkened stores; the merchants and the old men cocked their ears to him, and even from the big cars they sped by, their tires making lapping sounds in the softened highway, you could hear his voice, being carried past you out into the delta.

The Old Scotchman's real name was Gordon McLendon, and he described the big-league games for the Liberty Broadcasting System, which had outlets mainly in the South and the Southwest. He had a deep, rich voice, and I think he was the best rhetorician, outside of Bilbo and Nye Bevan, I have ever heard. Under his handling a baseball game took on a life of its own. As in the prose of the *Commercial Appeal's* Walter Stewart, his games were rare and remarkable entities; casual pop flies had the flow of history behind them, double plays resembled the stark clashes of old armies, and home runs deserved acknowledgment on earthen urns. Later, when I came across Thomas Wolfe, I felt I had heard him before, from Shibe Park, Crosley Field, or the Yankee Stadium.

One afternoon I was sitting around my house listening to the Old Scotchman, admiring the vivacity of a man who said he was a contemporary of Connie Mack. (I learned later that he was twenty-nine.) That day he was doing the Dodgers and the Giants from the Polo Grounds. The game, as I recall, was in the fourth inning, and the Giants were ahead by about 4 to 1. It was a boring game, however, and I began experimenting with my father's short-wave radio, an impressive mechanism a couple of feet wide, which had an aerial that almost touched the ceiling and the name of every major city in the world on its dial. It was by far the best radio I had ever seen; there was not another one like it in town. I switched the dial to short-wave and began picking up African drum music, French jazz, Australian weather reports, and a lecture from the British Broadcasting Company on the people who wrote poems for Queen Elizabeth. Then a curious thing happened. I came across a baseball game—the Giants and the Dodgers, from the Polo Grounds. After a couple of minutes I discovered that the game was in the eighth inning. I turned back to the local station, but here the Giants and Dodgers were still in the fourth. I turned again to the short-wave broadcast and listened to the last inning, a humdrum affair that ended with Carl Furillo popping out to shortstop, Gil Hodges grounding out second to first, and Roy Campenella lining out to center. Then I went back to the Old Scotchman and listened to the rest of the game. In the top of the ninth, an hour or so later, a ghostly thing occurred; to my astonishment and titillation, the game ended with Furillo popping out to short, Hodges grounding out second to first, and Campanella lining out to center.

I kept this unusual discovery to myself, and the next day, an hour before the Old Scotchman began his play-by-play of the second game of the series, I dialed the short-wave frequency, and, sure enough, they were doing the Giants and the Dodgers again. I learned that I was listening to the Armed Forces Radio Service, which broadcast games played in New York. As the game progressed I began jotting down notes on the action. When the first four innings were over I turned to the local station just in time to get the Old Scotchman for the first batter. The Old Scotchman's account of the game matched the short-wave's almost perfectly. The Scotchman's, in fact, struck me as being considerably more poetic than the one I had heard first. But I did not doubt him, since I could hear the roar of the crowd, the crack of the bat, and the Scotchman's precise description of foul balls that fell into the crowd, the gestures of the base coaches, and the expression on the face of a small boy who was eating a lemon popsicle in a box seat behind first base. I decided that the broadcast was being delayed somewhere along the line, maybe because we were so far from New York.

That was my first thought, but after a close comparison of the two broadcasts for the rest of the game, I sensed that something more sinister was taking place. For one thing, the Old Scotchman's description of the count on a batter, though it jibed 90 percent of the time, did not always match. For another, the Scotchman's crowd, compared with the other, kept up an ungodly noise. When Robinson stole second on short-wave, he did it without drawing a throw and without sliding, while for Mississippians the feat was performed in a cloud of angry, petulant dust. A foul ball that went over the grandstand and out of the park for short-wave listeners in Alaska, France, and the Argentine produced for the firemen, bootleggers, farmers, and myself a primitive scramble that ended with a feeble old lady catching the ball on the first bounce to the roar of an assembly that would have outnumbered Grant's at Old Cold Harbor. But the most revealing development came after the Scotchman's game was over. After the usual summaries, he mentioned that the game had been "recreated." I had never taken notice of that particular word before, because I lost interest once a game was over. I went to a dictionary, and under "recreate" I found, "To invest with fresh vigor and strength; to refresh, invigorate (nature, strength, a person or thing)." The Old Scotchman most assuredly invested a game with fresh vigor and strength, but this told me nothing. My deepest suspicions were confirmed, however, when I found the second definition of the word—"To create anew."

So there it was. I was happy to have fathomed the mystery, as perhaps no one else in the whole town had done. The Old Scotchman, for all his wondrous expressions, was not only several innings behind every game he described but was no doubt sitting in some air-conditioned studio in the hinterland, where he got the happenings of the game by news ticker; sound effects accounted for the crack of the bat and the crowd noises. Instead of being disappointed in the Scotchman, I was all the more pleased by his genius, for he made pristine facts more actual than actuality, a valuable lesson when the day finally came that I started reading literature. I must add, however, that this appreciation did not obscure the realization that I had at my disposal a weapon of unimaginable dimensions.

Next day I was at the short-wave again, but I learned with much disappointment that the game being broadcast on short-wave was not the one the Scotchman had chosen to describe. I tried every afternoon after that and discovered that I would have to wait until the Old Scotchman decided to do a game out of New York before I could match his game with the one described live on short-wave. Sometimes, I learned later, these coincidences did not occur for days; during an important Dodger or Yankee series, however, his game and that of the Armed Forces Radio Service often coincided for two or three days running. I was happy, therefore, to find, on an afternoon a few days later, that both the short-wave and the Scotchman were carrying the Yankees and the Indians.

I settled myself at the short-wave with notebook and pencil and took down every pitch. This I did for four full innings, and then I turned back to the town station, where the Old Scotchman was just beginning the first inning. I checked the first batter to make sure the accounts jibed. Then, armed with my notebook, I ran down the street to the corner grocery, a minor outpost of baseball intellection, presided over by my young Negro friend Bozo, a knowledgeable student of the game, the same one who kept my dog in bologna. I found Bozo behind the meat counter, with the Scotchman's account going full blast. I arrived at the interim between the top and bottom of the first inning.

"Who's pitchin' for the Yankees, Bozo?" I asked.

"They're pitchin' Allie Reynolds," Bozo said. "Old Scotchman says Reynolds really got the stuff today. He just set 'em down one, two, three."

The Scotchman, meanwhile, was describing the way the pennants were flapping in the breeze. Phil Rizzuto, he reported, was stepping to the plate.

"Bo," I said, trying to sound cut-and-dried, "you know what I think? I think Rizzuto's gonna take a couple of fast called strikes, then foul one down the left-field line, and then line out straight to Boudreau at short."

"Yeah?" Bozo said. He scratched his head and leaned lazily across the counter.

I went up front to buy something and then came back. The count worked to nothing and two on Rizzuto—a couple of fast called strikes and a foul down the left side. "This one," I said to Bozo, "he lines straight to Boudreau at short."

The Old Scotchman, pausing dramatically between words as was his custom, said, "Here's the windup on nothing and two.

Here's the pitch on its way—There's a hard line drive! But Lou Boudreau's there at shortstop and he's got it. Phil hit that one on the nose, but Boudreau was right there."

Bozo looked over at me, his eyes bigger than they were. "How'd you know that?" he asked.

Ignoring this query, I made my second prediction. "Bozo," I said, "Tommy Henrich's gonna hit the first pitch up against the right-field wall and slide in with a double."

"How come you think so?"

"Because I can predict anything that's gonna happen in baseball in the next ten years," I said. "I can tell you anything."

The Old Scotchman was describing Henrich at the plate. "Here comes the first pitch. Henrich swings, there's a hard smash into right field!... This one may be out of here! It's going, going—*No!* It's off the wall in right center Henrich's rounding first, on his way to second. Here's the relay from Doby... Henrich slides in safely with a double!" The Yankee crowd sent up an awesome roar in the background.

"Say, how'd you know that?" Bozo asked. "How'd you know he was gonna wind up at second?"

"I just can tell. I got extra-vision," I said. On the radio, far in the background, the public-address system announced Yogi Berra. "Like Berra right now. You know what? He's gonna hit a one-one pitch down the right-field line—"

"How come you know?" Bozo said. He was getting mad.

"Just a second," I said. "I'm gettin' static." I stood dead still, put my hands up against my temples and opened my eyes wide. "Now it's comin' through clear. Yeah, Yogi's gonna hit a one-one pitch down the right-field line, and it's gonna be fair by about three or four feet—I can't say exactly—and Henrich's gonna score from second, but the throw is gonna get Yogi at second by a mile."

This time Bozo was silent, listening to the Scotchman, who described the ball and the strike, then said: "Henrich takes the lead off second. Benton looks over, stretches, delivers. "Yogi swings." (There was the bat crack). "There's a line drive down the right side! It's barely inside the foul line. It may go for extra bases! Henrich's rounding third and coming in with a run. Berra's moving toward second. Here comes the throw!... And they *get* him! They get Yogi easily on the slide at second!"

Before Bozo could say anything else, I reached in my pocket for my notes. "I've just written down here what I think's gonna happen in the first four innings," I said. "Like DiMag. See, he's gonna pop up to Mickey Vernon at first on a one-nothing pitch in just a minute. But don't you worry. He's gonna hit a 380-foot homer in the fourth with nobody on base on a full count. You just follow these notes and you'll see I can predict anything that's gonna happen in the next ten years." I handed him the paper, turned around, and left the store just as DiMaggio, on a one-nothing pitch, popped up to Vernon at first.

Then I went back home and took more notes from the short-wave. The Yanks clobbered the Indians in the late innings and won easily. On the local station, however, the Old Scotchman was in the top of the fifth inning. At this juncture I went to the telephone and called Firehouse No. 1.

"Hello," a voice answered. It was the fire chief.

"Hello, Chief, can you tell me the score?" I said. Calling the firehouse for baseball information was a common practice.

"The Yanks are ahead, 5–2."

"This is the Phantom you're talkin' with," I said.

"Who?"

"The Phantom. Listen carefully, Chief. Reynolds is gonna open this next inning with a popup to Doby. Then Rizzuto will single to left on a one-one count. Henrich's gonna force him at second on a two-and-one pitch but make it to first. Berra's gonna double to right on a nothing-and-one pitch, and Henrich's goin' to third. DiMaggio's gonna foul a couple off and then double down the left-field line, and both Henrich and Yogi are gonna score. Brown's gonna pop out to third to end the inning."

"Aw, go to hell," the chief said, and hung up.

This was precisely what happened, of course. I phoned No. 1 again after the inning.

"Hello."

"Hi. This is the Phantom again."

"Say, how'd you know that?"

"Stick with me," I said ominously, "and I'll feed you predictions. I can predict anything that's gonna happen anywhere in the next ten years." After a pause I added, "Beware of fire real soon," for good measure, and hung up.

I left my house and hurried back to the corner grocery. When I got there, the entire meat counter was surrounded by friends of Bozo's, about a dozen of them. They were gathered around my notes, talking passionately and shouting. Bozo saw me standing by the bread counter. "There he is! That's the one!" he declared. His colleagues turned and stared at me in undisguised awe. They parted respectfully as I strolled over to the meat counter and ordered a dime's worth of bologna for my dog.

A couple of questions were directed at me from the group, but I replied, "I'm sorry for what happened in the fourth. I predicted DiMag was gonna hit a full-count pitch for that homer. It came out he hit it in two-and-two. There was too much static in the air between here and New York."

"Too much *static?*" one of them asked.

"Yeah. Sometimes the static confuses my extra-vision. But I'll be back tomorrow if everything's okay, and I'll try not to make any more big mistakes."

"Big mistakes!" one of them shouted, and the crowd laughed admiringly, parting once more as I turned and left the store. I wouldn't have been at all surprised if they had tried to touch the hem of my shirt.

That day was only the beginning of my brief season of triumph. A schoolmate of mine offered me five dollars, for instance, to tell him how I had known that Johnny Mize was going to hit a two-run homer to break up one particularly close game for the Giants. One afternoon, on the basis of a lopsided first four innings, I had an older friend sneak into The Store and place a bet, which netted me $14.50. I felt so bad about it I tithed $1.45 in church the following Sunday. At Bozo's grocery store I was a full-scale oracle. To the firemen I remained the Phantom, and firefighting reached a peak of efficiency that month, simply because the firemen knew what was going to happen in the late innings and did not need to tarry when an alarm came.

One afternoon my father was at home listening to the Old Scotchman with a couple of out-of-town salesmen from Greenwood. They were sitting in the front room, and I had already managed to get the first three or four innings of the Cardinals and the Giants on paper before they arrived. The Old Scotchman was in the top of the first when I walked in and said hello. The men were talking business and listening to the game at the same time.

"I'm gonna make a prediction," I said. They stopped talking and looked at me. "I predict Musial's gonna take a ball and a strike and then hit a double to right field, scoring Schoendienst from second, but Marty Marion's gonna get tagged out at the plate."

"You're mighty smart," one of the men said. He suddenly sat up straight when the Old Scotchman reported, "Here's the wind-up and the pitch coming in.... Musial *swings!*" (Bat crack, crowd roar.) "He drives one into right field! This one's going up against the boards!.... Schoendienst rounds third. He's coming on in to score! Marion dashes around third, legs churning. His cap falls off, but here he *comes!* Here's the toss to the plate. He's nabbed at home. He is *out* at the plate! Musial holds at second with a run-producing double."

Before I could parry the inevitable questions, my father caught me by the elbow and hustled me into a back room. "How'd you know that?" he asked.

"I was just guessin'," I said. "It was nothin' but luck."

He stopped for a moment, and then a new expression showed on his face. "Have *you* been callin' the firehouse?" he asked.

"Yeah, I guess a few times."

"Now, you tell me how you found out about all that. I mean it."

When I told him about the short-wave, I was afraid he might be mad, but on the contrary he laughed uproariously. "Do you remember these next few innings?" he asked.

"I got it all written down," I said, and reached in my pocket for the notes. He took the notes and told me to go away. From the yard, a few minutes later, I heard him predicting the next inning to the salesmen.

A couple of days later, I phoned No. 1 again. "This is the Phantom," I said. "With two out, Branca's gonna hit Stinky Stanky with a fast ball, and then Alvin Dark's gonna send him home with a triple."

"Yeah, we know it," the fireman said in a bored voice. "We're listenin' to a short-wave too. You think you're somethin', don't you? You're Ray Morris' boy."

I knew everything was up. The next day, as a sort of final

gesture, I took some more notes to the corner grocery in the third or fourth inning. Some of the old crowd was there, but the atmosphere was grim. They looked at me coldly. "Oh, man," Bozo said, "*we* know the Old Scotchman ain't at that game. He's four or five innings behind. He's makin' all that stuff up." The others grumbled and turned away. I slipped quietly out the door.

My period as a seer was over, but I went on listening to the short-wave broadcasts out of New York a few days more. Then, a little to my surprise, I went back to the Old Scotchman, and in time I found that the firemen, the bootleggers, and the few dirt farmers who had short-wave sets all did the same. From then on, accurate, up-to-the-minute baseball news was in disrepute there. I believe we all went back to the Scotchman not merely out of loyalty but because, in our great isolation, he touched our need for a great and unmitigated eloquence.

One day that spring, two months before I was to graduate from high school, my father gave me some unexpected advice. He was reading the *Commercial Appeal* in our front room, and he turned to me and told me, quite simply, to get the hell out of Mississippi. I do not quite know why. Perhaps he knew something about doom, though his argument, he said, was based on a lack of *opportunity*.

At first I ignored this advice. I was obsessed with Belle Prairie and the blond belle who graced its gullies, swamps, and tenant shacks. I had my heart set, at the age of seventeen, on entering Mississippi's educated landed gentry—by taking a degree at Ole Miss, as all my friends planned to do, and by returning to that plantation with my majorette, to preside there on the banks of the Yazoo over boll weevils big enough to wear dog tags, pre-Earl Warren darkies, and the young squirearchy from the plantations abutting on Carter, Eden, Holly Bluff, Sidon and Tchula.

I saw no reason to leave. I was athlete, sports announcer, valedictorian, and, my greatest pride, editor of the *Flashlight*. I knew Mississippi and I loved what I saw. I had just been voted mostly likely to succeed. In Yazoo I knew every house and every tree in the white section of town. Each street and hill was like a map on my consciousness; I loved the contours of its land, and the slow changing of its seasons. I was full of the regional graces and was known as a perfect young gentleman. I was pleasant, enthusiastic, and happy. On any question pertaining to God or man I would have cast my morals on the results of a common plebiscite of the white voters of Yazoo County. "One shudders at the thought of the meaninglessness of life," I read years later in *Winesburg, Ohio*, in a moment when I was trying to remember these years, "while at the same instant, and if the people of the town are his people, one loves life so intensely that tears come into the eyes."

Yet more than being desperately in love, I was sorrowfully ignorant—ignorant of myself, ignorant of the world of moving objects I was about to enter. One hundred miles to the north of Yazoo, Faulkner was writing his great tales of violence and the destruction of honor. In the spring of my senior year, when I was at Oxford for a convention, I watched as they filmed the jail scenes for the movie *Intruder in the Dust*, yet this did not inspire me much one way or the other. Had I known that great books were for one's own private soul rather than mere instrumentalities for achieving those useless trinkets on which all American high schools, including small ones in Mississippi, base their existence, perhaps I would have found in Faulkner some dark chord, some suggestion of how this land had shaped me, how its isolation and its guilt-ridden past had already settled so deeply into my bones. Unfortunately this was to come later. Then I joined easily and thoughtlessly in the Mississippi middle-class consensus that Faulkner, the chronicler and moralist, was out for the Yankee dollar.

My first seventeen years had been lived rich in experience—in sensual textures, in unusual confrontations. I had moved easily among many kinds of people, I had seen something of cruelty and madness, and I had survived fundamentalist religion. My father had taught me the woods; from everyone I had had love. The town in which I had grown up had yet to be touched by the great television culture, or by the hardening emotions and the defensive hostilities unloosed by the Supreme Court in 1954. Something was left, if but an oblique recollection: a Southern driftlessness, a closeness to the earth, a sense of time standing still, a lingering isolation from America's relentless currents of change and homogeneity. Something else also remained, some innocent and exposed quality that made possible, in the heart of a young and vulnerable boy, an allegiance and a love for a small, inconsequential place. Only retrospect would tell me I was to take something of these things with me forever, through my maturing into my manhood. But then I could not connect them, because I had yet to go beyond the most fundamental awareness of myself.

What was it, then, that led me to leave, to go to a place where I did not know a soul, and eventually to make such a sharp break with my own past that I still suffer from the pain of that alienation? Was there some small grain of sand there, something abrasive and unrecognized in my perception of things, some hidden ambition and independence that finally led me away from everything I knew and honored? Was there something in me that needed some stark removal from my deepest loyalties?

In trying to recapture a turning point in one's life at such an age, it is almost impossible to ascribe tangible motives to some great change in one's direction, to isolate a thought, or a decision. But there are a handful of things that stand out so clearly that they become, after many years, almost symbol. They embody in retrospect the very substance of one's existence at a given moment. They may be fleeting recollections, chance encounters, the thread of an old thought, but they are revealing in themselves, and they become more than memory.

My father took out one day for Austin, Texas, to see the campus of what we had sometimes heard was the best and certainly the biggest state university in the South. Four or five days later, my friend Bubba Barrier and I, quite by chance, ran into him in the lobby of the Edwards House in Jackson. He had just returned. "That's one hell of a place they got out there," he said. They had a main building 30 stories high, a baseball field dug right out of stone, artificial moonlight for street lamps, the biggest state capitol in the Republic, and the goddamndest student newspaper you ever saw. "I think you ought to go to school out there," he said. "Can't nuthin' in *this* state match it."

I would wander off by myself to that place of my childhood, the town cemetery. Here I would walk among all those graves I knew that had given me such a sense of the town when I was a boy—of the reprobates and early settlers, the departed gospelists and bootleggers, and all the boys we had buried with the American Legionnaires. I cannot remember what my thoughts were on these excursions, except that I had the most dramatic conception of imminent departure. Something different was stirring around in my future, and I would brood over the place where I was and some place where I would end up, and for days I carried a map of the University of Texas in my shirt pocket. I was bathing in self-drama; perhaps it was my *imagination*, which had never failed me even as a child, that sought some unknown awakening.

I had been commissioned to write the prophecy of the Class of 1952 of Yazoo High School, and I delivered it on class day that spring in the school auditorium. Afterward one of the senior class teachers cornered me and said it was the most disgusting thing she had ever heard, that only the day before she had recommended me to two FBI agents as promising material for that agency, but that she was going to write a letter telling them I was unfit for their service. These were unusual words for me, the favorite of every teacher in school and the winner of the American Legion Citizenship Award, but on rereading this curious statement I saw what had aroused her. I had consigned each member of the fifty-two-member graduating class to destruction. Honest Ed Upton, the salutatorian, was to die an agonizing death in quick-sand in a Mississippi swamp. Billy Bonner would be shot down by Italians in the streets of Brooklyn. All the others were to go the way of violence, treachery, corruption, and oblivion, except my-self, their chronicler, who did not figure in the predictions. "You just as well get out of here to Texas," that teacher said, "because it's pretty clear you don't appreciate the people around you." On graduation night in the school gymnasium, on a wet spring night in June, my comrades who were doomed to destruction and I stood finally on the podium and sang the last lines of our alma mater: "*Yazoo, Yazoo, in closing let us say . . . that forever and a day . . . we'll be thinking of you, Yazoo . . . Yazoo.*"

And one cold, dark morning in the early fall, sick with leaving for the first time the place where I grew up, and the blond majorette whom I had said goodbye to for the first and as it proved the last time in my old DeSoto car near the railroad tracks the night before, I caught a Southern Trailways bus in Vicksburg for Austin. My mother, as the story always goes, cried, and my father looked thin as death as the bus pulled out to cross the great bridge into Louisiana. I turned on the red portable radio the local radio station had given me as a farewell present, and I remember the song that came on over in Louisiana, a popular song of that time:

> *Fly the ocean in a silver plane,*
> *See the jungle when it's wet with rain,*
> *Just remember 'til you're home again*
> *You belong to me.*

Lanterns on the Levee

WILLIAM ALEXANDER PERCY

THE RETURN OF THE NATIVE

PROBABLY THERE IS NO nostalgia so long-lived and hopeless as that of the college graduate returning to his native town. He is a stranger though he is home. He is sick for a communal life that was and can never be again, a life merry with youth and unshadowed by responsibilities. He is hungry for the easy intimacies which competitive anxious living does not provide. He is unproved when proof is demanded on every side. In this alien environment, the only one he may now call his own, he is unknown, even to himself.

My case was no different from most, I suppose, and I hated it: eight years of training for life, and here I was in the midst of it—and my very soul whimpered. I had been pushed into the arena and didn't even know the animals' names. Besides, I labored under individual disabilities: I had been to Europe; I had been to Harvard; my accent, though not Northern, was—well, tainted; I had had it easy; I probably considered myself *it*. For crowning handicap, I was blessed with no endearing vices: drunkenness made me sick, gambling bored me, rutting per se, unadorned, I considered overrated and degrading. In charitable mood one might call me an idealist, but, more normally, a sissy.

It must have been difficult for Father too. Enjoying good liquor, loving to gamble, his hardy vices merely under control, he sympathized quizzically and said nothing. But his heart must often have called piteously for the little brother I had lost, all boy, all sturdy, obstreperous charm. Fortunately I wasn't meek and I wasn't afraid. When put upon, I discovered that a truculent tongue did more to save than a battalion of virtues. But it wasn't fun. I had attacks of nausea, but not of tears.

Yet these handicaps on my debut were a minor worry. My real

351

concern was what the show was all about and what role I should or could play in it, queries which, since the curtain was up and I on the stage, seemed fairly belated.

For eight years—in fact, for twenty-three—a great number of people had been pouring out money, skill, time, devotion, prayers to create something out of me that wouldn't look as if the Lord had slapped it together absent-mindedly. Not Alexander the Great nor Catherine II had been tended by a more noble corps of teachers. It humbles me to call their roster, but calling it is no penance: Nain and Mur, Mère and Père, Sister Evangelist and Judge Griffin, Father Koestenbrock and Mr. Bass, Dr. Henneman and Professor Williston, the Roman Catholic Church and Browning, the sea and the sun, Beethoven and Wagner, Michelangelo and Andrea del Sarto, loneliness and friendship, Sinkler and Harold, Mother and Father. They made a longer procession than the Magi and the shepherds combined, and the gifts they brought were more precious. Obviously I was cast to justify the ways of man to God, as it were. But how? What does one do with a life, or at any rate intend to do? It was time to inventory my ambitions and, having selected one as paramount, to pursue it whole-heartedly. For months (maybe for years, maybe until now) I hunted about for a good ambition. Money? No, positively—not because my financial future was assured or my financial present anything more than adequate to supply my simple needs, but it wasn't interesting and it wasn't worthy. Nothing to debate here. Fame as a lawyer? I had been a B man at the law school, which is eminently respectable but not brilliant as Harold and George had been. I suspected that if I should give everything I had to the law I might realize such an ambition, but I had no notion of doing any such thing. I wanted to do whatever piece of work fell to my care as well as I could, but beyond that I wasn't concerned over what opinion my brethren of the bar held of me. Power? I knew nothing about it and it certainly wasn't my métier. Civic usefulness? Perhaps; that was getting warmer, but I had no desire to hold office and I knew no way of dedicating one's unendowed life to usefulness. Other things, I did not know what, except that they were things inside, seemed realities, while money, fame, power, civic virtue seemed things which required an audience to become real. So with my ruminations I reached nowhere, a lonesome sort of spot. Now that the show is nearly over, I'm only just beginning to see what one may truthfully call the good life, but of the plot I still know so little that I can't swear whether it's been tragedy or comedy, though I have an inkling. Perhaps, after all, stumbling through life by ear, though slower, makes more exciting traveling, and if you have a good ear you're just as apt to arrive as if you'd dipped about in the wake of one of those twitchy compasses.

I didn't exactly plunge into life, rather I tipped in, trepidly. In spite of doubts and misgivings, there was living to be done and I set about it. Our town wasn't a thing of beauty in those days. The residences looked like illegitimate children of a French wedding cake. Besides all the icing they usually sported a turret or cupola to which Sister Ann couldn't have climbed if she *knew* somebody was coming, for it never had stairs. The brick stores, most of them still in situ, as we lawyers say, managed to look stark without looking simple. Curbs, gutters, and open ditches, while satisfactory to such stalwart conservatives as crawfish and mosquitoes, still abided hopefully the coming of the W.P.A. Sidewalks were often the two-board sort that grow splinters for barefoot boys, and the roads, summer or winter, were hazards. There were lovely trees and crape myrtles but where they grew was their business. There were flowers, but no gardens. Just a usual Southern town of that period, and its name was Greenville. There must be something in that name attractive to towns because every state in the Union has one. It's a name without charm for me. I prefer Alligator or Rolling Fork or Nitta Yuma or Rosedale, our neighbors— at least they have individuality, of one sort or another. But, aside from all that, in 1909 I retook Greenville for my home (and kept it) and could boast that I was a full-fledged practicing attorney-at-law.

While not what you might call indispensable in the office, I looked up authorities for Father with great interest and once or twice stumbled on an original legal theory, the discovery of which pleased him even more than myself. I was terrified at the thought of arguing a case, particularly before a jury, but somehow I steeled myself to do it and with some passion, though never brilliantly and never to this day without a spasm of nerves before and after. But the law was the least of my troubles. Making a rut, for comfort, was a grimmer endeavor, one that required years of effort—probably it is one of those lifetime jobs, and just when you are beginning to feel snug you are routed out permanently.

In those days the center of social life for the young people was the Elysian Club. The oldsters played poker at the Mississippi Club and the middling mature indulged their usual bacchanalian bent, unassisted by pards and maenads, at the Elks'. No doubt about it, our town was plumb social. Although it cherished a "reading-room" and a poolroom, our club's raison d'être was its dance floor. It was a fine floor, but it was housed in a room replete with unsynchronized angles and curves which it must have taken the local builder months to conceive and no time to execute. Beyond question it was the ugliest room in the world, but thoroughly entrancing when Handy appeared and the dancing started. Delta girls are born dancing and never stop, which is as it should be, for surely it is the finest form of human amusement except tennis and talking. The club's dances were famous from Hushpuckna to Yazoo City, and they were the right sort of affairs, with rows of broad-bosomed lares and penates against the wall and so many good-looking animated girls drawling darkest Southernese and doing intricate steps by instinct or inspiration that no one could think of going home before daylight. Drinking was not permitted in the clubhouse and there were no parked cars for intermissions. An intoxicated youth was a crying scandal and an intoxicated female would certainly have caused harakiri or apoplexy among the penates. There are dances now in the Delta, a never ending round, but I am told they are more stimulated and less stimulating.

Now and then Father and Mother appeared at our functions and remained an hour or two because they loved young people. Father himself would occasionally indulge in a whirl on the dance floor, but, being practically tone deaf, he was an awful dancer and knew it, though fairly unabashed and invariably amused. Mother never understood or forgave in me a certain lack of enthusiasm for things social. People, whole throngs of them, delighted her, and her delight was infectious. Everyone became a little more charming than he was meant by God to be when she was around. I liked people, too, but individually and separately, not in throngs. I soon learned, when surrounded, not to go bounding off like a flushed fawn, but crowds were not then and are not now my natural habitat, and even individuals, no matter how fascinating, I find more exhausting than hard work or boredom. Mother regarded my antisocial tendencies as pure mulishness, but Father, although disappointed no doubt, never showed it except by a far-away expression and a little smile.

I often took to the levee in sheer lonesomeness and confusion of soul. Our woods are not made for walking because the vines and bushes are too rampant and the rattlesnakes too much at home. But the high levee is perfect for a stroll, which you can extend, if so minded, a hundred miles in either direction. Across the river you see Arkansas, a state almost as unfamiliar to us as Montana, but we know it has one great virtue—it grows willows and cottonwoods right down to the water line. In spring they are done by Puvis de Chavannes in pastel green, in summer they are banked in impenetrable tiers of lushness, in fall they have a week of pale flying gold, and in winter they are at their best with their wands rose- and copper-colored and their aisles full of blue smoke. There wasn't a time of year I didn't walk there and watch them across the vari-colored river, which, though it seems home, seems too the most remote and secret stretch of all God's universe. It is most itself and to my liking when with the first crystal rush of winter the ducks and geese and water-turkeys, in wedges, follow its pale protecting sandbars south. At first I walked there alone, but later I discovered three familiar spirits who also enjoyed walking and talking. Will Francis and Lyne Starling and George Roth certainly tided me over a bad passage and are with me still.

It was on these levee walks that I began to think of poetry and to jot down lines. At Sewanee I had tried my hand at lyrics and unfortunately, as I was editor of the college magazine, some of them found their way, anonymously, into print. I reread them a few years ago and I cannot imagine an experience more embarrassing. In Paris I had written a feeble sonnet on Chatterton and at Harvard I improved slightly with two winter songs, one of which, to my amazement and delight, *McClure's* published, still anonymously. All these were secret indulgences and only Miss Carrie knew of them.

This is not an account of my poetry nor of me as a poet. But since much of my life has gone into the making of verse which I hope is poetry, I may as well state now and as briefly as I can how and why I wrote.

What I wrote seemed to me more essentially myself than anything I did or said. It often gushed up almost involuntarily like automatic writing, and the difficulty lay in keeping the hot gush continuous and unselfconscious while at the same time directing it with cold intellect into form. I could never write in cold blood. The results were intensely personal, whatever their other defects. But by some quirk I was always aware in the act of putting words to paper that what I was feeling and thinking had been felt and thought by thousands in every generation. Only that conviction would have permitted me to publish without feeling guilty of indecent exposure.

I judge there's nothing at all unusual about such mental processes, or about these:

When you feel something intensely, you want to write it down—if anguish, to stanch the bleeding; if delight, to prolong the moment. When after years of pondering you feel you have discovered a new truth or an old one which suddenly for you has the excitement of a new one, you write a longish poem. To keep it free from irrelevant photographic details you set it in some long-ago time, one, of course, you love and perhaps once lived in.

That is how I wrote and why I wrote. As to technique I tried to make it sound as beautiful and as fitting as I could. Old patterns helped, but if rhyme seemed out of place, the choruses of *Samson Agonistes,* some of Matthew Arnold's unrhymed cadences, and Shakespeare's later run-on pentameters suggested freer and less accepted modes of communication. As far as I can make out, the towering bulk of English poetry influenced me tremendously, but not any one poet, though I hope I learned as much as I think I owe to Browning's monologues and to Gilbert Murray's translations of Euripides.

Thinking of these lonely trial years would be impossible for me without thinking of Caroline Stern. Everybody in town called her Miss Carrie. The first time I saw her I was far gladder than she realized. One of the convent boys, a fattish one who loomed huge to my apprehensive vision, had announced to me as we dawdled on the corner that I would have to fight him then and there. As in so many conflicts, the casus belli was obscure and immediately forgotten. I accepted the challenge with the least possible enthusiasm and began taking off my coat very deliberately, to give the Lord time to take a hand. At this moment Miss Carrie appeared, surveyed the scene, and paused. The conflict petered out before a blow was struck. Evidently my guardian angel had taken the form of Miss Carrie. It was an unusual guise. She was as tiny as Sister Evangelist, but birdlike. She must have weighed eighty pounds. She had a sensitive face, pale, with a large Jewish nose and enormous brown eyes, lustrous and kind. Her hair, which curled pleasantly, was just darker than wasp red. But I found later there was nothing else waspish about her, though she was a gallant fighter. She never thought anything was worth fighting for except moral issues, and it sickened her when an individual or a nation refused to fight for them. On this occasion she stopped and viewed our bellicose stance, meaning no doubt to whirl in if developments required. Then as always she looked tidy but a tiny bit disheveled, as if a not very rough breeze had just deposited her unexpectedly. She had the air of a volunteer as we gardeners use the term, and that air always kept Mother from appreciating her, because Mother by instinct and training was chic.

Miss Carrie—she must have been in her twenties then, though of course she seemed to me far gone in overblown maturity—had mistaken my unwilling preparations for battle for simon-pure heroism and, since she admired nothing more than knightly prowess, I found myself a few days later a visitor in her little house. It was a bare little place with an improvised look and hardly enough furniture for convenience. Her dwarf of a father, an Alsatian Jew, lived with her, a querulous old fellow who had failed as a country merchant and, now idle, lived by her scanty earnings as a teacher. She tended and scolded him as if he were a child. Her passionate adoration had been for her mother, whose death a few years before had left her the bread-winner and spiritually in solitary confinement. It would have been mortally lonely for her had she not known Judge Griffin, who gave her the nourishment she needed, his deep patriarchal love.

Miss Carrie's passion for painting was beyond bounds, consuming. While still in her teens, by impossible denials and scrapings, she had managed to save enough money to study in New York for a year. I think she must have lived in a state of ecstasy that whole year—she needed to, for I am sure she went hungry half the time. She would tell me about the classes, about copying the head of Bastien-Lepage's *Joan of Arc*, about her friend Annie Goldthwaite, who became famous, about all the young doings of the League. She loved to remember it and longed to go back. But hardly had she returned home to her school work than she developed lead poisoning. Her doctor forbade her to paint again. Against orders she was trying it when I met her. While sketching me, she would say with shy pride: "At the League they said I had a real sense of color. Someone once mistook one of my oils for a Henner," and she laughed softly at the delightful recollection. But in a year or two the blood-poison returned and she had to give up painting again, this time forever. It was her whole life and that meant she had lost her life and must find another. If this had been different and that had not happened, she might have become a great painter. Instead she became a great soul.

She was a teacher born. Mr. Bass recognized her gift and soon had her teaching anything, everything—painting, history, English, whatever classes happened to be without a teacher at the moment. She was always exhausted, generally undernourished, and always eager. The children adored her. She read me my first poetry (Milton and Shakespeare didn't count, they were just Milton and Shakespeare) and I resisted it mightily. This resistant attitude of mine lasted for years—in fact, until I read *Dover Beach* at Sewanee. Perhaps it was due to Father's having read me when I was a little fellow Tennyson's *I'm to be Queen of the May, Mother,* which I had found so unbearably pathetic I had burst into tears. Or perhaps I did actually detest poetry's inversions and circumlocutions as much as I thought I did. But poetry fascinated me, like a fearful sin, and Miss Carrie kept on reading it to me. Mother disapproved of these goings-on and observed, accurately enough, that there was no telling what kind of impractical notions Carrie was putting into my head, and my visits to her must stop. Father wondered if they did any harm anyway. But I announced I was going to see her when I wanted to. Mother closed the discussion, not weakly but impotently, by remarking that for an obedient child I was the most hard-headed she had ever encountered.

I kept on seeing Miss Carrie until I could see her no more. Many of the young people, mostly her former students, felt similarly drawn to her, and those who had moved from town were eager to visit her on their return trips. We came to her as to a clean upland spot smelling of pine. There was a childish gaiety about her, and her great wisdom was completely innocent. Apparently she made no effort to be right, she just was right. She gave you the fine feeling you were shielding her when in fact you were drawing from her your strength.

While I was at college she joined the Episcopal Church. That must have been a cruel decision for her to feel she must make, for it meant, and she knew it meant, breaking with her own people and with the faith of her fathers. The Jews at home never forgave her for it. After a few years she stopped attending church, and that too must have meant a grievous struggle. So she went her way alone and built her own lonely altar. She must have been a very Jacob for wrestling with God, but when I knew her best, after her youth, she didn't wrestle anymore, she merely walked with Him and leaned on Him when she was tired. It's a good thing He was there because she was often tired and she had no one else to lean on.

Beginning with my return home from Harvard, every scrap I ever wrote I showed Miss Carrie or mailed to her, coming by her house Sundays for her criticism. Though a partial critic in my case, she was a sensitive and a fearless one. We fought over words and cadences and sometimes I was worsted. She knew far better than I when I was growing didactic, and vehemently opposed the tendency. One week I sent her three or four short pieces and when I arrived I was pleased and astonished to hear her say ardently: "At last you have written a perfect poem!" I didn't know to which one she was referring, but it was *Overtones*, the one poem of mine which critics and anthologists, almost without dissent, have liked. At the very time she was giving me so much, she was making a selection of her own poems and saving every nickel to have them published. For years she had been writing poetry and a good many of her lyrics had appeared in the more distinguished magazines. At last she named her collection and found a publisher, one of those who advertise little and charge much. Denied an outlet in painting, she had turned to poetry, and now her very own book—*At the Edge of the World*, by Caroline Stern—in a pretty yellow binding was to appear in the kindly world. She was so excited and hopeful, she often wore a cherry-red ribbon at her throat, but though it was not her color, none of us would tell her so because that ribbon made her feel reckless and mischievous. Although there was plenty of Joan of Arc and St. Theresa in her, she was fundamentally a little girl. Her book appeared, and that was all. The critics ignored it, there were no sales, after a year the publisher wrote no copies were available. It did not deserve such treatment. Though she had more fancy than imagination, more feeling than art, and though she was not endowed with the sense of the magic word, they were good poems, charming, and so like her. She was hurt inside, but she did not complain and she never grew accusatory or bitter. When she read favorable reviews of my volume, a little later, she was thrilled, and when the reviews were unfriendly she was furious. All the while she continued to teach with undiminished enthusiasm hundreds of children and to give cheer or comfort to her numerous young friends in their happiness or troubles.

After her father's death she had built herself a small home with two extra rooms which she rented as an apartment. Between paying by the month for it and paying for the publication of her poems she had little enough left to fill her birdlike needs. When I think of the stark little living-room where I found so much peace and encouragement and of the scanty meals she referred to vaguely and when I remember I never gave her a present worth having or thought of helping out in any one of a hundred possible ways, I am appalled at the self-centered egotism of youth and its incapacity for real understanding or pity.

Once in a while you would find she had visited the doctor or was not feeling so well, but none of us was disturbed or really interested—people were always getting sick and Miss Carrie was naturally frail. She was alone most of the time and bought a Ouija board for company. It did astounding things for her—wrote hours on end faster than anyone except her could read, leaped into the air, went into frenzies, or moodily refused to budge. It amused us enormously. But I found after a while it wasn't so amusing to her. Her mother would speak to her, and God, and Matthew Arnold would send me long messages. She was puzzled and incredulous, but Ouija became almost alive, almost a person to her. She had no one else to live with except God, and He isn't enough by Himself. One night when Ouija had announced God was speaking and she was listening intently to the strange poetic moralizing, the wretched three-legged thing suddenly bounded into the air and spelled out violently: "Carrie, you are a damn fool. This isn't God. Good night," and could not be coaxed into further comment. The incident distressed her more than she would confess.

Once as I was leaving she told me quietly she was going to the hospital next day—an operation, she didn't know what for; she'd be out in two weeks. She was out in a few days, although they had operated. Then she began to waste away before our eyes. Soon she was taken to the hospital again, and this time for good. Although she didn't complain she asked everyone what was the matter with her. At last they took Ouija away from her. One afternoon when I came in she smiled and said: "I know the truth now. I asked the nurse and as she was leaving without answering I picked up a pencil and said: 'Ouija, tell me,' and it wrote: 'Cancer'." The last time I saw her she had drawn a heavy white veil across her face and her body weighed no more than a bird's.

Miss Carrie was not "my favorite Jew." I have had dozens of favorites. To no people am I under deeper spiritual obligation. But I am not unaware of the qualities in them (absent in her) which have recurrently irritated or enraged other people since the Babylonian captivity. Touch a hair of a Jewish head and I am ready to fight, but I have experienced moments of exasperation when I could willingly have led a pogrom. No, Miss Carrie was not my favorite Jew. She was my favorite friend. She never failed me, but looking back I am not certain I did not fail her despicably—I suspect I was patronizing. She was so different, so unworldly, so fundamentally innocent, and her friendship was so unwithheld and shameless. I don't often trouble to be ashamed, but if I was patronizing, Miss Carrie and her God would have to forgive me. I never could.

Miss Carrie had failed in everything—in painting, in poetry, in making money, in winning love, in dying easy. Yet she was one of the few successes I ever knew. I think I learned more from her of what the good life is and of how it may be lived than from almost anyone else.

Growing Out of Shadow

MARGARET WALKER

WHEN I WAS FIVE, I was busy discovering my world, and it was a place of happiness and delight. Then, one day, a white child shouted in my ears "nigger" as if he were saying "cur," and I was startled. I had never heard the word before, and I went home and asked what it meant, and my parents looked apprehensively at each other as if to say, "It's come." Clumsily, without adding hurt to the smart I was already suffering, they sought to explain but they were unable to destroy my pain. I could not understand my overwhelming sense of shame, as if I had been guilty of some unknown crime. I did not know why I was suffering, what brought this vague uneasiness, this clutching for understanding.

When I went to school, I read the history books that glorify the white race and describe the Negro either as a clown and a fool or a beast capable of very hard work in excessive heat. I discovered the background of chattel slavery behind this madness of race prejudice. Once we were slaves and now we are not, and the South remains angry. But when I went home to the good books and the wonderful music and the gentle, intelligent parents, I could see no reason for prejudice on the basis of a previous condition of servitude.

I went to church and I wondered why God let this thing continue. Why were there segregated churches and segregated hospitals and cemeteries and schools? Why must I ride behind a Jim-Crow sign? Why did a full-grown colored man sit meekly behind a Jim-Crow sign and do nothing about it? What could he do? Then I decided perhaps God was on the side of the white people because after all God was white. The world was white, and I was Black.

Then I began to daydream: It will not always be this way. Someday, just as chattel slavery ended, this injustice will also end; this internal suffering will cease; this ache inside for understanding will exist no longer. Someday, I said, when I am fully grown, I will understand, and I will be able to do something about it. I will write books that will prove the history texts were distorted. I will write books about colored people who have colored faces, books that will not make me ashamed when I read them.

But always I was seeking for the real answer, not the daydream. Always I wanted to know. I lay awake at night pondering in my heart, "Why? Why? Why?"

I heard Roland Hayes and Marian Anderson sing, and James Weldon Johnson and Langston Hughes read poetry. In the audiences were well-dressed, well-behaved colored people. They were intelligent, yet they were not allowed to sit beside white people at concerts and recitals. Why? Every night Negro cooks and maids and chauffeurs and nursemaids returned home from the white people's houses where their employers were not afraid to sit beside them.

I learned of race pride and consciousness and the contribution of the Negro to American culture. Still I was bewildered. America was a place of strange contradictions. The white grocery man at the corner who was so friendly when I was in his store thought it a crime for a white and a colored boxer to fight in the ring together. But he did not think it a crime for a Negro to be drafted to fight for America.

I decided vaguely the white man must think these things because of fear; because he felt insecure. Perhaps he was a little afraid of what would happen in a free America.

How did I first discover the color of my skin? I had only to look in my mirror every morning to know. I must say it appeared to me a good healthy color. But there is a difference in knowing you are Black and in understanding what it means to be Black in America. Before I was ten I knew what it was to step off the sidewalk to let a white man pass; otherwise he might knock me off. I had had a sound thrashing by white boys while Negro men looked on helplessly. I was accustomed to riding in the Jim Crow streetcars with the Negro section marked off by iron bars that could not be moved. For a year and a half I went to school in a one-room wooden shack. One year when my father's schoolwork took him out of town constantly, my mother lived in fear of our lives because there was no man in the house to protect us against the possibility of some attack. Once, we climbed the fire escape to see a movie, because there was no Negro entrance, and after that we saw no movies. Another time my mother stood for hours upstairs in a darkened theatre to hear a recital by Rachmaninoff because there were no seats for colored. My father was chased home one night at the point of a gun by a drunken policeman who resented a fountain pen in a "nigger's" pocket. My grandmother told the story of a woman tarred and feathered in the neighborhood. A mob came and took her from her home because it was rumored that a white man was visiting her. Although they took her deep into the woods, her screams were heard by relatives and neighbors. My grandmother heard them, too. Next day the woman's family went to the woods and brought her home. She was still alive, so they removed the tar and feathers with turpentine. She was horribly burned and scarred.

And always the answer and the question in a child's mind to each of these was "Why? Why do they do these things?"

Negroes congregating on a city block to argue and talk about the race question imitated what they heard from the pulpits or what the white folks told them: "The trouble with the Negro problem in America is just we needs to git together... We don't co-operate... We always kicking one another... This is a white man's country and Black man ain't got no place in it... We just cursed by God, sons of Ham, hewers of wood and drawers of water... Our leaders are crooked and they betray us... We need to get a little money and make ourselves independent of the white man... If it wasn't for the white man we'd be way back in the jungles of Africa somewhere... We oughta thank the white man for bringing us to this country and making us civilized... Trouble is we scared to fight, scared to stick up for our rights... We'll fight for the white man but we won't fight for ourselves... All the progress we've made we owe to the white man... I hates a white man worsener I hates poison, left to me I'd kill up every paleface in the world... Don't let 'em fool you when they grinning in your face, they want something... Only God can help us... It takes time, that's all, to solve the Negro problem... All we got to do is humble ourselves and do right and we'll win out... Colored man hurts hisself most of the time... All we got to do is do like the children of Israel and the slaves done way back yonder, pray...

Colored people oughta get out of the notion that they are Negroes... That word *Negroes* is what hurts us...."

But all of it was no real answer to the anxious questioning of a child burdened constantly with the wonder of what race prejudice is.

When I went away to college in my teens, I left the South with mingled emotions. I had been told that Negroes in the North were better off than Negroes down South; they had more sense and more opportunities; they could go any place, enjoy recreational facilities such as parks and movies, eat in restaurants without discrimination; there were no Jim Crow transportation restrictions, and if Negroes were subjected to any indignity, they could sue the person or company involved; there was no such thing as lynching. Best of all, Negroes could vote.

I was, nevertheless, shy and afraid over the prospect of going to a white school; I might prove backward as a result of my southern training. I had also perforce become somewhat anti-white myself and I feared coming into close contact with white people. Yet I anticipated a new kind of freedom once I crossed the Mason-Dixon line.

Imagine my great hurt to discover that few of the wonderful promises came true. I was refused service in restaurants in Evanston and Chicago time and again. In the South I had suffered no similar embarrassment because there I had known what to expect. I discovered that most of the Negroes in the northern colleges and universities were from the South, for the majority of Negroes in the Middle West had no money with which to take advantage of higher education.

What was most amazing was my discovery of my own prejudices and my first realization of the economic problem.

Because of the nature of segregated life in America many Negroes have misconceptions of white life. I was no exception. As servants, Negroes know certain elements of white life and we characterize the whole in this way. My first step toward understanding what it means to be Black in America was understanding the economics of the United States.

In the South I had always thought that, naturally, white people had more money than colored people. Poor white trash signified for me the lazy scum of the marginal fringe of society with no excuse for poverty. Now I discovered there are poor white working people exploited by rich white people. I learned that all Jews are not rich. I discovered that all Negroes are not even in the same economic class. While there were no Negro multi-millionaires, there were many wealthy Negroes who made money by exploiting poor Negroes, who have some of the same attitudes toward them that rich whites have toward poor whites and that prejudiced whites have toward all Negroes. Imagine my amazement to hear a white girl tell me she was forced to leave Northwestern because she had no money. But I, a poor Negro girl, had stayed even when I had no money. They never threatened me with expulsion. Yet I did not find a white school in the Middle West free of prejudice. All around me was prejudice. To understand the issues out of which it grew became my life's preoccupation.

A year out of college found me working with poor whites—Jew and Gentile—and poor Negroes, too. In Chicago, for the first time I began to see that Negroes, as almost entirely a working-class people, belong with organized labor. My background was so thoroughly petty-bourgeois with parents who belonged to a professional small-salaried class, that I had not understood that people who worked with their brains were also workers. I knew we were poor and decent, and that was all I knew. In the South, many, if not most, petty-bourgeois Negroes are anti-union, anti-strike, and anti-white. This, of course, is not strange when one considers the history of Negroes in unions in the South, their forced role as scabs, the brutal treatment they received as such, prior to the Congress of Industrial Organizations (CIO), the general nature of Negro life in the South, threatened always by sinister undertones of white violence.

Thus there began for me in Chicago a period in which I learned about class in the United States. As soon as I began working in close contact with whites, I discovered startling things peculiar to both racial groups, all adding up to one main conclusion: that whites suffer psychologically from the problem of race prejudice as much as Negroes. I began to see race prejudice as a definite tool to keep people divided and economically helpless: Negroes hating whites and whites hating Blacks, with conditions of both groups pitiful, both economically and psychologically. I saw, too, that it was not beyond the ability of both groups to reach understanding and to live peaceably side by side, that the organization of Negroes and whites by labor was certainly one step forward toward that end.

The second step toward understanding what it means to be Black in America came in understanding the political problem. By 1932 and 1936, Negroes had, out of the dire necessity of destitution, become politically conscious even in the Deep South, where they had no real voice in politics. In the North, the East, and particularly the Middle West, the Negro vote assumed significant proportions and in many instances proved effective in the balance of power.

In 1936 I cast my first vote in Chicago in a Presidential election. It was a great time to come of age. There had been four years of the New Deal, and many of the ills and evils of our society, as they immediately touched Negroes and all poor people, had been somewhat alleviated. We had benefited from the Works Progress Administration (WPA), the National Youth Administration (NYA), the Federal Housing and Federal Farm Administration, Social Security, and the WPA adult education program; we had benefited in many instances where there had previously been evil practices of discrimination. I began to dig into the historical background of politics in America, to read the record where Negroes were concerned. I began to see parallels. When the thirteen colonies revolted, they revolted on the premise that taxation without representation is tyranny. Yet that is precisely what the Negro suffered in the South still. Moreover, poor white people as well had no voice in their government. If the truth were nationally known and understood, the small number of votes cast in electing southern representatives and senators to Congress, as compared with the population, would not merely appear ridiculous but alarming. Not that these citizens of America were too indifferent to vote; they were disfranchised under the pretense of a poll tax not paid or a grandfather clause. The old saying that a voteless people is a helpless people became a basic fact in my understanding of the Negro problem.

A third step came from a growing world perspective. As a child, reading the history books in the South, I was humiliated by some unhappy picture or reference to a Negro. Such items made me burn all over. It was as if we were cut off from humanity, without sensitivity. I could make no connection between my life as a Negro child in the South and the life of Chinese children or Indian children or children in South Africa. I grew up and became self-supporting, yet I had not connected myself with working women all over the world, with poor peasant women who are white as well as Black. Now I began to reach out. I saw it was eternally to the credit of Negroes in America that we were represented in Spain on the side of the Loyalists with soldiers, nurses, volunteer workers, our humble gift of an ambulance, our moral support. We can be proud that Ethiopia found a willing ear for help from us. While white America is far too prone to appreciate the struggle of people in distant lands and forget the problems on its own doorstep, its disadvantaged groups are often too obsessed with their own problems to see further than the bridge of their nose. I realized it was essential for Negroes to be identified with every heroic struggle of an oppressed people, with the brave Chinese, the Indians, the South Africans, the Negroes in the West Indies who fight for liberty. Now that we are engaged in a global war, it is even more essential that all peoples of the earth gain a world perspective and become conscious of our common humanity and struggle to be free.

Yet I am sure that economic, political, and social understanding is not all. There is need for a new type of spiritual understanding, and I use the word not in its narrow religious meaning. I am concerned with something far more meaningful in the lives of individual men and women, of greater practical value and far better potentialities for personal and social growth. Once the human spirit is washed clean of prejudices, once the basic needs of people are considered, and not the pocketbooks of the few nor the power of a handful, once institutionalized religion is liberated into religious meaning, of necessity there must begin to bloom upon the earth something spiritually more durable than any of the mystic conceptions of religion that humankind has thus far brought forth. Then no person will look at another with fear, patronage, condescension, hatred, or disparagement, under pain of one's own spiritual death.

A Christmas Remembered

DEAN FAULKNER WELLS

WHEN I WAS a little girl, at Christmas I always went to Rowan Oak, Pappy's fine white house not far from where my mother and I lived with Nanie, my grandmother.

One of the first Christmases I remember was a warm, sultry day, much too hot for the long-sleeved, green velvet dress I proudly wore. I rode to Pappy's in the rumble seat of Nanie's yellow Buick roadster. I could not see over the sides of the car, so I spent most of the short ride admiring my long white stockings and shiny new black patent-leather Mary Janes.

But as soon as the small car bounced and lurched into the first pothole, I knew we had turned into Pappy's driveway. It was dark for a moment. Then, through thick branches, the sunlight made yellow patterns dance on my hands and dress. I looked up into the tall cedars, closed my eyes and knew just from their smell that we were almost there. At the end of the driveway, the house loomed—bigger than a courthouse and twice as grand to my child's eyes.

Pappy stood on the gallery alone, arms folded across his chest, staring down the driveway. We chugged past him, Nanie tooted the horn, and I waved exuberantly. I was still waving when we stopped by the steps.

He did not look at us. My fat little arm wilted into my lap, and as the moments passed, I began to fidget in my seat. Pappy continued to stand motionless, his gaze riveted to the drive-way. I sat back there in the rumble seat for what seemed an eternity, feeling increasingly exposed and vulnerable as the austere figure within 6 feet of me held his pose. Finally, he turned toward us. He seemed to see the car for the first time, and with characteristically precise movements, he rebuttoned his tweed jacket, tugged its corners straight, and walked toward the car.

I sank lower and lower in the leather seat. I could hear Nanie and my mother chatting amicably. I knew they were busily pulling on their gloves and gathering up their handbags, totally unaware of his approach and of my impulse to bolt.

Then he was at the side of the car. I looked up into his tired, familiar face, at the fine lines etched around his eyes, the great hawk nose, the mustache which always hid his mouth and never let anyone see whether or not he was smiling. I wanted to reach out and touch him. He bent slightly to help my mother out of the car, and the moment he spoke to her, even though I could not make out the words, I knew everything was all right. The sound of his voice was warm and gentle. We were where we belonged.

He opened my mother's door with all the courtliness of an 18th-century gallant, and when he took her hand, she stepped out of the car as if she were walking on air or, at the very least, on somebody's coat. He came around the car and helped Nanie out with the same care and formality. He pulled her gently to him; then they joined my mother. They made a stately procession as they mounted the steps, one lady on each of his arms.

Alone and seemingly ignored, I was about to howl when Pappy said in a stage voice, much louder than his usual tone: "Oh, have we forgotten somebody?" He turned back to the car, chuckling.

I scrambled over the side into his arms. He stopped me on the steps to straighten my dress and whispered: "I like pretty girls in pretty dresses." Hand in hand, we joined my mother and Nanie. He took their arms again, and I brought up the rear, attempting a swaybacked stance in imitation of Pappy's distinctive walk, bent slightly backwards from the waist.

The front door was open to the balmy afternoon, and the smells of roasting turkey drifted out to the gallery. Aunt Estelle and members of the family, big and little, greeted us in the hall. Amid all the to-do, I scurried into the front parlor.

The tree was as big as I knew it would be, a cedar which touched the ceiling and smelled almost as good as the ones outside. My eyes caught on the presents piled beneath it.

This was the first Christmas I remember hearing Pappy say, "Don't buy me anything, just make me something." And the first thing I looked for under the tree was my present for him. The white tissue paper was smudged and torn at the corners, and its red ribbon, one of my tired hair ribbons—Nanie did not believe in buying fancy wrappings—had come undone. But there it was, atop the other presents with my labored Christmas message in full view: "I luve Papi."

In years to come, the same edict would hold, and Pappy's daughter Jill, his granddaughter Vicki and I would begin work on Christmas presents for Pappy right after Thanksgiving. Over the years, he received countless drawings of horses, several bad poems and, when Nannie decided I was old enough to learn the ladylike art of needlework, even more scandalous failures. The first year he got 16 rows of a navy wool scarf with the knitting needles and unused skeins of yarn wrapped up in a shoe box; the next, one-half of one argyle sock. Finally, when I was much older, I gave him a handhooked, red wool rug—all finished, I might add. He kept it by his bed until he died.

But this gift in tattered tissue was my first homemade present, and when he opened it and smiled at what was in all likelihood the single most hideous rendering in oils of an Indian tepee at dawn, I almost burst with pride. I had painted for weeks at Nanie's side in her dining room, with my own small easel and pallet, until I forced my squat fingers to make some sort of pattern on a cardboard square. It was signed with a big "DF," and I thought it was wonderful. I knew he thought so too.

Then it was Nanie's turn. The box from Pappy was enormous, shiny and splendid. Obviously store-bought and store-wrapped, I thought to myself with the condescension of an original-present-maker. She took her time opening it, as we all crowded around to see. Inside the gold cardboard box lay a beaded, blue chiffon evening gown. She didn't touch it for a moment, then shook it out with a precise gesture, letting the tail end trail across the floor. It was the most gorgeous thing I'd ever seen. Nanie muttered, "It's probably too big," and let it drop back into the box. She gave Pappy a funny look and said, "Thank you, Billy." I wondered if he knew, too, that she was going to take it back.

Then it was my turn. The box was almost as big as Nanie's. I tore the fancy wrappings away in short order. Inside was a beautiful, long-sleeved yellow sweater. But it was the plaid skirt, all red and green and with a tiny yellow stripe, that took my breath away. I felt very grown-up just looking at it.

I could hardly wait to rush upstairs and try it on, but Pappy held my squirming body still, long enough to convince me that I might miss dinner entirely if I left right then. When I was quieted, he told me about the skirt. The plaid was the Murry tartan, handed down from the Murrys and the MacAlpines from a long time ago in Scotland. It belonged to our family. "This skirt is part of your heritage," Pappy said, "and you must wear it with pride."

Next day, when I tried it on, I found that it swallowed me—but I wore it anyway. It was too big for the next two years; two years after that, it was too small. I put it on whenever I was sad or scared, or whenever I needed to be strong or brave. I seem to have it on in every snapshot taken of me for the next four years. I cried when I couldn't wear it anymore.

As Pappy finished his story about our past, Jack, the houseboy, came in and announced dinner. The adults moved in a formal procession to the dining room.

I scooted ahead of my elders to catch the first glimpse of the long table—elegant as always, with fine linens heavily starched, shining crystal, silver water goblets, and bread and butter plates that reflected the lights of many candles as well as one's own wonderfully distorted image. I circled the table, trying to decide which was the best spot for me.

I had just made my choice, right next to Pappy, when I felt his hand on my shoulder, gently but firmly guiding me away from the long table—that was for the grown-ups—to a smaller one for us children, set up in the east corner of the room. It was laid in equally fine style, with china and crystal and silver.

I sat down eagerly with a ravenous appetite that would no longer be denied. After all, Christmas or not, it was 2 o'clock, far past my dinner hour. I unfolded the heavy, linen napkin, plunked it in my lap, swung my legs impatiently, and waited for Pappy to get on with the carving and serving and passing of plates.

Then Jack appeared at the pantry door bearing a perfect, golden-brown turkey. Instead of placing it before Pappy, however, he promenaded around the room and offered just a glimpse to everyone there. Finally, he placed the bird in front of Pappy.

I reared back in my seat, anticipating every mouthful that was to come. At the head of the table, Pappy rose and in his most solemn voice began: "A toast, ladies and gentlemen." Then the adults stood, their chairs pushed far back from the table, their wine glasses raised, their faces serious and intent, their eyes on Pappy. Then the children stood. Everyone in the dining room was on his feet, except me. Blissfully unaware, I kept my seat.

Pappy left his place and made his way to my table. I felt his hand touch the top of my head softly, as he bent close and whispered. "We all stand when toasts are given."

"Me, too?"

"Everybody."

My toes searched for the floor.

I felt the blood rush to my face. My chair moved slowly backward beneath me. I looked around anxiously, just as I felt Pappy's hand on my arm. I took it gratefully, found my footing, and hefted my bottom off the chair.

"You get to sit down and eat soon as this is done," he whispered. Then he walked back to his place, raised his glass and, with only a slight nod toward my table, began: "A toast . . ." The watered wine nearly gagged me.

Jack and Pappy's cook Narcissus outdid themselves. Each course was perfect, and for the first time I managed to serve myself, thanks to Jack's steadying hand at my elbow. I made my way through turkey and dressing, Aunt Estelle's homemade jellies, three vegetables, rolls, the finger bowls, and flaming plum pudding.

We sat impatiently until the grown-ups finished; and finally it was time to go outside and play. As we headed out the front door, the ladies went into the front parlor for coffee, and the gentlemen, with one exception, moved to the library for after-dinner drinks. Pappy came outside with us.

What a fine, raucous afternoon we had. After sitting fairly still for nearly two hours, listening to soft conversations that we could not understand, concentrating on not spilling and on sitting up straight, we were as worn out with the adult world as we were with turkey and dressing. The giggles started before we left the table and picked up volume as we tore through the front hall. A perfunctory "don't run in the house" was lost in the banging of the heavy screen door as we scampered down the front steps to freedom.

The shadows were already long as Pappy organized the first of many games, and we played with uninhibited fury, as if we knew that soon this perfect day would be over. We had relay races and endless contests: who-can-jump-the-farthest, and who-can-stand-on-her-head-longest.

We ended with a series of disastrous cartwheels and our favorite, "Sling the Statue." Pappy was judge. The older children grabbed the younger ones by the hands and began turning faster and faster in place until our feet flew out behind us. The whole world was upended. The cedars and the house were upside down. Even Pappy, with pipe in hand, seemed to be standing on his head. Then they let us go. We sprawled onto the soft grass, holding our positions until Pappy passed slowly by, judging the shapes that the "statues" took, offering comments such as "This one might be a mule..." He chuckled often, and occasionally his face would redden, he would make a funny snorting sound through his nose, and all of us would laugh until our bodies crumpled into the wet grass.

Then it was over. My mother and Nanie came down the brick walk and talked quietly to Pappy. Other mamas gathered up their grass-stained, muddy-kneed, bedraggled offspring. It was almost dark, and the night was cool against my face.

Pappy walked us to the car. He carefully handed my mother and Nanie into the front seat and deposited me in the rumble seat. I snuggled down against the leather, my energies spent, a tired, happy little girl. As we headed out the driveway, I looked up over the back seat. Pappy stood alone on the gallery.

"Merry Christmas," I called. He raised his hand in a stiff, formal salute. I faced forward again and watched the beams from the Buick's headlights bounce off the tall cedars.

Suddenly I wanted one last look at the big white house, and I scrambled to my knees, riding backwards in the car. Lights from the downstairs windows shone softly onto the yard. Somebody turned on the gallery light behind Pappy, and I couldn't see his face anymore. He was just a small, dark figure silhouetted against the house.

"Oh, Pappy," I called again, as we rounded the bend in the driveway and the house grew smaller and smaller, and he was farther and farther away from me. "Thank you."

I hope he heard me.

A Sweet Devouring

EUDORA WELTY

WHEN I USED TO ask my mother which we were, rich or poor,
she refused to tell me. I was then nine years old and of course
what I was dying to hear was that we were poor. I was reading a
book called *Five Little Peppers* and my heart was set on baking a
cake for my mother in a stove with a hole in it. Some version of
rich, crusty old Mr. King—up till that time not living on our
street—was sure to come down the hill in his wheelchair and
rescue me if anything went wrong. But before I could start a cake
at all I had to find out if we were poor, and poor *enough;* and my
mother wouldn't tell me, she said she was too busy. I couldn't
wait too long; I had to go on reading and soon Polly Pepper got
into more trouble, some that was a little harder on her and easier
on me.

Trouble, the backbone of literature, was still to me the original
property of the fairy tale, and as long as there was plenty of
trouble for everybody and the rewards for it were falling in the
right spots, reading was all smooth sailing. At that age a child
reads with higher appetite and gratification, and with those two
stars sailing closer together, than ever again in his growing up.
The home shelves had been providing me all along with the usual
books, and I read them with love—but snap, I finished them. I
read everything just alike—snap. I even came to the *Tales from
Maria Edgeworth* and went right ahead, without feeling the
bump—then. It *was* noticeable that when her characters suffered
she punished them for it, instead of rewarding them as a reader
had rather been led to hope. In her stories, the children had to
make their choice between being unhappy and good about it and
being unhappy and bad about it, and then she helped them to
choose wrong. In *The Purple Jar,* it will be remembered, there
was the little girl being taken through the shops by her mother

and her downfall coming when she chooses to buy something beautiful instead of something necessary. The purple jar, when the shop sends it out, proves to have been purple only so long as it was filled with purple water, and her mother knew it all the time. They don't deliver the water. That's only the cue for stones to start coming through the hole in the victim's worn-out shoe. She bravely agrees she must keep walking on stones until such time as she is offered another choice between the beautiful and the useful. Her father tells her as far as he is concerned she can stay in the house. If I had been at all easy to disappoint, that story would have disappointed me. Of course, I did feel, what is the good of walking on rocks if they are going to let the water out of the jar too? And it seemed to me that even the illustrator fell down on the characters in that book, not alone Maria Edgeworth, for when a rich, crusty old gentleman gave Simple Susan a guinea for some kind deed she'd done him, there was a picture of the transaction and where was the guinea? I couldn't make out a feather. But I liked *reading* the book all right—except that I finished it.

My mother took me to the Public Library and introduced me: "Let her have any book she wants, except *Elsie Dinsmore*." I looked for the book I couldn't have and it was a row. That was how I learned about the Series Books. The *Five Little Peppers* belonged, so did *The Wizard of Oz*, so did *The Little Colonel*, so did *The Green Fairy Book*. There were many of everything, generations of everybody, instead of one. I wasn't coming to the end of reading, after all—I was saved.

Our library in those days was a big rotunda lined with shelves. A copy of *V.V.'s Eyes* seemed to follow you wherever you went, even after you'd read it. I didn't know what I liked, I just knew what there was a lot of. After *Randy's Spring* there came *Randy's Summer, Randy's Fall* and *Randy's Winter*. True, I didn't care very much myself for her spring, but it didn't occur to me that I might not care for her summer, and then her summer didn't prejudice me against her fall, and I still had hopes as I moved on to her winter. I was disappointed in her whole year, as it turned out, but a thing like that didn't keep me from wanting to read every word of it. The pleasures of reading itself—who doesn't remember?—were like those of a Christmas cake, a sweet devouring.

The "Randy Books" failed chiefly in being so soon over. Four seasons doesn't make a series.

All that summer I used to put on a second petticoat (our librarian wouldn't let you past the front door if she could see through you), ride my bicycle up the hill and "through the Capitol" (shortcut) to the library with my two read books in the basket (two was the limit you could take out at one time when you were a child and also as long as you lived), and tiptoe in ("Silence") and exchange them for two more in two minutes. Selection was no object. I coasted the two new books home, jumped out of my petticoat, read (I suppose I ate and bathed and answered questions put to me), then in all hope put my petticoat back on and rode those two books back to the library to get my next two.

The librarian was the lady in town who wanted to be it. She called me by my full name and said, "Does your mother know where you are? You know good and well the fixed rule of this library: *Nobody is going to come running back here with any book on the same day they took it out.* Get both those things out of here and don't come back till tomorrow. And I can practically see through you."

My great-aunt in Virginia, who understood better about needing more to read than you *could* read, sent me a book so big it had to be read on the floor—a bound volume of six or eight issues of *St. Nicholas* from a previous year. In the very first pages a serial began: *The Lucky Stone* by Abbie Farwell Brown. The illustrations were right down my alley: a heroine so poor she was ragged, a witch with an extremely pointed hat, a rich, crusty old gentleman in—better than a wheelchair—a runaway carriage; and I set to. I gobbled up installment after installment through the whole luxurious book, through the last one, and then came the words, turning me to *unlucky* stone: "To be concluded." The book had come to an end and *The Lucky Stone* wasn't finished! The witch had it! I couldn't believe this infidelity from my aunt. I still had my secret childhood feeling that if you hunted long enough in the book's pages, you could find what you were looking for, and long after I knew books better than that, I used to hunt again for the end of *The Lucky Stone.* It never occurred to me that the story had an existence anywhere else outside the pages of that single green-bound book. The last chapter was just something I would have to do without. Polly Pepper could do it. And then suddenly I tried something—I read it again, as much as I had of it. I was in love with books at least partly for what they looked like; I loved the printed page.

In my little circle books were almost never given for Christmas, they cost too much. But the year before, I'd been given a book and got a shock. It was from the same classmate who had told me there was no Santa Claus. She gave me a book, all right—*Poems by Another Little Girl*. It looked like a real book, was printed like a real book—but it was *by her*. *Homemade* poems? Illusion-dispelling was her favorite game. She was in such a hurry, she had such a pile to get rid of—her mother's electric runabout was stacked to the bud vases with copies—that she hadn't even time to say, "Merry Christmas!" With only the same raucous laugh with which she had told me, "Been filling my own stocking for years!" she shot me her book, received my Japanese pencil box with a moonlight scene on the lid and a sharpened pencil inside, jumped back into the car and was sped away by her mother. I stood right where they had left me, on the curb in my Little Nurse's uniform, and read that book, and I had no better way to prove when I got through than I had when I started that this was not a real book. But of course it wasn't. The printed page is not absolutely everything.

Then this Christmas was coming, and my grandfather in Ohio sent along in his box of presents an envelope with money in it for me to buy myself the book I wanted.

I went to Kress's. Not everybody knew Kress's sold books, but children just before Christmas know everything Kress's ever sold or will sell. My father had showed us the mirror he was giving my mother to hang above her desk, and Kress's is where my brother and I went to reproduce that by buying a mirror together to give her ourselves, and where our little brother then made us take him and he bought her one his size for fifteen cents. Kress's had also its version of the Series Books, called, exactly like another series, "The Camp Fire Girls," beginning with *The Camp Fire Girls in the Woods*.

I believe they were ten cents each and I had a dollar. But they weren't all that easy to buy, because the series stuck, and to buy some of it was like breaking into a loaf of French bread. Then after you got home, each single book was as hard to open as a box stuck in its varnish, and when it gave way it popped like a firecracker. The covers once prized apart would never close; those books once open stayed open and lay on their backs helplessly fluttering their leaves like a turned-over June bug. They were as light as a matchbox. They were printed on yellowed paper with corners that crumbled, if you pinched on them too hard, like old graham crackers, and they smelled like attic trunks, caramelized glue, their own confinement with one another and, over all, the Kress's smell—bandannas, peanuts and sandalwood from the incense counter. Even without reading them I loved them. It was hard, that year, that Christmas is a day you can't read.

What could have happened to those books?—but I can tell you about the leading character. His name was Mr. Holmes. He was not a Camp Fire Girl: he wanted to catch one. Through every book of the series he gave chase. He pursued Bessie and Zara—those were the Camp Fire Girls—and kept scooping them up in his touring car, while they just as regularly got away from him. Once Bessie escaped from the second floor of a strange inn by climbing down a gutter pipe. Once she escaped by driving away from Mr. Holmes in his own automobile, which she had learned to drive by watching him. What Mr. Holmes wanted with them—either Bessie or Zara would do—didn't give me pause; I was too young to be a Camp Fire Girl; I was just keeping up. I wasn't alarmed by Mr. Holmes—when I cared for a chill, I knew to go to Dr. Fu Manchu, who had his own series in the library. I wasn't fascinated either. There was one thing I wanted from those books, and that was for me to have ten to read at one blow.

Who in the world wrote those books? I knew all the time they were the false "Camp Fire Girls" and the ones in the library were the authorized. But book reviewers sometimes say of a book that if anyone else had written it, it might not have been this good, and I found it out as a child—their warning is justified. This was a proven case, although a case of the true not being as good as the false. In the true series the characters were either totally different or missing (Mr. Holmes was missing), and there was too much time given to teamwork. The Kress's Campers, besides getting into a more reliable kind of trouble than the Carnegie Campers, had adventures that even they themselves weren't aware of: the pages were in wrong. There were transposed pages, repeated pages, and whole sections in upside down. There was no way of telling if there was anything missing. But if you knew your way in the woods at all, you could enjoy yourself tracking it down. I read the library "Camp Fire Girls," since that's what they were there for, but though they could be read by poorer light they were not as good.

And yet, in a way, the false Campers were not better either. I wonder whether I felt some flaw at the heart of things or whether I was just tired of not having any taste; but it seemed to me when I had finished that the last nine of those books weren't as good as the first one. And the same went for all Series Books. As long as they are keeping a series going, I was afraid, nothing can really happen. The whole thing is one grand prevention. For my greed, I must have unwittingly dealt with myself in the way Maria Edgeworth dealt with the one who put her all into the purple jar—I had received word it was just colored water.

And then I went again to the home shelves and my lucky hand reached and found Mark Twain—twenty-four volumes, not a series, and good all the way through.

The Little Store

EUDORA WELTY

TWO BLOCKS AWAY from the Mississippi State Capitol, and on the same street with it, where our house was when I was a child growing up in Jackson, it was possible to have a little pasture behind your backyard where you could keep a Jersey cow, which we did. My mother herself milked her. A thrifty homemaker, wife, mother of three, she also did all her own cooking. And as far as I can recall, she never set foot inside a grocery store. It wasn't necessary.

For her regular needs, she stood at the telephone in our front hall and consulted with Mr. Lemly, of Lemly's Market and Grocery downtown, who took her order and sent it out on his next delivery. And since Jackson at the heart of it was still within very near reach of the open country, the blackberry lady clanged on her bucket with a quart measure at your front door in June without fail, the watermelon man rolled up to your house exactly on time for the Fourth of July, and down through the summer, the quiet of the early-morning streets was pierced by the calls of farmers driving in with their plenty. One brought his with a song, so plaintive we would sing it with him:

> Milk, milk,
> Buttermilk,
> Snap beans—butterbeans—
> Tender okra—fresh greens . . .
> And buttermilk.

My mother considered herself pretty well prepared in her kitchen and pantry for any emergency that, in her words, might choose to present itself. But if she should, all of a sudden, need another lemon or find she was out of bread, all she had to do was call out, "Quick! Who'd like to run to the Little Store for me?"

I would.

She'd count out the change into my hand, and I was away. I'll bet the nickel that would be left over that all over the country, for those of my day, the neighborhood grocery played a similar part in our growing up.

Our store had its name—it was that of the grocer who owned it, whom I'll call Mr. Sessions—but "the Little Store" is what we called it at home. It was a block down our street toward the capitol and half a block further, around the corner, toward the cemetery. I knew even the sidewalk to it as well as I knew my own skin. I'd skipped my jumping-rope up and down it, hopped its length through mazes of hopscotch, played jacks in its islands of shade, serpentined along it on my Princess bicycle, skated it backward and forward. In the twilight I had dragged my steamboat by its string (this was homemade out of every new shoebox, with candle in the bottom lighted and shining through colored tissue paper pasted over windows scissored out in the shapes of the sun, moon and stars) across every crack of the walk without letting it bump or catch fire. I'd "played out" on that street after supper with my brothers and friends as long as "first-dark" lasted; I'd caught its lightning bugs. On the first Armistice Day (and this will set the time I'm speaking of) we made our own parade down that walk on a single velocipede—my brother pedaling, our little brother riding the handlebars, and myself standing on the back, all with arms wide, flying flags in each hand. (My father snapped that picture as we raced by. It came out blurred.)

As I set forth for the Little Store, a tune would float toward me from the house where there lived three sisters, girls in their teens, who ratted their hair over their ears, wore headbands like gladiators, and were considered to be very popular. They practiced for this in the daytime; they'd wind up the Victrola, leave the same record on they'd played before, and you'd see them bobbing past their dining-room windows while they danced with each other. Being three, they could go all day, cutting in:

> *Everybody ought to know-oh*
> *How to do the Tickle-Toe*
> *(how to do the Tickle-Toe)—*

they sang it and danced to it, and as I went by to the same song, I believed it.

A little further on, across the street, was the house where the principal of our grade school lived—lived on, even while we were having vacation. What if she would come out? She would halt me in my tracks—she had a very carrying and well-known voice in Jackson, where she'd taught almost everybody—saying "Eudora Alice Welty, spell OBLIGE." OBLIGE was the word that she of course knew had kept me from making 100 on my spelling exam. She'd make me miss it again now, by boring her eyes through me from across the street. This was my vacation fantasy, one good way to scare myself on the way to the store.

Down near the corner waited the house of a little boy named Lindsey. The sidewalk here was old brick, which the roots of a giant chinaberry tree had humped up and tilted this way and that. On skates, you took it fast, in a series of skittering hops, trying not to touch ground anywhere. If the chinaberries had fallen and rolled in the cracks, it was like skating through a whole shooting match of marbles. I crossed my fingers that Lindsey wouldn't be looking.

During the big flu epidemic he and I, as it happened, were being nursed through our sieges at the same time. I'd hear my father and mother murmuring to each other, at the end of a long day, "And I wonder how poor little *Lindsey* got along today?" Just as, down the street, he no doubt would have to hear his family saying, "And I wonder how is poor *Eudora* by now?" I got the idea that a choice was going to be made soon between poor little Lindsey and poor Eudora, and I came up with a funny poem. I wasn't prepared for it when my father told me it wasn't funny and my mother cried that if I couldn't be ashamed for myself, she'd have to be ashamed for me:

> There was a little boy and his name was Lindsey.
> He went to heaven with the influinzy.

He didn't, he survived it, poem and all, the same as I did. But his chinaberries could have brought me down in my skates in a flying act of contrition before his eyes, looking pretty funny myself, right in front of his house.

Setting out in this world, a child feels so indelible. He only comes to find out later that it's all the others along his way who are making themselves indelible to him.

* * *

Our Little Store rose right up from the sidewalk; standing in a street of family houses, it alone hadn't any yard in front, any tree or flowerbed. It was a plain frame building covered over with brick. Above the door, a little railed porch ran across on an upstairs level and four windows with shades were looking out. But I didn't catch on to those.

Running in out of the sun, you met what seemed total obscurity inside. There were almost tangible smells—licorice recently sucked in a child's cheek, dill-pickle brine that had leaked through a paper sack in a fresh trail across the wooden floor, ammonia-loaded ice that had been hoisted from wet croker sacks and slammed into the icebox with its sweet butter at the door, and perhaps the smell of still-untrapped mice.

Then through the motes of cracker dust, cornmeal dust, the Gold Dust of the Gold Dust Twins that the floor had been swept with, the realities emerged. Shelves climbed to high reach all the way around, set out with not too much of any one thing but a lot of things—lard, molasses, vinegar, starch, matches, kerosene, Octagon soap (about a year's worth of octagon-shaped coupons cut out and saved brought a signet ring addressed to you in the mail. Furthermore, when the postman arrived at your door, he blew a whistle). It was up to you to remember what you came for, while your eye traveled from cans of sardines to ice cream salt to harmonicas to flypaper (over your head, batting around on a thread beneath the blades of the ceiling fan, stuck with its testimonial catch).

Its confusion may have been in the eye of its beholder. Enchantment is cast upon you by all those things you weren't supposed to have need for, it lures you close to wooden tops you'd outgrown, boy's marbles and agates in little net pouches, small rubber balls that wouldn't bounce straight, frazzly kitestring, clay bubble-pipes that would snap off in your teeth, the stiffest scissors. You could contemplate those long narrow boxes of sparklers gathering dust while you waited for it to be the Fourth of July or Christmas, and noisemakers in the shape of tin frogs for somebody's birthday party you hadn't been invited to yet, and see that they were all marvelous.

You might not have even looked for Mr. Sessions when he came around his store cheese (as big as a doll's house) and in front of the counter looking for you. When you'd finally asked him for, and received from him in its paper bag, whatever single thing it was that you had been sent for, the nickel that was left over was yours to spend.

Down at a child's eye level, inside those glass jars with mouths in their sides through which the grocer could run his scoop or a child's hand might be invited to reach for a choice, were wineballs, all-day suckers, gumdrops, peppermints. Making a row under the glass of a counter were the Tootsie Rolls, Hershey Bars, Goo-Goo Clusters, Baby Ruths. And whatever was the name of those pastilles that came stacked in a cardboard cylinder with a cardboard lid? They were thin and dry, about the size of tiddlywinks, and in the shape of twisted rosettes. A kind of chocolate dust came out with them when you shook them out in your hand. Were they chocolate? I'd say rather they were brown. They didn't taste of anything at all, unless it was wood. Their attraction was the number you got for a nickel.

Making up your mind, you circled the store around and around, around the pickle barrel, around the tower of Cracker Jack boxes; Mr. Sessions had built it for us himself on top of a packing case, like a house of cards.

If it seemed too hot for Cracker Jacks, I might get a cold drink. Mr. Sessions might have already stationed himself by the cold-drinks barrel, like a mind reader. Deep in ice water that looked black as ink, murky shapes that would come up as Coca-Colas, Orange Crushes, and various flavors of pop, were all swimming around together. When you gave the word, Mr. Sessions plunged his bare arm in to the elbow and fished out your choice, first try. I favored a locally bottled concoction called Lake's Celery. (What else could it be called? It was made by a Mr. Lake out of celery. It was a popular drink here for years but was not known universally, as I found out when I arrived in New York and ordered one in the Astor bar.) You drank on the premises, with feet set wide apart to miss the drip, and gave him back his bottle.

But he didn't hurry you off. A standing scales was by the door, with a stack of iron weights and a brass slide on the balance arm, that would weigh you up to three hundred pounds. Mr. Sessions, whose hands were gentle and smelled of carbolic, would lift you up and set your feet on the platform, hold your loaf of bread for you, and taking his time while you stood still for him, he would make certain of what you weighed today. He could even remember what you weighed the last time, so you could subtract and announce how much you'd gained. That was goodbye.

Is there always a hard way to go home? From the Little Store, you could go partway through the sewer. If your brothers had called you a scarecat, then across the next street beyond the Little Store, it was possible to enter this sewer by passing through a privet hedge, climbing down into the bed of a creek, and going into its mouth on your knees. The sewer—it might have been no more than a "storm sewer"—came out and emptied here, where Town Creek, a sandy, most often shallow little stream that ambled through Jackson on its way to the Pearl River, ran along the edge of the cemetery. You could go in darkness through this tunnel to where you next saw light (if you ever did) and climb out through the culvert at your own street corner.

I was a scarecat, all right, but I was a reader with my own refuge in storybooks. Making my way under the sidewalk, under the street and the streetcar track, under the Little Store, down there in the wet dark by myself, I could be Persephone entering into my six-month sojourn underground—though I didn't suppose Persephone had to crawl, hanging onto a loaf of bread, and come out through the teeth of an iron grating. Mother Ceres would indeed be wondering where she could find me, and mad when she knew. "Now am I going to have to start marching to the Little Store *for myself?*"

I couldn't picture it. Indeed, I'm unable today to picture the Little Store with a grown person in it, except for Mr. Sessions and the lady who helped him, who belonged there. We children thought it was ours. The happiness of errands was in part that of running for the moment away from home, a free spirit. I believed the Little Store to be a center of the outside world, and hence of happiness—as I believed what I found in the Cracker Jack box to be a genuine prize, which was as simply as I believed in the Golden Fleece.

But a day came when I ran to the store to discover, sitting on the front step, a grown person, after all—more than a grown person. It was the Monkey Man, together with his monkey. His grinding-organ was lowered to the step beside him. In my whole life so far, I must have laid eyes on the Monkey Man no more than five or six times. An itinerant of rare and wayward appearances, he was not punctual like the Gipsies, who every year with the first cool days of fall showed up in the aisles of Woolworth's. You never knew when the Monkey Man might decide to favor Jackson, or which way he'd go. Sometimes you heard him as close as the next street, and then he didn't come up yours.

But now I saw the Monkey Man at the Little Store, where I'd never seen him before. I'd never seen him sitting down. Low on that familiar doorstep, he was not the same any longer, and neither was his monkey. They looked just like an old man and an old friend of his that wore a fez, meeting quietly together, tired, and resting with their eyes fixed on some place far away, and not the same place. Yet their romance for me didn't have it in its power to waver. I wavered. I simply didn't know how to step around them, to proceed on into the Little Store for my mother's emergency as if nothing had happened. If I could have gone in there after it, whatever it was, I would have given it to them—putting it into the monkey's cool little fingers. I would have given them the Little Store itself.

In my memory they are still attached to the store—so are all the others. Everyone I saw on my way seemed to me then part of my errand, and in a way they were. As I myself, the free spirit, was part of it too.

All the years we lived in that house where we children were born, the same people lived in the other houses on our street too. People changed through the arithmetic of birth, marriage and death, but not by going away. So families just accrued stories, which through the fullness of time, in those times, their own lives made. And I grew up in those.

But I didn't know there'd ever been a story at the Little Store, one that was going on while I was there. Of course, all the time the Sessions family had been living right overhead there, in the upstairs rooms behind the little railed porch and the shaded windows; but I think we children never thought of that. Did I fail to see them as a family because they weren't living in an ordinary house? Because I so seldom saw them close together, or having anything to say to each other? She sat in the back of the store, her pencil over a ledger, while he stood and waited on children to make up their minds. They worked in twin black eyeshades, held on their gray heads by elastic bands. It may be harder to recognize kindness—or unkindness, either—in a face whose eyes are in shadow. His face underneath his shade was as round as the little wooden wheels in the Tinker Toy box. So was her face. I didn't know, perhaps didn't even wonder: were they husband and wife or brother and sister? Were they father and mother? There were a few other persons, of various ages, wandering singly in by the back door and out. But none of their relationships could I imagine, when I'd never seen them sitting down together around their own table.

The possibility that they had any other life at all, anything beyond what we could see within the four walls of the Little Store, occurred to me only when tragedy struck their family. There was some act of violence. The shock to the neighborhood traveled to the children, of course; but I couldn't find out from my parents what had happened. They held it back from me, as they'd already held back many things, "until the time comes for you to know."

You could find out some of these things by looking in the unabridged dictionary and the encyclopedia—kept to hand in our dining room—but you couldn't find out there what had happened to the family who for all the years of your life had lived upstairs over the Little Store, who had never been anything but patient and kind to you, who never once had sent you away. All I ever knew was its aftermath: they were the only people ever known to me who simply vanished. At the point where their life overlapped into ours, the story broke off.

We weren't being sent to the neighborhood grocery for facts of life, or death. But of course those are what we were on the track of, anyway. With the loaf of bread and the Cracker Jack prize, I was bringing home the intimations of pride and disgrace, and rumors and early news of people coming to hurt one another, while others practiced for joy—storing up a portion for myself of the human mystery.

Black Boy

RICHARD WRIGHT

GRANNY WAS AN ardent member of the Seventh-Day Adventist Church and I was compelled to make a pretense of worshiping her God, which was her exaction for my keep. The elders of her church expounded a gospel clogged with images of vast lakes of eternal fire, of seas vanishing, of valleys of dry bones, of the sun burning to ashes, of the moon turning to blood, of stars falling to the earth, of a wooden staff being transformed into a serpent, of voices speaking out of clouds, of men walking upon water, of God riding whirlwinds, of water changing into wine, of the dead rising and living, of the blind seeing, of the lame walking; a salvation that teemed with fantastic beasts having multiple heads and horns and eyes and feet; sermons of statues possessing heads of gold, shoulders of silver, legs of brass, and feet of clay; a cosmic tale that began before time and ended with the clouds of the sky rolling away at the Second Coming of Christ; chronicles that concluded with the Armageddon; dramas thronged with all the billions of human beings who had ever lived or died as God judged the quick and the dead...

While listening to the vivid language of the sermons I was pulled toward emotional belief, but as soon as I went out of the church and saw the bright sunshine and felt the throbbing life of the people in the streets I knew that none of it was true and that nothing would happen.

Once again I knew hunger, biting hunger, hunger that made my body aimlessly restless, hunger that kept me on edge, that made my temper flare, hunger that made hate leap out of my heart like the dart of a serpent's tongue, hunger that created in me odd cravings. No food that I could dream of seemed half so utterly delicious as vanilla wafers. Every time I had a nickel I would run to the corner grocery store and buy a box of vanilla wafers and walk back home, slowly, so that I could eat them all up without having to share them with anyone. Then I would sit on the front steps and dream of eating another box; the craving would finally become so acute that I would force myself to be active in order to forget. I learned a method of drinking water that made me feel full temporarily whether I had a desire for water or not; I would put my mouth under a faucet and turn the water on full force and let the stream cascade into my stomach until it was tight. Sometimes my stomach ached, but I felt full for a moment.

No pork or veal was ever eaten at Granny's, and rarely was there meat of any kind. We seldom ate fish and then only those that had scales and spines. Baking powder was never used; it was alleged to contain a chemical harmful to the body. For breakfast I ate mush and gravy made from flour and lard and for hours afterwards I would belch it up in my mouth. We were constantly taking bicarbonate of soda for indigestion. At four o'clock in the afternoon I ate a plate of greens cooked with lard. Sometimes on Sundays we bought a dime's worth of beef which usually turned out to be uneatable. Granny's favorite dish was a peanut roast which she made to resemble meat, but which tasted like something else.

My position in the household was a delicate one; I was a minor, an uninvited dependent, a blood relative who professed no salvation and whose soul stood in mortal peril. Granny intimated boldly, basing her logic on God's justice, that one sinful person in a household could bring down the wrath of God upon the entire establishment, damning both the innocent and the guilty, and on more than one occasion she interpreted my mother's long illness as the result of my faithlessness. I became skilled in ignoring these cosmic threats and developed a callousness toward all metaphysical preachments.

But Granny won an ally in her efforts to persuade me to confess her God; Aunt Addie, her youngest child, had just finished the Seventh-Day Adventist religious school in Huntsville, Alabama, and came home to argue that if the family was compassionate enough to feed me, then the least I could do in return was to follow its guidance. She proposed that, when the fall school term started, I should be enrolled in the religious school rather than a secular one. If I refused, I was placing myself not only in the position of a horrible infidel but of a hardhearted ingrate. I raised arguments and objections, but my mother sided with Granny and Aunt Addie and I had to accept.

The religious school opened and I put in a sullen attendance. Twenty pupils, ranging in age from five to nineteen and in grades from primary to high school, were crowded into one room. Aunt Addie was the only teacher and from the first day an acute, bitter antagonism sprang up between us. This was the first time she had ever taught school and she was nervous, self-conscious because a blood relative of hers—a relative who would not confess her faith and who was not a member of her church—was in her classroom. She was determined that every student should know that I was a sinner of whom she did not approve, and that I was not to be granted consideration of any kind.

The pupils were a docile lot, lacking in that keen sense of rivalry which made the boys and girls who went to public school a crowd in which a boy was tested and weighed, in which he caught a glimpse of what the world was. These boys and girls were will-less, their speech flat, their gestures vague, their personalities devoid of anger, hope, laughter, enthusiasm, passion, or despair. I was able to see them with an objectivity that was inconceivable to them. They were claimed wholly by their environment and could imagine no other, whereas I had come from another plane of living, from the swinging doors of saloons, the railroad yard, the roundhouses, the street gangs, the river levees, an orphan home; had shifted from town to town and home to home; had mingled with grownups more than perhaps was good for me. I had to curb my habit of cursing, but not before I had shocked more than half of them and had embarrassed Aunt Addie to helplessness.

As the first week of school drew to a close, the conflict that smoldered between Aunt Addie and me flared openly. One afternoon she rose from her desk and walked down the aisle and stopped beside me.

"You know better than that," she said, tapping a ruler across my knuckles.

"Better than what?" I asked, amazed, nursing my hand.

"Just look at that floor," she said.

I looked and saw that there were many tiny bits of walnut meat scattered about; some of them had been smeared into grease spots on the clean, white pine boards. At once I knew that the boy in front of me had been eating them; my walnuts were in my pocket, uncracked.

"I don't know anything about that," I said.

"You know better than to eat in the classroom," she said.

"I haven't been eating," I said.

"Don't lie! This is not only a school, but God's holy ground," she said with angry indignation.

"Aunt Addie, my walnuts are here in my pocket..."

"I'm Miss Wilson!" she shouted.

I stared at her, speechless, at last comprehending what was really bothering her. She had warned me to call her Miss Wilson in the classroom, and for the most part I had done so. She was afraid that if I called her Aunt Addie I would undermine the morale of the students. Each pupil knew that she was my aunt and many of them had known her longer than I had.

"I'm sorry," I said, and turned from her and opened a book.

"Richard, get up!"

I did not move. The room was tense. My fingers gripped the book and I knew that every pupil in the room was watching. I had not eaten the nuts; I was sorry that I had called her Aunt Addie; but I did not want to be singled out for gratuitous punishment. And, too, I was expecting the boy who sat in front of me to devise some lie to save me, since it was really he who was guilty.

"I asked you to get up!" she shouted.

I still sat, not taking my eyes off my book. Suddenly she caught me by the back of my collar and yanked me from the seat. I stumbled across the room.

"I spoke to you!" she shouted hysterically.

I straightened and looked at her; there was hate in my eyes.

"Don't you look at me that way, boy!"

"I didn't put those walnuts on the floor!"

"Then who did?"

My street gang code was making it hard for me. I had never informed upon a boy in the public school, and I was waiting for the boy in front of me to come to my aid, lying, making up excuses, anything. In the past I had taken punishment that was not mine to protect the solidarity of the gang, and I had seen other boys do the same. But the religious boy, God helping him, did not speak.

"I don't know who did it," I said finally.

"Go to the front of the room," Aunt Addie said.

I walked slowly to her desk, expecting to be lectured; but my heart quickened when I saw her go to the corner and select a long, green, limber switch and come toward me. I lost control of my temper.

"I haven't done anything!" I yelled.

She struck me and I dodged.

"Stand still, boy!" she blazed, her face livid with fury, her body trembling.

I stood still, feeling more defeated by the righteous boy behind me than by Aunt Addie.

"Hold out your hand!"

I held out my hand, vowing that never again would this happen to me, no matter what the price. She stung my palm until it was red, then lashed me across my bare legs until welts rose. I clamped my teeth to keep from uttering a single whimper. When she finished I continued to hold out my hand, indicating to her that her blows could never really reach me, my eyes fixed and unblinking upon her face.

"Put down your hand and go to your seat," she said.

I dropped my hand and turned on my heels, my palm and legs on fire, my body taut. I walked in a fog of anger toward my desk.

"And I'm not through with you!" she called after me.

She had said one word too much; before I knew it, I had whirled and was staring at her with an open mouth and blazing eyes.

"Through with me?" I repeated. "But what have I done to you?"

"Sit down and shut up!" Aunt Addie bellowed.

I sat. I was sure of one thing: I would not be beaten by her again. I had often been painfully beaten, but almost always I had felt that the beatings were somehow right and sensible, that I was in the wrong. Now, for the first time, I felt the equal of an adult; I knew that I had been beaten for a reason that was not right. I sensed some emotional problem in Aunt Addie other than her concern about my eating in school. Did my presence make her feel so insecure that she felt she had to punish me in front of the pupils to impress them? All afternoon I brooded, wondering how I could quit the school.

The moment Aunt Addie came into the house—I reached home before she did—she called me into the kitchen. When I entered, I saw that she was holding another switch. My muscles tightened.

"You're not going to beat me again!" I told her.

"I'm going to teach you some manners!" she said.

I stood fighting, fighting as I had never fought in my life, fighting with myself. Perhaps my uneasy childhood, perhaps my shifting from town to town, perhaps the violence I had already seen and felt took hold of me, and I was trying to stifle the impulse to go to the drawer of the kitchen table and get a knife and defend myself. But this woman who stood before me was my aunt, my mother's sister, Granny's daughter; in her veins my own blood flowed; in many of her actions I could see some elusive part of my own self; and in her speech I could catch echoes of my own speech. I did not want to be violent with her, and yet I did not want to be beaten for a wrong I had not committed.

"You're just mad at me for something!" I said.

"Don't tell me I'm mad!"

"You're too mad to believe anything I say."

"Don't speak to me like that!"

"Then how can I talk to you? You beat me for throwing walnuts on the floor? But I didn't do it!"

"Then who did?"

Since I was alone now with her, and desperate, I cast my loyalties aside and told her the name of the guilty boy, feeling that he merited no consideration.

"Why didn't you tell me before?" she asked.

"I don't want to tell tales on other people."

"So you lied, hunh?"

I could not talk; I could not explain how much I valued my code of solidarity.

"Hold out your hand!"

"You're not going to beat me! I didn't do it!"

"I'm going to beat you for lying!"

"Don't, don't hit me! If you hit me I'll fight you!"

For a moment she hesitated, then she struck at me with the switch and I dodged and stumbled into a corner. She was upon me, lashing me across the face. I leaped, screaming, and ran past her and jerked open the kitchen drawer; it spilled to the floor with a thunderous sound. I grabbed up a knife and held it ready for her.

"Now, I told you to stop!" I screamed.

"You put down that knife!"

"Leave me alone or I'll cut you!"

She stood debating. Then she made up her mind and came at me. I lunged at her with the knife and she grasped my hand and tried to twist the knife loose. I threw my right leg about her legs and gave her a shove, tripping her; we crashed to the floor. She was stronger than I and I felt my strength ebbing; she was still fighting for my knife and I saw a look on her face that made me feel she was going to use it on me if she got possession of it. I bit her hand and we rolled, kicking, scratching, hitting, fighting as though we were strangers, deadly enemies, fighting for our lives.

"Leave me alone!" I screamed at the top of my voice.

"Give me that knife, you boy!"

"I'll kill you! I'll kill you if you don't leave me alone!"

Granny came running; she stood thunderstruck.

"Addie, what are you doing?"

"He's got a knife!" she gasped. "Make 'im put it down!"

"Richard, put down that knife!" Granny shouted.

My mother came limping to the door.

"Richard, stop it!" she shouted.

"I won't! I'm not going to let her beat me!"

"Addie, leave the boy alone," my mother said.

Aunt Addie rose slowly, her eyes on the knife, then she turned and walked out of the kitchen, kicking the door wide open before she as she went.

"Richard, give me that knife," my mother said.

"But, mama, she'll beat me, beat me for nothing," I said. "I'm not going to let her beat me; I don't care what happens!"

"Richard, you are bad, bad," Granny said, weeping.

I tried to explain what had happened, but neither of them would listen. Granny came toward me to take the knife, but I dodged her and ran into the back yard. I sat alone on the back steps, trembling, emotionally spent, crying to myself. Grandpa came down; Aunt Addie had told him what had happened.

"Gimme that knife, mister," he said.

"I've already put it back," I lied, hugging my arm to my side to conceal the knife.

"What's come over you?" he asked.

"I don't want her to beat me," I said.

"You're a child, a boy!" he said.

"But I don't want to be beaten!"

"What did you do?"

"Nothing."

"You can lie as fast as a dog can trot," Grandpa said. "And if it wasn't for my rheumatism, I'd take down your pants and tan your backside good and proper. The very idea of a little snot like you threatening somebody with a knife!"

"I'm not going to let her beat me," I said again.

"You're bad," he said. "You better watch your step, young man, or you'll end up on the gallows."

I had long ceased to fear Grandpa; he was a sick old man and he knew nothing of what was happening in the house. Now and then the womenfolk called on him to throw fear into someone, but I knew that he was feeble and was not frightened of him. Wrapped in the misty memories of his young manhood, he sat his days out in his room where his Civil War rifle stood loaded in a corner, where his blue uniform of the Union Army lay neatly folded.

Aunt Addie took her defeat hard, holding me in a cold and silent disdain. I was conscious that she had descended to my own emotional level in her effort to rule me, and my respect for her sank. Until she married, years later, we rarely spoke to each other, though we ate at the same table and slept under the same roof, though I was but a skinny, half-frightened boy and she was the secretary of the church and the church's day-school teacher. God blessed our home with the love that binds...

I continued at the church school, despite Aunt Addie's never calling upon me to recite or go to the blackboard. Consequently I stopped studying. I spent my time playing with the boys and found that the only games they knew were brutal ones. Baseball, marbles, boxing, running were tabooed recreations, the Devil's work; instead they played a wildcat game called popping-the-whip, a seemingly innocent diversion whose excitement came only in spurts, but spurts that could hurl one to the edge of death itself. Whenever we were discovered standing idle on the school grounds, Aunt Addie would suggest that we pop-the-whip. It would have been safer for our bodies and saner for our souls had she urged us to shoot craps.

One day at noon Aunt Addie ordered us to pop-the-whip. I had never played the game before and I fell in with good faith. We formed a long line, each boy taking hold of another boy's hand until we were stretched out like a long string of human beads. Although I did not know it, I was on the tip end of the human whip. The leading boy, the handle of the whip, started off at a trot, weaving to the left and to the right, increasing speed until the whip of flesh was curving at breakneck gallop. I clutched the hand of the boy next to me with all the strength I had, sensing that if I did not hold on I would be tossed off. The whip grew taut as human flesh and bone could bear and I felt that my arm was being torn from its socket. Suddenly my breath left me. I was swung in a small, sharp arc. The whip was now being popped and I could hold on no more; the momentum of the whip flung me off my feet into the air, like a bit of leather being flicked off a horsewhip, and I hurtled headlong through space and landed in a ditch. I rolled over, stunned, head bruised and bleeding. Aunt Addie was laughing, the first and only time I ever saw her laugh on God's holy ground.

In the home Granny maintained a hard religious regime. There were prayers at sunup and sundown, at the breakfast table and dinner table, followed by a Bible verse from each member of the family. And it was presumed that I prayed before I got into bed at night. I shirked as many of the weekday church services as possible, giving as my excuse that I had to study; of course, nobody believed me, but my lies were accepted because nobody wanted to risk a row. The daily prayers were a torment and my knees became sore from kneeling so long and often. Finally I devised a method of kneeling that was not really kneeling; I learned, through arduous repetition, how to balance myself on the toes of my shoes and rest my head against a wall in some convenient corner. Nobody, except God, was any the wiser, and I did not think that He cared.

Granny made it imperative, however, that I attend certain all-night ritualistic prayer meetings. She was the oldest member of her church and it would have been unseemly if the only grandchild in her home could not be brought to these important services; she felt that if I were completely remiss in religious conformity it would cast doubt upon the staunchness of her faith, her capacity to convince and persuade, or merely upon her ability to apply the rod to my backside.

Granny would prepare a lunch for the all-night praying session, and the three of us—Granny, Aunt Addie, and I—would be off, leaving my mother and Grandpa at home. During the passionate prayers and the chanted hymns I would sit squirming on a bench, longing to grow up so I could run away, listening indifferently to the theme of cosmic annihilation, loving the hymns for their sensual caress, but at last casting furtive glances at Granny and wondering when it would be safe for me to stretch out on the bench and go to sleep. At ten or eleven I would munch a sandwich and Granny would nod her permission for me to take a nap. I would awaken at intervals to hear snatches of hymns or prayers that would lull me to sleep again. Finally Granny would shake me and I would open my eyes and see the sun streaming through stained-glass windows.

Many of the religious symbols appealed to my sensibilities and I responded to the dramatic vision of life held by the church, feeling that to live day by day with death as one's sole thought was to be so compassionately sensitive toward all life as to view all men as slowly dying, and the trembling sense of fate that welled up, sweet and melancholy, from the hymns blended with the sense of fate that I had already caught from life. But full emotional and intellectual belief never came. Perhaps if I had caught my first sense of life from the church I would have been moved to complete acceptance, but the hymns and sermons of God came into my heart only long after my personality had been shaped and formed by uncharted conditions of life. I felt that I had in me a sense of living as deep as that which the church was trying to give me, and in the end I remained basically unaffected.

My body grew, even on mush and lard gravy, a miracle which

the church certainly should have claimed credit for. I survived my twelfth year on a diet that would have stunted an average-sized dog, and my glands began to diffuse through my blood, like sap rising upward in trees in spring, those strange chemicals that made me look curiously at girls and women. The elder's wife sang in the choir and I fell in love with her as only a twelve-year-old can worship a distant and unattainable woman. During the services I would stare at her, wondering what it was like to be married to her, pondering over how passionate she was. I felt no qualms about my first lust for the flesh being born on holy ground; the contrast between budding carnal desires and the aching loneliness of the hymns never evoked any sense of guilt in me.

It was possible that the sweetly sonorous hymns stimulated me sexually, and it might have been that my fleshy fantasies, in turn, having as their foundation my already inflated sensibility, made me love the masochistic prayers. It was highly likely that the serpent of sin that nosed about the chambers of my heart was lashed to hunger by hymns as well as dreams, each reciprocally feeding the other. The church's spiritual life must have been polluted by my base yearnings, by the leaping hunger of my blood for the flesh, because I would gaze at the elder's wife for hours, attempting to draw her eyes to mine, trying to hypnotize her, seeking to communicate with her with my thoughts. If my desires had been converted into a concrete religious symbol, the symbol would have looked something like this: a black imp with two horns; a long, curving, forked tail; cloven hoofs, a scaly, naked body; wet, sticky fingers; moist, sensual lips, and lascivious eyes feasting upon the face of the elder's wife . . .

A religious revival was announced and Granny felt that it was her last chance to bring me to God before I entered the precincts of sin at the public school, for I had already given loud and final notice that I would no longer attend the church school. There was a discernible lessening in Aunt Addie's hostility; perhaps she had come to the conclusion that my lost soul was more valuable than petty pride. Even my mother's attitude was: "Richard, you ought to know God through *some* church."

The entire family became kind and forgiving, but I knew the motives that prompted their change and it drove me an even greater emotional distance from them. Some of my classmates—

who had, on the advice of their parents, avoided me—now came to visit and I could tell in a split second that they had been instructed in what to say. One boy, who lived across the street, called on me one afternoon and his self-consciousness betrayed him; he spoke so naïvely and clumsily that I could see the bare bones of his holy plot and hear the creaking of the machinery of Granny's maneuvering.

"Richard, do you know we are all worried about you?" he asked.

"Worried about me? Who's worried about me?" I asked in feigned surprise.

"All of us," he said, his eyes avoiding mine.

"Why?" I asked.

"You're not saved," he said sadly.

"I'm all right," I said, laughing.

"Don't laugh, Richard. It's serious," he said.

"But I tell you that I'm all right."

"Say, Richard, I'd like to be a good friend of yours."

"I thought we were friends already," I said.

"I mean true brothers in Christ," he said.

"We know each other," I said in a soft voice tinged with irony.

"But not in Christ," he said.

"Friendship is friendship with me."

"But don't you want to save your soul?"

"I simply can't feel religion," I told him in lieu of telling him that I did not think I had the kind of soul he thought I had.

"Have you really tried to feel God?" he asked.

"No. But I know I can't feel anything like that."

"You simply can't let the question rest there, Richard."

"Why should I let it rest?"

"Don't mock God," he said.

"I'll never feel God, I tell you. It's no use."

"Would you let the fate of your soul hang upon pride and vanity?"

"I don't think I have any pride in matters like this."

"Richard, think of Christ's dying for you, shedding His blood, His precious blood on the cross."

"Other people have shed blood," I ventured.

"But it's not the same. You don't understand."

"I don't think I ever will."

"Oh, Richard, brother, you are lost in the darkness of the world. You must let the church help you."

"I tell you, I'm all right."

"Come into the house and let me pray for you."

"I don't want to hurt your feelings..."

"You can't. I'm talking for God."

"I don't want to hurt God's feelings either," I said, the words slipping irreverently from my lips before I was aware of their full meaning.

He was shocked. He wiped tears from his eyes. I was sorry.

"Don't say that. God may never forgive you," he whispered.

It would have been impossible for me to have told him how I felt about religion. I had not settled in my mind whether I believed in God or not; His existence or nonexistence never worried me. I reasoned that if there did exist an all-wise, all-powerful God who knew the beginning and the end, who meted out justice to all, who controlled the destiny of man, this God would surely know that I doubted His existence and He would laugh at my foolish denial of Him. And if there was no God at all, then why all the commotion? I could not imagine God pausing in His guidance of unimaginably vast worlds to bother with me.

Embedded in me was a notion of the suffering in life, but none of it seemed like the consequences of original sin to me; I simply could not feel weak and lost in a cosmic manner. Before I had been made to go to church, I had given God's existence a sort of tacit assent, but after having seen His creatures serve Him at first hand, I had had my doubts. My faith, such as it was, was welded to the common realities of life, anchored in the sensations of my body and in what my mind could grasp, and nothing could ever shake this faith, and surely not my fear of an invisible power.

"I'm not afraid of things like that," I told the boy.

"Aren't you afraid of God?" he asked.

"No. Why should I be? I've done nothing to Him."

"He's a jealous God," he warned me.

"I hope that He's a kind God," I told him.

"If *you* are kind to Him, He *is* a kind God," the boy said. "But God will not look at you if you don't look at Him."

During our talk I made a hypothetical statement that summed

up my attitude toward God and the suffering in the world, a statement that stemmed from my knowledge of life as I had lived, seen, felt and suffered it in terms of dread, fear, hunger, terror, and loneliness.

"If laying down my life could stop the suffering in the world, I'd do it. But I don't believe anything can stop it," I told him.

He heard me but he did not speak. I wanted to say more to him, but I knew that it would have been useless. Though older than I, he had neither known nor felt anything of life for himself; he had been carefully reared by his mother and father and he had always been told what to feel.

"Don't be angry," I told him.

Frightened and baffled, he left me. I felt sorry for him.

Immediately following the boy's visit, Granny began her phase at the campaign. The boy had no doubt conveyed to her my words of blasphemy, for she talked with me for hours, warning me that I would burn forever in the lake of fire. As the day of the revival grew near, the pressure upon me intensified. I would go into the dining room upon some petty errand and find Granny kneeling, her head resting on a chair, uttering my name in a tensely whispered prayer. God was suddenly everywhere in the home, even in Aunt Addie's scowling and brooding face. It began to weigh upon me. I longed for the time when I could leave. They begged me so continuously to come to God that it was impossible for me to ignore them without wounding them. Desperately I tried to think of some way to say no without making them hate me. I was determined to leave home before I would surrender.

Then I blundered and wounded Granny's soul. It was not my intention to hurt or humiliate her; the irony of it was that the plan I conceived had as its purpose the salving of Granny's frustrated feelings toward me. Instead, it brought her the greatest shame and humiliation of her entire religious life.

One evening during a sermon I heard the elder—I took my eyes off his wife long enough to listen, even though she slumbered in my senses all the while—describe how Jacob had seen an angel. Immediately I felt that I had found a way to tell Granny that I needed proof before I could believe, that I could not commit myself to something I could not feel or see. I would tell her that if I were to see an angel I would accept that as infallible evidence that there was a God and would serve Him unhesitatingly; she would surely understand an attitude of that sort. What gave me courage to voice this argument was the conviction that I would never see an angel; if I had ever seen one, I had enough common sense to have gone to a doctor at once. With my bright idea bubbling in my mind, wishing to allay Granny's fears for my soul, wanting to make her know that my heart was not all black and wrong, that I was actually giving serious thought to her passionate pleadings, I leaned to her and whispered:

"You see, Granny, if I ever saw an angel like Jacob did, then I'd believe."

Granny stiffened and stared at me in amazement; then a glad smile lit up her old wrinkled white face and she nodded and gently patted my hand. That ought to hold her for a while, I thought. During the sermon Granny looked at me several times and smiled. Yes, she knows now that I'm not dismissing her pleas from my mind . . . Feeling that my plan was working, I resumed my worship of the elder's wife with a cleansed conscience, wondering what it would be like to kiss her, longing to feel some of the sensuous emotions of which my reading had made me conscious. The service ended and Granny rushed to the front of the church and began talking excitedly to the elder; I saw the elder looking at me in surprise. Oh, goddamn, she's telling him! I thought with anger. But I had not guessed one-thousandth of it.

The elder hurried toward me. Automatically I rose. He extended his hand and I shook it.

"Your grandmother told me," he said in awed tones.

I was speechless with anger.

"I didn't want her to tell you that," I said.

"She says that you have seen an angel." The words literally poured out of his mouth.

I was so overwhelmed that I gritted my teeth. Finally I could speak and I grabbed his arm.

"No . . . N-nooo, sir! No, sir!" I stammered. "I didn't say that. She misunderstood me."

The last thing on earth I wanted was a mess like this. The elder blinked his eyes in bewilderment.

"What did you tell her?" he asked.

"I told her that if I ever saw an angel, then I would believe," I said, feeling foolish, ashamed, hating and pitying my believing granny. The elder's face became bleak and stricken. He was stunned with disappointment.

"You . . . you didn't see an angel?" he asked.

"No, *sir!*" I said emphatically, shaking my head vigorously so that there could be no possible further misunderstanding.

"I see," he breathed in a sigh.

His eyes looked longingly into a corner of the church.

"With God, you know, anything is possible," he hinted hopefully.

"But I didn't see *anything*," I said. "I'm sorry about this."

"If you pray, then God will come to you," he said.

The church grew suddenly hot. I wanted to bolt out of it and never see it again. But the elder took hold of my arm and would not let me move.

"Elder, this is all a mistake. I didn't want anything like this to happen," I said.

"Listen, I'm older than you are, Richard," he said. "I think that you have in your heart the gift of God." I must have looked dubious, for he said: "Really, I do."

"Elder, please don't say anything to anybody about this," I begged.

Again his face lit with vague hope.

"Perhaps you don't want to tell me because you are bashful?" he suggested. "Look, this is serious. If you saw an angel, then tell me."

I could not deny it verbally any more; I could only shake my head at him. In the face of his hope, words seemed useless.

"Promise me you'll pray. If you pray, then God will answer," he said.

I turned my head away, ashamed for him, feeling that I had unwittingly committed an obscene act in rousing his hopes so wildly high, feeling sorry for his having such hopes. I wanted to get out of his presence. He finally let me go, whispering:

"I want to talk to you sometime."

The church members were staring at me. My fists doubled. Granny's wide and innocent smile was shining on me and I was filled with dismay. That she could make such a mistake meant that she lived in a daily atmosphere that urged her to expect something like this to happen. She had told the other members and everybody knew it, including the elder's wife! There they stood, the church members, with joyous astonishment written on their faces, whispering among themselves. Perhaps at that moment I could have mounted the pulpit and led them all; perhaps that was to be my greatest moment of triumph!

Granny rushed to me and hugged me violently, weeping tears of joy. Then I babbled, speaking with emotional reproof, censuring her for having misunderstood me; I must have spoken more loudly and harshly than was called for—the others had now gathered about me and Granny—for Granny drew away from me abruptly and went to a far corner of the church and stared at me with a cold, set face. I was crushed. I went to her and tried to tell her how it had happened.

"You shouldn't've spoken to me," she said in a breaking voice that revealed the depths of her disillusionment.

On our way home she would not utter a single word. I walked anxiously beside her, looking at her tired old white face, the wrinkles that lined her neck, the deep, waiting black eyes, and the frail body, and I knew more than she thought I knew about the meaning of religion, the hunger of the human heart for that which is not and can never be, the thirst of the human spirit to conquer and transcend the implacable limitations of human life.

Later, I convinced her that I had not wanted to hurt her and she immediately seized upon my concern for her feelings as an opportunity to have one more try at bringing me to God. She wept and pleaded with me to pray, really to pray, to pray hard, to pray until tears came...

"Granny, don't make me promise," I begged.

"But you must, for the sake of your soul," she said.

I promised; after all, I felt that I owed her something for inadvertently making her ridiculous before the members of her church.

Daily I went into my room upstairs, locked the door, knelt, and tried to pray, but everything I could think of saying seemed silly. Once it all seemed so absurd that I laughed out loud while on my knees. It was no use. I could not pray. I could never pray. But I kept my failures a secret. I was convinced that if I ever succeeded in praying, my words would bound noiselessly against the ceiling and rain back down upon me like feathers.

My attempts at praying became a nuisance, spoiling my days; and I regretted the promise I had given Granny. But I stumbled on a way to pass the time in my room, a way that made the hours fly with the speed of the wind. I took the Bible, pencil, paper, and a rhyming dictionary and tried to write verses for hymns. I justified this by telling myself that, if I wrote a really good hymn, Granny might forgive me. But I failed even in that; the Holy Ghost was simply nowhere near me...

One day while killing my hour of prayer, I remembered a series of volumes of Indian history I had read the year before. Yes, I knew what I would do; I would write a story about the Indians... But what about them? Well, an Indian girl... I wrote of an Indian maiden, beautiful and reserved, who sat alone upon the bank of a still stream, surrounded by eternal twilight and ancient trees, waiting... The girl was keeping some vow which I could not describe and, not knowing how to develop the story, I resolved that the girl had to die. She rose slowly and walked toward the dark stream, her face stately and cold; she entered the water and walked on until the water reached her shoulders, her chin; then it covered her. Not a murmur or a gasp came from her, even in dying.

"And at last the darkness of the night descended and softly kissed the surface of the watery grave and the only sound was the lonely rustle of the ancient trees," I wrote as I penned the final line.

I was excited; I read it over and saw that there was a yawning void in it. There was no plot, no action, nothing save atmosphere and longing and death. But I had never in my life done anything like it; I had made something, no matter how bad it was; and it was mine... Now, to whom could I show it? Not my relatives; they would think I had gone crazy. I decided to read it to a young woman who lived next door. I interrupted her as she was washing dishes and, swearing her to secrecy, I read the composition aloud. When I finished she smiled at me oddly, her eyes baffled and astonished.

"What's that for?" she asked.

"Nothing," I said.

"But why did you write it?"

"I just wanted to."

"Where did you get the idea?"

I wagged my head, pulled down the corners of my mouth, stuffed my manuscript into my pocket and looked at her in a cocky manner that said: Oh, it's nothing at all. I write stuff like this all the time. It's easy, if you know how. But I merely said in an humble, quiet voice:

"Oh, I don't know. I just thought it up."

"What're you going to do with it?"

"Nothing."

God only knows what she thought. My environment contained nothing more alien than writing or the desire to express one's self in writing. But I never forgot the look of astonishment and bewilderment on the young woman's face when I had finished reading and glanced at her. Her inability to grasp what I had done or was trying to do somehow gratified me. Afterwards whenever I thought of her reaction I smiled happily for some unaccountable reason.

Bodies & Soul

AL YOUNG

BLACK, BROWN AND BEIGE
DUKE ELLINGTON ORCHESTRA, 1947
(—OR, MIZ CHAPMAN TELLS US THE SCORE)

"NOW SON, I know you can do better than that. You've *got* to do better. You know how come? Because you're black, that's why. Nothing's going to come easy in this world that's laying for you out there, so you might as well get used to having to be twice as good as white folks at whatever you do if you intend to ever make anything out of yourself."

The woman speaking wasn't my mother. It was Miz Chapman, my second-grade teacher at Kingston Primary School for Colored in Laurel, Mississippi, 1947. My mother, who later bombarded me with similar warnings, was still quite young then. Unable to look after and provide for all of her children, she had sent me and a much younger brother back from Detroit to our native state to spend a couple of years with her sister, my Aunt Doris, and her family. This practice wasn't unusual then, long before such notions as the Nuclear Family, the Civil Rights Struggle and Black Pride were widespread.

Zora Neale Hurston, the late and eminent novelist and folklorist, spoke of being "passed around the family like a bad penny." Perhaps because I was only seven at the time, I didn't feel as though I were being farmed out. Still, it felt peculiar to be separated from my true parents—that is until I landed in Miz Chapman's room in that big, dilapidated, gray wooden structure surrounded by mud.

She was indeed a remarkable woman, this scolder and molder of minds, this Miz Chapman. Dark-skinned, white-haired, scalding of eye and seemingly telepathic, she was often given to warm laughter. Moreover, she possessed an uncanny ability, common to

409

the elderly in those days, of being able to train her laser-like sight on your very soul. With a look that variously melted or chilled, Miz Chapman was capable of reading everything there was to know about you—past, present or future—at a glance. And she was memorably tough on her secret favorites, pupils from whom she expected nothing short of excellence. Unfortunately, I happened to be one of those.

One chilly Friday morning in late autumn, while we were putting away our readers and bringing out arithmetic homework, Miz Chapman casually announced that anyone who wanted to stick around after school to "learn a little something about the history of the Negro race" was welcome to do so. "It's important that you all know about that," she added.

Given all the activities, sanctioned and unsanctioned, that went on after school in our sad little corner of that textile mill and cannery town, I was surprised to find myself remaining after class had let out just to learn what Miz Chapman had to teach us. Leontyne Price, a native of Laurel, might have been weaving her girlish, operatic dreams at that very moment. Since it was all entirely voluntary—and that went for our teacher's time as well—only a handful of us had been curious enough to take up the invitation.

Drawing a long face, the twinkle never leaving her eye, Miz Chapman gave us each a special look, then seated us in a semicircle around the rotund wood heater, now grown cold, that squatted in one corner of the rickety room. Chilly, we had to keep on our coats and jackets and sweaters. This arrangement, of course, was far more intimate than when she presided over us from her mean-looking desk up front by the blackboard.

"You poor things," she began, removing her glasses and pinching the bridge of her nose. "Poor babies. I wish there were more of you here because this here is something you really need to know about. We'll just have to start where we have to. Nothing makes a failure but a trial."

Those cryptic, prefatory remarks of Miz Chapman's were making me giddy with anticipation. I was innocently fascinated and yet, at the same time, slightly frightened. What on earth was she about to tell us that was so important that she found it necessary to lower her voice so mysteriously, so ominously?

"I reckon we'll have to begin with slavery," she said. "Now, you all know about slavery, don't you?"

Some of us knew vaguely about slavery and some of us didn't. It must be remembered that public school classrooms back then were often filled with pupils of varying ages. Not everyone was automatically passed on the way they are now, and certainly not in Miz Chapman's class. You simply had to master the material she was teaching before she would advance you to the next grade. There was no getting around it. In that second-grade class of hers, there were kids old enough to be third-graders, and several lanky, strapping ones of fourth, fifth or possible sixth grade age.

"Miz Chapman, ma'am," I raised my hand and asked, "would you please explain what slavery was?"

She folded her hands in her lap and leaned forward on her chair. "There was a time—and it wasn't all that long ago either—when colored people were in slavery. That was how we started out, in this country anyway, in these United States, this place we call America."

A stickler for correct speech and grammar, Miz Chapman, in her role as teacher, customarily spoke in gentle, cultivated Southern tones. Her voice was musical and proper when she wanted it to be. Naturally, she was also very much one of the people: a public servant who was on familiar terms with practically everybody in the community. She knew who your parents or guardians were and made a point of socializing with them as regularly as she could. In fact, chances were better than reasonable that she'd taught them when they were children. At the drop of a ruler, she could shift linguistic gears and become vigorously—if not wickedly—colloquial when the occasion called for it.

There was many a youngster, myself included, who knew what it was like to look up and blink just in time to duck an oncoming blackboard eraser hurled at top speed by Miz Chapman herself right at your unsuspecting head. "Next time I'll take better aim" she might shout down the aisle of desks at the offender. "Since you so doggone hardheaded, maybe that's the only way I can get through to you. Don't worry. I *will* get through!" Those old erasers weren't the soft felt kind in use today. They were chalky strips of heavy cloth glued to hard blocks of wood. Used accurately as missiles, they could cause severe concussions.

This afternoon, however, nobody was fooling around. We were all giving Miz Chapman our best attention. The message that she was warming up to was as clear and cold as ice water.

"Slavery," she continued, rising from her seat and pointing, "is when you—and by you I do mean *you, you and you*—are owned by somebody else, the same way somebody might own a dog or a cat or a mule or a cow. Now, the way the Creator meant for things to go, there wasn't supposed to be any such thing as slavery. People all over the world, all they are is brothers and sisters. But we don't always go by God's laws. We're like a world full of wayward children. We forget about the Lord and do things our way, and what that means is any old kinda way."

She paced around the heater momentarily, as though pulling her urgent thoughts together, "People out of Spain, England, France, Holland and different places, they hopped in their little boats and sailed over here to start them up a new country, so they say. Now, you all remember when we were studying about Christopher Columbus and the Pilgrims and all those folks? Remember how the Indians were already here when they stepped off the boat? Well, keep that in mind because that's important. We'll get back to that and talk about it some more because all that fits in with what I'm fixing to tell you."

Somewhere down inside my stomach, a little knot was beginning to tighten. I looked around at the other faces to see how my classmates were taking this old woman's words. Like the rest of this motley assemblage, I had seen my share of western movies, but had never stopped to consider why the Indians were always going on the warpath, or why Tom Mix, Bob Steele, Hopalong Cassidy and other cowboy heroes were forever shooting at them. Everybody sat engrossed, entranced and wide-eyed.

"You see," said Miz Chapman, peeping around furtively before sitting again, "you can go buy yourself a mule and hitch that mule up to pull your wagon or plow your land. You don't have to pay that mule a salary. All you have to do is give him feed and give him water, and maybe have a barn or a shed to put him in at night or when the weather gets rough. I mean, who ever heard of a mule or a cow or a chicken drawing a paycheck?"

When she broke out into a smile, we all knew that it was OK to follow her lead. We smiled back and a couple of us laughed nervously.

"Wellsir," she went on, "Back in those days, going way, way back—three four hundred years at least—you could buy yourself a person. That's right, a person, a human being, a man, a woman, a child—depending on what you needed 'em for—and you could train that person and put 'em to work just like you might any other poor beast of burden. And that's what was done with us. Slavetraders—men who made their living catching and selling slaves—traveled all up and down the coast of Africa, packing their slaveships with the strongest men and women and little bitty children they could round up and bringing 'em back over here to sell."

"But why'd they have to go all the way over there?" some girl wanted to know. "Couldn't they capture 'em some white folks and Indians right here?"

Miz Chapman shook her head and smiled again. "Whoa, now, that's a good question! Bless your heart! Shows me you got your thinking cap on. What you say! Fact of the matter is they did have a right sizeable few of their own kind in slavery all along. There used to be something called debtors prison. You owe so much money and can't pay off your debts and bills. Well, over yonder in England, say, they might slap you in prison and then you might could work out a deal where you'd get shipped over here to the Colonies and be put in slavery—indentured servitude, they called it—until you worked off what you owed. But, you see, white folks, it looked like, could always buy their way out of slavery somehow, but the Negro couldn't, not in most places anyway. You have to remember something, though—and if you don't remember this, then nothing else I'm trying to tell you today'll make much sense—so pay attention. White folks won't treat us the same way they treat other white folks. Listen at what I'm saying. White folks treat colored people different. They always have, and they still do!"

"And the Indians?" I asked.

"This Indian," she said, shaking her head. "Seems like they never could get him to work for them the way they could us. See, child, it's one thing when you pile in and take over somebody else's country, and another thing when you go yanking people from out their home and drag and carry 'em off someplace that's thousands of miles across the ocean, put 'em in chains, then dare 'em to run away or do anything about their condition. That's how they did us. They snatched us up the way you might go out in the woods and catch a rabbit or a possum or a squirrel, then they pent and cooped us up. They put us to planting cotton, chopping cotton, picking cotton, cooking, sewing, scrubbing, building, mending, riding shotgun on one another and every other kinda chore you can think of, even raising their little privileged children and—"

"But why?" It was the same girl's voice interrupting her. "I need to know why!"

"Girl, I already told you! It was cheaper to do it that way than it was to pay somebody, that's why. It's always cheaper to make somebody work for you for nothing than it is to pay 'em."

Miz Chapman's gaze turned suddenly toward the row of tall windows in back of us—kept sparkling clean by pupils forced to work off violations—where the late afternoon light had begun to fade.

"You know," she told us, getting to her feet, "for all that, we're still here. We are still here. We're still struggling, but we're still here. Y'all know that old spiritual we sing about 'I Been 'Buked and I Been Scorned'? Well, for all that, for all they have done to us and're trying to do to us, we are still here, right here, carrying on . . . still trying to make that journey home."

Her face softened wistfully. A tear slipped down one of her tall cheekbones. "Everything they could see to take away from us, they took. They took away our homeland, our families and the people we loved, our language, our customs, our music, our history. . . . But you know what? All we are is children of God, and the Almighty will take care of His own. No need for you to worry about *that*. Just like He parted the waters of the Red Sea and led the Israelites out of bondage in Egypt, the Lord is looking after all of His children.

"And for everything they took away, we came up with something new. We commenced to making a new religion. We sang us some new songs and danced us some new dances. We created new families, built us some new homes, and commenced to making some new history, too. See, you can put a hurting on the body, but you can't touch the soul. You know how come that is? It's because the soul of man, the same as God's love, is everlasting. The Good Book says, 'And I will dwell in the house of the Lord *forever*'!

"Now, it also says in the Good Book that God helps those who help themselves, and that's just what we've been doing and what we're bound to do more of. The way we go about doing that is first by learning *how* we can help ourselves. You young 'uns have opportunities we didn't have when I was coming along. You can go to school and study. You all are in a position to do a whole lot more than we could. But you're still dealing with the same situation. You don't have to be all that smart to look around at the way we're being treated and cheated to see that we aren't a free people yet. No, not yet.

"I feel like it's part of my job to tell you all what I know about what our people have been through before you got here, before you were born. I want you all to know about the Negro race and some of the people, *great* people, who didn't sit around and lay around waiting for somebody else to get busy. There were some who saw what had to be done, who went on ahead and did it, and what they did *stayed* done! I'm talking about folks like Phillis Wheatley, Harriet Tubman, Sojourner Truth, Frederick Douglass, Paul Laurence Dunbar, Booker T. Washington, W. E. B. DuBois, George Washington Carver, Mary McCleod Bethune, A. Philip Randolph, Langston Hughes, and plenty other Negro geniuses you aren't liable to find out too much about in history books these white folks put out."

One older boy seated next to me screwed up his face and raised his hand. "Miz Chapman," he asked, "how come white folks so doggone mean?"

"Now, that's something you've got to be careful about," she told him. "Not everybody's the same. Even with the white folks, some're different. You can't go putting good white folks, quality white folks, in the same category as crackers and peckerwoods. Y'all are old enough to know by now that there's a big difference between good and bad anything. If it wasn't for good-thinking white folks, then the Underground Railroad wouldn't have worked as well as it did."

"The Underground Railroad," I asked. "What was that?"

"I see we have a lot of catching up to do," said Miz Chapman. "That's why I want you all to listen and think about some of this stuff I'm telling you, then I want you to come back here with some questions. You know, there's such a thing as slavery of the mind too. You have to think. Next time we meet, we'll be talking about some of these Negro geniuses, like, now, you take Dr. George Washington Carver. By the way, who can tell me who he was?"

A girl raised her hand. "He invented the peanut, didn't he?"

Miz Chapman laughed. "No, child, he didn't exactly *invent* the peanut, but you're on the right track. George Washington Carver took the common little peanut, studied it real hard, then did things with it that people all over the world are still benefiting by. He was a botanist, one of our great scientists known the world over. Fact of business, he just died a few years ago over in Tuskegee. And when people would ask him how he got to know so much, Dr. Carver would explain how important it was to study *and* to have faith in the Lord. It was by listening to God that he was able to figure out so much and get to be so great.

"All of us are children of God, don't care what anybody else tells you—and before you turn grown, you'll be hearing a whole gang of explanations about how the world was created and how mankind got here. You just take your strength from the Almighty, trust in Him, use your own good sense and go on about your business. Anybody with any kind of sense knows good and well that man did *not* make this world and the stars and the planets and the seasons and all that comes with it. This earth is our home for *now*, that's all. We just pass through here on our way someplace else. But, see, that doesn't mean we won't have to fight for what we have a right to. There are going to be trials and there are going to be tribulations. Nobody's going to give you a durn thing! When they wrote the Constitution, white folks weren't thinking about us because Negroes were considered the same as property and livestock. 'Kill a mule and I'll hire another'n; kill a nigger and I'll buy another'n!' That's how the old saying went. But after the Civil War and President Abraham Lincoln signed the Emancipation Proclamation, that was a step in the right direction. Yet and still, nobody's going to just walk up and hand you nothing for free. You've got to work and struggle for it, and most times you've got to fight for it. 'Here, old So-and-So, we want you to have this here freedom on accounta you all right with us.' Hunh, what you say? That isn't how it works. You have got to earn it; but before you can earn, first you have to learn. Get something in your head and then—no matter what they do to you, no matter how lowdown the world becomes—they can't knock it out of you! But you can't operate on muscle and nerve and brains alone. You need heart; you need God. You need the Master to lean on and guide you."

Then rising and resting her hands in the pockets of her well-worn coat, Miz Chapman looked at the wall clock and said, "Now, who wants to lead us in reciting the 'Twenty-Third Psalm'?"

Looking back now from a vantage point of some thirty-odd years, it's easy to see how there must have been countless Miz Chapmans in Black classrooms all over the country who loved their calling devotedly, and who strove to give Black, Brown and Beige children charged to their care the skills, both practical and spiritual, that they would be needing to build halfway meaningful lives for themselves in a society that has traditionally spurned and rejected their kind. From that day on, I heeded such shibboleths as "What you get in your head, nobody can knock out." I heard them echoed so repeatedly, in fact, that they began to sound platitudinous. The vividness, however, of Miz Chapman's pronouncements at the first of those after-school study sessions has lasted.

I remember that it was growing dark as I made my way home from the schoolyard. Clutching my books wrapped in grocery bag paper, I hurried along the dirt roadways and partially asphalted paths, cutting across trash-strewn vacant lots and fields of weeds leaping over sluggish puddles and mud holes, some of them rumored to be mined with quicksand.

"*Yea, though I walk through the valley of the shadow of death, I will fear no evil; for Thou art with me....*"

Finally I was sprinting past the broken-down fences and ramshackle houses of my own little block in that part of Laurel known as Kingston Bottom.

"*Thou preparest a table before me in the presence of mine enemies ...*"

The smell of suppers cooking filled the air. I could see lights burning in the windows of our place, the last house on the road before you came to the creek. My Aunt Doris would be inside where it was warm, preparing a meal of neckbones and rice, turnip greens, cornbread, molasses, buttermilk. To top it all off, there'd be no school tomorrow!

I didn't know exactly yet who "mine enemies" were but, like the distant croaking of frogs hidden in darkness by the creek, I knew that they were out there somewhere, crouched, setting their traps, laying for me like wild game hunters. And I knew that I was either going to learn to be strong, clever and swift or forever play dead.

A surge of pure joy was bubbling inside me as I raced down the final stretch home.

Three

POETRY

Genealogy

JAMES A. AUTRY

You are
in these hills
who you were and who you will become
and not just who you are

>*She was a McKinstry*
>*and his mother was a Smith*

And the listeners nod
at what the combination will produce
those generations to come
of thievery or honesty
of heathens or Christians
of slovenly men or working

>*'Course her mother was a Sprayberry*

And the new name rises
to the shaking of heads
the tightening of lips
the widening of eyes

>*And his daddy's mother was a McIlhenney*

Oh god a McIlhenney
and silence prays for the unborn children
those little McKinstry Smith Sprayberry McIlhenneys

>*Her daddy was no count and her daddy's daddy*
>*was no count*

Old Brother Jim Goff said it
when Mary Allen was pregnant

>*Might's well send that chile*

> *to the penitentiary soons he's born*
> *gonna end up there anyway*

But that lineage could also forgive
with benign expectation
or transgressions to come

> *'Course, what do you expect*
> *his granddaddy was a Wilkins*

or

> *The Whitsells are a little crazy*
> *but they generally don't beat up nobody outside the family*

or

> *You can't expect much work out of a Latham*
> *but they won't steal from you*

In other times and other places
there are new families and new names

> *He's ex P&G*
> *out of Benton and Bowles*
> *and was brand management with Colgate*

And listeners sip Dewar's and soda or puff New True Lights
and know how people will do things
they are expected to do
New fathers spring up and new sons and grandsons
always in jeopardy of leaving the family

> *Watch young Dillard*
> *if you can work for Burton he's golden*
> *but he could be out tomorrow*

And new marriages are bartered for old-fashioned reasons

> *If you want a direct marketing guy*
> *get a headhunter after someone at Time Inc.*

Through it all
communities new and old watch and judge and make sure
the names are in order
and everyone understands

Childhood Remembrances

CHARLIE R. BRAXTON

i remember w-a-a-a-y back
when i was young
the make-believe games
we played for fun
like hopscotch and hide-and-go-seek
the roving reporter-the man on the street
i also remember
how crowded it was
when we played house
we shared the crib
with the family mouse
now we weren't rich
so we couldn't afford
no pool
instead we danced in front
of the hydrant
to keep our cool
i remember trading bottle taps
for ginger snaps
sitting on the corner
popping paper caps
with rocks
(we couldn't afford guns)
naw i never played cowboy
(we couldn't afford the hats)
but we played cops and robbers
and wore funny mask
made of brown paper sacks
the rich boys from across the tracks
laughed at us
(as if we were fools)
but it never bothered me

in fact it was cool
because my heroes
were never cowboys

Jazzy St. Walk:
An improvisational poem

hip hitting riffs
split my brain on past
the sullen refrains
of trane's free jazz movement

going on and on and on and on and on

and now
even though i don't know exactly
where it all begins
or ends
   i do know that i've
spent decades untold
doing a old blues walk/dance
       down these old mean & empty streets
sweating between the sheets
of satin dolls and many moochers
singing good night irene
'cause papa's got a brand new bag
of rhythms (& blues)
rocking and rolling all the way live
down mainstreet harlem
by way of muddy springs mississippi
you see
contrary to the all popular belief
jazz aint no kind of music
it's an artful way of life
spiced like a pickled pig tail
steaming on a peppermint twist stick
   dig what i mean

YEAH
i walk alone along
those rough rugged robust roads
                              of jazz
the same damn way
i walked the dirty/dusty rows of cotton way
back
      down in the
                    deep
                          deep
                                south
nobody knows the trouble i've seen
glory glory
hallelujah
lord have mercy ... mercy ... mercy
hallelujah

see you don't know what
it's like to live a
lyricless life of a poet
in exile
             lost   &   wandering without vision
with only the bittersweet
rutabaga memories of life
back home

HOME

                    where the heart beats
                    tom tom voodoo chants

HOME

                    where a small pin in
                    the bottom of a rag
                    doll is a sudden sharp
                    pain in the ass of
                    masta jack

HOME

                    where shango's hammer
                    swings like basie's big

band on a one night stand
in a funky joint north of
gutbucket u.s.a.

i say

YEAH

i do walk alone
along these pitch black back streets
crying & bleeding blue/jazzy sounds
from the raw pockets of my fatal wounds
i plead for ancestral elders wisdom
to close the gaping holes
in my soul before
i expose too much
   too quick
   too soon
for these old angry streets are just
too too mean to be seen without
an axe to grind behind...
if you dig my meaning

Southern Roads/City Pavement

VIRGIA BROCKS-SHEDD

SOUTHERN ROADS
  Held me virgin and
  barefoot in the dust
  that circled up to cover my face,
  my hair, and engaged my nostrils
  to inhale the dust of life
  for me to become when I am dead.

MY SOUTHERN DUSTY ROADS
  Led me from the deep piney woods
  of my shacky home to the
  pavement of Highway number 49

to see cars going to or coming
from the city 30 miles away;
waving my blackberry buckets,
hoping the riders would stop
and leave fifty cents for
my three hours of picking, and dodging snakes,
and getting untangled, while
envisioning money to leave
at the white folks' store
for nickel bars of delightful
but seldom had candy bars,
and then go home and say to
my daddy's widow,
"Mama, I made some money today."

MY SOUTHERN ROADS

In the little world of my life;
didn't know our folks could not afford
to take us to see the city streets;
I wonder now if I knew they existed;
and we thought everyone was like us,
except the folks in cars;
and me and my sisters and brothers
were jumping up and shouting everytime
we saw Black folks in cars as we
exclaimed which car was our own;
the cars, passing us, and now I recall,
some riders, glancing with pity
at those poor, poor children,
and stopping to buy our
fifty cents syrup bucket of blackberries.

The only other world we knew was
in the cowboy movies that we saw
in a tent during one season on unused,
unplowed dusty or grassy grounds,
because it was early 60s before we saw
television regularly to reject
our own lives, to imagine ourselves

dancing to Welk's champagne music
and wearing fine clothes.

SOUTHERN ROADS

That held and carried us barefoot
and occasionally with new cheap shoes
to school and our country church,
where we tried to look and be
without sin and important, too,
among those who were; and,
trying to get to heaven in one day
from the preaching and shouting and the
baptizing in our white sheets of goodness;
and going back home just before night
to play, fight, court and whisper
and glance and touch the boyfriends
and girlfriends we paired with unnoticed,
we thought, by our parents, and grandparents,
and aunts and uncles and senior cousins
who told us ghost tales and
superstitions and family histories,
as we listened to fox sounds and panther wails
and saw community, not homebox, entertainment
in pennies disappearing from and reappearing to
my daddy's hands while he lived to 1951

To wake and kill home raised chickens,
and cook them on the fires we stoked
in our wood stoves; pick greens, pull corn,
pick plums; stomp on clothes in a big tin tub,
stir them up in a big black pot,
and wait for hog killing time when we knew
we would eat homemade skins and the pig's feet;
and when with no meat, have homemade
buttermilk and cornbread

SOUTHERN ROADS

In the grassy, dusty paths that led
to Mrs. Eleases's house, Mrs. Clara's
and Mr. J.P.'s, Mr. Horse's,
Lynette's and Nooky's, Herman's and Billy's

on rutted walkways, or little craggy clay hills,
leading to springs of water for drinking,
branches of water for washing the clothes
from the bodies, the lives of sawmill, paperwood
workers; men touching women and children in the
new corners of our everyday life,
after our mommies came home from cleaning
the white folks' homes and our daddies bringing
very tired bodies home in their overalls
on

SOUTHERN ROADS

A peaceful haven for
floating southern spirits,
rejuvenating their times when they
physically touched the soil,
protecting living lives in the
meekness of us as we moaned together
in blackness of nationwide black care and
love for the Emmett Tills and the
Mack Charles Parkers; and, saying
deeply inside of us,
"Lord, have mercy; please have mercy."
And cry and shout at Mahalia's throaty notes
singing, "Precious Lord," and to later
feel the fleeting joy when we would
wind and grind to the lightning music of
Brother Hopkins or scream in pleasure
to know that B.B. was singing about women
who could love and cause or leave misery.

SOUTHERN ROADS

Leading to death in the lynch sites of
forest of trees; to burial grounds in rivers,
in the soil of dams; in carports and living
rooms of modern homes; in unpillowed beds
on railroad cars; on lawns adjacent to
dormitories; in the paved streets of cities,
at Parchman, Whitfield, and even the whiskey stills

SOUTHERN ROADS
>Tapping and rooting and growing to and with
the lives that left for Chicago, L A, New York,
the army, Oakland, Detroit, Milwaukee,
the street corners, bars, heroin, coke—
the best of life, we thought, in escape from

SOUTHERN ROADS
>I miss you since all I now touch
is asphalt or concrete or carpet;
gritty dust, not the fine kind
that blew with the clean winds through trees,
or kicked up with dusty barefoot feet
in the rows of fields we chopped to
make food for ourselves or money for the others
who hired us for $3.00 a day,
and then to shop at their stores for processed
foods we thought better than our natural
homemade brands or the fish we caught and ate
from creeks and natural lakes.

SOUTHERN ROADS
>I now seldom walk anywhere,
but I do drive back to visit
the roads of my youth;
touching the soil, bringing some of its rocks,
its dirt to my city street;
and bringing the memories and the caresses
of the senior ones and the younger ones
who never left whom I see
still shaped and living in the
southern dust, home with me.

SOUTHERN ROADS
>From the dust of you I have risen,
and have come and produced from me
two other lives to replenish you, too,
along with all the juniors from my sisters
of every race;
children to teach us loving and how to care

as those who were taught before
to care for the present us.
And, I wish to leave you naturally made
by bare or animal skinned feet;
to leave you laying paths to a world of peace
in unpaved, unpolluted by concrete and asphalt,
and gasoline and machine air;
and that airplanes will always pass by you
and not land too near;
that the blues and spirituals you give
will be orchestrated by southern homing birds
which won't ever have to fly away;
all creature; including me, who need you
to remain dusty or muddy when wet,
just dusty or muddy, good southern roads.

SOUTHERN ROADS
    Foundation of my life,
    holding all that made me,
    my expired families and friends,
    my ancestral anchors, so far
    from where I am now.
    But, what sorrows at each birth
    these ancestors must have given in hopes
    and prayers that the children
    of black lives and black spirits
    would have lives better than their own . . .
    to try and not ever miss the early lives
    of their scrotums and wombs which had died
    from disease or natural miscarriages;
    yet,

SOUTHERN ROADS,
    You've paved a permanence in my life,
    for I am bounded by gentle southern spirits
    that travel you, too, and still,

SOUTHERN ROADS,
    You will lead those to me
    when I lie still, covered in death,

under southern love,
returning myself to you,
O precious southern soil.

Hank and Peg

WILLIAM BURT

He was as skinny
As I was
But wiry
The kid next door
Who was everything
Summer was made of
White t-shirt
Freckles
An ugly crew-cut
An uglier dog
A red bike
Without fenders
His name was Hank
Together
We cultivated boredom
As though it were
A rare orchid
In the shade
Of the carport
Beside the fallout shelter
Beside the house
Where his family lived
The pavement there
Cool to the touch
Was a hot-bed
Of get-rich-quick schemes
And Charles Atlas ads
Experiments with firecrackers
That didn't go off

On the Fourth
And still didn't go off
On the twenty-fourth
Experiments in creative talking
Backwards
Who could talk the longest
The fastest
With water in your mouth
Warm hose water
Acting out the final scene
Of Bataan
Careful not to die
In the oil puddle
Acting out
Godzilla Meets Werewolf
While the sun
Not even moving
An inch
Baked front yards
And gnats crawled the lips
Of the ugly dog sleeping
Her name was Peg
And she was old
Before there were
People on the earth
There was Peg
Toothless
Panting
We thought she was smiling
It was canine air-conditioning
We thought she was a bulldog
She was a Boston Terrier
Ugly, bloated, unafraid
Even of death
Which was on her
Like a smell
Bored enough to provoke Peg
We would grab at her club feet
And make fun

Of old Peg
Old blind Peg
Old fat Peg
Until a death-rattle snarl
Became a neckless lurch
Peg gummed the air
And sometimes
An inch of finger
Reminded her
Of the taste
Of sweeter days
Peg the fighter
Triumphant
Cat killer
The world
May not remember
But the heart
Never forgets
And so it is
That I recall
Mississippi summers
And a carport
And the sound of a screen door
An aimless whistled tune
I would look out the window
There was Hank
Coming through the hedge
Peg at his heel
And the day would begin

Preserves

JACK BUTLER

Great love goes mad to be spoken: you went out
to the ranked tent-poles of the butterbean patch,
picked beans in the sun. You bent, and dug

the black ground for fat purple turnips.
You suffered the cornstalk's blades, to emerge
triumphant with grain. You spent all day in a coat
of dust, to pluck the difficult word
of a berry, plunk in a can. You brought home
voluminous tribute, cucumbers, peaches,
five-gallon buckets packed tightly with peas,
cords of sugar-cane, and were not content.

You had not yet done the pure, the completed,
the absolute deed. Out of that vegetable ore,
you wrought miracles: snap-beans broke
into speech, peas spilled from the long slit pod
like pearls, and the magical snap of your nail
filled bowls with the fat white coinage of beans.

Still, you were unfinished. Now fog swelled
in the kitchen, your hair wilted like vines.
These days drove you half-wild—you cried, sometimes,
for invisible reasons. In the yard, out of your way,
we played in the leaves and heard
the pressure-cooker blow out its musical shriek.

Then it was done: you had us stack up the jars
like ingots, or books. In the dark of the shelves,
quarts of squash gave off a glow like late sun.

That was the last we thought of your summer
till the day that even the johnson grass died.
Then, bent over sweet relish and black-eyed peas,
over huckleberry pie, seeing the dog outside
shiver with cold, we would shiver, and eat.

The Country Idiot

SYBIL PITTMAN ESTESS

Not many remember him anymore, my cousin
who had epileptic fits in the bottoms of holes
and other abysses he had to be in
by necessity—like the life he was in
with no means to control. No medicine
that they could pay for or wanted to know about
for their son named Leon in that land, at that time.
Now that he is little more than a vague memory,
I still see the country men taunt him
to climb down the fresh-dug well
late that night. He swallowed his tongue
and his mouth foamed
when the loud crowd turned its head. I remember
the giggles, the jests, and how he grinned afterward,
as if having come through some trial,
some accomplishment. And it was:
his mere living. Another extravagance
from my red rural past—like my grandmother's house
with no bathroom, no electricity;
like the king snake she found in her dresser drawer once.
And like Leon's two brothers, also dead: one in a carwreck,
drunk doing ninety; the other burned
in the gasoline housefire.
(He only wanted to clean the paintbrushes
near the heater.) Each grave has a picture by their
mother, my aunt. I was seven
and fresh from town when I fled,
so late, from Leon in black water
to grandmother's beside for her to cover
my eyes from Leon whom I hated,
Leon, who never missed Sunday School
once in his thirty-one years. Full mid-moons,
now I fear him.

The Best Meal I Ever Had Anywhere

ELLEN GILCHRIST

At the wonderful table of my grandfather
Bunky got the high chair
Dooley got the Webster's Unabridged Dictionary
and I got the Compton's Pictured Encyclopedia
Volumes A, B, D, and E.

The best meal I ever had anywhere
was one Sunday Pierce Noblin
wired the salt shaker to a dry cell battery
Dolly got a fishbone caught in her throat
and almost died
Sudie went into the parlor to sulk
and when no one was looking
I stabbed Bunky in the knee
with Onnie Maud's pearl handled wedding fork.

Diphtheria

REBECCA HOOD-ADAMS

Seventh summer
Sister took sick,
Hottest time I ever knew;
Sweat beads choke my neck
And dust devils dance
In fields behind the house.

Back of the buckboard
Raymond, Baby, and me
Sit quiet,
Even Dolly is sad-faced;
Secrets everywhere
But no one tells me.

All the way to Aunt Pet's
Papa never says a word;
He reins up sharp,
His shoulders shake
The one time Raymond coughs.

Sister sleeps with me
Since before I can remember,
Aunt Pet says crawl in beside her,
But I fidget until dawn;
Dreams of fever
Flash through sleep,
Striking Sister like a lightning bolt
That hit old man McWilliams
But never touched his horse;
I hear the grown-ups talk,
Some mystery, says they,
The way God chooses children.

Make/n My Music

ANGELA JACKSON

my colored child/hood wuz mostly music
    celebrate/n be/n young an Black (but we din know it)
        scream/n up the wide alleys
an holler/n afta the walla-mellon-man.

sun-rest time
my mama she wuz yell/n
    (all ova the block
            sang/n fa us
ta git our butts in
            side.

we grew up run/n jazz rhythms
    an watch/n mr. wiggins downstairs
        knock the blues up side   his woman's
                            head

we rocked.   an the big boys they snuck
an rolled   dice/ in the hallways   at nite.

i mean. we laughed love.   an the teen
     agers they jus slow dragged thru smokey
                            tunes.
        life wuz a ordinary miracle   an
        have/n fun wuzn no temptation

        we just dun it.
an   u know
i think we grew.   thru them spirit-uals
        the saint-tified folks wud git happy off
        of even if we *wuz* jus clown/n
        when we danced the grizzly bear an
        felt good when the reverend
        wid the black cadillac   said:

        let the holy ghost come in
        side you

that music makes you/feel sooo/ good!

any how   i wuz a little colored girl
        then . . .

so far
my Black woman/hood ain't been noth/n but music

        i found billie
            holiday   an learned
                 how
                 to cry.

Home Trainin

      my father never did
      heal my smart talkin
      mouth. no matter
      how many pursuits

aroun and unda the kitchen table
with belt or extension cord.

i had two smartin legs
              and ass
but my mouth
              continued to sass

mary mariah

my grandmother
mary mariah is sitting
by the window
her face   etched smooth
              into the day
        in her cheek/bones i
        see my aunt
bee bee who died when she was a little
over thirty   i see my aunts
bay-suh maude mary and hattie
and some of aunt jenny too
              i see
the young lines of my sister
bettys face

mary mariah is sitting silent
by the window   carrying generations
in her bones.

A Poem for Myself
(or Blues for a Mississippi Black Boy)

ETHERIDGE KNIGHT

I was born in Mississippi;
I walked barefooted thru the mud.

Born black in Mississippi,
Walked barefooted thru the mud.
But, when I reached the age of twelve
I left that place for good.
My daddy he chopped cotton
And he drank his liquor straight.
Said my daddy chopped cotton
And he drank his liquor straight.
When I left that Sunday morning
He was leaning on the barnyard gate.
Left her standing in the yard
With the sun shining in her eyes.
And I headed North
As straight as the Wild Goose Flies,
I been to Detroit & Chicago
Been to New York city too.
I been to Detroit & Chicago
Been to New York city too.
Said I done strolled all those funky avenues
I'm still the same old black boy with the same old blues.
Going back to Mississippi
This time to stay for good
Going back to Mississippi
This time to stay for good—
Gonna be free in Mississippi
Or dead in the Mississippi mud.

Our Fathers at Corinth

WILLIAM MILLS

For William J. Mills, Co. A., 24th Mississippi Infantry Regiment. Died June 18, 1862. Buried in an unknown soldier's grave, Enterprise, Mississippi

"Let the impending battle decide our fate, and add one more illustrious page to the history of our Revolution, one to which our children will turn with noble pride, saying, 'Our fathers were at the battle of Corinth.'"

P.G.T. Beauregard, General, Commanding

Winter in Mississippi and your sons stand before you,
All of us together now, here between Chunky River and
Okatibbe Creek. You lie unmarked in these four hundred
Gray stones, still in formation and like enlisted men
Everywhere mostly unknown. It was this
That haunted your children,
That we didn't even know your name,
Only that you never came home.

The specter of our forgetfulness drove us
To front porches of the old of Greene County
Wanting to put a name to your wraith,
An end to our neglect.
As we rocked our way to eighteen hundred and sixty-two,
A hundred-year-old cousin remembered
You had walked the long way to Corinth.
That your young son got a licking
For trying to follow you.

She also said your name, great-grandfather.
With this we followed you to these cracked stones.

The records showed it to be
A late spring of blood.
You clustered at the courthouse
With your brash and ruddy cousins
Come to watch the lieutenant dressed in gray
Come to hear him talk about the fight.
He spoke of April at Shiloh and the butcher's bill,
Of General Johnston dying,
Of Mississippians buried there.
He spoke of Halleck with twice our number
Moving on Corinth.
He read a letter from Jeff Davis:
"Beauregard must have reinforcements . . .
The case of vital importance.
Send forward to Corinth
All the armed men you can furnish."
What parts of the late spring day
Warred in your Anglo-Saxon mind
As you moved slowly from the dock

of rhythmical certainties in Greene County
To the caesura of war, that pause
As the blood boils before its final thickening
Before it is left to cool in Corinth, in Enterprise?
Young yeoman, rude in your blue eyes,
Straw hat cocked in the county's latest style
Was it defense, not wanting to miss the big event,
Or just being shy about staying home?
No matter. You walked to Corinth. You went.

Well, not being cavalry because you had no horse
Means nothing to us now who conjure your ghost.
We have been mostly the infantrymen
Of the country's armies—Hill 209, Hill 800.
Yes sir, they have numbers.
We feel the earth as we walk to the world's wars,
And remembering, we return to care again,
Planting the seeds to tide us until the next
Rearing of the Apocalyptic face.

In the middle of May you found yourself
Not only in Company A, but in Polk's First Corp.
You also found what enlisted men know—
Being scared is only half.
There was typhoid, measles, and dysentery;
Also nothing to eat.
Instead of the clear water of the Chickasawhay
Here muddy, stagnant holes
Held what there was to drink.
How you soldiered and how you died
We don't know. Diaries tell us
What days it rained. We know Polk's Corp
Was beyond the entrenchments skirmishing day and night.
Everyone prepared for the coming fight.

As always the enlisted men were the last to know—
All units would fall back to Tupelo.
Perhaps this was your last bright sight
As the torches were put
To the trunks and tents, the blankets and beds,
As eighteen thousand in hospitals moved

Farther south.
No great battle, just plenty dead.
Grandfather, as you leaked away in June
Did you think at all of generation?
Your wife even then carried a son.
Did dreaming take its hands and urge you
Past Corinth to her labor to come,
To us, unnumbered, unknown
But coming, grandfather . . . coming.
Your blood may have thickened in Corinth
Yet your seed twisted to a birthing scream,
Your blood surged to now,
Surges like a sea in my head
Even as it may have spoken to you lying there
In your cocked hat,
Now tipped to shade your eyes, now tipped to die.
What now for the unknown soldier?
Somewhere in this plot of four hundred Confederates
Your bones stopped
But your blood salts leached the ground
On their way to the Chunky and Okatibbe,
Or down the Chickasawhay, past the summer corn,
And the homestead you left unfinished,
On to larger holdings. Your salt blood
Moved now down the Pascagoula,
Out to the Gulf of Mexico, out to the salt seas
Embracing the earth, holding us all.
Your home is large now, your wraith has a name.
You rest in your sons
Who must keep you to keep themselves.

The Eating Hill

KAREN MITCHELL

Going to get some eating dirt, special dirt
For my mother.

Going to take a pail, a fork
And dig in the special ground,
Until the pail is full
With baked brown, sweet soil.

Grandma took me to the brown hill, eating hill
When I was much younger.
We the dust, ate the dirt
When very cooked
In Grandma's great oven.

Down the well, the deep well
I went to get some rainwater.
Passed lined clothes, wet clothes,
Passed great-aunt's cabin
Snatching her great red rose.

Take a honeysuckle, take a blackberry,
Must take a pail of rainwater
And sit on the eating hill, special hill
Until my heart stop running,
I stop racing,
Quiet, so quiet
On the eating hill.

Closed my eyes, my brown eyes
And watched the colors bleed in darkness.
Did I hear birds? Grandma's voice?
Or was it my grasshoppers
Singing behind my shoulder?

Don't sing too loud, my Grandma's still.

"Nothing's like eating dirt,
Nothing's quick and easy to fill,"
My Grandma said, sitting on the eating hill.

Great, great, great, who?
The water restored my lips.
Remember, remember, remember when?
Grandma, you remember
Us laughing on top of
The eating hill.

My torn dress, flower dress,
Blows in my small face.
Laughing sister, younger sister,
Come to me
And let mud mix with our lace.

Cool water

Chopped wood burns
Cold rooms.
Laughing sister, sleep next to me
Living under covers.

Beans in the garden,
Oil lamps in the box,
Green leaves in my hands crumble,
Red berries grow smaller.

Too dark my dear,
My Grandma dear,
To eat with you much longer.

She is mine—
My daughter moving,
Old sister,
Old mother,
Brown-eyed dirt, lovely dirt
Waking in my arms.

Mother, mother
Grandma said
Don't take away eating dirt, special dirt
From me,
To me,
Eating dirt
Would stay.
So I must climb the eating hill, special hill
In the morning.
Must walk the road, the path
Slide between trees, cedar trees
And clear caves by mid-morning.

Birmingham, Alabama: 1963

The choir kept singing
while the preacher screamed through the walls
Miss Anderson testified that she
was cured because she believed
and we all got the Holy Ghost
drinking his blood
eating his body
I clapped my hands and cried "Jesus!"
saw Baby sleeping on Mama's lap
his dime rolled into the aisle
"Glory!" Miss Anderson cried "Glory hallelujah!"
and then I heard a sound
saw my pink dress tear
something colored my stockings my shoes
I heard my black face split
"Mama!" I cried
and we four went up with the dust.

Don't come to this wake
or touch this small cold body
lying in velvet
I am Job's child
dead from the Lord and Satan's wager
dead when the wind closed its eyes
and smote the four corners of the house
I have been left dry
without knowing why
I have not read the papers of Birmingham.
Braid my hair
in the rain-washed morning
I want to come back to you
stand beside the stove
and watch you stir steam
curl my finger around your ear

and make you hear the beating inside you
I want to breathe through the pores of this wood.

The choir keeps singing
Steal away, steal away, steal away to Jesus
the preacher keeps shouting
"So young! And she's gone!"
"Lord!" Miss Anderson cries "Lord have mercy!"
I ain't got long to stay here
Steal away, steal away home

I Remember 1929

JOHN NIXON, JR.

I remember 1929.
The cotton gins went Boom-boom-Boom-boom-Boom.
At five, in Mississippi, I was fine.
Hot noons, that summer, in the dining room

They let me sip diluted home brew, though
My mother was the most belligerent dry
The world has known. Daddy built bungalows.
My sister, cutest gal in junior high,

Had cut her curls "wind-blown" and had a pink
Silk hat with glitters on it. Black Aunt Ann
Died and was buried with some pomp. I think
Boob was my favorite funny paper man.

Our neighbors in the vast brick house across
The road imported bands from Memphis twice
That year for dances. Sweating brine, a horse
Brought us a wagon, an ice man, and some ice.

The cotton gins went Boom-boom-Boom. One fall
Day Mother took the bottled brew behind
The barn and smashed it there. And that was all
The crash I heard in 1929.

Confessions from Childhood

STEPHEN OWEN

(Class Reaction to *Lord of the Flies*)

1

With chairs in a circle
We become an island
Staring deep into chasms
Of ourselves.

From the fear and anger
So shallow in our flesh
The beast awakens
In confessions from childhood:
Stories of hanging sisters' dolls
With jump ropes,
Aiming toy pistols
At heads that spout
Blood mushrooms,
And exploding firecracker bombs
In cat skulls.

The beast lunges,
Digging out our backbones.
Leaving them snarled vines.
Our flesh rages
While our spirits cower
In the mouth of pig lore.

2

Afterwards on our island
A final wave breaks
Covering us with shame
And wonderment.

The beast recoils
And settles back
Under our quivering flesh
While in animal silence
We sit afraid
With human masks
At our feet.

Blues

STERLING D. PLUMPP

Blues. And the morning lifts
night from its dishrag
of darkness, commences to moan
vines of light climbing
over the horizon
in a vested crimson summoning.
Blues. And the day arrives
spitting pieces of rays
on darkness in transitions.
Blues. And time wakes me
to another pain before executioners
arrive, with commands
from mythology to wipe me
from being. But I'm ready,
ready as anybody can be,
ready for you,
hope you ready for me.
I got ax-handled tears
in the ball of my hand,
drinking bruises and blood
in a alcohol vein,
ain't in no mood
for no jive commands;
ain't in no mood
for no jive commands.

Blues. When I got
out the womb. All red
and underfed. Couldn't lay down
cause the blues all in my bed.
I got this pinching memory
so bad/I don't know
'xactly what to do.
I call on god
but he can't answer;
I call on the devil
but he can't hear;
and I call on the wind
and it comes here. Moved me
round so long
that I can't rest at all.
Blues. I got this pinching memory
so bad/my mind notices
everything that crawls.
Blues. Won't somebody come
tell me the good news.
Feel so low/feel like an empty cistern
in a six month drought.
Everytime I try to move the dust
gits up and dances about.
I got the blues.
And if I forget, I got
everything to lose. But don't
git me wrong cause I ain't
gonna lay down dead. I will
just sing, feel pain, and keep
going ahead . . .

I Hear the Shuffle
of the People's Feet

i am a name clanging
against circles

i go round
in what's been said and done
the old puts leashes
on my eyes
i go round
in tribal wisdom

men walking from the sea
as if it is dry land
enter my circle
put me in a straight line
from profit to death
i turn from now
back to the past
they fold my future
in their bank accounts

they take me from hands
to memory
i move from knowledge
to obedience
i plant tobacco
i train sugarcane
i yessir masters
i go straight from sunrises
to death
when i remember
i chant shango
i sing ogun
i dance obatala
i hum orishas

i am folded in work
i get up
i obey
i rebel
i runaway
they beat production
from my bones
and track up my mind
with their language

after one generation
i go round in silence
while my children work
without ever knowing tribal hands
they echo my songs
until whips dull their voices

i survive dungeons
by singing songs shaped by brutality:
i sing new necessities
in a strange band
my songs carry
rhythmic cries of my journey
and when i dance
yes, when i dance
i revive tribal possessions
the elders' hands
twist my eyes on right
and let my body go

true believer, the whip
tells my mind
what to dream
i feel the blood of africa
dripping down my back

though my pride rises
in what i do
to destroy the masters' blade
sinning against my skin
true believer, i survive
yes, i survive, i keep going
though they take everything away
i survive america

my name is written
in blood-wrapped days
untold centuries of cruelty
but i survive
come into the union
through a crack

my fist made
i had experienced
breaking freedom holes
by laying underground railroads
by plotting at night
by striking blows

they closed equality's door
before i could enter
they sent me bluesing towns
facing hostility
with open-eyed moans
i get my woman
from the master's bed
but lose her to his kitchen
learn every road
from all my searching
and not one of them end at opportunity
they send me bluesing towns

when i get the vote
terror drives me into fear
the tar, ropes, and evil men
scar my name with blood

they puke their fright and weaknesses
on me
instead of on those who own our bones
though they slaughter
still they cannot stop my efforts
i survive
following rivers to cities
putting my story on brass and winds

i live tyranny down
by swinging with jazz
but the white man's word
places hinges on my sky
from the shadows
i hear plantations talk
the civil war

sets me free from legal whippings
but not from lashes

when booker t prayed conformity
at backseat rites
i could hear lynchees scream
i could hear frightened men cry
i walked with DuBois
at Niagara
they jailed my reputation
in smelly epithets
yet i survive their onslaught
distance between freedom and chains
is measured by steps from backseats
to defiance

i move by going
where there ain't no fields
going where bondage is to production
to the factory's commands
in detroit
chicago
cleveland and milwaukee
away from hot suns
away from boll weevils
away from droughts
to a new world
my music affirms demons
barking resistence in my veins
and i sing ragtime gospels
hi-de-hi-hos hoochie coochies
my girls and temptation walks
in leaving the land
my legacy is transformed
in citified jive sayings

they take me to the work line
but leave my freedom at the station
listening to rails retell the places
i have not arrived at yet

i am still motherless
yet a hip-cat-rhinehart-zoot-suiting
malcolming wolf-waters shoeshine stone
i am a bigger bad trigger greedy
no-name boy prowling chitown
they put ethel in my waters
and she emerges lady day
pestering orchards of my soul
she-goddess of this strangeness
lady instrumentalized voice
tingling new sounds in new times

what the whip and lynchings
didn't get on the land
hard work, high prices, and the hawk
took away on these streets
they send me bluesing towns
"i ain't got nobody/got nobody
just me and my telephone"
i burn from exploitation
i empty my soul on fads
powdery substances Messiahs stand on

i mau-mau stampedes
against racist stalls
bellowing "for your precious love
means more to me
than any love can ever be"
the work songs rise
to become freedom anthems

the Supreme Court hears my lyrics
and its laws change beats
"separate but equal"
becomes "equality for all"
malcolm speaks/speaks so sweet
i hear the shuffle of the people's feet
we move in montgomery
we move in little rock
we move

we move at sit-in counters
we move on freedom rides
we move
we move in birmingham
we move on registration drives
we move
malcolm speaks/speaks so sweet

doin the riot/i fall from new bags
with a world fighting back
in viet nam
in angola
in mozambique
in the panther walks
poppa gotta rebellion thing
momma wears a freedom ring
freedom rings
from every alley and hole
brother, come here quick
take this struggle stick
freedom rings
the get black
burning too
take all the streets
do the boogaloo
freedom rings
feel so good
black out loud
dancing in the streets
with the fighting crowd

doing the riot
the burning too
throwing molotov cocktails
making black power new

we move
malcolm speaks/speaks so sweet.
i hear the shuffle of the people's feet

How to Tell a Story

SAMUEL PRESTRIDGE

Jesus the South is fine, isn't it. It's better than the theatre, isn't it. It's better than Ben Hur, isn't it. No wonder you have to come away now and then, isn't it.
—Absalom, Absalom!
William Faulkner

Unravel it
slowly, but tautly, the last strand
of rope, turning, turning, slowly separating
as the hero scuttles over the burning bridge,
the starlet in his arms. Then,
let everything crash down.

Say in 1933, a farmer with a lot of kids—
specifics and details—19 kids, all sons
to strap and carry, all deaf, all look-alikes,
planned Christmas on a cotton bale,
his last, and him with a large family,
though this needn't be mentioned again,
except to say, implicitly, how old
the man must be; the kids too, old enough
to have their own minds—not mean, but knowing
just enough to ruin Christmas.

He'd meant to swap the bale for gifts
and couldn't have them with him.
This too is implicit: *old enough to have their own minds*
demonstrates the use of idiom, succinct,
the twist of salt, adding authenticity.

By problem and solution, let the plot develop.
"He'd gotten up that morning
before the kids awoke.—This being a farm,
it would have to be, say, 3:00 a.m.,
the wife up too, cold breakfast, cold stars outside,
the bale already loaded,

and the hand-cranked, flat-bed waiting to be started.
The participle will imply that something's pending,
and the situation will create itself,
but also problems: "hand-cranked" denotes
the setting of the spark,
tinkering with magnetos, and the danger
of the crank kicking back, breaking your arm for you.

By now, he'd be in the yard,
trying to crank the sullen truck, when WHAM!—
a useful interjection, "wham"—
the crank kicked back and broke his arm.

Now, we forget Christmas and the bale,
everything but pain and the urgency
to crank that truck.
"So, he set the spark again . . ."

Here, pause.

They'll know what's coming, but won't believe.
Then WHAM! And understatement:
"He couldn't even raise his arms
to wipe tears from his eyes."

This may seem an ending,
but you can't just leave it there—
him, hopping around the yard, his arms twin trout,
Christmas pending, the kids asleep.
What happens next is toe-nailing,
a carpenter's effect.
"So, the wife woke up the oldest,
the dumb one, who could drive the truck."

The boy took out the spark plugs,
put them on the hearth to warm,
siphoned gas into a syrup bucket—
again, details authenticate—
took off the breather, put gas in the carburetor.
A cat jumped to the fender while he held the breather,
rubbed the syrup bucket, sloshing gasoline.
The boy got mad, ran the cat.

Here, quicken the pace.
The cat hid under a white pine stump.
They'll know what's going to happen.
The boy doused it with gasoline.
Here, the reader winces.
Struck a match.
Say "whoosh!"

The rest is denouement.
Talk slowly.
Be deliberate.
The fire-cat ran across the yard,
setting it on fire,
across the cotton bale,
setting it on fire,
into the barn where goats were kept,
setting it on fire.
And everything burned, even the goats,
and the boy stood looking dumb.
And the farmer, arms broken, couldn't even beat him.
And Christmas was potatoes buried in the yard.

Next, tie the story off,
relate your own life to it:
"The boy grew up to be the guard
at the Fox Run city dump, the image of his father."

To close, insist it's true.
That it happened in your family.
If there must be a moral,
let it always be the same:
God works in wondrous ways.

Now:

The Rolling Store

PAUL RUFFIN

It came,
his grandmother reported,
as regular as Sunday morning service,
grinding up the gravel slope
to her mailbox:
"White as Easter and
long as the arm of God!"
And there on shelves
high as a tall man's head
lay trays of butter, sacks
of beans, printed cloth,
soap, nails, jugs of kerosene:
"All a body could pray for."

Asphalt lies to the mailbox now.
("The ride to the grave will be
quick and smooth," he has heard her say.)
Her kitchen stinks of disuse
and roaches haunt her shelves
where a few jars of beans and peaches
squat in dust.
("A body just don't need much any more.")

On a hillside two hollows over,
when the air is right and the
leaves are gone, he can see
from the porch the rusty rolling store
lying on its side like a brown severed arm
in a glacier of grass.

Frozen Over

In Mississippi I recall only once
how the cold came down like a lid of iron,
clamping the landscape, stilling the trees,
and all the ponds froze over: not
just a skim for crashing rocks through,
but thick and hard enough to walk on.
The gravel pit where we swam in summer
spanged and creaked as I edged out
toward the gray, awful middle where,
if I went through, no one could reach.
I moved like a bird coming to terms
with glass, sliding one foot, then
the other, holding back my weight
and breath until they had to come.
I could see, beyond the far shore,
cars moving on the highway, slowing,
faces in the window ringed with frost,
the little ones waving, pointing
to that child walking on water.

It All Comes Together
Outside the Restroom in Hogansville

JAMES SEAY

It was the hole for looking in
only I looked out
in daylight that broadened
as I brought my eye closer.
First there was a '55 Chevy
shaved and decked like old times
but waiting on high-jacker shocks.

Then a sign that said J. D. Hines Garage.
In J. D.'s door was an empty Plymouth
with the windows down and the radio on.
A black woman was singing in Detroit
in a voice that brushed against the face
like the scarf
turning up in the wrong suitcase
long ago after everything came to grief.
What was inside we can only imagine—
men I guess trying to figure what would make it
work again. Beyond them
beyond the cracked engine blocks and thrown pistons
beyond that failed restroom
etched with our acids beyond that American Oil Station
beyond the oil on the ground
the mobile homes all over Hogansville
beyond our longing
all Georgia was green.
I'd had two for the road
a cheap enough thrill
and I wanted to think
I could take only what aroused me.
The interstate to Atlanta was wide open.
I wanted a different life.
So did J. D. Hines. So did the voice on the radio.
So did the man or woman
who made the hole in the window.
The way it works is this:
we devote ourselves to an image
we can't live with and try to kill
anything that suggests it could be otherwise.

Indian Mound • Winter • The Search

JES SIMMONS

Men planting cotton rows
would come to this pecan tree on the mound,
sole shade in acres of dirt
grooved to points at my eyes' limit.

This is my father-in-law's farm
deep in the Mississippi Delta.
This winter he is converting yet another
field into catfish ponds:
> two million pounds of farm-raised catfish
> swimming above cotton stalks buried,
> rotted in the soil.
"Don't plant 'em too deep, son."

> Among dried leaves on the mound
> I search for arrowheads, stone beads,
> and shards of pottery,
find where a scratching dog or possum
unearthed a brown bowl edge
becoming a dried out hipbone in my hand.

A distant cry, a hawk rides
the cold air, its spread-wing
shadow breaking
> out of hawk-shape
> on the rough-clod field,
reassembling itself in the packed dirt
floor of a newly-dug pond, then
> flowing over the mound, bending
> around me to weave itself
> into the gray limbs above my head.
Eyes that catch a mouse at 300 yards
are fixed like death on the bone in my palm.

I drop the Indian bone to cover it
with the black soil in which it cannot grow,
filling in the deep claw marks
which brought the dead to me.
Let these bones stay in the soil;
let the old tree remain on the mound,
the hawk steady over my head;
farm the soil in any way you can.
          let me connect all of this,
          walk away with all of this.

Piano Lessons

JOHN STONE

She wanted me to stretch my fingers
into next week   and next week.
I mean stretch them,
pull the tendons in their joints,
loosen bone from bone a bit.
My hands were too small
for octaves,
too little for recitals,
Chopin and Brahms,
which she would have had me
playing even now
except I escaped
by moving to a larger town.
Here she will never think
to look for me.
My fingers can be normal.
And I can disguise myself
as a clarinet,
march past her in the crowd
lining the street for parades
and blow her eardrums out
with a high held G.

Lola Forest

OVID VICKERS

We lived near
A Southern flag stop.
Two shorts, we knew
The dinner train would stop.
Through net curtains
We could see the platform.
The conductor stepped off first
and then Miss Lola Forest.

Miss Lola wore a cloche hat
And jet beads.
Her rouge was high.
Her lips were full, very red,
Pouting just a little
At the midday July sun.

A big patent leather purse
Under her arm
Had a gold L F on the front flap.
Even in the heat she wore gloves
And carried a little jacket
On her arm.

"Lola has come to see her sister,"
Mama said.
"Lola has seen a lot of men,"
Papa said.

Mama looked at Papa
And passed the squash.

Miss Pearl Parkerson

When high school was over
she took a test
at the county court house.
She listed the rivers and cities,
knew who Woodrow Wilson was,
worked the equations with ease,
and got certified.

They gave her a school
on the River road.
The first day
sixteen students came.
The youngest was five,
the oldest fifteen.

While some recited,
others did seat work.
The girls giggled,
and the boys were shy;
but she taught them all
to sing and to spell,
to read and to write,
to cypher and to parse.

Some summers
she went to the Normal,
but one day the state
required a degree.
Forty winters had passed
since she opened school
on the River road.
So, Miss Pearl went home,
sat on the porch,
and crocheted.

For My People

MARGARET WALKER

For my people everywhere singing their slave songs repeatedly:
their dirges and their ditties and their blues and jubilees,
praying their prayers nightly to an unknown god, bending their
knees humbly to an unseen power;

For my people lending their strength to the years, to the gone
years and the now years and the maybe years, washing ironing
cooking scrubbing sewing mending hoeing plowing digging
planting pruning patching dragging along never gaining never
reaping never knowing and never understanding;

For my playmates in the clay and dust and sand of Alabama
backyards playing baptizing and preaching and doctor and jail
and soldier and school and mama and cooking and playhouse
and concert and store and hair and Miss Choomby and
company;

For the cramped bewildered years we went to school to learn
to know the reasons why and the answers to and the people
who and the places where and the days when, in memory of
the bitter hours when we discovered we were black and poor
and small and different and nobody cared and nobody wondered
and nobody understood;

For the boys and girls who grew in spite of these things to be
man and woman, to laugh and dance and sing and play and
drink their wine and religion and success, to marry their
playmates and bear children and then die of consumption and
anemia and lynching;

For my people thronging 47th Street in Chicago and Lenox
Avenue in New York and Rampart Street in New Orleans, lost
disinherited dispossessed and happy people filling the cabarets
and taverns and other people's pockets needing bread and shoes
and milk and land and money and something—something all
our own;

For my people walking blindly spreading joy, losing time being lazy, sleeping when hungry, shouting when burdened, drinking when hopeless, tied and shackled and tangled among ourselves by the unseen creatures who tower over us omnisciently and laugh;

For my people blundering and groping and floundering in the dark of churches and schools and clubs and societies, associations and councils and committees and conventions, distressed and disturbed and deceived and devoured by money-hungry glory-craving leeches, preyed on by facile force of state and fad and novelty, by false prophet and holy believer;

For my people standing staring trying to fashion a better way from confusion, from hypocrisy and misunderstanding, trying to fashion a world that will hold all the people, all the faces, all the adams and eves and their countless generations;

Let a new earth rise. Let another world be born. Let a bloody peace be written in the sky. Let a second generation full of courage issue forth; let a people loving freedom come to growth. Let a beauty full of healing and a strength of final clenching be the pulsing in our spirits and our blood. Let the martial songs be written, let the dirges disappear. Let a race of men now rise and take control.

Kissie Lee

Toughest gal I ever did see
Was a gal by the name of Kissie Lee;
The toughest gal God ever made
And she drew a dirty, wicked blade.

Now this here gal warn't always tough
Nobody dreamed she'd turn out rough
But her Grammaw Mamie had the name
Of being the town's sin and shame.

When Kissie Lee was young and good
Didn't nobody treat her like they should

Allus gettin' beat by a no-good shine
An' allus quick to cry and whine.

Till her Grammaw said, "Now listen to me,
I'm tiahed of yoah whinin', Kissie Lee.
People don't never treat you right,
An' you allus scrappin' or in a fight.

"Whin I was a gal wasn't no soul
Could do me wrong an' still stay whole.
Ah got me a razor to talk for me
An' aftah that they let me be."

Well Kissie Lee took her advice
And after that she didn't speak twice
'Cause when she learned to stab and run
She got herself a little gun.

And from that time that gal was mean,
Meanest mama you ever seen.
She could hold her likker and hold her man
And she went thoo life jus' raisin' san'.

One night she walked in Jim's saloon
And seen a guy what spoke too soon;
He done her dirt long time ago
When she was good and feeling low.

Kissie bought her drink and she paid her dime
Watchin' this guy what beat her time
And he was making for the outside door
When Kissie shot him to the floor.

Not a word she spoke but she switched her blade
And flashing that lil ole baby paid:
Evvy livin' guy got out of her way
Because Kissie Lee was drawin' her pay.

She could shoot glass doors offa the hinges,
She could take herself on the wildest binges.
And she died with her boots on switching blades
On Talladega Mountain in the likker raids.

Molly Means

Old Molly Means was a hag and a witch;
Chile of the devil, the dark, and sitch.
Her heavy hair hung thick in ropes
And her blazing eyes was black as pitch.
Imp at three and wench at 'leben
She counted her husbands to the number seben.
  O Molly, Molly, Molly Means
    There goes the ghost of Molly Means.

Some say she was born with a veil on her face
So she could look through unnatchal space
Through the future and through the past
And charm a body or an evil place
And every man could well despise
The evil look in her coal black eyes.
  Old Molly, Molly, Molly Means
    Dark is the ghost of Molly Means.

And when the tale begun to spread
Of evil and of holy dread:
Her black-hand arts and her evil powers
How she cast her spells and called the dead,
The younguns was afraid at night
And the farmers feared their crops would blight.
  Old Molly, Molly, Molly Means
    Cold is the ghost of Molly Means.

Then one dark day she put a spell
On a young gal-bride just come to dwell
In the lane just down from Molly's shack
And when her husband came riding back
His wife was barking like a dog
And on all fours like a common hog.
  O Molly, Molly, Molly Means
    Where is the ghost of Molly Means?

The neighbors come and they went away
And said she'd die before break of day
But her husband held her in his arms
And swore he'd break the wicked charms;
He'd search all up and down the land
And turn the spell on Molly's hand.
  O Molly, Molly, Molly Means
  Sharp is the ghost of Molly Means.

So he rode all day and he rode all night
And at the dawn he come in sight
Of a man who said he could move the spell
And cause the awful thing to dwell
On Molly Means, to bark and bleed
Till she died at the hands of her evil deed.
  Old Molly, Molly, Molly Means
  This is the ghost of Molly Means.

Sometimes at night through the shadowy trees
She rides along on a winter breeze.
You can hear her holler and whine and cry.
Her voice is thin and her moan is high,
And her cackling laugh or her barking cold
Bring terror to the young and old.
  O Molly, Molly, Molly Means
  Lean is the ghost of Molly Means.

Don't Be Fourteen (in Mississippi)

JERRY W. WARD, JR.

Don't be fourteen
black and male in Mississippi
    they put your mind
    in a paper sack, dip it
    in a liquid nitrogen
    for later consumption
Don't be fourteen

black and male in Mississippi,
have two 20/20 eyes,
feet that fail to buck, wing, and tap,
a mouth that whistles
    they castrate you, wrap
    you in cotton-bailing wire
    while your blood still feels,
    feed you to the Tallahatchie
    as guilt-offering to blue-eyed susans
Don't be fourteen
black and male in Mississippi
    they say you a bad nigger
    named Bubba, a disgrace
    to the race in your first offense,
    and give you to Parchman
    for forty-eight years.
    You need, they say, a change to grow.
Don't be fourteen
black and male in Mississippi
    they say you a man at two.
    be one.
    when white boys ask
    why don't you like them,
    spit on them
    with your mouth closed.

He Remembers Something from the War

JAMES WHITEHEAD

In Kansas during the war
  my grandfather made a big thing
  of a car left out in our alley—
There's bullet holes and human blood
  so hurry up and eat your supper.

And the whole world would jiggle a little
   like Jello, when he was nervous.
Mother and grandmother were gone
   to the movies to see my father winning
   the war in Europe—grandfather
   never went to the movies or church
   and for the same reasons.
This is a lot like the real trouble
   your father is having in Germany,
   he said, as we walked past our victory garden
   then down our alley.

The things themselves were plain—
   a blue Nash and a windbreaker
   stiff with blood
   but I wasn't scared
   even by the stain itself
   until he told the story
   about how for some reason
   a hitch-hiker had murdered a farmer
   then left the car and jacket in our alley
   after dumping out the dead farmer
   in the woods of northern Arkansas.
About the time the police arrived
   I asked why in our alley?
He was the only father I had
   those long years during the war
   my mother was gone to in the movies.

Later that night mother and grandmother
   scolded him for getting drunk
   because they didn't know the things
   behind the garden
   and wouldn't until the morning news
   that told another story
   which was a lie grandfather said,
   like Roosevelt.
Upstairs he staggered near the door
   outside my room and close to my bed
   where that night in a sweaty dream

I saw a German soldier
catching a ride
with my own father
in my own father's M-4 tank
that was standing out in our alley.

Teaching

AL YOUNG

There's no such thing as a student,
only abiding faces unwilling
to change except with time,
the oldest force that still fools us

So you teach a feeling,
a notion learned the hard way,
a fact, some figures,
a tract, some rigors of childhood

The face out there
interacting with yours
knows how to grin & play with its pen
but misses the point so charmingly

A thousand moves later
that same shiny face
moving thru the world with
its eyes glazed or fully closed
reconnects with one of its own childhoods

Loosely we call this learning

A Little More Traveling Music

A country kid in Mississippi I drew water from the well
& watched our sun set itself down behind the thickets,
hurried from galvanized baths to hear music

over the radio—Colored music, rhythmic & electrifying,
more Black in fact than politics & flit guns.

Mama had a knack for snapping juicy fruit gum
& for keeping track of the generation of chilrens
she had raised, reared & no doubt forwarded,
rising thankfully every half past daybreak
to administer duties the poor must look after
if theyre to see their way another day, to eat, to live.

I lived & upnorth in cities sweltered & froze,
        got jammed up & trafficked
in everybody's sun going down but took up with the moon
as I lit about getting it all down up there
where couldnt nobody knock it out.

Picking up slowly on the gists of melodies, most noises softened.
I went on to school & to college too, woke up cold
& went my way finally, classless, reading all poems,
        some books & listening to heartbeats

Well on my way to committing to memory the ABC reality,
I still couldnt forget all that motherly music,
those unwatered songs of my babe-in-the-wood days
until, committed to the power of the human voice,
I turned to poetry & to singing by choice,
reading everyone always & listening, listening for a
        silence deep enough
to make out the sound of my own background music.

1962–1967

Written at My Mother's Grave

STARK YOUNG

It was in the early spring you fell asleep,
For I brought violets to your dear hands
Next day when they had laid you in the still
Dark room. And now from travelling many lands,

From many a stranger shore of level sands,
Made musical with waves, I come to fill
My weary eyes with my own native scene.
And now once more the spring brings everywhere
The warm southwind, these quiet trees are green,
And all along the ancient graveyard wall,
Amid the tangled sedge, the daisies bear
Their crowding stars. So all the memories
I have of you are green and fresh and pure,
Of that sweet childhood season when the flower
Blows fair, ere petals fall and the mature
Fresh-fruit of manhood ripening to its hour
Cumbers the plant. Listen! the dove's voice
In the distant brake sounding her sad pain,
Sadly, I hear, and in her mournful note
I catch the measure of my sorrow's strain.

Had I but had you longer, mother, then
Haply my hours and deeds should miss you more,
But then my heart should have you always near,
Having your words and ways heaped up in store,
Sweet company for many a weary year.

Such as I have are but the clambering
Upon your patient knees to kiss your lips,
Or look long in your blue eyes wondering,
Or put the dark hair from your gentle brow,
Feeling a wondrous sweetness steal somehow
From out your hands through all my little frame.
Once I remember, when my terrier died,
Through all the long stretches of the night I cried,
And when at last I slept, they say I fell
Amoaning in my childish sleep, but you
Closed not your eyes, but held me always well
Pressed into your heart and kissed my face
As a mother can. And then the swift years flew,
Seating grim manhood in the innocent place,
And many-mouthed cares are knocking at the gate.
Yet though I have no comforter so strong,
I would not call you from your well-won peace,

From the sweet silence of rich death. The wrong
Men did upon your shoulders heavy sat,
Your summer of goodness had too full increase
And brought an early harvest of your life.

Would call? What mummery! Too well I know
That those we love and those we hate must go,
Down the dim avenues of death must pass
Out to the fields of the great forever—lo,
Are gone from us like shadows on the grass
To the dark region of their last abode.

The Mississippi hills are blue and faint,
The air grows stiller and the sounds more sweet,
The gray shades cluster round each marble saint,
And in the long box walks the shadows meet.
And on your grave, rich-ripe with golden days,
Nasturtium cups are lit with level rays
From the low-sunk sun. Still would I be a child,
And come with flowers here for your dear praise,
And with *Good morrow, Mother,* pause to tell
The marvels of the day—nay, nay, I know,
I only fancy, mother, ere I go
To say *Farewell forever,* and *farewell.*

Four

DRAMA

The Freedom Kick

Shelby Foote

Lights come up on a rather chubby, middleaged Negro who stands on an open platform beside an old-fashioned, hooded camera on a tripod. The time is 1910. He wears a well-cut suit and a high hard collar, a flowing bow-tie, and button shoes. His air is one of congenial well-being, and he gives the impression of being as much at ease under stress as he is now, with time on his hands and nothing pressing. He checks his camera, then speaks as if in answer to a question from an invisible companion. This companion is the audience.

You ask about that old time. It aint nothing I cant tell you. Kluxers, smut ballots, whipping-bees, all that: I'm in a position to know and I remember, mainly on account of my mama. That woman loved freedom like nothing ever was. She was the daughter of a free man, a barber, and when she married my daddy it like to killed him—the barber I mean. A barber had a position in those days: the shop was kind of a gathering place where the white men would sit around and talk, so he knew all the business deals and the scandal, who-all was messing with who-all's wives, and so forth. When he got the news his only child had up and married, he butted his head against the wall, kicked at the baseboard so hard he lamed himself in the foot for week, and threw two of his best porcelain shaving mugs clean across the shop. My daddy, you see, was a slave from the beginning, and he had looked a good deal higher for her than that. I'm still talking about the barber, but the fact was I didn't know him. He died of a sudden seizure around the time I was born, five months after the wedding. He just thought she'd been putting on weight, when all the time it was me.

He should have known better how to handle her. Ever since

481

she was a little girl, if you wanted her to have something, even medicine, no matter how bitter-tasting it might be, all you had to do was act like you were going to keep it from her. I know, for Ive got children of my own, including one marriageable daughter, and I wouldnt cross her for the world. Then too, he had a lot of blood-pride—claimed we had African chiefs somewhere in the background. But I dont know; I never put much stock in all that talk. You used to hear lots of such claims among the colored. If it wasnt chiefs it was French blood. Maybe we caught it from the white folks. Anyhow, he certainly didnt want the son-in-law he got.

You see, my daddy was a kind of artist, high-strung and determined. He belonged at one time to a rich lady, a widow; she gave him his freedom in her will when she died. Maybe she sort of spoiled him. Anyhow he always wore a black silk tie under a soft collar and kept his hands smooth. He was a photographer, like me; had his tent right down by the levee, the same as me, at the foot of Marshall Avenue, and country people theyd get their picture taken every time they came to town with twenty cents. Whatever else Mamma's daddy wanted, he certainly didnt want any twenty-cent artist.

But that was what he got, all right, and he butted his head and took it. What else could he do? That was during the war; I was born the day after Vicksburg fell on the Fourth. I dont remember the war, howsomever, though sometimes I think I do. The first I remember, really, was afterwards—what I'm telling now. Reconstruction, some called it. . . . The surrender was some time back and I was maybe six or seven. My daddy didnt come home one night. Then next morning here he came, with a lump beside one eye. "Where you been?" Mamma asked him, hands on hips, eyes blazing. She was worried and angry too. But he just stood there in the doorway, kind of weavy on his feet. So she got the camphor bottle off the shelf and some cotton and began to swab at the lump. The camphor fumes helped to clear his head, and while she swabbed he told her.

"I'll tell you the plain truth, Esmy," he said. Mamma's full name was Esmeralda; Daddy called her Esmy. "I was standing on the corner Third and Bird, minding my business. It wasnt even late. This man comes up, big, so tall, with a derby and a cigar, a

mouth full of gold. Say, 'What you doing, boy?' I aint no boy. I
look back at him, eye to eye. Then I look away, across to where the
Pastime Pool Hall was. Say, 'Answer up!'—like he had every right.
Did I say he was wearing a brass watch chain? Well, he was, and
every breath he took it made a little line of fire run cross his vest.
I said, 'Whats it to you what I'm doing?' Thats what I told him."
(This is still my daddy talking.) "He was already solemn but now
he got more-so. He clouded up: say, 'Dont jaw back at me I ask
you something. Come along.' Then it happen; I see what he was
wearing. He let his coat kind of slide ajar and there it was. A
badge. I turn to run and Blip! all I saw was stars and colored
lights; the Pastime Pool Hall run round in a circle. He done hit
me slap up side the head with one them billy things, birdshot
wrapped in leather. Next thing I knew it was the jailhouse and a
white man looking at me through the bars. I said, 'Captain,
what was that?' 'Was what?'—the white man talking; he run his
hand through the front of his hair where he had his hat tipped
back. 'That man, Captain,' I ask him, 'was that a colored
policeman?' "

He stopped talking. Mamma went on swabbing the lump. I was
sitting there watching, smelling the camphor. She was so mad her
face just swole up with it. I could see what was coming next, and
here it came.

"Sue," she says.

"Sue who?" my daddy says; as if he didnt know, the same as me
that was going on seven or eight.

"The town of Bristol," Mamma says. "The Law. Who else? They
cant knock you round for sport and then just turn you loose like
nothing happened."

"Cant?" my daddy says. He sat there for a minute, saying
nothing. He was a high-strung man; God knows he was. But not
that high-strung. So he told her: "You sue," he says, "but not in
my name. I already got one knot up side my head."

. . . (It was the times, thats what it was, the carpetbaggers
coming to town with cotton receipts already signed and the
number of bales left blank to be filled in later; the fine-dressed
man selling bundles of four painted sticks for you to use to stake
off your forty acres come Emancipation Day again; the nightriders

pounding the roads in their bedsheets with the pointy hoods and the hoofs like somebody beating a drum along the turnpike. They burnt crosses every night all round us—and a man who'll burn what he prays to, he'll burn anything. It was the times, the whole air swirling full of freedom and danger; it was catching, you see, and Mamma already had it bad in the first place.)...

What happened next I didnt see, for she didnt take me with her. She left, walked out the door with that swole-up look still bulging her face, and was gone a good long time, till afternoon. Then here she come, back again, looking a good deal worse than Daddy did. He just had him a lump on the head but she had that and more. I broke out crying.

She went there looking for damages: "For what you done to my husband," she told them, right there in the town jail with the prisoners watching through the bars. At first the constable and this other man thought it was some kind of joke or something; they couldnt believe it. But then she got angry and started to yell in a loud voice about freedom and justice, right in their faces, and of course they couldnt stand for that, right there in their own jail house with the prisoners looking on. So they hit her, knocked her down. They almost had to, to get her to stop. But she wouldnt. She was still hollering in a high voice about freedom and justice and the vote, lying there on the floor where they had knocked her; she wouldnt quit. And then one of the men did something I cant justify, even considering all the disruption she was making. He kicked her full in the mouth, twice; cut both her lips and knocked several of her teeth right down her throat. That stopped her, for the time being at least, and then he kicked her once more, to make certain. They didnt arrest her—which they could have done. When she came to, she picked herself up, holding her mouth, and came on home. . . . I took one look at her and burst out crying; I was high-strung like my daddy in those days. But she wouldnt tell us anything. She went to bed without even the camphor bottle, and pulled the quilt up over her face and lay there.

Next day she had a nervous diarrhea, passed three of the teeth, and she picked them out of the slopjar, rinsed them off, and put them on the mantel to remember freedom by. That might sound like an ugly thing to you; I can see how it might. But to me it always seemed real fine, since it showed how much her love of freedom meant to her even after all it got her was three hard kicks in the mouth. . . . (It was the time, I say again; all that new, untested liberty and equality coming so sudden before we had a chance to get used to them. But it worked both ways, I can tell you. You think we didn't laugh at all those white men cutting head-holes in their wives' best sheets and eye-holes in the pillow-cases? We did indeed. It was a two-sided thing.) . . .

For a while then—most of her teeth being missing on one side, I mean—she didnt much look like herself. She'd always been such a fine-looking woman; her barber daddy had kept her dressed in style. But we got used to it in time, and Mamma was downright proud. It was like she'd sued and won. She held her head high, showing the missing teeth and the sunk-in cheek. You couldnt down her.

A pause; not sad—more wistful. Then he goes on.

She didnt live long, though. She had some kind of stomach ailment; it went into a tumor and she died. I was nine or ten. The night she died she put her arms around me and her tears fell onto the back of my head. "Youll be free, Emanuel," she told me; her last words. "Youll have freedom and the vote and youll be free."

But I dont know. It was true: I got them, but it seems like they dont mean so much as they did back then with the Kluxers riding the roads to take them from you. Thats how it is with most things, even freedom. You do most of your honing before you get it. Then it pales.

My daddy he outlived her many years. He had two more wives in fact, including the one that outlived him. I inherited all his clothes—and wore them, too, till I started putting on all this weight. Now all I can wear is these ties, a whole drawerful of silky bow ones. I got the business, too, this box and all; I'm a artist like my daddy, with a wife and four grown children, one on Beale, one in Detroit, one in New Orleans, and one to help my wife keep house. You want me take your picture?

Lights down. End of play

This Property Is Condemned

TENNESSEE WILLIAMS

Characters

WILLIE a young girl.

TOM a boy.

Scene: A railroad embankment on the outskirts of a small Mississippi town on one of those milky white winter mornings peculiar to that part of the country. The air is moist and chill. Behind the low embankment of the tracks is a large yellow frame house which has a look of tragic vacancy. Some of the upper windows are boarded, a portion of the roof has fallen away. The land is utterly flat. In the left background is a billboard that says "GIN WITH JAKE" and there are some telephone poles and a few bare winter trees. The sky is a great milky whiteness: crows occasionally make a sound of roughly torn cloth.

The girl Willie is advancing precariously along the railroad track, balancing herself with both arms outstretched, one clutching a banana, the other an extraordinarily dilapidated doll with a frowsy blond wig.

She is a remarkable apparition—thin as a beanpole and dressed in outrageous cast-off finery. She wears a long blue velvet party dress with a filthy cream lace collar and sparkling rhinestone beads. On her feet are battered silver kid slippers with large ornamental buckles. Her wrists and her fingers are resplendent with dimestore jewelry. She has applied rouge to her childish face in artless crimson daubs and her lips are made up in a preposterous Cupid's bow. She is about thirteen and there is something ineluctably childlike and innocent in her appearance despite the makeup. She laughs frequently and wildly and with a sort of precocious, tragic abandon.

The boy Tom, slightly older, watches her from below the embankment. He wears corduroy pants, blue shirt and a sweater and carries a kite of red tissue paper with a gaudily ribboned tail.

TOM Hello. Who are you?

WILLIE Don't talk to me till I fall off. (*She proceeds dizzily. Tom watches with mute fascination. Her gyrations grow wider and wider. She speaks breathlessly.*) Take my—crazy doll—will you?

TOM (*scrambling up the bank*) Yeh.

WILLIE I don't wanta—break her when—I fall! I don't think I can—stay on much—longer—do you?

TOM Naw.

WILLIE I'm practically—off—right now! (*Tom offers to assist her.*) No, don't touch me. It's no fair helping. You've got to do it—all—by yourself! God, I'm wobbling! I don't know what's made me so nervous! You see that water-tank way back yonder?

TOM Yeah?

WILLIE That's where I—started—from! This is the furthest—I ever gone—without once—falling off. I mean it will be—if I can manage to stick on—to the next—telephone—pole! Oh! Here I go! (*She becomes completely unbalanced and rolls down the bank.*)

TOM (*standing above her now*) Hurtcha self?

WILLIE Skinned my knee a little. Glad I didn't put my silk stockings on.

TOM (*coming down the bank*) Spit on it. That takes the sting away.

WILLIE Okay.

TOM That's animal medicine, you know. They always lick their wounds.

WILLIE I know. The principal damage was done to my brace-let, I guess. I knocked out one of the diamonds. Where did it go?

TOM You never could find it in all them cinders.

WILLIE I don't know. It had a lot of shine.

TOM It wasn't a genuine diamond.

WILLIE How do you know?

TOM I just imagine it wasn't. Because if it was you wouldn't be walking along a railroad track with a banged-up doll and a piece of a rotten banana.

WILLIE   Oh, I wouldn't be so sure. I might be peculiar or something. You never can tell. What's your name?

TOM   Tom.

WILLIE   Mine's Willie. We've both got boy's names.

TOM   How did that happen?

WILLIE   I was expected to be a boy but I wasn't. They had one girl already. Alva. She was my sister. Why ain't you at school?

TOM   I thought it was going to be windy so I could fly my kite.

WILLIE   What made you think that?

TOM   Because the sky was so white.

WILLIE   Is that a sign?

TOM   Yeah.

WILLIE   I know. It looks like everything had been swept off with a broom. Don't it?

TOM   Yeah.

WILLIE   It's perfectly white. It's white as a clean piece of paper.

TOM   Uh-huh.

WILLIE   But there isn't a wind.

TOM   Naw.

WILLIE   It's up too high for us to feel it. It's way, way up in the attic sweeping the dust off the furniture up there!

TOM   Un-huh. Why ain't you at school?

WILLIE   I quituated. Two years ago this winter.

TOM   What grade was you in?

WILLIE   Five A.

TOM   Miss Preston.

WILLIE   Yep. She used to think my hands was dirty until I explained that it was cinders from falling off the railroad tracks so much.

TOM   She's pretty strict.

WILLIE   Oh, no, she's just disappointed because she didn't get married. Probably never had an opportunity, poor thing. So she has to teach Five A for the rest of her natural life. They started teaching algebra an' I didn't give a goddam what X stood for so I quit.

TOM   You'll never get an education walking the railroad tracks.

WILLIE   You won't get one flying a red kite neither. Besides...

TOM   What?

WILLIE   What a girl needs to get along is social training. I learned all of that from my sister Alva. She had a wonderful popularity with the railroad men.

TOM   Train engineers?

WILLIE   Engineers, firemen, conductors. Even the freight sup'rintendent. We run a boarding-house for railroad men. She was I guess you might say The Main Attraction. Beautiful? Jesus, she looked like a movie star!

TOM   Your sister?

WILLIE   Yeah. One of 'em used to bring her regular after each run a great big heart-shaped red-silk box of assorted chocolates and nuts and hard candies. Marvelous?

TOM   Yeah. (*The cawing of crows sounds through the chilly air.*)

WILLIE   You know where Alva is now?

TOM   Memphis?

WILLIE   Naw.

TOM   New Awleuns?

WILLIE   Naw.

TOM   St. Louis?

WILLIE   You'll never guess.

TOM   Where is she then? (*Willie does not answer at once.*)

WILLIE   (*very solemnly*) She's in the bone-orchard.

TOM   What?

WILLIE   (*violently*) Bone-orchard, cemetery, graveyard! Don't you understand English?

TOM   Sure. That's pretty tough.

WILLIE   You don't know the half of it, buddy. We used to have some high old times in that big yellow house.

TOM   I bet you did.

WILLIE   Musical instruments going all of the time.

TOM   Instruments? What kind?

WILLIE   Piano, victrola, Hawaiian steel guitar. Everyone played on something. But now it's—awful quiet. You don't hear a sound from there, do you?

TOM   Naw. Is it empty?

WILLIE   Except for me. They got a big sign stuck up.

TOM   What does it say?

WILLIE   (*loudly but with a slight catch*) "THIS PROPERTY IS CONDEMNED!"

TOM   You ain't still living there?

WILLIE   Uh-huh.

TOM   What happened? Where did everyone go?

WILLIE   Mama run off with a brakeman on the C. & E. I. After that everything went to pieces. (*A train whistles far off.*) You hear that whistle? That's the Cannonball Express. The fastest thing on wheels between St. Louis, New Awleuns an' Memphis. My old man got to drinking.

TOM   Where is he now?

WILLIE   Disappeared. I guess I ought to refer his case to the Bureau of Missing Persons. The same as he done with Mama when she disappeared. Then there was me and Alva. Till Alva's lungs got affected. Did you see Greta Garbo in *Camille*? It played at the Delta Brilliant one time las' spring. She had the same what Alva died of. Lung affection.

TOM   Yeah?

WILLIE   Only it was—very beautiful the way she had it. You know. Violins playing. And loads and loads of white flowers. All of her lovers come back in a beautiful scene!

TOM   Yeah?

WILLIE   But Alva's all disappeared.

TOM   Yeah?

WILLIE   Like rats from a sinking ship! That's how she used to describe it. Oh, it—wasn't like death in the movies.

TOM   Naw?

WILLIE   She says, "Where is Albert? Where's Clemence?" None of them was around. I used to lie to her, I says, "They send their regards. They're coming to see you tomorrow." "Where's Mr. Johnson?" she asks me. He was the freight sup'rintendent, the most important character we ever had in our rooming-house. "He's been transferred to Grenada," I told her. "But wishes to be remembered." She known I was lying.

TOM   Yeah?

WILLIE   "This here is the pay-off!" she says. "They all run out on me like rats from a sinking ship!" Except Sidney.

TOM   Who was Sidney?

WILLIE   The one that used to give her the great big enormous red-silk box of American Beauty choc'lates.

TOM   Oh.

WILLIE   He remained faithful to her.

TOM   That's good.

WILLIE   But she never did care for Sidney. She said his teeth was decayed so he didn't smell good.

TOM   Aw!

WILLIE   It wasn't like death in the movies. When somebody dies in the movies they play violins.

TOM   But they didn't for Alva.

WILLIE   Naw. Not even a goddam victrola. They said it didn't agree with the hospital regulations. Always singing around the house.

TOM   Who? Alva?

WILLIE   Throwing enormous parties. This was her favorite number. (*She closes her eyes and stretches out her arms in the simulated rapture of the professional blues singer. Her voice is extraordinarily high and pure with a precocious emotional timbre.*)

> *You're the only star*
> *In my blue hea-ven*
> *And you're shining just*
> *For me!*

This is her clothes I got on. Inherited from her. Everything Alva's is mine. Except her solid gold beads.

TOM   What happened to them?

WILLIE   Them? She never took 'em off.

TOM   Oh!

WILLIE   I've also inherited all of my sister's beaux. Albert and Clemence and even the freight sup'rintendent.

TOM   Yeah?

WILLIE   They all disappeared. Afraid that they might get stuck for expenses I guess. But now they turn up again, all of 'em, like a bunch of bad pennies. They take me out places at night. I've got to be popular now. To parties an' dances an' all of the railroad affairs. Lookit here!

TOM   What?

WILLIE   I can do bumps! (*She stands in front of him and shoves her stomach toward him in a series of spasmodic jerks.*)

TOM   Frank Waters said that...

WILLIE   What?

TOM   You know.

WILLIE   Know what?

TOM   You took him inside and danced for him with your clothes off.

WILLIE   Oh. Crazy Doll's hair needs washing. I'm scared to wash it though 'cause her head might come unglued where she had that compound fracture of the skull. I think that most of her brains spilled out. She's been acting silly ever since. Saying an' doing the most outrageous things.

TOM   Why don't you do that for me?

WILLIE   What? Put glue on your compound fracture?

TOM   Naw. What you did for Frank Waters.

WILLIE   Because I was lonesome then an' I'm not lonesome now. You can tell Frank Waters that. Tell him that I've inherited all of my sister's beaux. I go out steady with men in responsible jobs. The sky sure is white. Ain't it? White as a clean piece of paper. In Five A we used to draw pictures. Miss Preston would give us a piece of white foolscap an' tell us to draw what we pleased.

TOM   What did you draw?

WILLIE   I remember I drawn her a picture one time of my old man getting conked with a bottle. She thought it was good, Miss Preston, she said, "Look here. Here's a picture of Charlie Chaplin with his hat on the side of his head!" I said, "Aw, naw, that's not Charlie Chaplin, that's my father, an' that's not his hat, it's a bottle!"

TOM   What did she say?

WILLIE   Oh, well. You can't make a school-teacher laugh. You're the only star In my blue hea-VEN... The principal used to say there must've been something wrong with my home atmosphere because of the fact that we took in railroad men an' some of 'em slept with my sister.

TOM   Did they?

WILLIE   She was The Main Attraction. The house is sure empty now.

TOM   You ain't still living there, are you?

WILLIE   Sure.

TOM   By yourself?

WILLIE   Uh-huh. I'm not supposed to be but I am. The property is condemned but there's nothing wrong with it. Some county investigator come snooping around yesterday. I recognized her by the shape of her hat. It wasn't exactly what I would call stylish-looking.

TOM   Naw?

WILLIE   It looked like something she took off the lid of the stove. Alva knew lots about style. She had ambitions to be a designer for big wholesale firms in Chicago. She used to submit her pictures. It never worked out.

You're the only star
In my blue hea-ven . . .

TOM   What did you do? About the investigators?

WILLIE   Laid low upstairs. Pretended like no one was home.

TOM   Well, how do you manage to keep on eating?

WILLIE   Oh, I don't know. You keep a sharp look-out you see things lying around. This banana, perfectly good, for instance. Thrown in a garbage pail in back of the Blue Bird Café. (*She finishes the banana and tosses away the peel.*)

TOM   (*grinning*) Yeh. Miss Preston for instance.

WILLIE   Naw, not her. She gives you a white piece of paper, says "Draw what you please!" One time I drawn her a picture of—Oh, but I told you that, huh? Will you give Frank Waters a message?

TOM   What?

WILLIE   Tell him the freight sup'rintendent has bought me a pair of kid slippers. Patent. The same as the old ones of Alva's. I'm going to dances with them at Moon Lake Casino. All night I'll be dancing an' come home drunk in the morning! We'll have serenades with all kinds of musical instruments. Trumpets an' trombones. An' Hawaiian steel guitars. Yeh! Yeh! (*She rises excitedly.*) The sky will be white like this.

TOM   (*impressed*) Will it?

WILLIE   Uh-huh. (*She smiles vaguely and turns slowly toward him.*) White—as a clean—piece of paper . . . (*then excitedly*) I'll draw—pictures on it!

TOM   Will you?

WILLIE   Sure!

TOM   Pictures of what?

WILLIE   Me dancing! With the freight sup'rintendent! In a pair of patent kid shoes! Yeh! Yeh! With French heels on them as high as telegraph poles! An' they'll play my favorite music!

TOM   Your favorite?

WILLIE   Yeh. The same as Alva's. (*breathlessly, passionately*)
              You're the only STAR—
              In my blue HEA-VEN . . .

I'll—

TOM   What?

WILLIE   I'll—wear a corsage!

TOM   What's that?

WILLIE   Flowers to pin on your dress at a formal affair! Rosebuds! Violets! And lilies-of-the-valley! When you come home it's withered but you stick 'em in a bowl of water to freshen 'em up.

TOM   Uh-huh.

WILLIE   That's what Alva done. (*She pauses, and in the silence the train whistles.*) The Cannonball Express . . .

TOM   You think a lot about Alva. Don't you?

WILLIE   Oh, not so much. Now an' then. It wasn't like death in the movies. Her beaux disappeared. An' they didn't have violins playing. I'm going back now.

TOM   Where to, Willie?

WILLIE   The water-tank.

TOM   Yeah?

WILLIE   An' start all over again. Maybe I'll break some kind of continuous record. Alva did once. At a dance marathon in Mobile. Across the state line. Alabama. You can tell Frank Waters everything that I told you. I don't have time for inexperienced people. I'm going out now with popular railroad men, men with good salaries, too. Don't you believe me?

TOM   No. I think you're drawing an awful lot on your imagination.

WILLIE   Well, if I wanted to I could prove it. But you wouldn't be worth convincing. (*She smooths out Crazy Doll's hair.*) I'm going to live for a long, long time like my sister. An' when my lungs get affected I'm going to die like she did—maybe not like in the movies, with violins playing—but with my pearl earrings on an' my solid gold beads from Memphis. . . .

TOM   Yes?

WILLIE   (*examining Crazy Doll very critically*) An' then I guess—

TOM   What?

WILLIE   (*gaily but with a slight catch*) Somebody else will inherit all of my beaux! The sky sure is white.

TOM   It sure is.

WILLIE   White as a clean piece of paper. I'm going back now.

TOM   So long.

WILLIE   Yeh. So long. (*She starts back along the railroad track, weaving grotesquely to keep her balance. She disappears. Tom wets his finger and holds it up to test the wind. Willie is heard singing from a distance.*)

You're the only star
In my blue heaven—

(*There is a brief pause. The stage begins to darken.*)

An' you're shining just—
For me!

CURTAIN

WILLIAM ATTAWAY (1911–1986) was born in Greenville, Mississippi. An outstanding interpreter of the Great Migration, he was himself a member of a migrant professional family. When Attaway was still quite young, his family moved to Chicago.

After graduating from the University of Illinois, Attaway spent a year traveling around the country gathering materials for his first novel; he finally arrived in New York City to earn his living as a free-lance writer. There he was a part of the Harlem Renaissance and lived near artist Romare Bearden and writer Ralph Ellison. His first novel, *Let Me Breathe Thunder*, was published in 1939. In his second novel, *Blood on the Forge* (1941), he confronted directly many of the problems faced by blacks who migrated northward during the first decade of the twentieth century.

In the fifties he turned to writing for radio, films, and television programs such as "Wide Wide World" and "The Colgate Hour." One of his most famous scripts in the sixties was an hour-long special on black humor, "A Hundred Years of Laughter," which featured comedians Redd Fox, Moms Mabley, Flip Wilson, and others for the first time on television. Attaway was the first black writer to write scripts for television and for films. A composer as well as a writer, he arranged songs for Harry Belafonte and authored the *Calypso Song Book* (1957). In 1967 he published *Hear America Singing*, a children's book with an introduction by Belafonte. In this important work he tells the stories of about a hundred songs as sung by pioneers, soldiers, workers, and country and city dwellers.

JAMES A. AUTRY (1933) was born in Memphis, Tennessee, and grew up in Benton County, Mississippi, the son and grandson of Mississippi Baptist ministers. In 1955 he graduated from the University of Mississippi with a B.A. in journalism. Autry is president of Meredith Corporation's Magazine Group which publishes *Better Homes and Gardens*, *Ladies' Home Journal*, and *Successful Farming* among others. His book of poetry, *Nights Under a Tin Roof: Recollections of a Southern Boyhood* (1983), was published by the Yoknapatawpha Press.

LERONE BENNETT, JR. (1928) was born in Clarksdale, Mississippi. When he was young, his family moved to Jackson, Mississippi, where he received his education in the public schools. After high school, he went to Atlanta to attend Morehouse College, from which he graduated in 1949. After further study at Atlanta University, Bennett became a journalist and worked for the *Atlanta Daily World* (1949–53), *Jet* magazine (1953), and *Ebony* magazine as an associate editor from 1954 to 1957. In 1958 he became the senior editor of *Ebony*, a position he holds today. Bennett is a historian, critic, poet, essayist, and writer of short stories. His *Before the Mayflower: A History of the Negro in America, 1619–1966* is considered by many the "bible of black history."

In an interview with Felicia Lee of *USA Today* Bennett says, "Black history studies saved my life. It's made it possible for me to have some sense of why black people are where they are; why black people are what they are. It's given me a sense of optimism." His love for black history was ignited, as he was growing up in Jackson, by the "extraordinary" teachers in the public schools, and grew stronger as he sought understanding of Jackson. "I developed the mad idea that if I mastered the written word I could figure out why Mississippi existed, why black people lived as they did. I *had* to know," he said. "It was a matter of life and death. It had nothing to do with academics, it had nothing to do with books. I had friends who were whipped, attacked. I was threatened. It was rare for a black person to reach adulthood without having that kind of an experience."

In addition to *Before the Mayflower* (1962, revised 1969), Bennett is the author of *The Negro Mood and Other Essays* (1964), *What Manner of Man: A Biography of Martin Luther King, Jr.* (1964), *Confrontation: Black and White* (1965), *Black Power U.S.A.: The Human Side of Reconstruction, 1867–1877* (1967), and *Pioneers of Protest* (1968).

CHARLIE R. BRAXTON (1961) was born in McComb, Mississippi, and was educated in the public school system there. He received a degree from Jackson State University and has spent his entire life in Mississippi. Of this Braxton says, "When I look back on my life in the Magnolia State, thus far, I feel a strong sense of being. By that I mean, I feel that my soul is deeply rooted in the soil of this state. Like the bittersweet gutbucket blues of Robert Johnson, I belong here."

Braxton is the author of a volume of poems, *Obsidian from the Ashes*, published in 1990.

VIRGIA BROCKS-SHEDD (1943) was born in Carpenter, Mississippi. In 1948 her family moved to the community of the now-extinct Bel Pine, near the Piney Woods Country Life School; at the age of thirteen, she became a boarding student at the Piney Woods School and lived there until 1961. She was an avid reader and decided that she wanted to be a poet like Margaret Walker, with whom she was able to study when she went to Jackson State University.

Brocks-Shedd received a B.S. degree from Jackson State in 1964 and the M.S.L.S. from Atlanta University in 1965. Now head librarian at Tougaloo College, Brocks-Shedd was working at Tougaloo as an assistant librarian in 1966 when she met writer-in-residence Audre Lorde, black feminist poet, who urged her to publish some of her poems in the Tougaloo College literary magazine, *Pound*. During 1966 and 1971, she published many articles and poems in *Close-Up*, a Jackson-based magazine, through her affiliation as contributing writer and managing editor. Her work has also appeared in *Hoo-Doo II/III, Jackson Advocate, Northside Reporter*, and in chapbooks *Mississippi Woods* (1980), *Mississippi Earthworks* (1982) and the Farish Street Festival souvenir booklets.

LARRY BROWN (1951) was born in Oxford, Mississippi, and has lived in Lafayette County for most of his life. For the last fifteen years he has lived at Yocona with his wife, Mary Annie, and their three children. He was a firefighter from 1973 to 1990 for the Oxford Fire Department. He now writes full time.

His short stories have appeared in various literary magazines such as *Greensboro Review, Fiction International, Mississippi Review, Carolina Quarterly, St. Andrews Review*, and *Chattahoochee Review*. His short fiction has appeared in several anthologies, most notably *The Best American Short Stories 1989. Facing the Music*, his first collection of stories, won the literature award from the Mississippi Institute of Arts and Letters in 1989, and a second collection, *Big Bad Love*, appeared in 1990.

His first novel, *Dirty Work*, was published in 1989 and has been adapted by Brown for American Playhouse, which filmed a version of the play for PBS. Algonquin Books of Chapel Hill, North Carolina, has published all of his books.

WILLIAM BURT (1950) was born in Greenville, Mississippi, and has composed free verse since his days in Greenville High School, where he and poet Brooks Haxton spent world literature class passing their latest works to each other for criticism. Burt was honored with the William Alexander Percy Poetry Award and the Hodding Carter Award for Creative Writing before moving to Cambridge, Massachusetts, to study film. His short subject "Rapport" was the second-place winner at the 1972 Wachussett Film Festival. Burt has continued writing while pursuing a career in broadcasting which has taken him to Utah, Wyoming, Montana, and Arkansas, and back to Mississippi, where he has won four Mississippi Broadcasters Association Awards for news and sports reporting. He has written over a hundred songs and several short stories in addition to his poetry.

JACK BUTLER (1944) was born in Alligator, Mississippi. He received a B.A. in English, a B.S. in mathematics, and an M.F.A. in writing from the University of Arkansas. His books include *West of Hollywood* (1980),

Hawk Gumbo and Other Stories (1982), *The Kid Who Wanted to Be a Spaceman* (1984), *Jujitsu for Christ* (1986), and *Nightshade* (1989). He has also completed a new book of poems, *The Circles*. He has published frequently in *The New Yorker, Atlantic, Poetry, New Orleans Review, Texas Quarterly*, and other magazines.

Butler is assistant dean of students at Hendrix College in Conway, Arkansas.

ANNE CARSLEY (1935) has spent most of her life in Jackson, Mississippi, where she was born. She received a B.A. from Millsaps College in 1957 and an M.A. from the University of Mississippi in 1959. For her essays she has received awards from Millsaps College, the Southern Literary Festival, the Mississippi Arts Festival, and the Mississippi Commission on the Arts. In 1970 she received third prize for a screenplay in a contest sponsored by the Mississippi Authority for Educational Television.

Since 1980 Carsley has published six romantic novels with historical settings—*This Ravished Rose* (1980), *The Winged Lion* (1981), *This Triumphant Fire* (1982), *Defiant Desire* (1983), *The Golden Savage* (1984), and *Tempest* (1985). Her interest in archaeology led her to set *The Winged Lion* in Sumer (now Iran) in 2350 B.C. and *The Golden Savage* in Crete in 1650 B.C. Her work in progress is *The Sword and the Rose*, a novel of the Civil War.

HODDING CARTER (1907–1972) was born in Hammond, Louisiana. He attended public schools in Hammond and received a B.A. in 1927 from Bowdoin College in Maine. He studied at the Pulitzer School of Journalism at Columbia University (1927–28), taught freshman English at Tulane University (1928–29), and entered newspaper work in 1929 as a member of the staff of the New Orleans *Item-Tribune*. Night manager of the New Orleans bureau of the United Press in 1930, Carter began working for the Associated Press bureau in Jackson, Mississippi, in 1931.

In 1932 he returned to his hometown and started the Hammond *Daily Courier*, which he ran for the next four years. In 1936 he was persuaded by William Alexander Percy and David Cohn to move to Greenville, Mississippi, to start a paper to compete with the Greenville *Democrat-Times*. Soon afterward, the *Democrat-Times* sold out to Carter and his backers, and the *Delta Democrat-Times* was born.

Throughout his journalistic career Carter was a major advocate of racial justice and a fierce opponent of the system of state-supported racial segregation in Mississippi and in the South. For years Carter was one of the most hated white men in Mississippi. When the Mississippi legislature resolved in 1955 that he was a traitor for criticizing the white Citizens Council, he was at the time chairman of the Rotary Club's Ladies Night, a counselor to the Boy Scouts, a Cub Scout den father, a director of the Chamber of Commerce, a member of the Board of Visitors of Tulane University, president of the Mississippi Historical Society and a vestryman at St. James Episcopal Church.

Except for brief periods—1940 as a Nieman Fellow at Harvard, a few years with the United States Army during World War II, and some time in New Orleans as a writer-in-residence at Tulane—Carter spent the years 1936 to 1972 in Greenville. In 1946 he was awarded a Pulitzer Prize for editorials in the *Delta Democrat-Times*.

During his lifetime Carter published numerous books including *Lower Mississippi* (1942), *The Winds of Fear* (1944), *Flood Crest* (1947), *Southern Legacy* (1950), *Where Main Street Meets the River* (1953), *The Angry Scar: The Story of Reconstruction* (1959), *First Person Rural* (1963), and *So the Heffners Left McComb* (1965).

Ellen Douglas (1921) is the pen name of Josephine Ayres Haxton. Born in Natchez, Mississippi, she graduated from the University of Mississippi in 1942. Her books include *A Family's Affairs* (1962, winner of the Houghton Mifflin-Esquire Fellowship Award and named by the *New York Times* one of the five best novels of the year), *Black Cloud, White Cloud* (1963; her story, "On the Lake," which became a part of that book's novella, "Hold On," was first published in *The New Yorker* and won an O. Henry Prize Award), *Where the Dreams Cross* (1968), *Apostles of Light* (1973, nominated for the National Book Award), *The Rock Cried Out* (1979, a Book-of-the-Month Alternate Selection and the winner of the Mississippi Institute of Arts and Letters Literature Award), *A Lifetime Burning* (1982, awarded the Mississippi Institute of Arts and Letters Literature Award), and *Can't Quit You, Baby* (1988). In 1987, University Press of Mississippi published *The Magic Carpet and Other Tales*, stories retold by Douglas with illustrations by Walter Anderson, and in 1989 reissued *Black Cloud, White Cloud*. In addition to her fiction, Douglas has written a short study of Walker Percy's novel *The Last Gentleman*.

The first recipient of the Mississippi Institute of Arts and Letters Literature Award in 1979, Douglas has also been awarded a grant from the National Endowment for the Arts. In 1989 she was chosen for the Fellowship of Southern Writers award for her work. She has been writer-in-residence at Northeast Louisiana University, the University of Virginia, and the University of Mississippi. She lives in Jackson.

Sybil Pittman Estess (1942) was born in Hattiesburg, Mississippi, and grew up in Hattiesburg and Poplarville. She holds a B.A. from Baylor University, an M.A. from the University of Kentucky, and a Ph.D. from Syracuse University. Her critical articles and poems have appeared in *Modern Poetry Studies, Southern Review, Southern Poetry Review* and *Shenandoah*, among others. She is co-editor of *Elizabeth Bishop and Her Art*, and her collection of poems, *Seeing the Desert Green*, was published in 1987. Estess lives in Houston, Texas, and teaches creative writing at the University of St. Thomas.

William Faulkner (1897–1962) was born in New Albany, Mississippi.

When he was five years old his family moved to Oxford, Mississippi, where he lived most of his life except for brief periods spent in Hollywood and Charlottesville, Virginia. Faulkner's education was sporadic. Dropping out of high school in his senior year, he attended the University of Mississippi as a special student for only one year (1919–20). He was a voracious reader and, through his friend and earliest critic, Phil Stone, was introduced to modern writers, including the French Symbolist poets. Their influence, along with the influence of Thomas Hardy and William Butler Yeats, can be seen in Faulkner's first book, *The Marble Faun*.

Influenced by Sherwood Anderson, Faulkner wrote his first novel, *Soldiers' Pay*, which appeared in 1926. Its publication began an extraordinarily prolific career. The next decade produced eight novels, including many of the finest he would write: *The Sound and the Fury* (1929), *As I Lay Dying* (1930), *Light in August* (1932), and *Absalom, Absalom!* (1936). However, his creative output was not matched by financial returns, so, in 1932, Faulkner went to Hollywood as a screenwriter, a position he kept, under financial duress, until 1948, when the commercial success of *Intruder in the Dust* and its subsequent sale to the movies enabled him to return to Mississippi. With the exception of tours for the State Department and time spent as a writer-in-residence at the University of Virginia, he remained in Oxford the rest of his life. Faulkner won numerous awards for his fiction, including the 1949 Nobel Prize and two Pulitzer Prizes, one for *A Fable* (1954) and another for *The Reivers* (1962). His accomplished short fiction appears in *Collected Stories* (1950) and *Uncollected Stories* (1979).

Robert Penn Warren said, "The study of Faulkner's writing is one of the most challenging tasks in our literature. It is also one of the most rewarding." Faulkner, who admitted that he had learned to write "from other writers," advised hopeful poets and novelists to "read all you can."

Faulkner's manuscripts and papers are at the University of Virginia, the University of Texas at Austin, Yale University Library, the New York Public Library, and the University of Mississippi.

SHELBY FOOTE (1916) was born in Greenville, Mississippi, where he was educated in the public schools. He attended the University of North Carolina from 1935–37 and served in Europe as a captain of field artillery during World War II. According to Foote, his parents were not literary. He writes, "My principal connection with a literary home was through my friendship with the Percys (William Alexander Percy, author of *Lanterns on the Levee*, and his three nephews, among them Walker Percy). There were literally thousands of books in the Percy house. It's probable that if those Percy boys hadn't moved to Greenville, I might never have become interested in literary things.

"I wrote five novels in five years in Greenville," Foote said. "I wrote all of them on Washington Avenue. But that was the beginning of my writing life and sort of the first chapter of it." Twenty years elapsed after his first five novels, but in 1974 publication of his massive three-volume history, *The Civil War: A Narrative* was completed. According to Polk and Scafidel (*An Anthology of Mississippi Writers*, 1979, University Press of Mississippi), Foote "brought to the writing of his heavily researched history not just the historian's reservoir of facts and dates but also the novelist's eye for meaningful detail and the capacity for understanding and depicting character. In addition, his history reflects the novelist's natural way with storytelling and a superb, clear, prose style." It was a unique achievement and won him a nomination for the Pulitzer Prize.

His first five novels were *Tournament* (1949; reissued in 1987), *Follow Me Down* (1950), *Love in a Dry Season* (1951), *Shiloh* (1952), and *Jordan County* (1954). A sixth, *September, September*, was published in 1977. In 1990, he served as a consultant for the movie *Glory* and appeared frequently on the PBS series *The Civil War*. He lives in Memphis, Tennessee.

RICHARD FORD (1944) was born in Jackson, Mississippi, and lived in the state until he graduated from high school. He received a B.A. from Michigan State University and an M.F.A. from the University of California. His stories have appeared in such magazines as *Esquire, The Paris Review*, and *The New Yorker* and have been widely anthologized. A collection, *Rock Springs*, was published in 1987. That book and his four novels, *A Piece of My Heart* (1976), *The Ultimate Good Luck* (1981), *The Sportswriter* (1986), and *Wildlife* (1990) have all received much critical acclaim. The *New York Times* has called him "one of the most compelling and eloquent storytellers of his age." *The Sportswriter* was chosen by *Time* magazine as one of the five best novels of the year.

Ford has won fellowships from the Guggenheim Foundation and the National Endowment for the Arts. He was editor of Houghton Mifflin's *The Best American Short Stories 1990*. He lives in New Orleans.

ELLEN GILCHRIST (1935) was born in Vicksburg, Mississippi. She received a B.A. in philosophy from Millsaps College and did graduate work at the University of Arkansas in creative writing. She has served as contributing editor of *Courier* in New Orleans. Gilchrist's works have appeared in such publications as *Atlantic Monthly, California Quarterly, Mademoiselle, New York Quarterly, Poetry Northwest, Prairie Schooner*, and *Southern Living*. Her books include two collections of poetry, *The Land Surveyor's Daughter* (1979) and *Riding Out the Tropical Depression* (1986), two novels, *The Annunciation* (1983) and *The Anna Papers* (1988), five collections of short fiction, *In the Land of Dreamy Dreams* (1981), *Victory Over Japan* (1984), *Drunk with Love* (1986), *Light Can Be Both Wave and Particle* (1989), and *I Cannot Get You Close Enough* (1990). *Falling Through Space: the Journals of Ellen Gilchrist* was published in 1987.

Her awards include the Craft in Poetry Award from *New York Quarterly* (1978), National Endowment for the Arts Fellowship Grant in Fiction (1979), fiction award from *Prairie Schooner* (1981), and the 1981 and 1984 Mississippi Institute of Arts and Letters Literature Award for *In the*

Land of Dreamy Dreams and *Victory Over Japan.* In addition, Gilchrist received the American Book Award in 1984 for *Victory Over Japan.* She lives in Fayetteville, Arkansas.

BARRY HANNAH (1942) was born in Meridian, Mississippi, and grew up in Clinton. He received a B.A. from Mississippi College and an M.F.A. from the University of Arkansas. He has been writer-in-residence at Clemson University, Middlebury College, the University of Alabama, the University of Iowa, the University of Montana, and Memphis State University and is currently at the University of Mississippi.

His first novel, *Geronimo Rex* (1972), won a William Faulkner Prize. A second novel, *Nightwatchmen* (1973), was followed by *Airships* (1978), a collection of short stories, which won the Arnold Gingrich Short Fiction Award. His other books are *Ray* (1980), *The Tennis Handsome* (1983), *Captain Maximus* (1985), *Hey Jack!* (1987), and *Boomerang* (1989). He has been honored by the American Academy of Arts and Letters and has received, among his many honors, a Guggenheim Fellowship. He lives in Oxford, Mississippi.

REBECCA HOOD-ADAMS (1949) was born in Grenada, Mississippi, and has lived in Mississippi most of her life. She graduated from Delta State University and now is a features copy editor for the (Jackson) *Clarion-Ledger.* In addition to journalistic articles her writing has appeared in *Delta Scene* and *Best American Magazine Verse* (1979).

ANGELA JACKSON (1951) was born in Greenville, Mississippi; shortly thereafter her family moved to Chicago. She is considered to be one of the most talented writers to emerge from Chicago's Organization of Black American Culture (OBAC) Writers Workshop which celebrated its twentieth year by publishing *NOMMO: A Literary Legacy of Black Chicago (1967–1987).* Her writing has appeared in *Story Quarterly, Black Scholar, Chicago Review, Callaloo, Open Places,* and *TriQuarterly,* among others. Her four books of poetry are *Voo Doo/Love Magic* (1974), *The Greenville Club* (1977), *Solo in the Boxcar Third Floor E* (1985), *The Man with the White Liver* (1985), and *And All These Roads Be Luminous: Selected Poems* (1991). Jackson is the winner of the Conrad Kent Rivers Memorial Award from *Black World* magazine, the Academy of American Poets Award, the Edwin Schulman Fiction Prize, and a Before Columbus Foundation American Book Award. In 1977 she was selected to represent the United States at the Second World Festival of Black and African Arts and Culture (FESTAC) in Lagos, Nigeria. That same year she received one of the two premier Illinois State Arts Council Creative Writing Fellowships. In 1978 she received a creative writing fellowship from the National Endowment for the Arts. *Ebony* magazine, in its August 1982 issue, included her among "Women to Watch in the 1980s." Jackson received the second Hoyt W. Fuller Award for Literary Excellence in 1983 and that year was writer-in-residence at Stephens College in Columbia, Missouri. In 1986 Jackson returned to Chicago to teach and to complete revisions on her novel *Treemont Stone.*

ETHERIDGE KNIGHT (1931) was born in Corinth, Mississippi, and grew up in Mississippi and Paducah, Kentucky. While serving in the army in Korea, he was wounded and became addicted to narcotics. In 1960 he was convicted of a robbery committed to support his drug habit. In prison, poetry resurrected him. His first collection, *Poems from Prison,* was published in 1968 while he was an inmate in Indiana State Prison. When he was paroled he continued to write, absorbing Afro-American, Anglo-American, European, and African literary traditions.

Knight's other books are *Belly Songs and Other Poems* (1973), *Born of a Woman* (1980), and *The Essential Etheridge Knight* (1986). He has been awarded fellowships by the Guggenheim Foundation and the National Endowment for the Arts and in 1985 was awarded the Shelley Memorial Award by the Poetry Society of America in recognition of distinguished achievement in poetry.

WILLIAM MILLS (1935) was born in Hattiesburg, Mississippi. He holds a Ph.D. from Louisiana State University and a diploma from Goethe Institute, Blaubeuren, Germany. He is the author of three poetry collections, *Watch for the Fox* (1974), *Stained Glass* (1979), and *The Meaning of Coyotes* (1984). Among Mills's other books are *The Stillness in Moving Things: The World of Howard Nemerov* (1975), a collection of short stories, *I Know a Place* (1976), a novel, *Those Who Blink* (1986), and a nonfiction book with text and color photographs, *Bears and Men: A Gathering* (1986). Currently he travels and writes on nature and the environment.

KAREN MITCHELL (1955) was born in Columbus, Mississippi, and grew up in Holly Springs, Mississippi, where she graduated from high school in 1973. She graduated from Stephens College in 1977. Mitchell has published poetry in *13th Moon, Essence, Obsidian, Open Places,* and *Southern Exposure* and has been a fellow at the MacDowell Colony.

ANNE MOODY (1940) was born in Centreville, Mississippi. She attended local public schools and later enrolled at Natchez Junior College. In 1963 Moody received a B.S. degree from Tougaloo College where she took part in many civil rights activities. In 1964 she became a fund raiser and public speaker for the Council on Racial Equality (CORE), and from 1964 to 1965 she was civil rights project coordinator at Cornell University.

Her first book, *Coming of Age in Mississippi,* published in 1968, received the American Library Association "Best Book of the Year Award," the "Gold Medal Award" from the National Council of Catholics and Jews, and a citation from *Mademoiselle* magazine. Now in its eighteenth printing, *Coming of Age in Mississippi* has become a classic.

It is used as a high school and college textbook in many parts of the world and has been translated into seven languages.

After leaving Mississippi, Moody lived for nine years in Europe and has since lived in New York City as a teacher, lecturer, and writer. Her second book, *Mr. Death*, was published in 1975. A sequel to *Coming of Age in Mississippi* is her forthcoming publication.

WILLIE MORRIS (1934) was born in Jackson, Mississippi, but moved with his family in 1935 to Yazoo City, Mississippi. He attended the University of Texas where he received a degree in English and became editor of the *Daily Texan*. After graduation in 1956, he received a Rhodes Scholarship to Oxford University and studied modern history at New College until 1959. For three years (1960–63) he was editor of the *Texas Observer*, a political and literary journal based in Austin. In 1963 he was employed by *Harper's Magazine* in New York. In 1967, when he was thirty-two, he became editor-in-chief of *Harper's*, substantially attracting first-rate fiction and essays, but resigned in 1971 in an editorial dispute. He has, since then, worked as a free-lance writer and lecturer, and has produced numerous essays and books. Morris is the writer-in-residence at the University of Mississippi.

His books include *North Toward Home* (1967), which received a Houghton Mifflin Literary Fellowship Award, *Good Old Boy* (1971), *Yazoo: Integration in a Deep-Southern Town* (1971), *The Last of the Southern Girls* (1973), *James Jones: A Friendship* (1978), *Terrains of the Heart and Other Essays on Home* (1981), *The Courting of Marcus Dupree* (1983), *Always Stand in Against the Curve* (1983), *Homecomings* (1989), and *Faulkner's Mississippi* (1990).

JOHN NIXON, JR. (1924) was born in Batesville, Mississippi. With the exception of a brief residence in North Carolina (non-military) during World War II, all of his early life was spent "next door to Yoknapatawpha" in the northwestern corner of his native province. Many of his poems represent specific Panola County locales. Toward the end of 1948, Nixon moved to Fluvanna County, Virginia, where he now resides. For sixteen years he coedited the venerable quarterly of poetry, *Lyric*. His own work has appeared in *The New Yorker, Saturday Review, Commonweal, Mademoiselle, Arizona Quarterly*, and *Washingtonian*. Nixon has received, among other honors, the Bellamann Award.

STEPHEN OWEN (1946) was born in Starkville, Mississippi, and was educated mostly in Clinton where he attended Mississippi College and earned a B.A. and an M.A. in English. Owen has taken courses in creative writing and literature at the University of Mississippi, the University of West Florida, Vanderbilt University, and the Writer's Workshop at Long Island University, Southampton Campus. He lives in Meridian and teaches English at Meridian Community College. Publications by Owen include a book about Meridian's endurance flyers Fred and Al Key, entitled *The Flying Key Brothers and Their Flight to Remember*, and various prose and poetry published in magazines and journals such as *Mississippi* magazine, *Writer's Digest*, *Piedmont Literary Review*, and *Teaching English in the Two-Year College*.

WALKER PERCY (1916–1990) was born in Birmingham, Alabama. After the death of his parents, he and two brothers were adopted by their father's first cousin, William Alexander Percy, and raised in Greenville, Mississippi. He graduated from the University of North Carolina in 1937 with a B.A. in chemistry and upon graduation became a student at the College of Physicians and Surgeons, Columbia University. He received his M.D., with honors, in 1941. During his internship at Bellevue Hospital in New York, Percy contracted tuberculosis and was forced in 1942 to convalesce in the Adirondacks. In 1944 he returned to Columbia to teach, but suffered a relapse, after which he retired from medicine.

While convalescing Percy read the great Russian novelists, the modern French novelists, Kierkegaard, and many of the other existentialists. In 1961 his first novel, *The Moviegoer*, was published; in 1962 it won the National Book Award. His other books include *The Last Gentleman* (1966), *Love in the Ruins* (1971), *The Message in the Bottle* (1975), *Lancelot* (1977), *The Second Coming* (received the 1980 Mississippi Institute of Arts and Letters Literature Award), *Lost in the Cosmos* (1983), and *The Thanatos Syndrome* (1987). He was one of the most highly regarded American novelists.

WILLIAM ALEXANDER PERCY (1885–1942) was born in Greenville, Mississippi, where he grew up in a secure atmosphere that was rich with music and books. His early education took place at the Sisters of Mercy convent. He graduated from the University of the South in 1904 and spent the next year traveling across Europe and into Egypt.

Upon his return to the United States, Percy entered the Harvard School of Law; he received his degree in 1908 and returned to Greenville to enter practice with his father. It was during this period that Percy began to write poetry.

After spending time in Europe during World War I, Percy returned to Greenville to face a troubled time. In 1922 there was a resurgence of activity by the Ku Klux Klan, and Percy's stand against them, along with his father's, endangered both Percy and his family. In 1927 the Mississippi River overflowed its banks, creating the worst flood in recorded history. In 1929, both his parents died within a few weeks of each other, leaving Percy with his father's law practice and possession of Trail Lake, 3,000 acres of some of the richest land in the South. In 1931 Percy adopted his three young cousins, Walker, LeRoy, and Phinizy Percy, after the death of their parents, and he turned his energies toward giving these orphaned boys the best opportunities he knew how to give them. Of his efforts, and of Will Percy, Walker Percy has said, "I will say no more than that he was the most extraordinary man I have ever known and that I owe him a debt which cannot be paid."

Among Percy's books of poetry are *Sappho in Levkas and Other Poems* (1915), *In April Once* (1920), *Enzio's Kingdom, and Other Poems* (1924), *Selected Poems* (1930), *The Collected Poems of William Alexander Percy* (1943), and *Of Silence and Stars* (1953).

Of his 1941 memoirs, *Lanterns on the Levee,* critic Herschel Brickell of the *New York Times Book Review* wrote that it was "a work of exceptional merit and importance. The high quality of the prose would entitle it to consideration for a permanent place in our literature, and it has numerous other virtues as well." It remains Percy's major work.

STERLING D. PLUMPP (1940) was born in Clinton, Mississippi. In 1955 his family moved to Jackson, Mississippi, where he completed school. After being selected for a scholarship, Plumpp studied for two years at St. Benedict's College and in 1968 received a B.A. in psychology from Roosevelt University. He is currently associate professor in the Black Studies Program at the University of Illinois at Chicago.

Plumpp's writings include six books of poetry, prose, and essays. In 1972 Third World Press published *Black Rituals,* a book of black psychological essays; it is a probing analysis of the black man's way of coping in a technological, urbanized, and industrialized society. His books of poetry include *Portable Soul* (1969), *Half Black, Half Blacker* (1970), *Steps to Break the Circle* (1974), *Clinton* (1976), and *The Mojo Hands Call, I Must Go* (1982). The latter, published by Thunder's Mouth Press, won the 1983 Carl Sandburg Literary Award for Poetry. In 1982 Plumpp edited a collection titled *Somehow We Survive: An Anthology of South African Writing.*

SAMUEL PRESTRIDGE (1952) was born in Columbus, Mississippi; he grew up in Mississippi, Texas, Alabama, and Georgia. His family returned to Mississippi in 1969, and he graduated from high school in Tupelo. Prestridge received a B.A. from Mississippi College in 1974 and an M.A. from the University of Southern Mississippi in 1977. For two years he was poet-in-the-schools for the Mississippi Arts Commission. During this time he worked toward an M.F.A. at Goddard College in Plainfield, Vermont, where he studied with Donald Hall and Thomas Lux. In 1980 Prestridge moved to south Louisiana where he worked in the oil fields. Since his return to Mississippi in 1981 he has supported himself as a para-legal, a credit manager, and a freelance writer. Presently he is employed by an advertising company in Jackson.

PAUL RUFFIN (1941) was born in Millport, Alabama, and grew up in Columbus, Mississippi. He received a Ph.D. in English from the Center for Writers at the University of Southern Mississippi and presently teaches creative writing, American literature, technical writing, and poetry at Sam Houston State University in Huntsville, Texas. He is director of the writing program there and is editor-in-chief of *Texas Review*.

Ruffin has published over 300 poems in such journals and anthologies as *Michigan Quarterly Review, Massachusetts Review, Georgia Review, New England Review, New Mexico Humanities Review, Kansas Quarterly, New Orleans Review, Mississippi Review, South Carolina Review, Southern Poetry Review, New Southern Poetry, Southwest Heritage,* and *Southern Humanities Review*. His books of poetry include *Lighting the Furnace Pilot* (1980), *Our Women* (1982), and *The Storm Cellar* (1985). In addition, he has edited three anthologies, *The Poets of Mississippi, The Texas Anthology,* and *Contemporary New England Poetry*. His poems have been anthologized in *Discoveries in Literature* (Scott-Foresman) and *Introduction to Poetry* (Little, Brown). His short stories have appeared in *Ploughshares: Southern Writers Edition, Florida Review, Southern Review, South Carolina Review,* and *Pembroke Magazine,* among others.

JAMES SEAY (1939) was born in Panola County, Mississippi. He received a B.A. from the University of Mississippi in 1964 and an M.A. from the University of Virginia in 1966. He taught English at the Virginia Military Institute, the University of Alabama, and Vanderbilt University before joining the English department of the University of North Carolina at Chapel Hill, where he is now the director of the creative writing program. Seay is the author of three books of poems, *Let Not Your Hart* (1970), *Water Tables* (1974), and *The Light As They Found It* (1970).

Limited editions of his poems have been issued by Deerfield Press/ Gallery Press of Ireland and Palaemon Press Limited. His poetry and critical writing have appeared in *American Review, Carolina Quarterly, Esquire, Nation, Southern Review,* and others. Among his honors are an Emily Clark Balch Prize and membership on the William Faulkner Fiction Award committee (currently PEN/Faulkner Award). In 1977 his work was selected for inclusion in an exhibit of poetry at the Centre Cultural Americain in Paris, and in 1987 he was part of a delegation of Mississippi writers invited to visit the Soviet Union.

JES SIMMONS (1954) was born in Farnborough, County Kent, England, and grew up in Natchez, Clinton, and Jackson, Mississippi, and in Carbondale, Illinois, and El Paso, Texas. Simmons received an M.A. and a Ph.D. in English from Texas A&M University, where he currently is an instructor in English.

Simmons's poems have appeared in *College English, River City Review, Mississippi Arts & Letters, New Poets Review, CEA Critic, Piddiddle,* and *Natchez Trace Literary Review*. He has had critical essays published in *Explicator* and in *Margaret Atwood: Reflections and Reality*.

ELIZABETH SPENCER (1921) was born in Carrollton, Mississippi, to a family that had lived in Carroll County since the 1830s. She received a

B.A. in English from Belhaven College in Jackson, Mississippi, and an M.A. from Vanderbilt University. She taught at Northwest Mississippi Junior College, Ward-Belmont School, and the University of Mississippi.

Her books include *Fire in the Morning* (1948), *This Crooked Way* (1952), *The Voice at the Back Door* (1956), *The Light in the Piazza* (1960), *Knights and Dragons* (1965), *No Place for an Angel* (1967), *Ship Island and Other Stories* (1968), *The Snare* (1972), *The Stories of Elizabeth Spencer* (1981), *Marilee* (1981), *The Salt Line* (1984), and *Jack of Diamonds and Other Stories* (1988). Her two-act play, *For Lease or Sale*, was produced by Playmakers Repertory Company, Chapel Hill, North Carolina, in 1989. Her short stories, which have appeared regularly for four decades in *The New Yorker, Atlantic, Southern Review*, and *McCall's*, have received many awards and have been included in *O. Henry Prize Stories* and *The Pushcart Prize: Best of the Small Presses*.

Spencer has received many awards for her writing, including a Guggenheim Fellowship (1953), the Rosenthal Foundation Award of the American Academy of Arts and Letters (1957), the Kenyon Review Fellowship in Fiction (1957), the McGraw-Hill Fiction Award (1960), the Henry Bellamann Award for creative writing (1968), the Award of Merit Medal for the Short Story by the American Academy of Arts and Letters (1983), election to the American Institute of Arts and Letters (1985), and a Senior Award Grant in Literature from the National Endowment for the Arts (1988).

Spencer lived for many years in Montreal, but now lives in Chapel Hill, where she teaches at the University of North Carolina. Her manuscripts and papers are located at the University of Kentucky Library in Lexington.

JOHN STONE (1936) was born in Jackson, Mississippi, and grew up in Jackson and Palestine, Texas. He graduated from Central High School and Millsaps College in Jackson, Mississippi. He received an M.D. degree from Washington University, completing postgraduate training in Internal Medicine and Cardiology at the University of Rochester and Emory University. Dr. Stone is now Professor of Medicine (Cardiology) and Community Health (Emergency Medicine) at Emory University School of Medicine, where he sees patients and teaches. Stone has published three books of poetry, *The Smell of Matches* (1972), *In All This Rain* (1980), and *Renaming the Streets* (1985), which received the literature award from the Mississippi Institute of Arts and Letters. His essays have appeared in the *New York Times Magazine* and *Discover*, and *In the Country of Hearts: Journeys in the Art of Medicine* was published in 1990. Stone's awards include citations from the Georgia Writers' Association and the Theobald Smith Award from Abany Medical College of Union University.

JAMES STREET (1903–1954) was born in Lumberton, Mississippi, and grew up in Poplarville, Hattiesburg, and Laurel. He began working for the Laurel *Daily Leader* at age fourteen and at seventeen, after a brief period of hoboing in the West, became a reporter for the *Hattiesburg American*. In 1924, after attending a Baptist seminary, he became the youngest ordained Baptist minister in the United States. He left the ministry in 1926 and became a reporter, eventually working for the *Arkansas Gazette*, then for the Associated Press in Memphis, Nashville, Atlanta, and New York. In New York a feature article he had written attracted the attention of William Randolph Hearst, and Street was hired to write for the New York *American* in 1933.

In 1936 he published a book of short sketches about the South titled *Look Away! A Dixie Notebook*. His first novel, *Oh, Promised Land*, appeared in 1940. In that same year he resigned his position and moved to Natchez, Mississippi, where he wrote *In My Father's House* (1941). Returning to New York the following year, he lived there until 1945. During that time he wrote his popular novel, *The Gauntlet* (1945). In 1945 Street settled in Chapel Hill, North Carolina. He remained a successful professional writer for the rest of his life. Nearly all his novels were best sellers, and some sold over a million copies. Three of his books, *The Biscuit Eater* (1941), *Tap Roots* (1942), and *Good-bye, My Lady* (1954), were made into films.

MILDRED D. TAYLOR was born in Jackson, Mississippi, and grew up in Toledo, Ohio, with yearly trips back to the South. After graduating from the University of Toledo, she spent two years in Ethiopia with the Peace Corps. Returning to the United States, she recruited for the Peace Corps before entering the School of Journalism at the University of Colorado. There, as a member of the Black Student Alliance, she worked with students and university officials in structuring a Black Studies program.

Song of the Trees (1975), Taylor's first book about the Logan family of Mississippi, won the Council on Interracial Books Award in the African-American category. It was also chosen as a *New York Times* Outstanding Book of the Year in 1975. Her second book, *Roll of Thunder, Hear My Cry* (1976), won many honors including the prestigious Newbery Award from the American Library Association. It was also made into a film. A sequel, *Let the Circle Be Unbroken*, was published in 1981.

OVID VICKERS (1930) was born in Gadsden, Alabama. He received a B.A., an M.A., and an ED.S. degree from George Peabody College. After serving in the military during the Korean conflict, he began teaching English at East Central Junior College in Decatur, Mississippi, where he is now chair of the division of humanities and fine arts. His short stories, articles, and poems have appeared in *Texas Review*, *Delta Scene*, *Southern Living*, *Mississippi*, *Teaching English in the Two-Year College*, and *Mississippi Folklore Journal*. In 1980 Vickers received an award of merit from the Mississippi Historical Society for his writing of over forty articles on the folklore of Mississippi.

MARGARET WALKER (1915) was born in Birmingham, Alabama; she grew up in Alabama, Louisiana, and Mississippi. Walker received a B.A. from Northwestern University in 1935 and an M.A. and a Ph.D. from the University of Iowa. In 1942, after working for the WPA on its Federal Writers Project, Walker began teaching at West Virginia State College in the English department. In the same year *For My People*, her first book, was published as a volume in the Yale Series of Younger Poets. In 1949 Walker joined the faculty at Jackson State University as a professor of English and later became director of the Institute for the Study of History, Life, and Culture of Black People. Her novel *Jubilee*, published in 1966, won a Houghton Mifflin Literary Fellowship Award and became an international best seller. Her other books include *Prophets for a New Day* (1970), *How I Wrote Jubilee* (1972), *October Journey* (1973), *A Poetic Equation: Conversations Between Nikki Giovanni and Margaret Walker* (1974), *The Daemonic Genius of Richard Wright* (1985), *This Is My Century: New and Collected Poems* (1989), and *How I Wrote Jubilee and Other Essays* (1990).

JERRY W. WARD, JR. (1943) was born in Washington, D.C. When he was six his family moved to Mississippi. He received a B.S. from Tougaloo College (1964), an M.S. from the Illinois Institute of Technology (1966), and a Ph.D. from the University of Virginia (1978). Ward's poetry and essays have appeared in the *Southern Quarterly*, *Obsidian*, and *Mississippi Folklore Register*, among other professional journals, magazines, and newspapers. Former chair of the English department at Tougaloo College, Ward has worked in the Division of Fellowships and Seminars at the National Endowment for the Humanities. He is currently researching the works of Lance Jeffers, Sterling D. Plumpp, and Ishmael Reed.

DEAN FAULKNER WELLS (1936) was born in Oxford, Mississippi, the daughter of Dean Swift Faulkner and Louise Hale. Her father, William Faulkner's youngest brother, was killed in a plane crash before she was born.

Published in magazines and journals, Wells is the author of *The Ghosts of Rowan Oak: William Faulkner's Ghost Stories for Children*, *Belle-Ducks at The Peabody* and editor of *The Great American Writers' Cookbook*. She makes her home in Oxford, Mississippi, and with her husband, Larry Wells, operates Yoknapatawpha Press.

EUDORA WELTY (1909) was born in Jackson, Mississippi. Educated in Jackson's public schools, she began writing and drawing very early, publishing poems and sketches in *St. Nicholas* magazine as early as 1920. After attending Industrial Institute and College (now Mississippi University for Women) for two years, she transferred to the University of Wisconsin, graduating with a B.A. in 1929. In 1930 she attended Columbia University School of Business, but returned to Mississippi in

1931 when her father died. In Jackson, she worked in a variety of jobs before going to work for the WPA, traveling across the state taking photographs and writing copy for several small newspapers.

Two of her short stories, "Death of a Traveling Salesman" and "Magic," were published in *Manuscript* magazine in 1936. Her first book, *A Curtain of Green*, appeared in 1941, and was a critical success. Her second volume, *The Robber Bridegroom*, appeared in 1942, and firmly established her reputation as a writer. Since the 1943 publication of *The Wide Net and Other Stories*, Welty has published *Delta Wedding* (1946), *The Golden Apples* (1949), *The Ponder Heart* (1954), *The Bride of the Innisfallen and Other Stories* (1955), *The Shoe Bird* (1964), *Losing Battles* (1970), *One Time, One Place* (1971), *The Optimist's Daughter* (1972), *The Eye of the Story* (1977), *The Collected Stories of Eudora Welty* (1980), *One Writer's Beginnings* (1984), and *Photographs* (1989). *Conversations with Eudora Welty*, interviews collected by Peggy Whitman Prenshaw, appeared in 1984.

Welty has received great international attention and praise. Her many honors include the Pulitzer Prize, the American Book Award for fiction, the Gold Medal for the Novel by the National Institute of Arts and Letters, and the Howells Medal for Fiction by the American Academy of Arts and Letters.

JAMES WHITEHEAD (1936) was born in St. Louis, Missouri, but grew up in Jackson, Mississippi. He earned a B.A. and an M.A. from Vanderbilt University and an M.F.A. in creative writing from the University of Iowa in 1965. He has taught at Millsaps College and the University of Iowa and is currently teaching in the creative writing program at the University of Arkansas. Whitehead was awarded the Robert Frost Fellowship of the Bread Loaf Writers' Conference in 1967 and a Guggenheim Fellowship in fiction in 1972. His poems have appeared in many reviews and journals including the *Southern Review, Mississippi Review, New Orleans Review, Poetry Now*, the *Vanderbilt Poetry Review*, and the *Greensboro Review*.

Domains, his first book of poems, was published in 1966. His first novel, *Joiner*, appeared in 1971 and received critical acclaim. Another book of poems, *Local Men*, was published in 1979.

TENNESSEE WILLIAMS (1911–1983) was born Thomas Lanier Williams in Columbus, Mississippi. After living his early years in various Mississippi towns, his family moved to St. Louis. This environment and its effect on the young Williams is described in his play *The Glass Menagerie* and his short story "Portrait of a Girl in Glass." Williams attended the University of Missouri from 1929 to 1931, when he was withdrawn by his father because of his failure to pass ROTC (Reserve Officers' Training Corps). He then worked for three years at the International Shoe Company in St. Louis and, as a way of escaping tedium, began to write more and more. Quitting his job, he attended Washington University before receiving a degree from the University of Iowa in 1938.

Williams revised an earlier script called *The Gentleman Caller* into *The Glass Menagerie*. It opened in Chicago on December 26, 1944, and was his first professional success. In 1945 it moved to Broadway. With this impressive start, Williams began his career as one of the world's most popular playwrights. He won two Pulitzer Prizes, one for *A Streetcar Named Desire* and another for *Cat on a Hot Tin Roof*, and four New York Drama Circle Critics Awards for these two plays, as well as for *The Glass Menagerie* and *The Night of the Iguana*. Many of Williams's plays have been made into films.

Williams divided much of his time between New Orleans, his home in Key West, and the Hotel Elysee on East 54th Street in New York where he died.

RICHARD WRIGHT (1908–1960) was born in Adams County, Mississippi, to a country schoolteacher mother and an illiterate sharecropper father. Because of his mother's illness and his father's eventual abandonment, his childhood was one of poverty, frequent moves from relative to relative, and interrupted schooling. His first published story, "The Voodoo of Hell's Half Acre," was printed in September 1924 in the *Southern Register*, the local black newspaper in Jackson, Mississippi. In 1925 he graduated from Jackson's Smith-Robertson Public School. It was the last year he spent in school.

Wright worked in Memphis, then in 1927 moved to Chicago, where he would remain for ten years. In 1932 he joined the American Communist Party, believing that he had finally found a group interested in the plight of the American black. He had begun writing poetry and short stories earlier, and now, on behalf of the Party, his work began to appear in such publications as *New Masses*, *Left Front*, and *Partisan Review*.

In 1937 Wright moved to New York, where he was Harlem editor of the *Daily Worker*. His first book, *Uncle Tom's Children*, was published in 1938. This was followed by his two most famous works. *Native Son*, published in 1940, is the tragic tale of a Mississippi-born black in Chicago. Its success was phenomenal, and assured Wright a place in American literature. In 1945 *Black Boy*, an autobiographical work based on his traumatic childhood in Mississippi, was released.

By 1944 Wright had left the Communist Party and in 1946, unreconciled to the continuing racism in the United States, he and his family moved to Paris, France. There he was to remain until his death. After moving to France he was active in establishing such organizations as the Society of African Culture and working with such African leaders as Leopold Senghor, later president of Senegal, and Aime Cesaire from Martinique. Among Wright's nonfiction works of this time are *Black Power* (1954) and *Pagan Spain* (1957).

Wright's fiction includes *The Outsider* (1953) and *Savage Holiday*

(1954). In addition, three works were published posthumously— *Eight Men* (1961), *Lawd Today* (1963), and *American Hunger* (1977).

Wright's manuscripts, papers, and letters are located in the Beinecke Library at Yale University, in the New York Public Library, and in the Princeton University Library.

AL YOUNG (1939) was born in Ocean Springs, Mississippi, and grew up in the South, the Midwest, and on the West Coast. He was educated at the University of Michigan and the University of California at Berkeley and has taught writing and literature at Stanford, Foothill Community College, Colorado College, the University of Washington, and the University of California at both Santa Cruz and Berkeley.

His novels include *Who Is Angelina?* (1975), *Sitting Pretty* (1976), *Ask Me Now* (1980), and *Seduction by Light* (1988). His books of poetry are *Dancing* (1969), *The Song Turning Back Into Itself* (1971), *Geography of the Near Past* (1976), *The Blues Don't Change* (1982), and the collected poems, *Heaven* (1988). Film assignments have included scripts for Dick Gregory, Sidney Poitier, Bill Cosby, and Richard Pryor. With poet-novelist Ishmael Reed, Young edits *Quilt*, an international journal devoted to multicultural writing. His work has been translated into Norwegian, Swedish, Italian, Japanese, Spanish, Polish, Russian, French, and Chinese.

Bodies & Soul (1981), *Kinds of Blue* (1984), and *Things Ain't What They Used to Be* (1987) are all books of musical memoirs inspired by such artists as James Brown, Ravel, Billie Holiday, Thelonious Monk, Glenn Miller, Janis Joplin, Miles Davis, and many more.

Young is the recipient of the Joseph Henry Jackson Award, National Arts Council Awards for editing and poetry, a Wallace Stegner Fellowship, a National Endowment for the Arts Fellowship, the Pushcart Prize, a Fulbright Fellowship, the Before Columbus Foundation American Book Award, and a Guggenheim Fellowship.

STARK YOUNG (1881–1963) was born in Como, Mississippi, and moved to Oxford, Mississippi, in 1895. He attended the University of Mississippi and received a B.A. with honors in 1901. In 1902 he earned an M.A. in English from Columbia University. Returning to Mississippi, he taught at Water Valley, then at the University of Mississippi. From 1907 to 1915, he taught at the University of Texas and from 1915 to 1921 at Amherst College, Amherst, Massachusetts. In 1921 Young resigned from academic life and began writing and reviewing on a full-time basis in New York. He became drama critic for the *New Republic* and an editor of *Theatre Arts Magazine*.

Over the next forty years, Young distinguished himself as a critic, poet, translator of Chekhov, novelist, essayist, editor, painter, and playwright. He wrote thirty plays, many of which he directed. He is best remembered for his novel, *So Red the Rose* (1934), a story of the Civil War that preceded *Gone with the Wind* but never attained its popularity or commercial success. He died in New York on January 6, 1963.

ACKNOWLEDGMENTS

THE EDITOR wishes to thank the following authors and publishers or magazines for permission to reprint the designated selections. Rights in all cases are reserved by the owner of the copyright.

Fiction

Excerpt from *Blood on the Forge* by William Attaway. Published by Doubleday & Company, Inc. Copyright © 1941 by Doubleday & Company, Inc. Reprinted by permission of the publisher.

Excerpt from *Facing the Music* by Larry Brown. Published by Algonquin Books Copyright © 1988 by Algonquin Books. Reprinted by permission of the publisher.

"On the Lake" by Ellen Douglas first appeared in *The New Yorker*. Copyright © 1961 by Houghton Mifflin Company; renewed 1985 by Ellen Douglas. Reprinted by permission of the author from *Black Cloud, White Cloud*.

"Barn Burning" by William Faulkner first appeared in *Harper's Magazine*. Copyright © 1939; renewed 1967 by Estelle Faulkner and Jill Faulkner Summers. Reprinted by permission of Random House, Inc., from *Collected Stories of William Faulkner*. "A Rose for Emily" from *Collected Stories of William Faulkner* by William Faulkner. Copyright © 1950 by Random House, Inc. Reprinted by permission of Random House, Inc.

Excerpt from *Shiloh* by Shelby Foote. Copyright © 1952 by Shelby Foote; renewed 1982. Reprinted by permission of Random House, Inc.

"Revenge" by Ellen Gilchrist first appeared in *Prairie Schooner*. Copyright © 1981 by Ellen Gilchrist. Reprinted by permission of Don Congdon Associate, Inc.

"Testimony of Pilot" by Barry Hannah first appeared in *Esquire*. Copyright © 1978 by Barry Hannah. Reprinted by permission of Alfred A. Knopf, Inc. from *Airships*.

Excerpt from *Good Old Boy* by Willie Morris. Copyright © 1971 by Willie Morris; renewed 1980. Published by Harper & Row, Publishers, Inc. Second edition published by Yoknapatawpha Press, Inc. Reprinted by permission of the author.

Excerpt from *The Moviegoer* by Walker Percy. Copyright © 1961 by Walker Percy. Reprinted by permission of Alfred A. Knopf, Inc.

"The Day Before" by Elizabeth Spencer first appeared in *Ship Island and Other Stories*. Copyright © 1968 by Elizabeth Spencer. Reprinted by permission of Doubleday & Company, Inc. from *The Stories of Elizabeth Spencer*.

"Weep No More, My Lady" by James Street. Copyright © 1941 by Curtis

Publishing Company; renewed 1969 by Lucy Nash Street. Reprinted by permission of the Harold Matson Company, Inc.

Excerpt from *Roll of Thunder, Hear My Cry* by Mildred D. Taylor. Copyright © 1976 by Mildred D. Taylor. Reprinted by permission of Dial Books for Young Readers, a Division of E.P. Dutton, Inc.

Excerpt from *Jubilee* by Margaret Walker. Copyright © 1966 by Margaret Walker Alexander. Reprinted by permission of Houghton Mifflin Company.

"A Memory" by Eudora Welty first appeared in *The Southern Review*. Copyright © 1937; renewed 1980 by Eudora Welty. Reprinted by permission of Harcourt Brace Jovanovich, Publishers, Inc., from *The Collected Stories of Eudora Welty*.

"Why I Live at the P.O." by Eudora Welty first appeared in *The Atlantic Monthly*. Copyright © 1941; renewed 1980 by Eudora Welty. Reprinted by permission of Harcourt Brace Jovanovich, Publishers, Inc., from *The Collected Stories of Eudora Welty*.

"Almos' a Man" by Richard Wright first appeared in *Harper's Bazaar*. Copyright © 1940 by Richard Wright; renewed 1961 by Ellen Wright. Published (with slight revision) in *Eight Men* by World Publishing Company. Reprinted by permission of Paul R. Reynolds, Inc.

Nonfiction

"Have We Overcome?" by Lerone Bennett, Jr., first appeared in *Have We Overcome? Race Relations Since "Brown,"* edited by Michael V. Namorato. Copyright © 1979 by the University Press of Mississippi. Reprinted by permission of the editor.

"Sunday Has a Different Smell" by Anne Carsley first appeared in *Mississippi*. Copyright © 1971 by Anne Carsley. Reprinted by permission of the author.

"Grandmother Was Emphatic" by Hodding Carter. Copyright © 1950 by the Louisiana State University Press. Reprinted by permission of the publisher from *Southern Legacy*.

Nobel Prize Acceptance Speech by William Faulkner. Delivered in Stockholm December 10, 1950. Reprinted by permission.

"My Mother, in Memory" by Richard Ford first appeared in *Harper's*. Copyright © 1989 by Richard Ford. Reprinted by permission of the author.

Excerpt from *Coming of Age in Mississippi* by Anne Moody. Copyright © 1968 by Anne Moody. Reprinted by permission of Doubleday & Company, Inc.

Excerpt from *North Toward Home* by Willie Morris. Copyright © 1967 by Willie Morris. Reprinted by permission of the author.

Excerpt from *Lanterns on the Levee* by William Alexander Percy. Copyright © 1941 by Alfred A. Knopf, Inc.; renewed 1968 by LeRoy Pratt Percy. Reprinted by permission of Alfred A. Knopf, Inc.

"Growing Out of Shadow" by Margaret Walker first appeared in *Common Ground*. Copyright © 1943; renewed 1985 by Margaret Walker. Reprinted by permission of the author.

"A Christmas Remembered" by Dean Faulkner Wells first appeared in *Parade*. Copyright © 1980 by Dean Faulkner Wells. Reprinted by permission of Raines and Raines.

"A Sweet Devouring" by Eudora Welty first appeared in *Mademoiselle*. Copyright © 1957; renewed 1978 by Eudora Welty. Reprinted by permission of Random House from *The Eye of the Story: Selected Essays and Reviews*.

"The Little Store" by Eudora Welty first appeared as "The Corner Store" in

Acknowledgments

Esquire. Copyright © 1975; renewed 1978 by Eudora Welty. Reprinted by permission of Random House from *The Eye of the Story: Selected Essays and Reviews.*
Excerpt from *Black Boy* by Richard Wright. Copyright © 1937, 1942, 1944, 1945 by Richard Wright. Reprinted by permission of Harper & Row, Publishers, Inc.
"Black, Brown and Beige" by Al Young. Copyright © 1981 by Al Young. Reprinted by permission of Creative Arts Book Company from *Bodies & Soul.*

Poetry

"Genealogy" by James A. Autry. Copyright © 1983 by James A. Autry. Reprinted by permission of Yoknapatawpha Press from *Nights under a Tin Roof.*
"Childhood Remembrances" and "Jazzy St. Walk" by Charlie R. Braxton. Copyright © 1988 by Charlie R. Braxton. Reprinted by permission of author.
"Southern Roads/City Pavement" by Virgia Brocks-Shedd first appeared in *Jackson Advocate.* Copyright © 1982 by Virgia Brocks-Shedd. Reprinted by permission of the author.
"Hank and Peg" by William Burt. Copyright © 1988 by William Burt. Reprinted by permission of the author.
"Preserves" by Jack Butler first appeared in *Cedar Rock.* Copyright © 1984 by Jack Butler. Reprinted by permission of August House from *The Kid Who Wanted to Be a Spaceman.*
"The Country Idiot" by Sybil Pittman Estess. Copyright © 1988 by Sybil Pittman Estess. Reprinted by permission of the author.
"The Best Meal I Ever Had Anywhere" by Ellen Gilchrist. Copyright © 1988 by Ellen Gilchrist. Reprinted by permission of Don Congdon Associates, Inc.
"Diphtheria" by Rebecca Hood-Adams first appeared in *Delta Scene.* Copyright © 1979 by Rebecca Hood-Adams. Reprinted by permission of the author.
"Make/n My Music" by Angela Jackson first appeared in NOMMO. Copyright © 1972 by Angela Jackson. "mary mariah" first appeared in *First World.* Copyright © 1987 by Angela Jackson. "Home Trainin" first appeared in *The Greenville Club* published by BkMk Press. Copyright © 1977 by Angela Jackson. Reprinted by permission of the author.
"A Poem for Myself (or Blues for a Mississippi Black Boy)" by Etheridge Knight. Copyright © 1986 by Etheridge Knight. Reprinted by permission of the University of Pittsburgh Press from *The Essential Etheridge Knight.*
"Our Fathers at Corinth" by William Mills. Copyright © 1979 by William Mills. Reprinted by permission of Louisiana State University Press from *Stained Glass.*
"The Eating Hill" by Karen Mitchell first appeared in *Thirteenth Moon.* Copyright © 1982 by Karen Mitchell. "Birmingham, Alabama: 1963" first appeared in *Open Places.* Copyright © 1979 by Karen Mitchell. Reprinted by permission of The Eight Mountain Press from *The Eating Hill.*
"I Remember 1929" by John Nixon, Jr., first appeared in *Georgia Review.* Copyright © 1958 by University of Georgia Press. Reprinted by permission of the publisher.
"Confessions from Childhood" by Stephen Owen first appeared in *Teaching English in the Two-Year College.* Copyright © 1980 by the National Council of Teachers of English. Reprinted with permission.

Drama